Flexibility Principles in Boolean Semantics

Flexibility Principles in Boolean Semantics

Yoad Winter

The Interpretation of Coordination, Plurality, and Scope in Natural Language

The MIT Press
Cambridge, Massachusetts
London, England

This book was set in Times Roman by Windfall Software using ZzTEX and was printed and bound in the United States of America.

First printing, 2001

Library of Congress Cataloging-in-Publication Data

Winter, Yoad.
  Flexibility principles in boolean semantics : the interpretation of coordination, plurality, and scope in natural language / Yoad Winter.
      p.   cm. — (Current studies in linguistics ; 37)
  Includes bibliographical references.
  ISBN 0-262-23218-9 (hc. : alk. paper)
  1. Grammar, Comparative and general—Coordinate construction. 2. Definiteness (Linguistics) 3. Semantics. 4. Algebra, Boolean. I. Current studies in linguistics series ; 37.
P293.W56   2002
401′.43—dc21   2001044334

Contents

Preface

In his 1970 article *"English as a Formal Language,"* Richard Montague introduced a revolutionary theory of the interpretation of human languages. Montague showed that non-trivial semantic facts about English can be explained using precise methods that had previously been employed only for the construction of artificial mathematical languages. A fundamental principle in Montague's program is that the *meaning* of a complex linguistic expression is tightly connected to its *form*. Under this conception, knowledge of the meaning of a natural language expression is reduced to knowledge of its internal structure and the meanings of its syntactic constituents. Accordingly, Montague's semantic theory contains a simple recursive procedure that computes the meaning of a sentence from its syntactic representation and the meaning of the words it contains.

Because of the close relationship it assumes between syntax and semantics, Montague's paradigm carries an enormous hope for linguistic theory. If it proves correct it will allow theories of natural language syntax, with the impressive advances they have achieved since the early works of Noam Chomsky, to significantly extend their empirical coverage. Syntactic theory would not only account for well-formedness of expressions, but could also be the basis for analyzing their informational content. On the other hand, the theory of natural language semantics in the Montagovian paradigm is no longer the dull exercise of merely formalizing *what* sentences mean. Montague semantics also addresses the scientifically more exciting question of *how* the meaning of language expressions is derived.

On the basis of Montague's answer to this question, a broader framework of *Boolean Semantics* has evolved. Boolean semantics is an extension of Montague grammar that pays special attention to the mathematical nature of the semantic domains it uses. It is observed that these domains all have the structure of *Boolean Algebras*. This observation allows a remarkably elegant treatment of coordination and negation phenomena. The boolean order that underlies Montague semantics is also the basis for the analysis of the noun phrase, which is treated using the boolean domain of *generalized quantifiers*. Boolean semantics and its sub-field of generalized quantifier theory have become the foundations of a modern framework where the meaning of natural language expressions is studied in close connection to their syntactic analysis.

The main claim of this book is that boolean semantics should be augmented by *flexibility principles*. In a flexible interpretation process, the computation of meaning involves operation of general semantic rules that do not have any direct counterpart in phonological form and are more specialized than the elementary logical operations that are needed in order to glue meanings together (e.g. function application). One familiar strategy underlying the application of flexibility operations is the *type-fitting* strategy. According to this strategy, flexibility operations are allowed to apply only when other composition operations fail and lead to so-called *type mismatch*. Another kind of flexibility principles are referred to in this book as *category-shifting principles*. These operations, unlike type-fitting principles, change the semantic category of an expression (e.g. from predicate to quantifier or vise versa) and are triggered by syntactic factors and not by type mismatch.

Both kinds of flexibility principles contribute to the solution of central problems in the analysis of *coordination, plurality* and *scope* that previous works have considered inherent to boolean semantics. Contrary to these beliefs, however, it will be shown that the flexibility paradigm in fact reveals further advantages of the boolean approach to natural language. Under the emerging new conception of flexibility, semantic theory includes a logical compositional component that is relevant for the interpretation of all languages, natural as well as artificial, in conformity of Montague's use of the term *Universal Grammar*. In addition to this logical component, the theory of natural language semantics includes an array of flexibility operations that are specific to human languages. These rules are therefore candidates for inclusion in 'Universal Grammar' in the Chomskyan sense of the term: they characterize general properties of natural language that are nonetheless not made necessary by any plausible abstract definition of language as a symbolic system.

This work is primarily intended for readers with background in theoretical linguistics who have some knowledge of formal semantics. However, many parts of the book are also of relevance for researchers and students in related disciplines that deal with natural language. The discussion throughout the book presupposes some sophistication in elementary set theory and logic, but a number of central principles and techniques in formal semantics of natural language are reviewed in the introduction.

Acknowledgments

This book is based on some of the main chapters of my dissertation (Winter, 1998). The main ideas of chapters 2 and 3 appeared in Winter (1996a) and Winter (1997). However, much of the text in these two articles was rewritten and many details were added or reformulated. Section 3.5.1 is also included in Winter (2000b). Parts of Winter (1997) and Winter (2000b) are reprinted here with the kind permission of Kluwer Academic Publishers.

Of the many people who contributed to this work I am especially grateful to Johan van Benthem, Martin Everaert, Danny Fox, Nissim Francez, Herman Hendriks, Ed Keenan, Fred Landman, Tanya Reinhart, Eric Reuland, Eddy Ruys, Roger Schwarzschild, Anna Szabolcsi, Henk Verkuyl, Joost Zwarts and two anonymous reviewers of the MIT Press.

Chapter 1
Introduction

Two aspects are central to any theory of natural language semantics. One aspect concerns the lexical meanings of simple morphemes and the relationships among them. Another part of the theory studies the interpretation of syntactically complex expressions, a process that is referred to as *meaning composition* or the *syntax-semantics interface*. This book concentrates on the second aspect in the linguistic domains of coordination, plurality and scope. The theory of *Boolean Semantics* is extended in order to account for some of the central problems that are introduced by the three phenomena and the interactions among them. The leading proposal is that the interpretation prcocess at the syntax-semantics interface is *flexible*: natural language involves a variety of semantic principles without counterpart in form, which shift meanings of linguistic expressions in the process of semantic composition. New flexible treatments of collective noun phrase coordination, the scope of indefinites and plural quantification are proposed. These mechanisms form a compact and combinatorially manageable array of operators, whose coverage is extended to include more general cases of coordination and quantification. This system eliminates ad hoc assumptions about syntax and lexical semantics that were previously needed. For example, in the treatment of the scope of indefinites unconstrained syntactic operations are avoided; problems of coordination and plurality are handled without any postulation of lexical ambiguity of coordinators or determiners; plural quantification is modeled using a uniform type shifting scheme.

This introductory chapter consists of the following parts. Section 1.1 gives a general overview of the problems of coordination, plurality and scope that are in the focus of this book. Section 1.2 outlines the central foundational assumptions of the semantic theory on which the present study of these phenomena draws. Section 1.3 is a general introduction to the notion of flexibility that is adopted in this book. Section 1.4 informally surveys the principles underlying the proposed solutions. Section 1.5 reviews essential technical details of the semantic tools that are used throughout the book. The organization of the book is described in section 1.6. The chapter concludes with some bibliographical remarks.

1.1 Questions about Coordination, Plurality and Scope

General questions A remarkable property of *coordination* is its cross-categorial nature: morphemes such as *and* and *or* can form coordinate structures of virtually all syntactic categories in English, and the same holds in numerous other languages. The sentences in (1) exemplify only a narrow range of this syntactic flexibility.

(1) a. [Mary is tall] and/or [John is thin]
    b. Mary is [tall and/or thin]
    c. [Mary and/or John] are tall

The lexical and compositional semantic questions that are raised by cross-categorial coordination are closely related to each other: a semantic theory of coordination should explain how the lexical value of one single coordinator can combine with the different meanings of expressions of various categories.

Sentences with *plural* noun phrases constitute another case where lexical and compositional questions are strongly related. A familiar puzzle is the intuitive distinction between distributive and collective interpretation. For example, consider the following sentences.

(2) a. The children smiled.
    b. Each child smiled.

(3) a. The children met.
    b. *Each child met.

Sentence (2a) is semantically close, or even equivalent, to (2b), where the predicate "distributes" to individual children. By contrast, sentence (3a) is not equivalent to the unacceptable sentence (3b), since the plural subject of (2a) is now interpreted as performing a "collective action." A theory of plurality should account for the lexical differences between predicates that give rise to distributivity/collectivity effects. Concomitantly, it should decide whether the compositional processes in the two cases are any different.

Inverse scope effects with various noun phrase constructions are another hard problem for theories of form and meaning. For instance, consider sentence (4a), which can be interpreted similar to (4b).

(4) a. A guard is standing in front of every building.
    b. Every building has a guard standing in front of it.

(5) A guard [is standing in front of [every building]]

Most theories of grammar assign (4a) a syntactic structure as roughly given in (5), where the noun phrase *every building* is within the syntactic scope of the subject *a guard*. However, this syntactically plausible structure makes it hard for semantic theory to account for the equivalence between (4a) and (4b). This situation is often described by saying that the "semantic scope" of a noun phrase can be different than its syntactic scope. Here the puzzle is to determine whether the standard syntactic analysis in (5) has to be modified or whether it is semantic theory that is to be enriched in order to directly operate on standard structures while still generating the inverse scope effect.

Summarizing, each of the three phenomena that were mentioned raises a general question of foundational interest for linguistic theory:

1. What is the mechanism that gives coordination its cross-categorial semantics?
2. What are the lexical and compositional sources of the distributive/collective distinction with plurals?
3. Are inverse scope phenomena syntactic or semantic in nature?

These questions motivate the investigations in this book, which concentrate on some of their specific aspects.

Specific questions   The many interactions between coordination, plurality and scope make the attempt to answer the above questions even more challenging. *Coordination and plurality* are most intimately related, as conjunctive coordination is one of the simple means to form plural noun phrases from singular ones. For example, while the proper names *Mary* and *John* are both singular, the conjunction *Mary and John* is plural. Quite expectedly, the distributivity/collectivity puzzle of sentences (2) to (3) reappears in sentences (6) and (7) below. Thus, while sentence (6a) is equivalent to the sentential conjunction (6b), sentence (7a) is not equivalent to the unacceptable sentence in (7b).

(6) a. Mary and John smiled.
     b. Mary smiled and John smiled.

(7) a.   Mary and John met.
     b. *Mary met and John met.

It is reasonable to expect that a cross-categorial semantics of *and* should naturally account for both distributivity and collectivity effects in NP coordinations. As it turns out this is not a straightforward enterprise. The main complication, as we shall see, is that the standard boolean treatment of coordination, which arguably gives the clearest account of its cross-categorial behaviour, does not immediately account for the absence of equivalence in simple cases as in (7). This problem is in the focus of chapter 2.

Another central question in this book is about the interactions between *plurality and scope*, and especially in what concerns *indefinite* noun phrases. One of the central observations made on inverse scope phenomena is that, while noun phrases like *every building* as in (4a) are quite restricted in their ability to display wide scope, indefinite NPs like *some building* are exceptionally free in their scopal behaviour. For instance, while sentence (8a) below cannot be interpreted as equivalent to (8b), sentence (9a) does have an interpretation equivalent to (9b).

(8) a. If every building in Washington is attacked by terrorists then US security will be
        threatened.
     b. For every building x in Washington, if x is attacked by terrorists then US security
        will be threatened. (*un*available interpretation)

(9) a. If some building in Washington is attacked by terrorists then US security will be
        threatened.
     b. For some building x in Washington, if x is attacked by terrorists then US security
        will be threatened. (available interpretation)

There are many proposals that try to account for this distinction between indefinites and
other noun phrases. One of the important ways to test these theories against other parts of
semantic theory is to study the interpretation of *plural indefinites*. Some of these indefinites,
like singular indefinites, have exceptional ability to take inverse scope. In addition, like
other plurals, they also show distributivity and collectivity effects. Consider for instance
the following example.

(10) If some/three building*s* in Washington are attacked by terrorists then US security will
      be threatened.

In chapter 3 it is observed that plural indefinites like *some buildings* or *three buildings*
show a "double scope" effect. This effect consists of *existential* scope, which is free like
the existential scope of the singular indefinite in (9a), and of *distributivity* scope, which
is restricted like the scope of the universal NP in (8a). For instance, it is argued that
sentence (10) has the reading paraphrased in (11a) below, with an existential quantifier
taking scope over the conditional and a universal quantifier (distributor) having scope within
the conditional. However, it is claimed that the sentence does not have any interpretation
like (11b), where also the distributor takes scope over the conditional.

(11) a. There *exist* some/three buildings such that *if each* of them is attacked by terrorists
         then US security will be threatened. (available interpretation)
      b. There *exist* some/three buildings such that for *each* of them, *if* it is attacked by
         terrorists then US security will be threatened. (*un*available interpretation)

Chapter 3 studies such effects and proposes to use the *choice function* mechanism of
Reinhart (1997) as the basis for their account.

   One of the main arguments of this book is that the problems discussed above can be
treated under the general assumption that some noun phrases can be interpreted as either
quantifiers or *predicates*. To study further the implications of this assumption, chapter 4
addresses another empirical problem that has important connections to coordination, plurality and scope phenomena: the interpretation of noun phrases in so-called *predicative
positions*. These are positions in the sentence that are normally reserved for adjectives and
prepositional phrases, as in the following examples.

(12) a. This is *interesting/completely out of the question*.

    b. Mary considers this *interesting/completely out of the question*.

However, some noun phrases also appear naturally in such positions, as the following sentences illustrate.

(13) a. This is *a good proposal/the best proposal*.

    b. Mary considers this *a good proposal/the best proposal*.

The problem that such constructions raise is how to classify the noun phrases that can appear in predicative positions and to explain their interpretation in these positions. Chapter 4 follows the proposal in Partee (1987) and argues that the predicative reading of certain noun phrases is connected to their quantificational reading using flexibility operations. It is further proposed that these flexibility principles are not special to predicative constructions, but are the same as the ones that were used in chapters 2 and 3 for the treatment of collective coordination and the scope of indefinites.

    Another central problem that is studied in this book is the quantification process with plural NPs and its relationships with the typology of predicates in natural language and plural inflection. To illustrate these complex relationships, consider the following sentences.

(14) a. The (five) students met.

    b. All the/exactly five students met.

(15) a.   The (five) students are a good team.

    b. *All the/exactly five students are a good team.

(16) a.   All the/no/at least two students met.

    b. *Every/no/more than one student met.

While most theories of plurals give a straightforward analysis of sentences as in (14a), with "referential" plurals, sentences with "quantificational" plurals as in (14b) are highly challenging. However, Dowty (1987) first pointed out that for some predicates, like *be a good team* in (15b), such effects of "collective quantification" are ruled out. Moreover, even with predicates like *meet*, plural inflection is a necessary condition for obtaining collectivity effects. This is illustrated by the contrasts in (16). These variations make the study of plural quantifiers even more challenging. Chapter 5 proposes a novel account of plural quantification within the flexible boolean framework of this book. This theory is based on a new typology of predicates in natural language and a simple account of the role of morphological number in the semantic interpretation process of these predicates.

    The discussion above summarized the main questions that this book will address. The following sections introduce the basic tools and principles that will be used in the analysis of these problems.

1.2   Foundational Assumptions

Any scientific theory should start from a specification of the empirical phenomena that it counts as relevant data and provide a limited set of assumptions about the ways in which these facts are to be described. This section surveys the basic assumptions of semantic theory that form the foundational background of the present study.

Entailments and model-theoretic semantics   One of the properties of natural language that make it a useful means for human communication is the fact that it enables to draw inferences. Speakers of all natural languages display a striking regularity in their judgements about whether it is right or wrong to assert a sentence on the basis of some given premise(s). For example, all English speakers will agree that sentence (18) is a valid conclusion from the sentences in (17).

(17) a. No cat that John likes is white.
      b. Tina is a cat that John likes.

(18) Tina is not white.

The sentences in (17) are said to *entail* sentence (18). We will indicate this intuitive entailment relation by the notation (17) $\Rightarrow$ (18). It can be noted that the fact that (17) $\Rightarrow$ (18) does not depend on whether the informants agree on details such as the (reasonably vague) set of cats that John likes, or even on the identity of John and Tina. Furthermore, speakers can have various understandings of what is to be a cat, what is for a cat to be white, etc., but still accept the validity of the entailment. Such robust judgements about inference are the primary source of data that any *truth-conditional* theory of meaning strives to explain.

There are two other truth-conditional intuitions that are strongly related to entailment. One is *equivalence*, which can simply be defined as mutual entailment between sentences. This is for example the relation between the sentence *Mary hit John* and the sentence *John was hit by Mary*. Another useful intuition about the truth-conditional connections between sentences is *contradiction*. An example is the intuitive connection between the sentences *Tina is white* and *Tina is not white*. Unlike the equivalence notion, it is harder to account for contradiction intuitions in pre-theoretical terms of entailment. This is for reasons that have to do with scope ambiguities of negation.

Model-theoretic semantics is a theory that is designed to account for truth conditional intuitions about meaning. A model-theoretic theory of natural language takes meanings to be objects in an abstract *model of discourse*. Natural language expressions *refer to* or *denote* objects in the model. Very often the model includes two special objects that are taken to be the possible denotations of sentences: the truth values *true* (1) and *false* (0). A model-theoretic semantics with these sentence denotations is considered descriptively adequate only if it satisfies the following criterion. Assume that $S_1, \ldots, S_n$ and S are natural language sentences and that the entailment $S_1, \ldots, S_n \Rightarrow S$ is accepted by speakers of the language. The theory has to make sure that whenever it takes all the sentences $S_1, \ldots, S_n$ to denote *true*, also S denotes *true*. Conversely, when this relation between the sentence denotations holds in the theory then sentences $S_1, \ldots, S_n$ should intuitively entail sentence S. This adequacy requirement for model-theoretic semantics is referred to as the *truth-conditionality criterion*.

Compositionality and non-representationalism   Model-theoretic semantics does not put particular restrictions on the way in which the truth value of a sentence is evaluated. In other words, it underdetermines the syntax-semantics interface. An independent well-known principle that does put a strong restriction on this interface is *compositionality*. This principle states that the meaning of a compound expression is derived solely from the meanings of its (immediate) syntactic parts and some general rule(s) of meaning composition. In the present study, compositionality is taken to be the core restricting assumption about the syntax-semantics interface. What makes this idea crucial is its unrivaled simplicity: given a theory of syntax and lexical meanings, compositionality leaves little room for speculation about how compound meanings are derived. This imposes a strong restriction on possible theories of sentence form and word meaning. Such theories fail if they do not allow a compositional derivation of adequate sentence meaning.

Apart from that, compositionality has little to say about how syntactic theory should be organized, or what lexical meanings can be. The generality of compositional semantics is retained as long as one makes as few ad hoc assumptions as possible about syntax and lexical semantics. An important guideline with respect to the latter is to avoid unmotivated lexical ambiguities. A rule of thumb regarding the former is to stick as closely as possible to phonological word order and commonly assumed constituency ("surface structure"). If this turns out to be impossible, some further solid syntactic assumptions should be adopted. Once the theory is developed in this way, compositionality establishes a strong linkage between syntactic theories and semantic theories.

However, it often happens that some structural operations that lack well-established syntactic motivation are assumed for semantic needs. Such a move deprives compositionality of its restrictiveness: whenever a syntactically motivated structure is not easily amenable to compositional methods, it enables one to impose ad hoc additional syntactic operations that eventually do make compositional interpretation possible. I refer to any assumption on structural operations, either at syntactic levels of representation or at (debatable) semantic levels, that is designed only in order to deal with truth-conditional effects, as a *representationalist* approach to meaning. This common practice is rejected in the present study.

Nevertheless, since humans are massive consumers of symbolism, some formal tool for naming model-theoretic objects in the metalanguage turns out to be handy. A common practice since Montague (1973) is to employ a logical language for this purpose. Under this practice, any logical expression that is used for representing the meaning of a natural language expression directly corresponds to a model-theoretic object. This makes the logical language redundant as a level of representation, and it will therefore be used as a convenience only.

The boolean coordination assumption   From a compositional point of view, the cross-categorial behaviour of coordination as illustrated in (1) may seem embarrassing. Given that the syntax is as roughly indicated there, the coordinators *and* and *or* seem to be highly ambiguous. For example, in (1a) the coordinator conjoins sentences, which denote truth values. In (1b) the conjuncts are adjective phrases, which standardly denote predicates (or sets of individuals). This may seem to necessitate the assumption of a lexical ambiguity of coordinators between two different semantic functions needed to conjoin truth values and predicates. Of course, the apparent ambiguity increases once more syntactic categories are considered.

Such undesired ambiguity was avoided by traditional versions of Transformational Grammar, where a rule of *Conjunction Reduction* maps sentential coordinations into phrasal coordinations as in (1b–c). Under that approach, the semantically relevant structure ("deep structure") of (1b) is not as indicated there, but rather as in (19) below.

(19) [Mary is tall] and/or [Mary is thin]

In this analysis, the semantics of coordination is invariably sentential, and coordinators are not ambiguous. However, there are numerous familiar problems for conjunction reduction, and in the non-representationalist view this method can hardly be called a solution, as it stipulates a syntactic operation for elementary semantic needs which has little further motivation.

The boolean approach to coordination adopts a completely opposite line. In this approach coordinators can function directly in different semantic domains because all these domains have something in common: they are all *Boolean Algebras*. Among other things, this means that they are ordered in a similar way. For example, the domain of truth values is ordered by *implication*: truth is "greater" than falsity, or $1 > 0$. Predicates are ordered by *set inclusion*: any set is "greater" than its proper subsets. In boolean terms, these are both manifestations of one order relation: domination (see below). This generality is also reflected in the boolean approach to coordination. In the domain of truth values, the coordinators *and* and *or* correspond to propositional conjunction and disjunction respectively. In the domain of predicates, they correspond to set intersection and set union. However, both the propositional and the set-theoretical operators are instances of the general boolean operators *meet* and *join*. Therefore, although the meanings of coordinators can compose with different kinds of semantic objects, they always denote "the same thing." In this way the boolean approach to coordination avoids the assumption of lexical ambiguity and still leaves the simple compositional picture of the syntax-semantics interface unaffected. Because of the centrality of this boolean treatment I henceforth refer to it as the *Boolean Assumption on coordination*.

A similar approach is adopted in boolean semantics with respect to *negation*. This is also a cross-categorial phenomenon, which is identified with the boolean operator of *complementation*. Negation problems are beyond the scope of the present book and therefore the boolean assumption on negation will be less frequently employed. However, even for a limited treatment of negation phenomena the boolean approach is a useful starting point. The linguistic relevance of negation to the treatment of coordination is especially clear when cases like *neither A nor B, A but not B*, etc. are considered.

Montagovian individuals and generalized quantifiers   Coordination of proper names as in (1c) is of remarkable importance for boolean semantics. Initially, perhaps the most intuitive way to think of proper names is as denoting *entities* in the model of discourse. The domain of entities is primitive, just as the domain of truth values: both domains are not defined in terms of other domains. Unlike the domain of truth values, however, the domain of entities is not boolean: there is no *a priori* order that is assumed for the set of entities. This seems to stand in opposition to the boolean assumption on coordination: as (1c) exemplifies, coordination applies to proper names as well. So, if proper names are interpreted in the domain of entities, then coordination cannot be strictly boolean and the elegant cross-categorial semantics of coordination must be given up.

Montague's treatment of proper names shows the way to a strikingly simple solution of this problem. The elementary linguistic observation is that proper names belong to a much larger syntactic category: they are noun phrases. Montague semantics takes noun phrases to denote *generalized quantifiers*. In extensional systems this means that they denote *sets of sets of entities*. Given Montague's conception of the syntax-semantics interface, it follows that proper names, as a special kind of noun phrases, must also denote sets of sets. A proper name, instead of denoting a certain entity, refers to the *set of sets that contain that entity as a member*. Now, since the domain of generalized quantifiers is boolean, coordination applies in (1c) in the standard way.

When it comes to more complex noun phrases than proper names, the theory of generalized quantifiers has of course much more to offer. As a starting point for this book, however, Montague's boolean treatment of proper names as generalized quantifiers deserves special mention.

An elementary example   To get an impression of the empirical power of boolean semantics and the theory of generalized quantifiers, we consider a familiar example: the interpretation of sentences with predicate coordination, as in the schemes of the following *a* examples.

(20) a. NP sang and danced
     b. NP sang and NP danced

(21) a. NP sang or danced
     b. NP sang or NP danced

Table 1.1
Equivalence of sentences with predicate conjunction and disjunction

Noun phrase	(20a) ⇔ (20b)?	(21a) ⇔ (21b)?
every woman	yes	no
some woman	no	yes
no woman	no	no
not every woman	no	no
Mary	yes	yes
Mary and John	yes	no
Mary or John	no	yes
neither Mary nor John	no	no
exactly one woman	no	no

A sentence with a conjunctive predicate as in (20a) can be equivalent or non-equivalent to the "expanded" sentential conjunction (20b), depending on the identity of the subject noun phrase. For the noun phrase *every woman*, for instance, the sentences (20a) and (20b) are equivalent (i.e. they entail each other). However, for the noun phrase *some woman* the two sentences are not equivalent. The equivalence pattern reverses with predicate *dis*junction as in (21): in this case the subject *some woman* gives rise to equivalence, whereas *every woman* does not. Some more data are summarized in table 1.1. Boolean semantics, unlike traditional transformational accounts of conjunction reduction, predicts such complex entailment patterns in a straightforward fashion.

1.3   Flexibility Principles in Boolean Semantics

The term *boolean semantics* refers to a branch of compositional model-theoretic semantics that studies the implications of the boolean properties of semantic domains for the analysis of natural language phenomena. The general view of this sub-field of semantic theory is the starting point for the investigations in this book. The boolean perspective on natural language was most thoroughly developed in the work of Keenan and Faltz (1978, 1985), which is a linguistic elaboration of some of the central aspects of Montague Grammar. Keenan and Faltz used the boolean approach in order to achieve a more general implementation of Montague's program for the semantic analysis of natural language. Their system did away with many of the translation rules in Montague (1973), which to a large extent obscured Montague's pure concept of compositionality. A similar move in another direction was taken by the influential article of Barwise and Cooper (1981), one of the first systematic studies of model-theoretic properties of noun phrases within the Montagovian framework. The theory of generalized quantifiers that evolved from Barwise and Cooper's article and related works of Keenan, Van Benthem, Westerståhl and their associates is a sub-field of boolean semantics that concentrates on boolean domains for quantification in natural language.

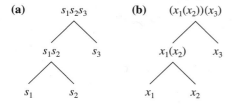

Figure 1.1
Meaning composition using function application

The assumptions of the boolean semantic framework about compositionality and the syntax-semantics interface are pleasingly minimal. The syntax is assumed to have the main propeller of compositional semantic processes: once the denotations of lexical expressions are determined, the denotations of complex expressions are completely predictable from the syntactic structures that are assigned to them. For instance, consider a complex linguistic expression that consists of the lexical expressions s_1, s_2, and s_3. Suppose that the syntax assigns this expression the structure given in figure 1.1a. Suppose further that the denotations of the lexical expressions s_1, s_2 and s_3 are x_1, x_2 and x_3, respectively. Now, the semantic component simply assumes that denotations of expressions that the syntax groups together stand in a function-argument relation to each other. For instance, since the syntax parses the signs s_1 and s_2 as one unit, we assume either that the denotation x_1 is a function that takes the denotation x_2 as its argument or that it is the other way around. The role of the compositional semantic component merely consists in correctly gluing together the denotations by letting the function apply to its argument. The application of this process to the syntactic structure of figure 1.1a is illustrated in figure 1.1b, where the standard notation $a(b)$ denotes the result of applying a function a to an argument b. This process of *function application* is so elementary that it is often hard to realize that it is one of the central assumptions on the syntax-semantics interface.

Unfortunately, boolean semantics that is only equipped with such a simple mechanism for compositional interpretation, has to face too many challenges when it comes to the actual semantic analysis of natural language. In particular, each of the questions that were raised in section 1.1 introduces a serious problem for existing compositional versions of boolean semantics. Some authors conclude from the existence of such problems that there is something fundamentally wrong in the basic assumptions that were described above. However, in this book I will argue that there is no reason for such a dramatic conclusion. To the contrary: the problems raised by phenomena of coordination, plurality and scope can fruitfully be addressed within the boolean framework. The critical step in using boolean semantics for the analysis of these problems is the introduction of a *flexible* mechanism that interfaces the syntax with the semantics, instead of having only one "rigid" rule of function application. The flexibility hypothesis was first put forth by Partee and Rooth (1983) and

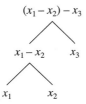

$$(x_1 - x_2) - x_3$$
$$x_1 - x_2 \qquad x_3$$
$$x_1 \qquad x_2$$

Figure 1.2
Meaning composition using subtraction

developed in Partee (1987) and—from different perspectives—in the categorial semantic literature, notably in Van Benthem (1991) and Hendriks (1993). I will now review in general terms the main idea of flexible systems.

We have seen above that a minimal assumption on the syntax-semantics interface takes function application to be the only operation available for meaning composition in natural language. Thus an expression like $s_1 s_2 s_3$ with the structure specified in figure 1.1a can only have meanings of the kind displayed in figure 1.1b, which are obtained by successive function application to lexical denotations according to the syntactic structure. This means that also the lexical denotations must stand in the right function-argument relations for allowing function application to compose them into a complex meaning. However, suppose for the sake of discussion that the denotations x_1, x_2 and x_3 are positive numerical values. Suppose further that we want the complex expression $s_1 s_2 s_3$ to denote the natural number that results from applying the operation of subtraction on these values according to the order of association that is imposed by the syntactic structure in figure 1.1a. To make the analogy with function application more transparent, assume that our subtraction operation always subtracts the smaller number from the bigger one if they are not equal. In this way the result of the operation is unique independently of the linear order of the two daughters, like the result of function application.

Of course, a compositional glue of function application would be of little help in achieving an operation of subtraction between numerical values. However, it is very easy to modify the system in such a way that it generates the desired meaning. All we need is, instead of the rule of function application that was employed in figure 1.1b, a rule of *subtraction* that takes as input any two numerical meanings a and b of sister nodes in the syntactic tree such that $a \geq b$. Our subtraction rule composes the values of these two nodes into the non-negative numerical value $a - b$ that will be used as the denotation of their mother. According to the structure we assume, the new process uses subtraction to generate the numerical meaning $(x_1 - x_2) - x_3$ for the string $s_1 s_2 s_3$, provided $x_1 \geq x_2$ and $x_1 - x_2 \geq x_3$. This is illustrated in figure 1.2.

Obviously, numerical values and their subtractions are hardly useful as meanings of linguistic expressions for the purposes of natural language semantics. However, the general point that the discussion above exemplifies is that whenever a compositional mechanism does not generate the desired meanings, this is not necessarily because the wrong structure or the wrong lexical denotations were assumed. Failure to derive the desired meanings may also result from a "compositional glue" that is not suitable for the purposes of the system. Here, function application is used as the basic compositional glue for the purposes of natural language semantics. However, there is no reason to think that this is the only compositional rule available in the system. Together with function application, the operations that are used for composing denotations but do not have any phonological realization, are referred to as the *flexibility principles* of linguistic theory. In this book a boolean semantics is supplemented with flexibility operations in addition to function application. A suitable configuration of such operations will permit an adequate account of many of the problems raised by the phenomena of coordination, plurality and scope.

To summarize the discussion so far, the diagram in figure 1.3 illustrates the architecture of (flexible) boolean semantics. The role of syntax is to recursively generate complex expressions from lexical items. The *model* contains *denotations* of lexical and complex expressions. However, while lexical expressions are directly assigned denotations in the model, complex expressions get their denotations via syntax-driven rules of semantic composition. In non-flexible boolean semantics the only rule of composition is function application, which is "hard wired" into the system. In a flexible version of boolean semantics, function application is only one of the flexibility principles assumed. These principles, and especially those that are specific to *natural* languages, are the focus of the present study.

What is the status of flexibility principles in the theory of natural language semantics? How are they related to the other modules of linguistic theory? As mentioned above, few linguists would debate on the necessity of function application as a semantic rule of meaning composition. As far as we know this rule should not be affected at all by language specific factors: it is needed in all languages and can freely apply to all constructions. Moreover, any language, natural as well as artificial, whose meanings involve functions and arguments is expected to involve a rule of function application. For this reason function application is a candidate for being a part of what I call the *logical base* of meaning composition. By this I refer to the theory of meaning composition in *all* languages, even in languages other than those spontaneously acquired by children and naturally spoken by adults. This logical module of meaning composition is part of Montague's notion of *Universal Grammar*: the general mathematical theory of symbolic systems. In categorial semantics, the framework assumed in this book, the logical base is a *categorial calculus* managing the types and meanings of linguistic expressions. This calculus may include other rules beside function application, a topic that is extensively explored in Van Benthem (1991).

Notwithstanding the centrality of function application, and perhaps other logical principles, as a central part of meaning composition, it is fairly uncontroversial that the theory of

Boolean Semantics

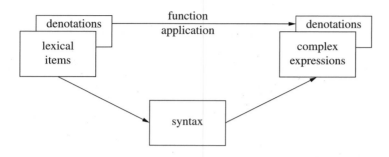

Flexible Boolean Semantics

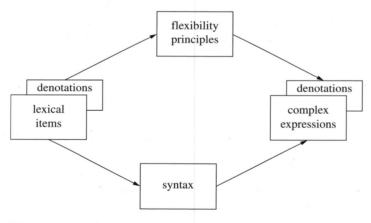

Figure 1.3
Boolean semantics and flexible boolean semantics

natural language should include some flexibility principles of a different kind. Consider for instance the simple Hebrew sentence below.

(22) yeled ba
      child came
      "*A* child came"

This sentence illustrates a cross-linguistically common situation: unlike English, in many languages an article or a determiner is not necessary for a singular noun phrase to be grammatical. Both the Hebrew noun *yeled* (child) and the verb *ba* (came) are assumed by most theories to denote one place predicates, or sets of entities. Two such semantic objects of the same type cannot compose by function application alone to derive a truth value. Hence, in order for sentence (22) to be meaningful the syntactic/semantic theory must involve a covert operation that carries a meaning other than function application. Some theories assume that sentences like (22) contain a phonologically silent indefinite article, which carries the semantics needed to compose the predicates denoted by the noun and the verb. This popular syntactic point need not affect our conclusion about the necessity of flexibility principles other than function application. It is clear that the analysis of sentences like (22) should involve a *phonologically* covert semantic principle in addition to function application, also in the cases where the theory decides to give this semantic principle a syntactic representation.

An invisible semantic operator in the analysis of sentences like (22) above is specifically required for such cases of bare descriptions. It is not a general semantic principle and hence it is unlikely to constitute a part of the logical base. In an influential article, Partee and Rooth (1983) start to explore the operation of such covert semantic operations outside the logical base (though examples like (22) above were not originally discussed in Partee and Rooth's paper, but only in Partee's (1987) subsequent work). Partee and Rooth propose that the semantic theory of natural language should involve various *type shifting principles* that may change types and denotations of natural language expressions in the process of meaning composition. An important part of Partee and Rooth's proposal is that such operators, unlike function application, are not freely introduced. Rather, type shifting in Partee and Rooth's sense applies only when function application fails to compose denotations into a new meaning of a complex expression. This situation is referred to as *type mismatch*. An example for such a situation is sentence (22), discussed above, where the predicates denoted by the noun and the verb in cannot be composed by function application. Hence this is a situation where type shifting is in principle allowed in Partee and Rooth's system. In situations where function application *can* do its job, type shifting principles are ruled out. I refer to this strategy of applying type shifting principles only when they are needed as a *type fitting* strategy.

This book argues that type fitting strategies, although useful for the treatment of some problems in semantic theory, do not exhaust the variety of flexibility principles needed for the analysis of natural language. Specifically, it is argued that type fitting is not the right tool for treating the semantics of simple sentences like (22) above. It is proposed that semantic theory should involve additional principles of a different nature, referred to as *category shifting* principles. These principles, unlike type fitting principles, modify the *semantic category* of an expression (without necessarily changing its type). For instance, in sentence (22) above, the noun has a semantic category of a *predicate*. This category can be shifted into a *quantifier* in the compositional analysis of the sentence. The category shifting operation, unlike type fitting, is not driven by type mismatch but rather by the syntactic configuration: the structure of the noun phrase. Thus, a syntactic theory that postulates a null article in such sentences qualifies as requiring a category shifting principle that is denoted by this null element or is triggered in different means by its presence in the structure.

The three kinds of flexibility discussed above—composition rules of the logical base, type fitting and category shifting operations—are the major principles that will be used to account for semantic data throughout this book.

1.4   Flexibility Principles in the Analysis of Coordination, Plurality and Scope

As mentioned above, two central ideas constitute the cornerstone of boolean semantics. The first idea is that all noun phrases denote generalized quantifiers. The second idea is that coordination is cross-categorially boolean: the coordinators *and* and *or* denote the *meet* and *join* operators in all the semantic domains where they apply. The obvious advantage of these two assumptions lies in their elegance and generality. However, the problems in the analysis of coordination, plurality and scope that were discussed in section 1.1 challenge any straightforward implementation of these uniform principles. The main argument of this book is that these problems can be elegantly solved within a boolean semantics enriched with flexibility principles along the lines introduced in the preceding section. Two semantic assumptions underly the implementation of flexibility principles in the proposed system:

1. Some noun phrases have a *predicative* denotation in addition to their generalized quantifier denotation.
2. Denotations of natural language expressions can range either over *atoms* (= primitive semantic entities) or over *sets* of atoms.

For the sake of exposition in this section we can use the feature values $+Q$ (quantifier) and $-Q$ (predicate) to refer to the first distinction, which classifies the *semantic category* of a denotation. The values $-S$ (atom) and $+S$ (set) correspond to the second distinction and are referred to as the *semantic number* of the denotation. Flexibility principles are used to shift meanings between the four kinds of denotations that these two features describe.

There are two kinds of flexibility principles that will be used to change meanings characterized by the $\pm Q \pm S$ features:

• The *category shifting* principles mentioned above, which map predicative ($-Q$) denotations to quantificational ($+Q$) denotations or vice versa, while (only) possibly affecting their $\pm S$ semantic number feature.
• *Type fitting* principles *à la* Partee and Rooth, which affect the semantic number ($\pm S$) of a denotation.

Below I introduce in informal terms the main flexibility operators that will be used to account for the specific problems presented in section 1.1 above:

The exceptional inverse scope effects of indefinites are analyzed using the *choice function* (CF) mechanism proposed in Reinhart (1997). Intuitively, a choice function is a function that maps any non-empty set (predicate) to an element of this set. Thus, if f is a CF and A is any non-empty set, then $f(A)$ is an element of A. Reinhart proposes that indefinites are syntactically free in their scopal behaviour because their interpretation involves existential quantification over CFs that can occur at any compositional level. For instance, the indefinite in sentence (9a), restated below, is scopally ambiguous because existential quantification over CFs can occur either within the scope of the conditional, as informally paraphrased in (23a), or outside the scope of the conditional, as in (23b).

(23) If some building in Washington is attacked by terrorists then US security will be threatened.
    a. if $\exists f[f$ is a CF and f(building) is attacked by terrorists] then US security will be threatened
    b. $\exists f[f$ is a CF and if f(building) is attacked by terrorists then US security will be threatened]

Reinhart's use of CFs describes correctly scopal effects with singular indefinites, and in chapter 3 it is furthermore extended to deal with more intricate scope phenomena with plural indefinites. However, an important problem for the choice function theory of indefinites appears when CFs are used to map a set A of atomic elements to one of its elements. By definition such an element comes from the non-boolean domain of entities. Therefore, it is no longer clear what to do when the set A happens to be empty: in such a case there is no element that the choice function can "choose." Why this is problematic becomes clear when we consider indefinites like *a unicorn*, whose noun is likely to denote the empty set in many normal situations. Chapter 3 argues that this problem for choice function semantics is mainly a result of the assumption that the non-boolean domain of entities should play an operative role in the theory. It is proposed to employ the standard Montagovian treatment of individuals in the generalized quantifier domain, so the general correspondence between NPs and GQs of boolean semantics is retained. Thus, CFs map sets to *generalized quantifiers*, which in the case of non-empty sets are simply Montagovian individuals. An empty set is mapped by a CF to the *empty quantifier*: the generalized quantifier (= set of sets) that includes no sets whatsoever. This definition naturally solves the problem raised by predicates with empty denotation. Once we readopt a quantificational analysis of indefinites in this way, we view the CF mechanism as a general *category shifting* flexibility principle that maps predicative $(-Q)$ denotations to quantificational $(+Q)$ denotations. As we will presently see, this principle is operative in other cases of NP interpretation besides the scope of indefinites.

Another extensive use of the boolean properties of generalized quantifiers is made in chapter 2, which treats NP coordinations as in the following examples.

(24) a. Mary and John met. (= (7a))
    b. Mary and [John or Bill] met.

Many theories treat sentences like (24a) using a "non-boolean" denotation of *and*. This function operates on objects like $\mathbf{m}'$ (for *Mary*) and $\mathbf{j}'$ (for *John*) in the non-boolean domain of entities to generate a "plural individual" corresponding to the set $\{\mathbf{m}', \mathbf{j}'\}$. However, the "non-boolean *and*" idea not only renounces the generality of the boolean cross-categorial account of *and*, it also does not help very much to analyze more complex cases of coordination with *or*, as in example (24b) above. The problem is that if *and* must apply in (24b) to non-boolean entities in order to generate the collectivity effect, it remains unclear what non-boolean entity can the disjunction *John or Bill* denote.

In chapter 2 it is argued that in fact, no complication of the boolean treatment of *and* (or *or*) is needed, and a flexible version of boolean semantics can naturally account for collective interpretations of NP coordination. As in the choice function account of indefinites, the key for the solution is the Montagovian-Boolean treatment of individuals as generalized quantifiers. Noun phrases like *Mary and John* and *Mary and John or Bill* basically denote quantifiers over atoms—semantic objects of the features $[+Q -S]$. However, an optional flexibility principle called the *minimum operator* maps such generalized quantifiers to predicates over their *minimal sets*. For instance, in (24a) the quantifier denoted by *Mary and John*, which is obtained by the standard boolean denotation of *and*, has only one minimal set: the set $\{\mathbf{m}', \mathbf{j}'\}$. In (24b) there are two minimal sets in the denotation of the subject: $\{\mathbf{m}', \mathbf{j}'\}$ and $\{\mathbf{m}', \mathbf{b}'\}$. The $[-Q +S]$ predicates that range over these sets are mapped by the choice function category shift to $[+Q +S]$ *quantifiers* over sets as in the analysis of the scope of indefinites. The resulting analyses of the sentences in (24) are informally given below.

(25) a. $\exists f[f$ is a CF and $f(\{\{\mathbf{m}', \mathbf{j}'\}\})$ met]
      b. $\exists f[f$ is a CF and $f(\{\{\mathbf{m}', \mathbf{j}'\}, \{\mathbf{m}', \mathbf{b}'\}\})$ met]

Note that in (25a) the choice function applies to a predicate that holds only of the set $\{\mathbf{m}', \mathbf{j}'\}$. This predicate therefore corresponds to a set with only one member, which in this case is itself a set. Consequently, the choice function in (25a) is left with "no choice" but to choose the set of Mary and John. In (25b) the predicate to which the CF applies consists of two different sets. As a result, sentence (24b) is correctly analyzed as equivalent to the sentence *Either Mary and John met or Mary and Bill did*.

The *minimum* and *choice function* flexibility principles mentioned above are also responsible for the interpretation of noun phrases in predicative positions. It is proposed that simple indefinites and definites are *basically* predicative. Thus, their natural appearance in predicative positions as in (13), restated below, is expected.

(26) a. This is *a good proposal/the best proposal*.
      b. Mary considers this *a good proposal/the best proposal*.

As we have seen, in argument positions $-Q$ denotations are mapped to $+Q$ denotations using the choice function category shifting principle. On the other hand, proper names and their coordinations like *Mary and John*, which are basically quantificational, can be mapped using the minimum operator to predicative denotations when they appear in predicative positions. It is proposed that this is the basis for the analysis of such NPs as in the following examples.

(27) a. The best teacher in school is Mary.
　　 b. The best teachers in school are Mary and John.

The application of category shifting principles to the analysis of predicative NPs is the subject of chapter 4. The chapter concentrates on NPs like the proper names, simple in/definites and their coordinations that were discussed above. These NPs can change their semantic category from $-Q$ to $+Q$ and vice versa. However, it is argued that many NPs are uniformly assigned a non-flexible quantificational denotation, which cannot be shifted to a predicate. Examples for such noun phrases are *every child*, *no child*, *most children* and *more/less than five children*. It is proposed that the difference between the two kinds of noun phrases lies in their different syntactic structure: under a simple version of the *DP Hypothesis* (Abney 1987), it is argued that DPs that can undergo category shifting principles are analyzed at the D′ level, with no filled SPEC position. Due to this analysis, such D′/DPs are *potentially predicative*: they have a predicative denotation in addition to their quantificational analysis. By contrast, DPs with a filled SPEC position do not allow category shifting operations and are consequently *purely* quantificational.

Chapter 5 studies the distinction between denotations ranging over atoms and denotations ranging over sets and the ways they are related to each other by means of *type fitting principles*. There are two parts to the proposal in this chapter. First, it is shown that the distinction Dowty (1987) observes between predicates that allow collectivity with *all* and predicates that do not, extends to the whole range of quantificational noun phrases in the plural. This is illustrated by the following contrast between (28a) and (28b).

(28) a. 　All the/exactly five/no/many/less than ten students met.
　　 b. 　*All the/exactly five/no/many/less than ten students are a good team.

Moreover, this observation allows us to develop a descriptive criterion that divides the class of natural language predicates (verbs, nouns and adjectives) into two sub-classes. One sub-class is insensitive to the replacement of a plural determiner (e.g. *all*, *at least two* and plural *no*) by its singular correlate (e.g. *every*, *more than one*, and singular *no* respectively). This sub-class includes collective predicates like *be a good team* and *be numerous*, but also distributive predicates like *sleep* or "mixed" predicates like *vote to accept the proposal*. Each of these predicates when substituted for **P** in the following examples gives rise to equivalent, though possibly unacceptable, sentences.

(29) a. All the/at least two/no student*s* **P**.
　　 b. Every/more than one/no student **P**.

However, for predicates like *meet, gather, be similar, praise each other* and many other predicates, there is a clear difference, either in acceptability or in truth conditions, between (29a) and (29b). The first sub-class of predicates is referred to as *atom predicates*, whereas the latter predicates are called *set predicates*. Note that this distinction is significantly different than the traditional typology of distributive, collective and "mixed" predicates, because, for instance, atom predicates are not necessarily distributive (cf. *be a good team*).

It is proposed that the descriptive distinction between atom predicates and set predicates is straightforwardly reflected in their denotation. Atom predicates range over atoms, thus they are classified as $-S$. Set predicates range over sets of atoms and hence are classified as $+S$. The standard "atomic" analysis of determiners in generalized quantifier theory is retained, but it is further proposed that type fitting operators can change a denotation ranging over atoms $(-S)$ to one ranging over sets $(+S)$. Simple assumptions on the type of the morphological number feature explain why this type fitting process is allowed only when the predicate is morphologically plural. From these assumptions it follows that set predicates can allow collectivity with determiners, but only when they are morphologically plural. Atom predicates, by contrast, are insensitive to morphological number because their basic denotation does not include sets to begin with. Collective interpretations of sentences with atom predicates are restricted to *potentially predicative* noun phrases as in the following examples.

(30) The students/Mary and John/some students I know are a good team.

It is proposed that such collective interpretations are a manifestation of a general number shifting operator from sets to atoms, following Landman (1989,1996), which is restricted to apply only with predicative denotations of noun phrases.

1.5   Technical Background

This section briefly summarizes some of the most useful definitions that are employed in the semantic analyses given in this book. Familiarity with elementary set theory and logic is presupposed.

Extensionally typed domains constitute an extensional model. These domains are the sets from which natural language extensional meanings (denotations) are taken. The extensional types are defined as follows.

Definition 1 (extensional types)   Let TYPE_0, the set of *primitive types*, be the set $\{e, t\}$, where e is the type of *entities* and t is the type of *truth values*. The set of *extensional types* is the smallest set TYPE containing TYPE_0 that satisfies for every $\tau, \sigma \in \text{TYPE}: (\tau\sigma) \in \text{TYPE}$.

Outermost parentheses of types are omitted. Each type classifies a domain according to the following definition.

Definition 2 (typed domains) D_e is an arbitrary non-empty set. $D_t = \{0, 1\}$. If τ and σ are types then $D_{\tau\sigma} = D_\sigma^{D_\tau}$, the set of functions from D_τ to D_σ. *Alternative notation*: $\mathbf{2} = D_t$, $D_\tau \to D_\sigma = D_{\tau\sigma}$.

Further, $D_{\tau t}$ can also be thought of as $\wp(D_\tau)$, the power set of D_τ. This is since every member of $D_{\tau t}$ is the characteristic function of a unique set in $\wp(D_\tau)$ and vice versa. This can be generalized in that objects in domains of type $\tau_1(\ldots(\tau_n t)\ldots)$ (the *boolean* domains, see below) characterize n-ary relations in the cartesian product $D_{\tau_1} \times \cdots \times D_{\tau_n}$. The letter E is sometimes used to refer to an arbitrary domain D_τ, most often D_e.

Let L be a natural language over a finite set of words (strings) Σ, which constitutes the *lexicon* (alphabet) of L. That is, L is a possibly infinite subset of Σ^*, the set of all concatenations of strings from Σ. Unlike the definition of formal languages like the predicate calculus, assume that the strings in Σ all have a denotation and hence do not include constructions like brackets or logical constants (e.g. $\forall$, $\exists$) whose meaning is introduced syncategorematicly in the definition of the language. Let **type** be a function mapping any member of Σ to an extensional type in TYPE. An extensional *model* of L is a pair $M = \langle D_e, F \rangle$, where D_e is the non-empty set of entities and F is the *lexical interpretation function* from Σ to $\cup_{\tau \in \text{TYPE}} D_\tau$ such that for every $x \in \Sigma$: $F(x) \in D_{\mathbf{type}(x)}$. The task of giving a model-theoretic semantics for L is to define an *interpretation function* $[\![\ ]\!]_M$ that for any given model M assigns each sentence of L a denotation. The subscript M in $[\![\ ]\!]_M$ is often omitted. Since the language L is usually infinite, L has to be defined using a finite *grammar* G. In compositional systems the interpretation function is defined as a recursive extension of F to all syntactic categories in G. Thus, if x is in Σ, then $[\![\ ]\!]$ satisfies $[\![x]\!] = F(x)$.

Notational convention: Lexical denotations are given in boldface. Types are often given in subscript. For instance, assume that the **type** function maps the word *child* in English to type et. Thus, in any model of English the interpretation function F assigns this word an (arbitrary) element of D_{et}. We denote $[\![\text{child}]\!] = \mathbf{child}'_{et}$.

In order to refer easily to non-arbitrary denotation assignments, an extensionally typed λ-theoretical language with identity is often employed. The technical details in the definition of the syntax and semantics of such languages are familiar and will not be repeated here. See Dowty et al. (1981: ch. 4) or Gamut (1991b: ch. 4) for easy introductions from a logical-linguistic perspective. Once the logical language is defined useful first-order logical constants like $\neg$, $\wedge$, $\vee$, $\to$, $\forall$, $\exists$ can be easily expressed in this language (see e.g. Van Benthem (1991: 7)). The notation φ_τ indicates that φ is an expression of type τ. In case φ is a λ-expression without free variables, $[\![\varphi]\!]$ stands for a corresponding object in a given model. We will switch occasionally between such lambda notation and ordinary set-theoretical notation.

Certain domains are called *boolean* domains. To review their special properties, let us first present the definition of *Boolean Algebras* and their basic supplement concepts (see Sikorski (1964): 1–7).

Definition 3 (boolean algebra)   Let A be a non-empty set. Let $\wedge$, $\vee$ and $^-$ be functions such that for every $x, y \in A$: $x \wedge y \in A$, $x \vee y \in A$ and $\overline{x} \in A$. A structure $\langle A, \wedge, \vee, ^- \rangle$ is called a *Boolean Algebra* iff the following holds for every $x, y, z \in A$:

(A$_1$) $x \wedge y = y \wedge x$, $x \vee y = y \vee x$

(A$_2$) $x \wedge (y \wedge z) = (x \wedge y) \wedge z$, $x \vee (y \vee z) = (x \vee y) \vee z$

(A$_3$) $(x \wedge y) \vee y = y$, $(x \vee y) \wedge y = y$

(A$_4$) $x \wedge (y \vee z) = (x \wedge y) \vee (x \wedge z)$, $x \vee (y \wedge z) = (x \vee y) \wedge (x \vee z)$

(A$_5$) $x \wedge \overline{x}) \vee y = y$, $(x \vee \overline{x}) \wedge y = y$

The operators $\wedge$, $\vee$ and $^-$ are called the *meet*, *join* and *complement* operators of the boolean algebra.

The axioms in (A$_1$) are called the *commutative* laws. (A$_2$) lists the *associative* laws, (A$_3$) the *absorption* laws, and (A$_4$) the *distributive* laws. A boolean algebra $\langle A, \wedge, \vee, ^- \rangle$ is often sloppily referred to as the "boolean algebra A" when the boolean operators are clear from the context.

   An important fact is that in any boolean algebra A, for all $x, y \in A$: $x \wedge y = y$ iff $x \vee y = x$. In case $x \wedge y = y$ (or $x \vee y = x$) holds we say that x *dominates* y.

Definition 4 (domination)   An element x in a boolean algebra A *dominates* an element y in A iff $x \wedge y = y$ iff $x \vee y = x$. This is denoted by $y \leq x$.

Provably, the "$\leq$" domination relation is a partial order for any Boolean Algebra. One consequence of this definition is that the meet and join operators can equivalently be defined as the *greatest lower bound* and *least upper bound* respectively for the partial order of domination. The definitions of these notions are given below.

Definition 5   Let x and y be two elements in a partially ordered set $\langle B, \leq \rangle$.

1. An element $z \in B$ is the *greatest lower bound* (glb) of x and y iff $z \leq x$, $z \leq y$ and for every $z' \in B$: if $z' \leq x$ and $z' \leq y$ then $z' \leq z$.
2. An element $z \in B$ is the *least upper bound* (lub) of x and y iff $x \leq z$, $y \leq z$ and for every $z' \in B$: if $x \leq z'$ and $y \leq z'$ then $z \leq z'$.

The correspondence between the meet/join operators and the glb/lub operators with respect to domination allows alternative axiomatizations of Boolean Algebra where the basic notions are domination and complementation rather than meet, join and complementation.

   Each boolean algebra A has the following property: for all $x, y \in A$: $x \wedge \overline{x} = y \wedge \overline{y}$ and $x \vee \overline{x} = y \vee \overline{y}$. This fact is crucial for identifying the (unique) *zero* and the *unit* elements of the algebra, which are defined as follows.

Definition 6 (zero and unit elements)   The *zero* and *unit* elements of a boolean algebra A are defined by $0 = x \wedge \overline{x}$, $1 = x \vee \overline{x}$, for arbitrary $x \in A$.

Boolean algebras intuitively generalize naive set theory. For example, given a non-empty set X, the power set $\wp(X)$ with set intersection, union and complementation is a boolean algebra. Set inclusion is the domination relation of this algebra, the empty set is the zero element and X is the unit element.

The connection between type theoretical domains and boolean algebras becomes transparent with the set of *boolean types*.

Definition 7 (boolean type)   An extensional type τ is *boolean* iff $\tau = t$ or $\tau = \sigma_1\sigma_2$, where σ_1 is any type and σ_2 is a boolean type.

All boolean types are of the form $\sigma_1(\sigma_2(\ldots(\sigma_n t)\ldots))$, for some natural $n \geq 0$. For the corresponding domains it is straightforward to define boolean operators in lambda format. This is done in the following definition.

Definition 8 (polymorphic boolean operators)   Let τ be a boolean type. Let $\wedge_{t(tt)}$, $\vee_{t(tt)}$, $\neg_{tt}$ and $\rightarrow_{t(tt)}$ be the standard propositional functions. Denote:

$$\sqcap_{\tau(\tau\tau)} = \begin{cases} \wedge_{t(tt)} & \text{if } \tau = t \\ \lambda X_\tau.\lambda Y_\tau.\lambda Z_{\sigma_1}.X(Z) \sqcap_{\sigma_2(\sigma_2\sigma_2)} Y(Z) & \text{if } \tau = \sigma_1\sigma_2 \end{cases}$$

$$\sqcup_{\tau(\tau\tau)} = \begin{cases} \vee_{t(tt)} & \text{if } \tau = t \\ \lambda X_\tau.\lambda Y_\tau.\lambda Z_{\sigma_1}.X(Z) \sqcup_{\sigma_2(\sigma_2\sigma_2)} Y(Z) & \text{if } \tau = \sigma_1\sigma_2 \end{cases}$$

$$\neg_{\tau\tau} = \begin{cases} \neg_{tt} & \text{if } \tau = t \\ \lambda X_\tau.\lambda Z_{\sigma_1}.\neg_{\sigma_2\sigma_2}(X(Z)) & \text{if } \tau = \sigma_1\sigma_2 \end{cases}$$

$$\sqsubseteq_{\tau(\tau t)} = \begin{cases} \rightarrow_{t(tt)} & \text{if } \tau = t \\ \lambda X_\tau.\lambda Y_\tau.\forall Z_{\sigma_1}[X(Z) \sqsubseteq_{\sigma_2(\sigma_2 t)} Y(Z)] & \text{if } \tau = \sigma_1\sigma_2 \end{cases}$$

$0_\tau = X \sqcap \neg X$, *for arbitrary* X_τ

$1_\tau = X \sqcup \neg X$, *for arbitrary* X_τ

The notations $X \sqcap Y$, $X \sqcup Y$ and $X \sqsubseteq Y$ are "sugarings" for $(\sqcap(X))(Y)$, $(\sqcup(X))(Y)$ and $(\sqsubseteq(X))(Y)$ respectively.

It is not hard to establish that $\langle D_\tau, [\![\sqcap_{\tau(\tau\tau)}]\!], [\![\sqcup_{\tau(\tau\tau)}]\!], [\![\neg_{\tau\tau}]\!]\rangle$ is a boolean algebra for every boolean type τ and every model. The function $[\![\sqsubseteq_{\tau(\tau t)}]\!]$ is the domination relation and $[\![0_\tau]\!]$ and $[\![1_\tau]\!]$ are the zero and unit element, respectively. In fact, when $\tau = \sigma_1\sigma_2$ this algebra is a special one: it is the *pointwise algebra* (see Keenan and Faltz (1985: 82)) from D_{σ_1} to the boolean algebra of D_{σ_2}. In boolean domains the correspondence between the type-theoretical constructs and their set-theoretical parallels is obvious. For instance, a function $X_{et} \sqcap Y_{et}$ characterizes the intersection $\mathbf{X} \cap \mathbf{Y}$ of the sets $\mathbf{X}$ and $\mathbf{Y}$ that are characterized by the conjuncts. For this reason the set-theoretical notation $\cap, \cup, \overline{X}, \subseteq, \emptyset$ and $\mathbf{U}$ is sometimes used for boolean domains instead of $\sqcap, \sqcup, \neg X, \sqsubseteq, 0$ and 1. Further standard notation, in the domain of truth values, lets $\bot$ and $\top$ denote 0_t and 1_t, respectively.

Remarks

1. The denotations ⊓, ⊔ and ¬ of the natural language words *and*, *or* and *not* are not ordinary typed denotations: they are *polymorphic* functions that are potentially assigned an infinite number of types. I do not specify in this book how to determine that, for instance, the sentential coordinator in sentence (1a) gets the type $t(tt)$, while the predicate coordinator in (1b) requires the type $(et)((et)(et))$. There are various mechanisms that can handle such type substitutions and I know no linguistic reason to decide between them.

2. A further polymorphism of the English coordinators *and* and *or* consists in the fact that they can syntactically coordinate an arbitrary number of conjuncts. Consider for example a coordination like *tall, rich, nice and handsome*, which has four conjuncts. This behaviour motivates a generalized definition of the ⊓ and ⊔ operators as *n*-ary rather than just binary operators. This extension is straightforward and I will ignore it throughout this book.

In the Keenan and Faltz treatment, *all* natural language categories have boolean types. This has the advantage of allowing a uniform treatment of coordination and negation, but also has the virtue of enabling one to classify linguistically relevant properties of expressions across different categories. One of the most useful among these is monotonicity.

Definition 9 (monotonicity)   Let σ_1 and σ_2 be boolean types. A function $f \in D_{\sigma_1\sigma_2}$ is:

monotone increasing iff for all $X, Y \in D_{\sigma_1} : X \leq Y \Rightarrow f(X) \leq f(Y)$;

monotone decreasing iff for all $X, Y \in D_{\sigma_1} : X \leq Y \Rightarrow f(X) \geq f(Y)$; and

monotone iff f is either monotone increasing or monotone decreasing.

Let us briefly review some central notions from Generalized Quantifier theory. A *generalized quantifier* (GQ) over a domain D_τ is any element of $D_{(\tau t)t}$. Useful set-theoretical notation: $Q_E \in \wp(\wp(E))$ is a generalized quantifier over E. Across models, a functor Q mapping a domain E to a generalized quantifier Q_E over E is a *global* generalized quantifier. A *determiner* over E is a function $D_E \in \wp(E) \to \wp(\wp(E))$, mapping subsets of E to generalized quantifiers. Alternatively, a determiner D_E over E can be viewed as a relation between subsets of E, that is as a subset of $\wp(E) \times \wp(E)$. Again across models, a *global* determiner D is a functor mapping a domain E to a determiner D_E over E. The subscript E is often omitted when no confusion between denotations and global functors should arise. Note that the letter D is ambiguously used both as a name for determiner functions and as notation for typed domains.

Examples

1. The GQ corresponding to the proper name *Mary* is the Montagovian individual $\{A \subseteq E : \mathbf{m'} \in A\}$, where $\mathbf{m'}$ is some arbitrary element of E.

2. Determiners:

every'$(X)(Y)$ iff $X \subseteq Y$
some'$(X)(Y)$ iff $X \cap Y \neq \emptyset$
no'$(X)(Y)$ iff $X \cap Y = \emptyset$

exactly_one$'(X)(Y)$ iff $|X \cap Y| = 1$
more_than_half$'(X)(Y)$ iff $|X \cap Y| > |X \cap \overline{Y}|$

There are three basic properties for characterizing determiners in GQ theory:

Definition 10 (conservativity)   A global determiner D is *conservative* iff for all $X, Y \subseteq E$:
$D_E(X)(Y) \Leftrightarrow D_E(X)(X \cap Y)$.

Definition 11 (extension)   A global determiner D satisfies *extension* iff for all $X, Y \subseteq E \subseteq E'$: $D_E(X)(Y) \Leftrightarrow D_{E'}(X)(Y)$.

Definition 12 (isomorphy)   A global determiner D is *isomorphism invariant* iff for every isomorphism $f : E \to E'$, for all $X, Y \subseteq E$: $D_E(X)(Y) \Leftrightarrow D_{E'}(f[X])(f[Y])$.

The notation $f[X]$ means $\{f(x) : x \in X\}$. The five determiner denotations defined above satisfy the three properties. In fact, it is commonly agreed that *all* determiners of natural language denote conservative functions, while most *lexical* denotations of natural language determiners satisfy extension and isomorphy. See section 3.5 for further discussion.

Having reviewed some basic model-theoretic concepts to be employed, let us briefly concentrate on the aspect of *meaning composition*: the general procedure for defining the interpretation function $[\![\ ]\!]$ in natural language on the basis of the lexical interpretation function F. On this point there is no consensus among existing theories of grammar. The general approach that is adopted throughout this book is that of *categorial semantics*, as extensively studied in Van Benthem (1991). The categorial semantic approach seems to be most general in that it can be applied in different syntactic frameworks, both generative and categorial ones. Its main characteristics are described below.

The basic "compositional glue" is *function application*. Two denotations $f_{\tau\sigma}$ and x_{τ} can combine by applying the function f to the argument x. Semantic composition is *non-directional* in that the function-argument order is irrelevant for the derived meaning. Technically, non-directionality is obtained by assuming a composition rule of *permutation* that switches the order of its input. Summarizing then, there are two type transition rules, which together make up the *Ajdukiewicz calculus* (after Ajdukiewicz (1935)), which is defined below in a natural deduction format.

Definition 13 (the Ajdukiewicz calculus)

Function Application (APP): $\dfrac{\tau\sigma \;\; \tau}{\sigma}$ (type transition)

$\dfrac{A \;\; B}{A(B)}$ (semantics)

Permutation (PERM): $\dfrac{\tau \;\; \sigma}{\sigma \;\; \tau}$ (type transition)

$\dfrac{A \;\; B}{B \;\; A}$ (semantics)

The Ajdukiewicz calculus is one of the simplest options for defining a module of flexibility principles in semantic theory. An attractive property of such a non-directional system is that it enables one to abstract from many syntactic idiosyncrasies in the compositional analysis of a given expression. For instance, in English the meaning of a constituent like *see John* is derived in the same way as the meaning of the constituent *Jan zien* is derived in Dutch. Another example concerns Italian, where a noun phrase like *every little girl* can be expressed either with a pre-nominal adjective is either pre-nominal as in English (*ogni piccola bambina*), or with a post-nominal adjective as in Hebrew (*ogni bambina piccola*). Both forms mean the same and in the Ajdukiewicz calculus they can be interpreted without encoding information about word-order into the semantics. This is exemplified in (31), where the semantics of the modified nominal is analyzed.

(31) a. $[\![$piccola bambina$]\!]$: $\mathbf{piccola}'_{(et)(et)}$ $\mathbf{bambina}'_{et}$ $\overset{\text{APP}}{\Longrightarrow}$ $\mathbf{piccola}'(\mathbf{bambina}')$

    b. $[\![$bambina piccola$]\!]$: $\mathbf{bambina}'_{et}$ $\mathbf{piccola}'_{(et)(et)}$ $\overset{\text{PERM}}{\Longrightarrow}$ $\mathbf{piccola}'$ $\mathbf{bambina}'$ $\overset{\text{APP}}{\Longrightarrow}$ $\mathbf{piccola}'(\mathbf{bambina}')$

Permutation in semantic analyses will often be used without mention.

In a non-directional semantic system some non-trivial assumptions about natural language syntax have to be made. For instance, sentence (32) must have the binary branching structure specified in (32a). This correctly allows the derivation of meaning (32b), whereas the incorrect meaning in (32d) is not derived.

(32) Every student ran.
    a. [[every student] ran]
    b. $(\mathbf{every}'(\mathbf{student}'))(\mathbf{run}')$
    c. [every student ran]
    d. $(\mathbf{every}'(\mathbf{run}'))(\mathbf{student}')$

If a flatter structure like (32c) is assumed, *both* meanings (32b) and (32d) are derived due to the possibility of applying permutation in the translation of the three daughter constituent *every student ran*. This kind of ambiguity is of course highly undesirable. Fortunately, the structure that is required for eliminating such effects is commonly assumed by most syntactic theories. In any case, there is no need for making a too strong commitment to the permutation rule of the Ajdukiewicz calculus as a general flexibility principle in the analysis of natural language. It is however a convenient assumption that can be easily adapted by various syntactic and semantic frameworks.

1.6   The Organization of the Book

Chapter 2 reviews previous accounts of non-boolean *and* and introduces the proposed alternative treatment of collectivity in NP coordination using the minimum operator. Chapter 3 develops the choice function theory of indefinites, both descriptively, for treating plural indefinites, and formally, by introducing the solution to the empty set problem and other details concerning the compositional implementation of choice functions. Chapter 4 combines the minimum operator and the choice function mechanism of chapters 2 and 3 into a general system of category shifting that also accounts for the interpretation of predicative NPs. Chapter 5 introduces the atom/set distinction and the number shifting principles that account for the interpretation of plural quantificational NPs. Chapter 6 recapitulates the general approach to distributivity that emerges from the proposals in the preceding chapters. Chapter 7 summarizes the overall system that emerges and specifies some general problems for further research.

1.7   A Bibliographical Note

The textbooks Chierchia and McConnel-Ginet (1990), Dowty et al. (1981), Gamut (1991a, 1991b) and Heim and Kratzer (1997) discuss at length many relevant foundational issues for semantic theory. The books by Dowty et al. and Gamut also contain detailed introductions to Montague Grammar as developed in Montague (1973). Janssen (1983) is a thorough study of compositionality and the foundations of Montague Grammar. Sikorski (1964), Halmos (1963) and Koppelberg (1989) are introductions to the mathematics of Boolean Algebras. Keenan and Faltz (1985) is a detailed application of Boolean Algebra to linguistic semantics within the Montagovian tradition. For Generalized Quantifier theory, the reader is referred to Barwise and Cooper (1981) and Keenan and Stavi (1986). Keenan (1996b), Keenan and Westerståhl (1996), and Van der Does and Van Eijck (1996) contain up-to-date surveys of this field from various angles. For a broad investigation of categorial semantics see Van Benthem (1991). Obviously, this list covers only a tiny portion of the large amount of relevant literature.

Chapter 2
Coordination and Collectivity

The apparent simplicity of natural language coordination is one of its most enigmatic aspects. Most people will find it amusing to know that the semantic analysis of expressions like *Mary and John* or *healthy and happy* requires some non-trivial abstractions. The boolean perspective in Montague's work opened the way for a semantic clarity in the analysis of coordination that matches its seemingly simple meaning. This chapter attempts to retain this clarity while broadening the empirical look. The collective interpretation of noun phrase coordinations, which is widely considered to constitute a major challenge for the Boolean/Montagovian account, is shown to follow in fact from straightforward properties of conjunction *within* this system. Collective interpretations are treated using a flexibility operator that applies to noun phrase denotations. The cross-categorially unified analysis of coordination in the boolean framework is retained. It is further proposed that the flexibility operator that achieves this unified treatment cannot be activated by the "last resort" principle of Partee and Rooth (1983), where type shifting operators apply only in cases of type mismatch. Rather, the operator applies freely in the simple coordinations that are treated in this chapter. The nature of the restrictions on its use will be clarified in chapter 4.

Section 2.1 describes the problem of collectivity and noun phrase coordination in general terms. Section 2.2 critically reviews previous treatments, and focuses on the proposal to treat conjunction using non-boolean operators. Section 2.3 introduces the proposed flexible approach together with elements of its implementation. Section 2.4 briefly discusses some principles in the boolean analysis of *predicate* conjunction.

2.1   The Plurality-Coordination Problem

The boolean semantic framework offers an account of a large equivalence pattern that is displayed by sentences with noun phrase coordinations. This kind of equivalence between sentences is sometimes referred to as *distributive predication*.[1] Some examples are given in (1) to (3).

(1) a. Mary and John slept.
     b. ⇔ Mary slept and John slept.

(2) a. Most women or most men are tall.
     b. ⇔ Most women are tall or most men are tall.

(3) a. Neither the milkman nor the postman arrived.
     b. ⇔ Neither did the milkman arrive nor did the postman.

Consider for example sentence (1a). The boolean treatment of the subject proceeds by intersecting two Montagovian individuals as specified in (4) below. The equality in (4) directly follows from the definitions that were given in chapter 1.

(4) $[\lambda P.P(\mathbf{m}')] \sqcap [\lambda P.P(\mathbf{j}')]$
     $= \lambda P.P(\mathbf{m}') \wedge P(\mathbf{j}')$

The intuitive equivalence (1a) ⇔ (1b) is accounted for due to the following formal equivalence:

(5) $[\lambda P.P(\mathbf{m}') \wedge P(\mathbf{j}')](\mathbf{sleep}')$
     ⇔ $\mathbf{sleep}'(\mathbf{m}') \wedge \mathbf{sleep}'(\mathbf{j}')$

The boolean analysis of distributive predication applies in an equally elegant way to (2) and (3), as well as to many more complex cases of NP coordination. In fact, standard versions of boolean semantics predict similar equivalences with NP coordinations for *all* NPs, for *all* kinds of coordination.[2] In general, this happens due to the pointwise definition of the boolean operators in chapter 1. Under this definition, whenever f and g are functions of type $\tau\sigma$ and x is an argument of type τ we gave the following equivalences.

(6) $(f \sqcap_1 g)(x) = f(x) \sqcap_2 f(y)$

(7) $(f \sqcup_1 g)(x) = f(x) \sqcup_2 f(y)$

(8) $(\neg_1 f)(x) = \neg_2(f(x))$

The boolean operators $\sqcap_{1/2}$, $\sqcup_{1/2}$ and $\neg_{1/2}$ are of the types specified below.

Operator	Type
$\sqcap_1, \sqcup_1$	$(\tau\sigma)((\tau\sigma)(\tau\sigma))$
$\sqcap_2, \sqcup_2$	$\sigma(\sigma\sigma)$
$\neg_1$	$(\tau\sigma)(\tau\sigma)$
$\neg_2$	$\sigma\sigma$

This general treatment, although advantageous in many cases, is not so successful in handling another large class of sentences with coordinated NPs. With many predicates, NP conjunctions with *and* do not give rise to distributivity equivalences. Such cases exemplify what is known as *collective predication*. For instance, compare the pair of sentences in (1) with the following pair of sentences.

(9) a. Mary and John weigh exactly 140 kg.

    b. $\nLeftrightarrow$ Mary weighs exactly 140 kg. and John weighs exactly 140 kg.

Unlike the previous examples, in (9) the two sentences are not equivalent: in a situation where Mary and John *together* weigh 140 kg., (9a) is true (at least under one of its interpretations) whereas (9b) is false. Some theories assume that sentences like (9a) are *ambiguous* between a "distributive reading," where the equivalence with sentence (9b) holds, and a "collective reading," where it does not. For the sake of the present discussion this ambiguity intuition can be ignored. Whatever the empirical status of this judgement may be (a point that is often debated), it is clear that the two *sentences* (9a) and (9b) are not equivalent. Similarly, sentence (10a) below is not equivalent to (10b). In fact, sentence (10b) is unacceptable.

(10) a. Mary and John met.

    b. $\nLeftrightarrow$ *Mary met and John met.

This unacceptability indicates that unlike sentence (9a), sentence (10a) can be understood *only* collectively. A boolean analysis of sentences like (9a) and (10a) along the lines of (4) and (5) ignores their collective interpretation and incorrectly predicts distributivity equivalence for these cases.

More complex cases occur when other coordinators are involved in addition to *and*. For instance, sentence (11a) below is equivalent to (11b). This equivalence makes it hard to qualify the predication in (11a) as "distributive" or "collective." More crucial than the applicability of such labels is the fact that this kind of data is not accounted for by the standard boolean analysis.

(11) a. Mary and the postman or the milkman met.

    b. Mary and the postman met or Mary and the milkman met.

Other problematic cases appear with various singular and plural NPs that are coordinated by *and*. The sentences in (12) below exemplify this. Since no one of these sentences is equivalent to its distributive counterpart, this is another problem for the standard theory.

(12) a. An American and a Russian played a duo together.

    b. Every American and every Russian spoke English to each other.

    c. The Americans and the Russians fought each other.

    d. Two Americans and three Russians made an excellent basketball team.

Examples as in (9) to (12) show that collectivity, or absence of distributivity, is a highly productive phenomenon that occurs with various NP coordinations. However, it should be noted that the appearance of the coordinator *and* is crucial for obtaining collective effects. Non-conjunctive coordinators like *or* and *neither . . . nor* always show the same distributive behaviour of (1) to (3). Compare, for example, sentences (13a) and (14a) below, which are equivalent to the respective *b* sentences, to sentence (15a)($= $(12c)), which is not equivalent to (15b).

(13) a. The Americans or the Russians fought each other.

    b. ⇔ The Americans fought each other or the Russians fought each other.

(14) a. Neither the Americans nor the Russians fought each other.

    b. ⇔ Neither did the Americans fight each other nor did the Russians.

(15) a. The Americans and the Russians fought each other.

    b. ⇎ The Americans fought each other and the Russians fought each other.

As noted in Payne (1985: 17–18), similar distinctions as the one between *and* and other coordinators in English appear with striking regularity across the different languages of the world. Observe, however, that there are also certain conjunctive NP constructions that show a purely distributive behaviour. For instance, the sentences in (16) below, unlike sentence (15a) above, *are* equivalent to the sentence in (15b).

(16) $\left\{ \begin{array}{l} \text{The Americans and the Russians } too \\ \text{Both the Americans and the Russians} \\ \text{The Americans as well as the Russians} \end{array} \right\}$ fought each other

    We conclude that a distinction between the collectivity potential of *and* and other coordinators has to be made by any comprehensive theory of natural language semantics. The boolean analysis seems to fail to make this distinction. Of course, it is impossible to either substantiate or remove this suspicion without a general theory of distributive and collective predication. Two closely related questions should therefore be distinguished:

i. What are the sources of the distributive/collective distinction?

ii. Is the boolean assumption inadequate for conjunctive coordination?

Let us refer to these questions as the *plurality-coordination problem*. The puzzle, although certainly not in this formulation, has a very long history. Lasersohn (1995: 12) in his historical review of the problem mentions that the discussion of related issues reaches as far back as Aristotle. The next section reviews some of the approaches to the problem in contemporary semantics.

2.2 Previous Proposals

2.2.1 On non-boolean conjunction

Different accounts of plurality and conjunction give significantly different answers to questions (i) and (ii) above. However, with respect to one central aspect there is overwhelming agreement: virtually all previous works on the topic consider the boolean assumption concerning *and* to be (at best) insufficient. The prominent view takes cases like (10a), restated here as (17), as straightforward evidence for the existence of *non-boolean conjunction*.

(17) Mary and John met.

A basic assumption in this approach is that sentences like (17) make an assertion about a *plural individual*. Intuitively, plural individuals, unlike singular individuals, are not primitive (atomic) and can be thought of as sets of singular individuals. For example, in (17) the conjuncts denote the singular individuals $\mathbf{m}'$ (for Mary) and $\mathbf{j}'$ (for John). The role of non-boolean *and* is to "amalgamate" these individuals into a plural individual $\{\mathbf{m}', \mathbf{j}'\}$. A predicate like *meet* can directly apply to such a plural entity. Now, as with all predicates, there is no a priori reason to assume 'distribution' of the predicate to parts of the plural individual it is applied to. For example, if John is happy, we do not expect his thumb to be happy as well. Similarly, if the plural individual $\{\mathbf{m}', \mathbf{j}'\}$ is in the extension of *meet*, it does not follow that any of the singular individuals that take part in it are also in the extension of *meet*. In (17) non-boolean conjunction has been used to generate such a plural individual, and this causes the collectivity effect.

Before discussing several variants of this idea, let us consider some of its general characteristics. First, the non-boolean semantics of *and* is not proposed as an *alternative* to the boolean assumption. All non-boolean accounts agree that the boolean treatment of *and* is at least needed for the conjunction of some categories (with little agreement on what those categories actually are). Typically, in many proposals sentence, predicate and quantifier conjunction remain boolean. The non-boolean approach therefore inherently embodies a two-part analysis of *and*, consisting of a boolean as well as a non-boolean component. Furthermore, the treatment of non-conjunctive coordinators like *or* and *neither . . . nor* remains strictly boolean. Thus the distinction between *and* and other coordinators is attributed to the existence of an additional non-boolean interpretation of the former. In the absence of any alternative hypothesis, this assumption must be considered an accidental lexical fact about certain languages. Thus, if in some languages a non-boolean meaning is attached to conjunctive coordinators (for historical reasons perhaps), it can be expected that other coordinators in different languages should arbitrarily show collective behaviour as well. As mentioned above, this is not the case: cross-linguistically, only the conjunctive coordinator gives rise to collectivity effects. In addition, the definition of non-boolean *and* is usually similar, or even identical, to boolean *join*, the denotation that is proposed for *or*. Hence, on semantic grounds it is reasonable to expect the non-boolean function to be accommodated by *or*, rather than assimilated to *and* (see Hoeksema (1988: 26)). But again, no natural language behaves in this way. Thus the non-boolean approach leaves the main linguistic question open: why do only *conjunctive* NP coordinations show collective behaviour?

At a more general methodological level, it should be pointed out that cross-categorially, distributivity equivalences are not at all characteristic of the boolean treatment of *and*. Only when boolean operations apply to *functions*, as in (6) to (8) above, is their pointwise definition responsible for their "distributive" behaviour. When the boolean operation is in the argument, in function-argument structures as in (18a) below, the existence of equivalence with the corresponding expression in (18b) depends on the identity of f.

(18) a. $f(x \sqcap y)$ $f(x \sqcup y)$ $f(\neg x)$
     b. $f(x) \sqcap f(y)$ $f(x) \sqcup f(y)$ $\neg(f(x))$

For instance, consider the following pairs of sentences, mentioned in chapter 1.

(19) a. Someone was singing and dancing.
     b. $\not\Leftrightarrow$ Someone was singing and someone was dancing.

(20) a. Everyone was singing and dancing.
     b. $\Leftrightarrow$ Everyone was singing and everyone was dancing.

The absence of the distributivity equivalence between (19a) and (19b), as well as its presence in cases like (20), are both accounted for straightforwardly by the boolean account of *and* and the generalized quantifier treatment of noun phrases like *everyone* and *someone*. Thus, since no theory takes the absence of equivalence in (19) as evidence for non-boolean *and*, there is no a priori reason why the plurality-coordination problem should be considered differently: the absence of distributivity equivalence with sentences like *Mary and John met* should not lead us (at least not a priori) to the conclusion that something special is going on with *and* in this case. In fact, this problem will only lead us to adopt a more sophisticated analysis of the function-argument relations in the sentence.

These general points apply to all existing accounts of non-boolean conjunction. Let us move now to particular aspects of some proposals.

2.2.2   The cross-categorial status of non-boolean conjunction

What are the syntactic categories and the semantic types in which non-boolean *and* occurs? An answer to this question may reveal how general the non-boolean approach is, compared to the fully general boolean assumption. Recall that in the Keenan and Faltz system boolean coordination applies to *all* categories, because all categories have boolean types.

Hoeksema (1983) adopts the standard boolean assumption with respect to coordination. In addition, a definition of "collective conjunction" is proposed, which Hoeksema only applies to the conjunction of generalized quantifiers. In Hoeksema's definition, *and* can be interpreted as the *union* of *minimal sets* in the conjoined quantifiers. For example, the minimal set in the quantifier denoted by the proper name *Mary* is the singleton $\{\mathbf{m}'\}$. Similarly, the singleton $\{\mathbf{j}'\}$ is the minimal set in the quantifier denoted by *John*. Union of the two singleton sets yields the set $\{\mathbf{m}', \mathbf{j}'\}$. The predicate *meet* applies to this plural individual, which gives the collective interpretation of (17).

An attractive property of Hoeksema's proposal is its applicability to various quantifiers. Because it involves the generalized quantifiers, the definition applies equally well in cases of mixed conjunction and disjunction like (11a). However, as it stands, the proposal is too general. For certain quantifiers the appeal to minimal sets leads to undesired truth conditions. For example, consider the following sentence:

(21) Less than three women and less than five men met.

The conjuncts in (21) are monotone decreasing quantifiers. The minimal set of such quantifiers is always the empty set. Since the empty set does not correspond to any plural individual, in Hoeksema's system the semantic value of (21) could have been analyzed as undefined. To avoid such results, Hoeksema proposes a constraint that restricts the set of quantifiers to which non-boolean conjunction can apply.

The ad hoc semantic nature of this necessary restriction of Hoeksema (1983) is criticized in Hoeksema (1988: 22). Instead, in the latter paper it is proposed that non-boolean conjunction applies in D_e, the domain of individuals. What we get is an initially clear-cut distinction between boolean types where only boolean *and* applies, and the non-boolean domain D_e, where *and* is non-boolean. Roughly speaking, in cases like (17) *and* is treated as a set formation operator, which maps the e-type entities $\mathbf{m}'$ and $\mathbf{j}'$ to the set $\{\mathbf{m}', \mathbf{j}'\}$. However, Hoeksema notes that this clear-cut distinction cannot be maintained in view of cases where the conjuncts have to live in the quantifier domain. One such case is the above example (11a). Hoeksema also gives another example, sentence (22), with a conjunction of universal quantifiers.

(22) Every soldier and every officer met.
    a. every soldier x (every officer y (meet(x and y)))

For a correct treatment of such cases, Hoeksema proposes an additional definition of non-boolean *and* for the quantifier domain. This definition is derived from the e-conjoining *and* with the help of the type calculus defined in Van Benthem (1986,1991). This is a modification of the Lambek Calculus (Lambek (1958)), which is known as the *LP* (Lambek + Permutation) *Calculus*. The effect of this mechanism in cases like (22) is that the quantifiers are "scoped" out of the conjunction, as roughly illustrated in (22a). This leads to an intuitively plausible analysis. Hoeksema argues that because lifting of non-boolean *and* to the quantifier domain follows from the LP calculus, it is not stipulated ad hoc. I would like to question this assertion. It is true to the extent that the LP calculus is an adequate meaning composition device in natural language. Unfortunately, this is dubious. First, as a scoping device, the LP calculus gives no explanation for restrictions on the scope of quantifiers, a point to which we return in chapter 3. Second, as noted in Van Benthem (1991: 124) and Hendriks (1993: 69–70), the LP calculus faces some other serious problems. For example, in LP the sentence *All men are teachers* gets a reading equivalent to *All teachers are men* (see also subsection 3.7). This overgeneration is accompanied by undergeneration in the domain of coordination: as observed in Van Benthem (1991: 40), even the elementary case of boolean predicate coordination is not accounted for in LP. Thus the fact that some complicated cases of non-boolean *and* are treated is not too impressive. Note that these problems are due to Hoeksema's appeal to the LP calculus. If, instead, a special definition were *stipulated* for non-boolean quantifier conjunction, these problems would not have appeared. However, this would go against the initial motivation of Hoeksema (1988) and would not leave much of the alleged conceptual advantage of this proposal over the former one.

Both proposals by Hoeksema can be characterized as serious attempts to *localize* the effects of non-boolean conjunction. In the 1983 paper, these effects are localized in a too large domain: the domain of quantifiers. As a consequence, certain unattractive restrictions have to be assumed. In Hoeksema (1988), they are localized in the domain of entities, which is too small. In order to repair this, a non-well-behaved generalization is proposed. On the other hand, most qualms concerning Hoeksema's proposals criticize the ad hoc nature of the local definitions for *and* and the necessary supplements. As descriptive attempts both mechanisms are fairly successful, and possibly require only some modifications that will be discussed below.

In Krifka (1990) and in Lasersohn (1995) two attempts are made to *globalize* the non-boolean effects of *and*. That is, to find broader motivation for a non-boolean definition that transcends NP conjunction. Krifka's account of examples like (17) is similar to Hoeksema (1988): two *e*-type individuals are amalgamated using the non-boolean semantics of *and*. The basis for Krifka's attempt at generalizing non-boolean conjunction to other domains is the special definition of *predicate* conjunction in Link (1983, 1984). The motivation for this definition is what Link calls the "hydra" construction, which is exemplified in (23).

(23) The boy and girl who dated each other are friends of mine.

Link's definition, which is based on his mereological ontology, roughly reads as follows:

(24) A predicate P_1 *and* P_2 holds of x iff x can be divided into two parts x_1 and x_2, such that $P_1(x_1)$ and $P_2(x_2)$ hold.

With this definition (23) is analyzed as in (25) below.

(25) There is a unique x that consists of a boy x_1 and a girl x_2 such that x is a plurality in the extension of *dated each other*. This x is also in the extension of the plural predicate *friends of mine*.

While Link stipulates definition (24) only for hydra constructions, Krifka proposes to use it as a general definition of predicate conjunction. One motivation brought up by Krifka is sentence (26) below, which is roughly analyzed as in (26a). Another example is (27), which is more or less analyzed as in (27a).[3]

(26) The flag is green and white.
      a. Part of the flag is green and the rest is white.

(27) The books are old and new.
      a. Some of the books are old and the others are new.

Furthermore, Krifka proposes to generalize (24) to *all* types. This generalization requires some weakening of Link's definition. Instead of (24), Krifka actually employs a *partial* condition for predicate conjunction. Namely:

(28) A predicate P_1 *and* P_2 holds of x if there are two parts of x, x_1 and x_2, such that $P_1(x_1)$ and $P_2(x_2)$ hold.

A result of this modification is that the truth conditions of sentences with predicate conjunction are never fully specified. All we know is that, for instance, *if* (26a) holds then also (26) does, but not vice versa. Krifka's argument for such a radical semantic practice comes from idioms (Krifka (1990: 171–172)). Something can be *a cold war* while neither being cold nor being a war. But if something is cold and it is a war, then it is a cold war by necessity.

I will not try to evaluate this argumentation here. However, surprisingly, even the approximation (28) overgenerates in many cases.[4] Consider the following example in (29).

(29) #The bridge is small and big.

(30) #The bridge is small and the bridge is big.

The standard boolean account takes (29) to be equivalent to (30). Given the plausible assumption that the denotations of the predicates *small* and *big* are disjoint, the oddness of (29) is explained by its being a contradiction. However, in Krifka's proposal, (29) is no longer equivalent to (30). In fact, it may reasonably follow from (31):

(31) The bridge is big.

This unwelcome prediction arises because if a tiny part b_1 of a big bridge b is taken, the remaining part, b_2, is still big. Consequently, the predicate *small and big* will hold of b on Krifka's definition: *small* holds of b_1 and *big* holds of b_2. Strangely, Krifka's semantics considers any big object to be small and big, though not necessarily small (cf. the bridge b described above). More generally, intuitively sound equivalences of the type exemplified in (32) do not hold under the proposed non-boolean definition.

(32) a. John is short and fat $\Leftrightarrow$ John is short and John is fat
      b. The house is nice and comfortable $\Leftrightarrow$ The house is nice and the house is comfortable

Krifka's proposal is also curious in some other respects. Unlike predicate conjunction, sentential *and* and *e*-type conjunction are fully defined. Whether such a distinction is attested in natural language is not clear. Furthermore, for many types it is not clear that even an approximation of conjunction is attained. This is because, unfortunately, Krifka's attempt to provide a general recursive definition of *and* (Krifka (1990: ex. (32)) does not formally yield the reported results.[5]

The empirical challenges that examples like (23), (26) and (27) pose to boolean predicate conjunction are intriguing, but Krifka's (fairly complicated) attempt at their general account does not seem to work. Also a local use of Link's definition for predicate conjunction is unsatisfactory, however, not only because of its ad hoc nature but also since it does not preserve the sound predictions of the boolean treatment of elementary cases like (29) and (32). As Hoeksema (1988: 19) and Lasersohn (1995: 282–283) claim, the boolean treatment is successful with most predicates. This suggests that a more fine-grained account of predicate conjunction is called for, and not simply a stipulative rejection of the boolean assumption. This point will be discussed in section 2.4.

2.2.3   Non-boolean conjunction: union or set formation?

The precise semantic definition of non-boolean *and* is of central importance for the theory of plurality. The relevant data have far-reaching consequences also for theories that do not adopt non-boolean conjunction. This subsection concentrates on the controversy surrounding the operation of non-boolean *and*, and its implications for the ontology of plurals.

Ignoring many semantic subtleties, we can distinguish two principal trends in the analysis of non-boolean conjunction. One approach takes *and* to stand for a *union* operation over plural individuals (that is: sets). An alternative approach analyses *and* as a *set formation* operator, which maps two or more individuals to the set they constitute. The two approaches are exemplified below by way of giving their analysis of the subject of sentence (17).

Union: $[\![\text{Mary and John}]\!] = \{\mathbf{m}'\} \cup \{\mathbf{j}'\} = \{\mathbf{m}', \mathbf{j}'\}$

Set formation: $[\![\text{Mary and John}]\!] = \mathbf{m}' sf\ \mathbf{j}' = \{\mathbf{m}', \mathbf{j}'\}$

In simple cases like (17) the two approaches yield the same result. Mathematically, however, they are significantly different: recursive unioning of sets of atomic individuals can only leave us with sets of atomic individuals. However, when we recursively apply set formation to atomic individuals we get sets containing atomic individuals, sets containing sets of atomic individuals and so on. We say that a union denotation of *and* can do with a *flat* ontology of plural individuals, while a set formation operator requires a *nested* ontology of plurals.

To exemplify this difference, suppose that the model contains two atomic individuals a and b. Recursive application of union to the singletons $\{a\}$ and $\{b\}$ can only lead to one new plural individual: $\{a, b\}$. Further unioning of this set with $\{a\}$ or $\{b\}$ (and obviously, itself) can only lead to the same result: the set $\{a, b\}$ that we already have. By contrast, when set formation is used to map a and b to the set $\{a, b\}$ we can continue and generate the sets $\{a, \{a, b\}\}, \{b, \{a, b\}\}, \{a, b, \{a, b\}\}$ and so on inductively.

Hoeksema (1983: 75) gives sentence (33), with its structures indicated in (33a) and (33b), as an example where the two strategies of union and set formation lead to different predictions.

(33) Blücher and Wellington and Napoleon fought against each other near Waterloo.
    a. [[Blücher and Wellington] and Napoleon] fought against each other near Waterloo.
    b. [Blücher and [Wellington and Napoleon]] fought against each other near Waterloo.

The union treatment of *and* assigns both structures (33a) and (33b) the same interpretation. This is shown by the equality of the denotations in (34a) and (34b). Set formation treats the two cases differently: the syntactic structure is reflected in the semantic denotation, as exemplified in (35a–b).

(34) a. $(\{\mathbf{b}'\} \cup \{\mathbf{w}'\}) \cup \{\mathbf{n}'\} = \{\mathbf{b}', \mathbf{w}'\} \cup \{\mathbf{n}'\} = \{\mathbf{b}', \mathbf{w}', \mathbf{n}'\}$
       b. $\{\mathbf{b}'\} \cup (\{\mathbf{w}'\} \cup \{\mathbf{n}'\}) = \{\mathbf{b}'\} \cup \{\mathbf{w}', \mathbf{n}'\} = \{\mathbf{b}', \mathbf{w}', \mathbf{n}'\}$

(35) a. $(\mathbf{b}' \ sf \ \mathbf{w}') \ sf \ \mathbf{n}' = \{\mathbf{b}', \mathbf{w}'\} \ sf \ \mathbf{n}' = \{\{\mathbf{b}', \mathbf{w}'\}, \mathbf{n}'\}$
       b. $\mathbf{b}' \ sf \ (\mathbf{w}' \ sf \ \mathbf{n}') = \mathbf{b}' \ sf \ \{\mathbf{w}', \mathbf{n}'\} = \{\mathbf{b}', \{\mathbf{w}', \mathbf{n}'\}\}$

Due to the equality between (34a) and (34b), the union approach predicts the structures (33a) and (33b) to have the same meaning. The set-formation treatment predicts the two structures to lead to different statements. Hoeksema claims that the second prediction is correct: (33a) should be analyzed as historically true, whereas the alignment of forces asserted by (33b) is not the one that actually took place near Waterloo. Therefore, Hoeksema concludes, the set-formation approach is preferable.

Landman (1989) follows this line, which is also proposed in Link (1984), but Schwarzschild (1992, 1996) challenges Landman's conclusions. The debate concentrates on examples such as (36) (due to Landman) and (37) (due to Schwarzschild), where, due to the lack of syntactic ambiguity, the empirical issue is clearer than in Hoeksema's example (33).

(36) a. The cards below seven and the cards from seven up are separated.
       b. The cards below ten and the cards from ten up are separated.

(37) a. The young animals and the old animals were separated.
       b. The cows and the pigs were separated.

Consider the sentences in (36) in a context where there is only one deck of cards. Landman argues that the difference between (36a) and (36b) shows up in this context: if the cards below seven are separated from the cards from seven up, then (36a) is true, whereas (36b) is false. The union approach analyzes the subjects by unioning two sets of cards. In both examples this leads to one and the same result: the whole deck of cards. Therefore, the two sentences are predicted to be equivalent. According to Landman, this prediction is incorrect. In the set-formation approach, on the other hand, the subjects in the two sentences are taken to denote different entities. In (36a) the subject denotes a set that has two sets as members: the set of cards below seven and the set of cards from seven up. In (36b) the subject denotes a different set, which also has two sets as members: the set of cards below ten and the set of cards from ten up. Consequently, no equivalence is predicted. This is a main reason for Landman (1989) to prefer the set-formation approach; Landman directly concludes that the ontology of plurals should be a nested ontology: plural individuals can consist of other plural individuals with no principled restriction on the level of nesting. This can be contrasted with the flat ontology of Link (1983), where plural individuals consist only of *atoms*—singular individuals that cannot be divided further.

Schwarzschild rejects Landman's main empirical claim. For Schwarzschild, sentences like (36a) and (36b) are *semantically* equivalent. Schwarzschild's argument is based on the examples in (37) that are to be considered in a situation where the only animals are the cows and the pigs. On first glance, (37a) and (37b) seem just as non-equivalent as Landman's examples in (36). However, Schwarzschild makes the following observation. In Landman's approach, sentence (37a) is analyzed as entailing the sentence *The animals were separated* BY AGE.[6] With this assumption, the intuitively valid line of reasoning in (38) can be made.

(38) a. The young animals and the old animals were separated. (= (37a))
      b. $\overset{L}{\Rightarrow}$ The animals were separated by age.
      c. ⇒ The cows and the pigs were separated by age.
      d. ⇒ The cows and the pigs were separated. (= (37b))

The entailment from (38a) to (38b) requires Landman's set-formation assumption and its empirical status is the center of the debate. The remaining entailments involve common reasoning. Schwarzschild concludes that (37a) entails (37b). Of course, a reverse line of reasoning, from (37b) to (37a), can similarly be made. Thus Schwarzschild claims that even on Landman's assumptions, the sentences (37a) and (37b) have to be analyzed as equivalent after all, so his theory fails to make the distinction that constitutes its main motivation.

This claim is quite surprising because in isolation the sentences in (37) do seem to convey different meanings, just as Landman argues with respect to the sentences in (36). Schwarzschild proposes that this has a pragmatic reason. For example, (37a) does not truth-conditionally entail, but rather conversationally *implies* that the animals were separated by age. This is due to the wording: if the speaker did not know the criterion for separation she could have simply asserted the shorter and less misleading sentence *The animals were separated*. Like any conversational implicature, and unlike entailment, this "age" implication of (37a) can be canceled. For instance, by the continuation *though not necessarily by age*. The same phenomenon is observed in sentence (38c): the continuation *by age* cancels the implicature that separation prcoeeded according to the species of the animals. Schwarzschild concludes that Landman's argument for unrestricted nesting of sets is refuted and the simpler flat ontology of plurals can be retained, with *and* functioning as a union operator.

Schwarzschild does not explain how such a pragmatic account would handle Landman's original example (36). However, it is not too hard to construct a case where the same reasoning applies. The discourse in (39), for instance, is completely acceptable.

(39) John separated the cards below 7 from the cards from 7 up and left two piles of cards. However, when he was away *the cards below 7 and the cards from 7 up were shuffled and separated again*, but this time by color. So, eventually, there were still two piles of cards, though not the ones that John had left.

Of course, the construction of such examples is harder than in Schwarzschild's case, but it shows that the general point still holds.

A subtle point should be added here. In fact, Landman (1989: 575) does not claim that sentences like (38a) entail (38b). Rather, (38a) only has (38b) as a *reading* in certain contexts (of which the exact specification is not given). In effect, Landman takes (38a) to be ambiguous between a set-formation reading and a union reading. Schwarzschild argues that this view on the data does not help much because in the absence of direct intuitions about semantic ambiguity the adoption of only the more general union reading is to be preferred.

As it turns out, Landman's ambiguity approach makes the set-formation account of cases like (36) and (37) superfluous.[7]

The argumentation of Schwarzschild (1992) is linguistically solid and beautifully constructed; the heart of the set-formation thesis is used for attacking it. Furthermore, the conclusion vindicates a simpler theory. However, there are still some problems for Schwarzschild's claim concerning the equivalence of sentences like (37a) and (37b). These are more obvious in an example taken from Schwarzschild (1996: 57). Schwarzschild considers the sentences in (40) in a situation where it is given that the authors and the athletes are just the women.

(40) a. The authors and the athletes are outnumbered by the men.
      b. The women are outnumbered by the men.

The two sentences in (40) do not seem equivalent. Sentence (40a) is entailed by (41) below given the additional information. However, this apparently does not hold for (40b).

(41) The authors are outnumbered by the men and the athletes are outnumbered by the men.

Schwarzschild (1996: 99) claims that also the sentences in (40) are in fact semantically equivalent. According to Schwarzschild, the difference between these sentences should follow from a pragmatic theory of distributivity. Although some of Schwarzschild's claims about pragmatic effects are relevant for other phenomena, his argument with respect to (40) is much weaker than his argument against nesting of set formation operations. No valid line of reasoning similar to (38) seems to justify an equivalence for the sentences in (40). However, if Schwarzschild's argument is correct then it is expected that an appropriate addition to (40b) would make the division of the set of women into athletes and authors pragmatically salient as it is in (40a). Consequently, this is supposed to strengthen the putative entailment (41) $\Rightarrow$ (40b). However, such a pragmatic process does not appear. Consider for instance the following example.

(42) ?The women are outnumbered by the men according to the women's professions.

This sentence is quite incoherent. If Schwarzschild's proposal were correct, the addition in (42) should have been felicitous and should have facilitated the inference of this sentence from (41). At the present state of Schwarzschild's proposal, this fact (vis-à-vis the clear entailment from (41) to (40a)) is not explained.

Landman (1989: 591–592) takes cases like (40a) as further evidence for the set-formation approach. But this is not a necessary conclusion. As noted independently in Schwarzschild (1996: 21), Hoeksema's cross-categorial proposals are fully compatible with a union analysis of non-boolean conjunction. If *and* is ambiguous between boolean and non-boolean conjunction as in Hoeksema's accounts, then the entailment (41) $\Rightarrow$ (40a) is expected on the *boolean* reading of *and* in (40a). In (40b) there is no conjunction, so the relevant entailment is, correctly, predicted to be absent. As noted by Link (1984: 249), a set-formation analysis of conjunction can perhaps be used in such cases to *replace* boolean conjunction. However, under Hoeksema's ambiguity approach this is no longer a case for set-formation.

2.2.4   Event-based approaches

The analyses discussed above have similar ontological starting points. They all assume plural individuals, and differ only in their implementations of this idea. The works discussed in the present section propose some more controversial ontological revisions.

Lasersohn (1995): events and non-boolean conjunction   Lasersohn's point of departure is an argument in favour of an event ontology. The argument is quite complex and involves discussion of the *together* adverbial and "pluractional markers" in various languages. I will not review Lasersohn's claims about these issues, but rather discuss his final proposal and its implications for the analysis of conjunction. First, the ontological primitive of *events* is assumed. This notion intuitively represents some "chunk of the world" (Lasersohn (1995: 227)). In the version of event semantics that Lasersohn adopts, a sentence no longer denotes a truth value, but rather the *set of events* in which the sentence is true. Lasersohn assumes a group (nested) ontology both for events and "ordinary" individuals so that we have two primitive domains (or sorted sub-domains of D_e) with a hierarchical group structure. Let us denote this by using the domain D_E for events and their groups, and the domain D_e for all other entities and their groups.

"Referring NPs" like *the teacher*, *John and Mary*, etc. are interpreted in the D_e domain. Adjectives and intransitive verbs are of type Et denote sets of events, just like sentences. Consequently, a rule is needed for the combination of an NP of type e and a predicate of type Et, to derive a sentence of type Et. Lasersohn's proposal, which is standard in event semantics, is that in addition to the Et predicate, verbs and adjectives contribute a Θ-role relation for each of their arguments. This theta role is formalized as a relation between events and entities (type $E(et)$). For example, the simple sentence in (43) is analyzed as in (43a), where both the denotation **dance**$'$ and the Θ-role relation are triggered by the verb.

(43) John danced.
   a. $\mathbf{j}'_e\,[\mathbf{dance}'_{Et}\ \Theta_{\mathbf{dance}'}]$
       predication rule $\Rightarrow$ $\lambda e_E.\mathbf{dance}'(e) \wedge \Theta_{\mathbf{dance}'}(e)(\mathbf{j}')$

Given this, Lasersohn claims that a compositional semantics with a unified treatment of *and* is within reach. The basic idea is to define *and* as a *group (*set*) formation operator* for both events and other objects. Thus, for simple NP conjunction, Lasersohn's analysis is similar to Landman (1989). For sentence conjunctions, *and* similarly forms a group of events. For more complex types, Lasersohn proposes a complex definition which is based on group formation. Consider an elementary kind of conjunction: predicate conjunction. Sentence (44) is analyzed as in (44a).

(44) John danced and sang.

    a. $\mathbf{j}'_e$ $[[\mathbf{dance}'_{Et}\ \Theta_{\mathbf{dance}'}]$ and $[\mathbf{sing}'_{Et}\ \Theta_{\mathbf{sing}'}]]$

       i. conjunction rule $\Rightarrow$

        $\mathbf{j}'$ $[\lambda e.\exists e_1 \exists e_2[e = \{e_1, e_2\} \wedge \mathbf{dance}'(e_1) \wedge \mathbf{sing}'(e_2)]$, $\Theta_{\mathbf{dance}'}$, $\Theta_{\mathbf{sing}'}]$

       ii. predication rule $\Rightarrow$

        $\lambda e.\exists e_1 \exists e_2[e = \{e_1, e_2\} \wedge \mathbf{dance}'(e_1) \wedge \mathbf{sing}'(e_2) \wedge \Theta_{\mathbf{dance}'}(e_1)(\mathbf{j}')$

          $\wedge \Theta_{\mathbf{sing}'}(e_2)(\mathbf{j}')]$

    b. ii$'$. predication rule $\Rightarrow$

        $\lambda e.\exists e_1 \exists e_2[e = \{e_1, e_2\} \wedge \mathbf{dance}'(e_1) \wedge \mathbf{sing}'(e_2) \wedge \Theta_{\mathbf{dance}'}(e_2)(\mathbf{j}')$

          $\wedge \Theta_{\mathbf{sing}'}(e_1)(\mathbf{j}')]$

The derivation in (44a) is based on Lasersohn's text. The outcome of the conjunction rule given in (i) is described in Lasersohn (1995: 278). Lasersohn does not explicitly specify a predication rule, but an output analogous to the one in (ii) is explicitly mentioned in Lasersohn (1995: 279).[8] The problem with such a putative predication rule is that it is non-compositional. The Θ-role predicates in (44a.ii) are assumed to apply to the parts e_1 and e_2 of an event e. However, it is not clear how to keep track of the matching between the Θ-role and the event. An unwelcome derivation as in (44b) is to be expected as well. This problem may perhaps be corrected, but since many other details are missing in Lasersohn's account, I will not try to do that here. Such omissions make it hard to evaluate Lasersohn's approach to non-boolean conjunction. Lasersohn's system is also intended to deal with cases like *the air was alternately hot and humid*, which are a challenge for the boolean assumption.[9] However, apart from the semantics of such adverbials, Lasersohn's proposal does not affect the classical boolean predictions concerning predicate conjunction (see Lasersohn (1995: 281–286)). This is an important difference from Krifka's approach to predicate conjunction.

Lasersohn's starting point is the sound ambition to develop a unified account of conjunction in a compositional framework. As noted above, it is not clear that the problems for compositionality that Lasersohn's proposal sets out to solve are more severe than the problems it generates. The event semantics for conjunction that is proposed in Schein (1992) does not take compositionality to be a major issue to begin with. Let us discuss briefly this proposal too.

Schein (1992): Events and conjunction reduction Sentences like *Mary and John met* (= (17)) are among the early problems noted for the transformational rule of Conjunction Reduction (see e.g. Lakoff and Peters (1969)). In Schein's proposal, such cases *are* nonetheless analyzed by conjunction reduction using a version of event semantics. According to Schein, the sentence is paraphrased roughly as follows:

(45) There is a meeting event e such that Mary is an agent of e and John is an agent of e.

As Lasersohn (1995: 46) observes, this renders an account of the unacceptability of (46) problematic. According to Schein's basic assumptions, the sentence is to be analyzed as in (46a).

(46) *Mary met and John met.
      a. There is a meeting event e_1 such that Mary is an agent of e_1 and there is a meeting event e_2 such that John is an agent of e_2.

Since (45) entails (46a), there is no straightforward explanation for why (46) is unacceptable in situations where the sentence *Mary and John met* is true.[10] Furthermore, there are many well-known problems to Conjunction Reduction that Schein does not discuss. For example, a conjunction reduction approach predicts that the sentences in (19), repeated below, are equivalent.

(47) a. Someone was singing and dancing.
      b. Someone was singing and someone was dancing.

Schein does not explain how such cases as the absence of equivalence between (47a) and (47b) are to be accounted for. On the other hand, Schein does claim that his mechanism deals correctly with sentences like (48), attributed to an unpublished MIT paper (1988) by Chris Collins.

(48) Mary and Sue and possibly Jane met.

Schein argues that such examples show that *and*, even in its commonly assumed "non-boolean" use, must be treated as a propositional coordinator of sentences. This is because modal adverbs are typically classified as sentential modifiers. Schein further submits that his conjunction reduction mechanism handles such cases correctly. Lacking a well-defined semantic procedure for interpreting Schein's notation, I will have to leave further evaluation of his linguistic argumentation to further study.

Schein's work embodies a radical representational approach to meaning that marks a complete departure from compositionality. Unfortunately, no alternative hypothesis about the syntax-semantics interface is proposed; an unrestricted arsenal of syntactic rules is allowed to map surface structure to some notation of "logical form." On the ontological side, Schein (1992) follows Schein (1993) and does away with plural individuals in favour of a non-compositional treatment in events semantics. Also this move will have to await a rigorous examination.

2.2.5 Concluding remarks

The proposals by Krifka, Lasersohn and Schein all approach the plurality-coordination problem by trying to develop a semantics whose implications go far beyond the interpretation of noun phrases. This is by itself an a priori possible move, but the specific accounts turn out to lead to serious complications and inadequacies. By contrast, Hoeksema's proposals to localize the problem are technically sound and, to a large extent, empirically adequate. By adopting Schwarzschild's views, both proposals by Hoeksema can also become ontologically parsimonious. It seems no coincidence that similar approaches, briefly brought up also by Keenan and Faltz (1985: 270) and Partee and Rooth (1983: appendix B), were adopted in many later work on plurality, including Roberts (1987), Schwarzschild (1996) and Carpenter (1997).

However, the general claims against non-boolean conjunction that were made in subsection 2.2.1 most strongly apply to Hoeksema's accounts. The ad hoc nature of the semantic definitions leaves much to be desired. An ontologically minimalist explanation that does not need to modify the boolean assumption or basic views about compositionality is to be preferred. The main tenet of the present chapter is that such a theory is within reach.

2.3   A Flexible Boolean Approach

One of the main claims of this book is that the plurality-coordination problem does not necessitate any modification of the boolean assumption. It is argued that the treatment of collective interpretations of noun phrase coordination does not require any withdrawal from the assumption that *and* cross-categorially denotes boolean *meet*. The strategy that will be adopted in order to attack the coordination-plurality problem is to have a closer look at the basic properties of boolean coordination and their relation to collectivity. Two main observations will be made:

i. There is a boolean property that distinguishes *and* from other coordinators in the generalized quantifier domain.
ii. Within a flexible framework of NP interpretation this property can account for collectivity effects with *and* coordinations.

This section concentrates on elementary cases of proper name coordination as in (1) to (11). Coordinations that involve semantically more complex singular NPs (e.g. *a woman, every woman*) or plural NPs (e.g. *three men, most men*) will be dealt with in the following chapters. The rest of the section is organized as follows. Subsection 2.3.1 gives an initial typology of collective predicates and reviews the type-theoretical approach to plurality. Subsection 2.3.2 presents the foundational mathematical property that underlies the solution that is developed in subsection 2.3.3, which is based on a type shifting operator that derives the collective meaning of boolean NP coordinations. Subsection 2.3.4 analyzes two examples that show the advantages of treating collectivity in boolean domains. Subsection 2.3.5 argues that the Partee and Rooth (1983) idea of using it as the trigger of type shifting principles is not the right implementation of the proposed type shifting operator, which will be of much relevance for the proposal in chapter 4. Subsection 2.3.6 addresses the infelicity of sentences like *Mary met* and argues that it stems from lexical selectional restrictions and not from formal considerations of type mismatch, as previously proposed in Bennett

(1974). The proposed division of labor between syntax and semantics in the treatment of coordination and collectivity is summarized in subsection 2.3.7. Subsection 2.3.8 briefly recapitulates some of the issues in this chapter. Subsection 2.3.9 provides a 'road-map' for remaining problems and their treatment later in the book.

2.3.1 Collective predicates and the type-theoretical approach to plural individuals

There are various kinds of English predicates that give rise to collectivity effects. Several representative examples are given below.

(49) Verbs
    a. lexically collective: *gather, disperse, meet* (when used as intransitive verbs), *outnumber* (both arguments)
    b. lexically "mixed" collective/distributive: the subject argument of *write, lift, eat* and *carry*
    c. *together* modification: *sing together, live together, write* NP *together*
    d. *between them* modification: *grade over 200 papers between them, ate 15 pizzas between them*
    e. reciprocal modification: *like each other, look at one another*

(50) Adjectives
    a. lexically collective adjectives: *numerous, similar, alike, parallel, antagonistic, equivalent, neighboring*
    b. *together* modification: *happy together, irritating together*
    c. reciprocal modification: *nice to each other, fond of one another*

(51) Predicative constructions with nominals:
    a. group denoting nominals:[11] *seem a big group, be the organizing committee, be a nice couple*
    b. relational nominals: *be brothers, sisters, friends*
    c. nominals modified by collective adjectives: *be numerous people, similar students, parallel lines*
    d. reciprocal possessives: *be teachers of each other, be admirers of one another*

All the constructions above will henceforth be referred to as *collective predicates*. This is certainly not an exhaustive typology, and even among the members of this small list there are some important differences, as will be discussed below and, more extensively, in chapter 5. The predicates in (49b) above are different from other collective predicates in allowing sentences with simple singular subjects (e.g. *Mary lifted a piano*). Predicates like these are referred to as *mixed* predicates, whereas the collective predicates in the list above that are ruled out with such singular arguments (e.g. as in *Mary met*) are referred to as *completely collective* (ccl) predicates. Despite this distinction, all the predicates involved show the same behaviour in the respect that is crucial for us: they do not give rise to distributivity equivalences when their argument is an *and* coordination. In fact, if we adopt a broader notion of distributivity, this is true of a larger class of plural NPs. Characteristic is the case of plural definites. For example, consider the contrast between sentences (52a) and (53a) below.

(52) a. The old members of this institution retired last year.
       b. Every old member of this institution retired last year.

(53) a. The old members of this institution constitute the managing board.
       b. Every old member of this institution constitutes the managing board.

While (52a) is very close in its meaning (in a sense that will be addressed in chapters 5 and 6) to (52b), this is clearly not the case with (53a) and (53b). Predicates like *retire, sleep,* and *laugh* are often classified as *distributive predicates.*

   In chapters 5 and 6 it will be argued that the distinction between distributive predicates and collective predicates is not very useful, as the absence of distributivity equivalences (= collectivity) is a general phenomenon with many NPs, even when they combine with so called distributive predicates (consider the difficulty to declare the two sentences in (52) "equivalent"). For the sake of our purposes in the present chapter, however, the intuitive class of "distributive predicates" can remain undefined. To sum up, for the time being we adopt a rather uncontroversial typology of predicates, without any attempt to define it more systematically than by enumeration of examples.

   As already mentioned, the common semantic approach to collectivity is fairly simple. Sentences like *Mary and John met* and *the students lifted a piano* are treated as predications of the form $\mathcal{P}(X)$. The calligraphic "$\mathcal{P}$" is used for the denotation of collective predicates, while the italic "*P*" is a standard notation for the denotation of distributive predicates. The argument X is the denotation of the subject, which is taken to be a *plural individual.* Such individuals account for the collectivity effect in a manner that was already indicated. Part of the debate that surrounds the semantic nature of plural individuals was discussed in subsection 2.2.3. We turn now to the precise mathematical definition. Ontologically, the most minimalist approach to plural individuals is the *type-theoretical* one, which is adopted in Bartsch (1973), Bennett (1974), Scha (1981), Van der Does (1992) and Verkuyl (1993), among others. Under this approach plural individuals, like classical intransitive predicates, live in the *et* domain. Thus, they can simply be conceived of as (characteristic functions of) *sets* of singular *e* type individuals. Thus, we say that the type-theoretical analysis of plural individuals is an instance of a *set-theoretical* approach to their definition. The type-theoretical approach is ontologically attractive, since objects of type *et* are already in the model anyway. The assumption that plural individuals are the same kind of thing requires no modification of the ontology. According to Bennett, all collective predicates (including of course the "mixed" ones) should be of type *(et)t* and distributive predicates remain of the classical type *et*. The same applies to quantifiers: their type varies according to the

Table 2.1
Extensional Bennett typing

	Singular/Distributive	Plural/Collective
Individual	e	et
Predicate	et	$(et)t$
Quantifier	$(et)t$	$((et)t)t$

type of individuals they range over. An important question is whether collective predicates (and especially—the mixed ones) need to get also the et type of distributive predicates. Also the opposite question, of whether we need to let distributive predicates denote ett functions, is of central interest to the theory. These questions will be one of the major topics of chapter 5, which will answer both of them affirmatively (Bennett himself answered the first question affirmatively but the latter question negatively). As these questions are not directly related to our main concerns in the present chapter, let us ignore them for a while. In any case, Bennett's type-theoretical distinction between predicates is adopted throughout this book. The simple version of this distinction that is useful for the purposes of this chapter is summarized in table 2.1.

Note that the type-theoretical treatment of plural individuals as et objects is ontologically flat: we assume that plural individuals are of type et, but not of the higher types in the set-theoretical hierarchy: $(et)t$, $((et)t)t$, etc. I prefer not to dwell too much on the subtle differences between the type-theoretical approach and alternative ontologies, for the following reasons:

1. As pointed out in Van der Does (1992: 25–27), the treatment of plural individuals as et objects or sets is compatible with the lattice-theoretic approach of Link (1983). As argued by Landman (1989: 565–568), the decision between these two kinds of implementations draws almost completely on metaphysical preferences.
2. As mentioned above, Schwarzschild's arguments in favour of a simple, 'flat' ontology for plurals, which is easy to model in typed frameworks, are convincing.
3. The status of "group-denoting" NPs like *the committee*, which is highly relevant for the ontology of plurals, is also highly controversial. These may be treated as special entities in the D_e domain (Link (1983)) or as intensional entities (Landman (1989)). In any case, the type-theoretical approach can be made compatible with both alternatives. See more on this issue in section 5.6.
4. The sound motivation of Link (1983) to keep the treatment of plurals semantically close to that of mass terms is satisfied by the recent elegant set-theoretical account of mass terms in Chierchia (1998b), which I believe can be translated fairly easily to a type-theoretical format.

In the absence of any clear-cut arguments against the type-theoretical approach, its technical and ontological simplicity is a major reason to adopt it as a solid basis for potential changes in the future.

2.3.2   The principal filter property

After the basic assumptions about collectivity have been introduced we can now get back to the original problem. How is collectivity in (17), repeated here as (54), obtained?

(54) Mary and John met.

Type-theoretically, (54) should be modeled as in (55), where a collective $(et)t$ predicate applies to a set of atomic individuals—a predicate of type et.

(55) $\mathbf{meet}'_{(et)t}(\{\mathbf{m}', \mathbf{j}'\})$

The question is how to produce the plural individual $\{\mathbf{m}', \mathbf{j}'\}$ from the standard denotations of the conjuncts. The "non-boolean" approach to *and*, reviewed in section 2.2, analyzes *and* as (some variation on) the boolean *join* operator. From the leading assumption in non-boolean accounts it follows that in (54) the conjuncts are not boolean objects and that the conjunction is not boolean *meet*, so that the boolean insight into the cross-categorial nature of *and* is lost.

But things are not necessarily that messy. Let us take a more careful look at the boolean analysis of NP conjunction. In a different notation than what was given in (4) above, the subject *Mary and John* of sentence (54) is analyzed as follows:

(56) $\{A : \mathbf{m}' \in A\} \cap \{A : \mathbf{j}' \in A\} = \{A : \{\mathbf{m}'\} \cup \{\mathbf{j}'\} \subseteq A\}$

What can be noticed is that the desired union set $\{\mathbf{m}'\} \cup \{\mathbf{j}'\}$ is in fact here, but it "hides," so to speak, within the standard generalized quantifier. This is because every set that contains both $\mathbf{m}'$ and $\mathbf{j}'$ is trivially a superset of the union set $\{\mathbf{m}'\} \cup \{\mathbf{j}'\} = \{\mathbf{m}', \mathbf{j}'\}$, and vice versa. Thus, in a way, the coordinator *and* in sentence (54) does behave like set union, but not because it denotes anything else than the familiar boolean *meet*. Rather, standard intersection of standard Montagovian individuals reduces to union at a "lower semantic level." This is due to the specific semantic nature of the conjuncts. In order to get a grip on the mathematics of this phenomenon, we need to introduce some basic boolean notions.

A *filter* of a boolean algebra is any subset of it that is closed under *meet* and domination of its members. More formally:

Definition 14 (filter)   Let A be a boolean algebra and let F be a non-empty subset of A. F is called a *filter* of A iff the following hold:

1. For all $x, y \in F$: $x \wedge y \in F$.
2. For all $x \in F$, $y \in A$: if $x \leq y$ then $y \in F$.

For example, the quantifier $\mathbf{J} = \{A \subseteq E : \mathbf{j}' \in A\}$ is a filter of $\wp(E)$. Proof: first, if $X \in \mathbf{J}$ and $Y \in \mathbf{J}$ then $\mathbf{j}' \in X$ and $\mathbf{j}' \in Y$. Thus, $\mathbf{j}' \in X \cap Y$, so $X \cap Y \in \mathbf{J}$. Second, if $X \in \mathbf{J}$ then

$\mathbf{j}' \in X$. If further $X \subseteq Y \in \wp(E)$ then it follows that $\mathbf{j}' \in Y$. Thus, $Y \in J$. We conclude that J is a filter.[12]

A quantifier like J is not just a filter. It is a special kind of filter, which is called a *principal filter*.

Definition 15 (principal filter)   Let A be a boolean algebra and $x \in A$. The *principal filter generated by* x is the set $\{y \in A : x \leq y\}$, which is denoted by F_x.

Obviously, every principal filter is a filter. The Montagovian individual J is the principal filter $F_{\{\mathbf{j}'\}}$ generated by $\{\mathbf{j}'\}$. A principal filter like this one, which is generated by a singleton $\{x\}$, is often referred to as the *principal ultrafilter generated by* x.[13]

The observation in (56) can now be stated as follows. The *intersection* of the principal filters generated by $\{\mathbf{m}'\}$ and $\{\mathbf{j}'\}$ is the principal filter generated by the *union* of the generators $\{\mathbf{m}'\} \cup \{\mathbf{j}'\}$. In formula: $F_{\{\mathbf{m}'\}} \cap F_{\{\mathbf{j}'\}} = F_{\{\mathbf{m}'\} \cup \{\mathbf{j}'\}}$. This is the basic fact that will lead to an account of the "union" behaviour of *and* in (54). In boolean terms, this property reads as follows.

Proposition 1 (the Principal Filter Property, PFP)   Let A be a boolean algebra and $x, y \in A$. Then $F_x \cap F_y = F_{x \vee y}$.

Note that in the way the PFP is stated, the set A can be any boolean algebra, hence the general join notation $x \vee y$ for the elements $x, y \in A$. By contrast, the filters F_x and F_y are members of the power-set algebra $\wp(A)$. This is the reason the specific meet operation of intersection is explicitly given in the expression $F_x \cap F_y$. The proof of proposition 1 follows directly from the following simple fact about boolean algebras.

Lemma 2 $x \leq z$ and $y \leq z$ iff $x \vee y \leq z$.

Proof
1. Assume $x \leq z$ and $y \leq z$.
By definition, $(x \wedge z) = x$ and $(y \wedge z) = y$.
By distributivity (A_4): $(x \vee y) \wedge z = (x \wedge z) \vee (y \wedge z)$.
Thus $(x \vee y) \wedge z = x \vee y$, and by definition, $x \vee y \leq z$.
2. Assume $x \vee y \leq z$.
By definition, $(x \vee y) \vee z = z$.
By associativity (A_2): $x \vee (y \vee z) = z$.
$(x \vee (y \vee z)) \wedge x = z \wedge x$
By absorption (A_3): $(x \vee (y \vee z)) \wedge x = x$.
Thus $x = z \wedge x$, and by definition, $x \leq z$.
Symmetrically, $y \leq z$.

In the propositional domain D_t, lemma 2 reduces to a classical equivalence: $x \to z$ and $y \to z$ iff $(x \vee y) \to z$.

In the sequel a more general fact that follows directly from the PFP will be used in the actual analysis. Consider first an example. In the coordinated subject of (11a), restated with slight changes in (57) below, the conjunction is not a principal filter coordination: the principal filter for *Mary* is intersected with a *union* of the principal filters for *Sue* and for *John*, which is no longer a principal filter. However, due to the boolean nature of the $D_{(et)t}$ somain of quantifiers, the distributive laws sanction the analysis of an intersection of unions as a union of intersections. Of these intersections the PFP does hold. This is exemplified in (57a–c).

(57) Mary and [Sue or John] met.
    a. $F_{\{\mathbf{m'}\}} \cap [F_{\{\mathbf{s'}\}} \cup F_{\{\mathbf{j'}\}}]$
    b. $\overset{A_3}{=} [F_{\{\mathbf{m'}\}} \cap F_{\{\mathbf{s'}\}}] \cup [F_{\{\mathbf{m'}\}} \cap F_{\{\mathbf{j'}\}}]$
    c. $\overset{PFP}{=} F_{\{\mathbf{m'},\mathbf{s'}\}} \cup F_{\{\mathbf{m'},\mathbf{j'}\}}$

This corollary of the PFP can be stated as follows.

Corollary 3   Let A be a boolean algebra, let $n \geq 1$ and let $m_i \geq 1$ for every i, $1 \leq i \leq n$. Let $x_{i,j} \in A$ for every i, j, $1 \leq i \leq n$, $1 \leq j \leq m_i$. Then the following holds:

$$\bigcap_{i=1}^{n} \bigcup_{j=1}^{m_i} F_{x_{i,j}} = \bigcup_{r_1=1}^{m_1} \bigcup_{r_2=1}^{m_2} \cdots \bigcup_{r_n=1}^{m_n} F_{x_{1,r_1} \vee x_{2,r_2} \vee \ldots \vee x_{n,r_n}}$$

To exemplify the notation, note that the equality (57a) = (57c) can be presented in terms of the equality in corollary 3, for $n = 2$, $m_1 = 1$, $m_2 = 2$, $x_{1,1} = \{\mathbf{m'}\}$, $x_{2,1} = \{\mathbf{s'}\}$ and $x_{2,2} = \{\mathbf{j'}\}$.

2.3.3   Collectivity as type shifting

Up to this point we have only been studying the *standard* boolean analysis of NP coordination. As noted above, this treatment is not successful in capturing collectivity effects. However, as soon as the PFP is observed a natural linguistic hypothesis is forthcoming.

Hypothesis 1 (the PFP hypothesis)   "Union" behaviour of *and* in NP coordination is a result of the principal filter property of its standard *intersective* denotation in the boolean domain of generalized quantifiers.

This subsection contains the first steps in the exploration of the PFP hypothesis. More specifically, the hypothesis will be used to develop a mechanism of *type shifting* that generates collective readings in a standard boolean framework. In order to understand the general background for this idea, we will briefly review some familiar guidelines for the syntax-semantics mapping in Montague Grammar.

In the classical grammar of Montague (1973), every syntactic category is given a unique semantic type. This is the *highest* type that is needed for allowing function application in any syntactic environment the grammar generates for the category. For example, as we have already seen, the boolean analysis requires that proper names have the quantificational type $(et)t$. In Montague Grammar this means that proper names are also *lexically* quantificational: they denote Montagovian individuals (principal ultrafilters). Independently, the uniform typing strategy implies that proper names must receive the quantificational type that is motivated for other NPs.

In an influential article, Partee and Rooth (1983) propose a significant modification in this paradigm. Partee and Rooth (henceforth P&R) renounce the uniform typing of syntactic categories. Notably, in P&R's proposal proper names are no longer lexical quantifiers. Rather, they originally come from the D_e domain. In many syntactic contexts this is obviously sufficient to guarantee function application. For example, the simple sentence (58) can be compositionally analyzed as in (58a).

(58) Mary slept.
    a. $\mathbf{m}'_e \ \mathbf{sleep}'_{et} \ \Rightarrow \ \mathbf{sleep}'(\mathbf{m}')$

However, in cases of coordinations as in (59) below, however, mere function application is not sufficient for composing the basic denotations of the NP constituents with the boolean operator. This circumstance, illustrated in (59a), is referred to as *type mismatch*.

(59) Mary or John slept.
    a. $\mathbf{m}'_e \ \sqcup \ \mathbf{j}'_e$ (type mismatch)
    b. $\mathbf{M}(\mathbf{m}') \sqcup \mathbf{M}(\mathbf{j}') = [\lambda P.P(\mathbf{m}')] \sqcup [\lambda P.P(\mathbf{j}')] = \lambda P.P(\mathbf{m}') \vee P(\mathbf{j}')$

To resolve such situations, P&R propose to use a variety of type-shifting operators: functions that can change the type of certain categories.[14] For proper names (= NPs of type e) the relevant operator is a mapping of an entity to a generalized quantifier. Partee (1987) labels this operator *Montague Raising*. Its definition is given in (60).[15] Application of $\mathbf{M}$ to the conjuncts in (59) resolves the type mismatch and leads to the familiar analysis of proper name coordination in (59b).

(60) **Montague Raising**: $\mathbf{M}_{e((et)t)} \overset{\text{def}}{=} \lambda x_e.\lambda P_{et}.P(x)$

This flexible treatment of proper name coordination does not seem to significantly improve on the Montague's uniform typing of proper names as generalized quantifiers. Thus, at this stage there is no need to be committed to P&R's non-boolean e-type treatment of proper names.[16] For this reason, and for simplicity of notation, I occasionally refer to the quantifiers corresponding to proper names like *Mary, John, Sue* and *Bill* with the capital letters M, J, S and B.

Now, according to Bennett's typing of predicates, what we get in collective predications like (54), restated below as (61), is similar to the situation P&R encounter in (59a).

(61) Mary and John met.
    a. $[\mathbf{M} \sqcap \mathbf{J}]_{(et)t} \ \mathbf{meet}'_{(et)t}$ (type mismatch)
    b. $[\mathbf{C}(\mathbf{M} \sqcap \mathbf{J})]_{((et)t)t}(\mathbf{meet}')$

Traditional function application cannot compose the collective predicate $\mathbf{meet}'_{(et)t}$ with the distributive quantifier M ⊓ J, since both functions are of the same type. This is the situation in (61a). The P&R strategy is to resolve such mismatches by using a type-shifting operator. For the time being we can leave open the question of whether type mismatch is the *only* situation where we need to apply type shifting. In subsection 2.3.5 it will be argued that this is not the case. A type-shifting operator that is used to derive collectivity with NP conjunctions is the only new machinery in the present proposal. Let us call the required operator **C**, for *Collectivity Raising*. We let it apply to the coordinate NP denotation to yield a quantifier over *plural* individuals. Thus, **C** is a function of type $((et)t)(((et)t)t)$. The meaning of sentence (61) is to be obtained as illustrated in (61b). How should **C** be defined in order to the right collective reading in (61b)? Here the principal filter property comes to our aid. As mentioned, the $(et)t$ quantifier denotation of the NP *Mary and John* is a principal filter generated by the set $\{\mathbf{m}', \mathbf{j}'\}$. Since this generator is precisely the plural individual we need, we have to get to it from the principal filter. A natural way to obtain this result is to consider the *minimal sets* of the quantifier.[17] A set A is a minimal set of a generalized quantifier Q iff A is in Q and every proper subset of A is not in Q. The operator min derives for each quantifier the collection of its minimal sets. In general, talking about minimal members of a set X only makes sense when X is a subset of a boolean algebra. In type theory, this means that X is of type τt, where τ is a boolean type. The general definition of min reads as follows.

(62) **Minimum Sort**

$$\min_{(\tau t)(\tau t)} \overset{\text{def}}{=} \lambda Q_{\tau t}.\lambda A_{\tau}.Q(A) \wedge \forall B \in Q[B \sqsubseteq A \to B = A]$$

It is easy to verify that $\{\mathbf{m}', \mathbf{j}'\}$ is a minimal set of the quantifier M ⊓ J. Moreover, it is the *only* minimal set of that quantifier. Formally: $\min(\text{M} \sqcap \text{J}) = \{\{\mathbf{m}', \mathbf{j}'\}\}$.

Application of min to a generalized quantifier generates a set of sets: min is a type *sort* operation, or a semantic modifier. Let us view the generated set of sets as a *predicate over plural individuals*. In argument positions, such a predicate still has to become a *quantifier* over plural individuals in order to combine by application with the main predicate in the sentence. This is a familiar situation in semantic theory. Most notably, *indefinite* NPs in Discourse Representation Theory are basically analyzed as predicates. This means that there has to be an operation of *existential closure* in order for an indefinite to have "quantificational force" in argument positions. The same holds of the predicate generated by the min operator. In chapter 4 this analogy between indefinites and collective predication will be shown to have some far-reaching theoretical implications. For the time being let us follow Partee (1987) and employ the standard definition of *Existential Raising* (**E**) of predicates of the general type τt into quantifiers of type $(\tau t)t$. This is just the definition of the existential determiner **some**' in generalized quantifier theory.

(63) **Existential Raising**

$$\mathbf{E}_{(\tau t)((\tau t)t)} \overset{\text{def}}{=} \lambda A_{\tau t}.\lambda P_{\tau t}.\exists X_{\tau}[A(X) \wedge P(X)]$$

Given this, the collectivity operator is simply shorthand for successive application of minimum sort and existential raising to a standard $(et)t$ quantifier.

(64) **Collectivity Raising**

$$\mathbf{C}_{((et)t)(((et)t)t)} \overset{\text{def}}{=} \lambda Q_{(et)t}.\mathbf{E}(\min(Q))$$

Let us now verify that this definition of **C** correctly substantiates the analysis of sentence (61) in (61b):

(65) $\min(\mathrm{M} \sqcap \mathrm{J}) = \{\{\mathbf{m}', \mathbf{j}'\}\}$

$\mathbf{E}(\min(\mathrm{M} \sqcap \mathrm{J})) = \mathbf{E}(\{\{\mathbf{m}', \mathbf{j}'\}\})$

$= \lambda \mathcal{P}_{(et)t}.\exists B \in \{\{\mathbf{m}', \mathbf{j}'\}\} [\mathcal{P}(B)]$

$= \lambda \mathcal{P}.\mathcal{P}(\{\mathbf{m}', \mathbf{j}'\})$

Therefore, $[\mathbf{C}(\mathrm{M} \sqcap \mathrm{J})](\mathbf{meet}')$

$\Leftrightarrow [\lambda \mathcal{P}.\mathcal{P}(\{\mathbf{m}', \mathbf{j}'\})](\mathbf{meet}')$

$\Leftrightarrow \mathbf{meet}'(\{\mathbf{m}', \mathbf{j}'\})$

This is the desired result.

All the mechanics we need in this chapter are now in place: (i) Bennett's typing of plurals. (ii) Partee and Rooth's flexible strategy. (iii) The new collectivity raising operator. In the following sections these will be used to obtain a broader empirical picture.

2.3.4 Collectivity in boolean domains

It may seem that the definition of collectivity raising contains an unnecessary complication. Recall that in the analysis of (61) it was noticed that the plural individual $\{\mathbf{m}', \mathbf{j}'\}$ is the only minimal set of the quantifier $\mathrm{M} \sqcap \mathrm{J}$. This set could have been reached directly by lowering $\mathrm{M} \sqcap \mathrm{J}$ into this plural individual, rather than lifting it into a quantifier over pluralities. However, this is only an apparent redundancy that is suggested by the simplicity of the example. Reconsider sentence (57), repeated below.

(66) Mary and (either) [Sue or John] met.

    a. $\mathrm{M} \sqcap [\mathrm{S} \sqcup \mathrm{J}] = \lambda P_{et}.P(\mathbf{m}') \wedge [P(\mathbf{s}') \vee P(\mathbf{j}')]$

       $\min(\mathrm{M} \sqcap [\mathrm{S} \sqcup \mathrm{J}]) = \{\{\mathbf{m}', \mathbf{s}'\}, \{\mathbf{m}', \mathbf{j}'\}\}$

       $\mathbf{E}(\min(\mathrm{M} \sqcap [\mathrm{S} \sqcup \mathrm{J}])) = \mathbf{E}(\{\{\mathbf{m}', \mathbf{s}'\}, \{\mathbf{m}', \mathbf{j}'\}\})$

         $= \lambda \mathcal{P}_{(et)t}.\exists B \in \{\{\mathbf{m}', \mathbf{s}'\}, \{\mathbf{m}', \mathbf{j}'\}\}(\mathcal{P}(B))$

         $= \lambda \mathcal{P}.\mathcal{P}.(\{\mathbf{m}', \mathbf{s}'\}) \vee \mathcal{P}(\{\mathbf{m}', \mathbf{j}'\})$

       $[\mathbf{C}(\mathrm{M} \sqcap [\mathrm{S} \sqcup \mathrm{J}])](\mathbf{meet}')$

         $\Leftrightarrow [\lambda \mathcal{P}.\mathcal{P}(\{\mathbf{m}', \mathbf{j}'\}) \vee \mathcal{P}(\{\mathbf{m}', \mathbf{j}'\})](\mathbf{meet}')$

         $\Leftrightarrow \mathbf{meet}'(\{\mathbf{m}', \mathbf{s}'\}) \vee \mathbf{meet}'(\{\mathbf{m}', \mathbf{j}'\})$

The quantifier $\mathrm{M} \sqcap [\mathrm{S} \sqcup \mathrm{J}]$, which is the basic interpretation of the subject, has *two* minimal sets: $\{\mathbf{m}', \mathbf{s}'\}$ and $\{\mathbf{m}', \mathbf{j}'\}$. Thus, **C** is not too general—it is required to get the correct analysis (66a), which captures the intuitive equivalence between (66) and (67) below.

(67) Mary and Sue met or Mary and John met.

This straightforward analysis of sentence (66) is obtained because in the approach presented here all kinds of coordination are uniformly boolean. Since virtually all compositional analyses of NP coordination take disjunctions like *Sue or John* to denote boolean $(et)t$ objects, there is nothing special the present analysis has to say about cases like (66), by contrast to the non-boolean approach to *and*, which cannot simply conjoin the denotation of *Sue or John* with an *e*-type denotation of individuals. One option for non-boolean theorists is to stipulate, like Hoeksema (1983, 1988), a special non-boolean *and* also for the boolean domain. An alternative is to let the disjunction *Sue or John* in sentence (66) take scope over the whole subject. Such an operation would be quite problematic, as it would violate the Coordinate Structure Constraint (see section 3.1.1 page 83), which is widely considered to restrict scope mechanisms.[18]

Further support for the treatment of collectivity in boolean domains comes from sentence (68) below, which is intuitively equivalent to (69).

(68) (Either) [Mary and John] or [Sue and Bill] met.

    a. $[(\mathbf{C}(M \sqcap J)) \sqcup (\mathbf{C}(S \sqcap B))](\mathbf{meet'})$

        $\Leftrightarrow [(\lambda \mathcal{P}.\mathcal{P}(\{\mathbf{m'}, \mathbf{j'}\})) \sqcup (\lambda \mathcal{P}.\mathcal{P}(\{\mathbf{s'}, \mathbf{b'}\}))](\mathbf{meet'})$

        $\Leftrightarrow \mathbf{meet'}(\{\mathbf{m'}, \mathbf{j'}\}) \vee \mathbf{meet'}(\{\mathbf{s'}, \mathbf{b'}\})$

    b. $[\mathbf{C}((M \sqcap J) \sqcup (S \sqcap B))](\mathbf{meet'})$

        $\Leftrightarrow \mathbf{meet'}(\{\mathbf{m'}, \mathbf{j'}\}) \vee \mathbf{meet'}(\{\mathbf{s'}, \mathbf{b'}\})$

(69) (Either) Mary and John met or Sue and Bill met.

In sentence (68), although the two *and*'s may seem to amalgamate individuals in a "non-boolean" way, their outputs are disjoined as ordinary boolean quantifiers and give rise to a distributivity equivalence. This is another argument for letting the operator $\mathbf{C}$ generate two plural generalized quantifiers. The treatment is illustrated in (68a). An alternative analysis consists of one application of $\mathbf{C}$ to the whole subject denotation, which in this case, as in (66), is a quantifier with two different minimal sets. The results of this analysis, which is given in (68b), are equivalent to (68a). Another example for such an effect is given in sentence (70) below, where the disjunction is between an *and* coordination and a single proper name.

(70) (Either) [Mary and John] or Sue lifted a piano.

In the non-boolean approach to *and*, sentences like (68) and (70) can be treated by conjoining *e*-type entities, while lifting the type of the result to $(et)t$, so it becomes conjoinable by *or*. However, this strategy necessitates the lifting operator of Montague Raising defined in (60) above. In the present account this operator is dispensable because collectivity is obtained in the boolean $(et)t$ domain to begin with.

2.3.5   The collectivity operator is not triggered by type mismatch

The null assumption that is employed in the analyses above is that the **C** operator can freely apply at any compositional level. For other type shifting operators this liberal strategy was adopted in Groenendijk and Stokhof (1989) and Hendriks (1993: 50). By contrast, Partee and Rooth's (1983) type shifting operators are triggered only in situations of "type mismatch," when function application fails to compose typed denotations in the compositional process. Since Partee and Rooth's strategy is to use type shifting only to fit the type of expressions to "unsuitable" environments, I henceforth refer to this strategy as *type fitting*.

Although the type fitting strategy will be extensively used in chapter 5 for other cases that involve collective interpretations, I argue that type fitting is not the right startegy for the application of the **C** operator. I will not adopt the Groenendijk and Stokhof/Hendriks free approach either, but the syntactic-semantic restrictions on the **C** operator will be studied only in chapter 4, after more of the proposed system will be introduced. For the time being let us see why Partee and Rooth's type fitting strategy cannot work with the **C** operator. One crucial piece of evidence for this claim is the following felicitous example due to Hoeksema (1988: 26).

(71) Dylan and Simon and Garfunkel wrote many hits in the 1960s.

Clearly, this sentence does not entail that Garfunkel wrote many hits in the 1960s.[19] In fact, it might have well been the case that Garfunkel wrote very few hits in the 1960s, but still sentence (71) is true because both Dylan and the *couple* Simon and Garfunkel wrote many hits in the 1960s. Roughly speaking, the NP conjunction in (71) may have a collective reading for the noun phrase *Simon and Garfunkel* while the whole subject under the structure *Dylan and [Simon and Garfunkel]* gets a distributive reading with respect to the main conjunction. In more accurate terms of entailment: the following sentences are not contradictory and yet they entail sentence (71).

(72) a. Dylan wrote many hits in the 1960s.
      b. Simon and Garfunkel wrote many hits in the 1960s.
      c. Garfunkel did not write many hits in the 1960s.

This kind of effect is of course unproblematic for a boolean/non-boolean ambiguity approach like Hoeksema's, which may treat the first *and* in (71) as boolean while taking the second *and* to be non-boolean. For the present approach this example is also unproblematic, but it tells us something important about the principles that govern the application of **C**. The way to obtain the "collective inside distributive" effect in the present treatment is to let **C** apply separately to the denotation of the conjunct *Dylan* and to the denotation of *Simon and Garfunkel*. This allows to collectivize the second conjunct while giving the first conjunct the higher type needed for conjoining it with the second conjunct. This analysis is given below.

(73) $[\mathbf{C}(D) \sqcap \mathbf{C}(S \sqcap G))](\mathbf{write\_many\_hits}')$
   $\Leftrightarrow \mathbf{write\_many\_hits}'(\{\mathbf{d}'\}) \wedge \mathbf{write\_many\_hits}'(\{\mathbf{s}', \mathbf{g}'\})$

This analysis is precisely the one we need above, but crucially, it cannot follow from Partee and Rooth's type fitting strategy: there is no type mismatch involved in the conjunction of the denotation D (for *Dylan*) and the denotation S ⊓ G (for *Simon and Garfunkel*). These denotations can be directly conjoined using the boolean *meet* operator denoted by *and*; hence application of **C** to them is ruled out by Partee and Rooth's "lazy" strategy.

The only stage at which type mismatch is detected is at the level of the whole conjunction, when we attempt to compose an (*et*)*t* subject with an (*et*)*t* predicate. This would only license application of the **C** operator to the whole subject's denotation as in the analysis below.

(74) $[\mathbf{C}(D \sqcap (S \sqcap G))](\mathbf{write\_many\_hits}')$
   $\Leftrightarrow \mathbf{write\_many\_hits}'(\{\mathbf{d}', \mathbf{s}', \mathbf{g}'\})$

This proposition can be paraphrased by the sentence *There are many hits that Dylan, Simon and Garfunkel wrote (as a group) in the 1960s.* Such a reading for sentence (71) is of course well-motivated (world knowledge aside), but it does not help to license the entailment from (72) to (71), which is what we are after. The conclusion from this observation is that the **C** operator is a type shifting principle that should not be restricted by Partee and Rooth's economy principle "apply only in cases of type mismatch." In other words: **C** is not a type fitting operator. Chapter 4 will discuss in more detail the status of such operators in flexible boolean semantics. Chapter 5 will argue that Partee and Rooth's type fitting strategy, although as we have seen is inappropriate for the **C** operator, is motivated for other collectivity type shifting principles.

One consequence of the free application of the **C** operator is that even in simple examples like *Mary and John met* (= (61)) there is an analysis that has not been considered yet. Namely, the analysis in which **C** applies to both conjuncts separately. The corresponding denotation of the subject is C(M) ⊓ C(J). In order to analyze systematically the application of **C**, let us concentrate now on one natural kind of restrictions on its use.

2.3.6 Selectional restrictions: Mrs. Slocombe's unanimity as a colorless green idea

Admirers of the TV comedy *Are you being served?* will affectionately remember Mrs. Slocombe's colorful character declaring assertively when a matter of debate was at stake:

(75) And I am unanimous in that!

Like *unanimous*, most collective predicates listed in (49) to (51) lead to bizarre sentences when they apply to a simple singular subject. For example, all the sentences in (76) are unacceptable.

(76) a. *John dispersed.

    b. *Mary is a nice couple.

    c. *The child liked each other.

    d. *The policeman lifted a piano together.

"Mixed" predicates like *lift a piano* or *write a book* are the exception to this paradigm within the class of collective predicates. For instance, sentence (77) below is fine.

(77) John wrote a book.

Recall that collective predicates like *disperse* and *be a nice couple*, which lead to unacceptabilities as in (76) above (hence are not mixed) are referred to by the label *completely collective* (ccl) predicates. Unacceptabilities with *ccl* predicates as the ones in (76) are not only due to the morpho-syntactic singular number of the subject. For example, it has been noted that some *ccl* predicates can appear with "group-denoting" singular subjects as in (78).

(78) The crowd *is* dispersing. (American English)

And conversely, problematic cases as in (76) are not restricted to singular subjects. For example, sentence (79a) is odd, even though (as noted by Sag et al. (1985)) the disjunctive subject does allow plural agreement in (79b).

(79) a. *Mary or John are meeting.

    b. Mary or John are sleeping.

Hence, the unacceptable sentences in (76) and (79a) are reasonably not purely syntactic and require a semantic or pragmatic account. A semantic explanation was proposed by Bennett (1974: 133). In Bennett's system cases as in (76) are ruled out due to type considerations: the subject in these sentences is unambiguously a quantifier of type $(et)t$. The *ccl* predicate is also of the same type. Therefore, function application fails and the sentence is ruled out. Bennett's system does not deal with NP coordination. On the other hand, the possibility of ruling out cases as in (76) for type mismatch considerations is not open for the present flexible approach, since it is precisely under these circumstances that application of the **C** operator can resolve the mismatch. Moreover, if we tried to rule out unacceptabilities as in (76) by stipulating that **C** does not apply to single proper names but applies to their coordinations, we would have had trouble with Hoeksema's example (71), restated below.

(80) Dylan and Simon and Garfunkel wrote many hits in the 1960s.

As we have seen, to get the prominent reading of this sentence we have to apply the **C** operator to the denotation of *Dylan*, hence singularity of the proper name cannot be the reason for the failure of **C** to apply in cases as in (76) above. Summing up, Bennett's type mismatch approach to these unacceptable cases is unsuitable to the needs of the present flexible system.

An alternative line of explanation is briefly proposed in Scha (1981), where cases like *John dispersed* are classified as a "semantic anomaly," similar to Chomsky's celebrated example in (81).

(81) ?Colorless green ideas sleep furiously.

Such strange sentences are analyzed as structurally well-formed by most theories of grammar. Their oddness is often attributed to "selectional restrictions." According to this line, there is a separate mechanism (grammatical or extra-grammatical) that encodes trivial information like the inability of a predicate like *sleep* to hold of a subject like *an idea*. Scha makes the same suggestion with respect to cases like the verb *disperse* and the subject *John*, or the other examples in (76) above. A similar position is taken in Dowty (1987), and Roberts (1987: 124) elaborates:

> What does it mean to gather or to disperse? By virtue of the meaning of such a predicate, its subject must denote a group of individuals. . . . Viewed in this way, these verbs are no more special than a verb such as *grasp*, which, on one of its senses, can only be true of an individual with a certain type of movable thumb.

Simplifying a bit,[20] we may model the Scha/Dowty/Roberts view by formulating a meaning postulate about possible denotations of *ccl* predicates:

(82) **The SDR postulate**
      Let $\mathcal{P}_{(et)t}$ be the denotation of a *ccl* predicate. Then the following holds: $\forall A[\mathcal{P}(A) \rightarrow |A| \geq 2]$.

In order to use this postulate to account for the unacceptability of the sentences in (76) there are two possible theoretical lines:

1. To argue that selectional restrictions like the SDR postulate are to be used as semantic/syntactic principles that rule out such sentences grammatically.
2. To consider principles like the SDR postulate as part of the common knowledge of speakers that cannot be contradicted, at least in everyday use of language.

For the sake of the present (limited) purposes, I adopt the second approach without argument. If the SDR postulate is part of the common ground of participants in a conversation then any utterance expressing a proposition that contradicts it becomes pragmatically deviant. For instance, in (76a), repeated below as (83), the **C** operator applies to the subject and yields the proposition in (83a). Accommodation of the SDR postulate for *disperse* then leads to the contradiction in (83b).

(83) *John dispersed.
      a. $[\mathbf{C}(J)](\mathbf{disperse'}) \Leftrightarrow \mathbf{disperse'}(\{\mathbf{j'}\})$
      b. $\mathbf{disperse'}(\{\mathbf{j'}\}) \wedge \forall A[\mathbf{disperse'}(A) \rightarrow |A| \geq 2] \Leftrightarrow \bot$

In cases of negation like (84) below the problem is the opposite one. Such sentences are *entailed* by the SDR postulate and hence they are pragmatically uninformative in any normal situation.

(84) *John did not disperse.

Disjunctions as in (79a) are treated in a similar fashion. In this sentence there are two possible ways to apply **C**: either to the whole coordination or to its parts. As illustrated in (85a-b) below, both lead to the same proposition, one that contradicts the SDR postulate as shown in (85c).

(85) *Mary or John met.
    a. $[\mathbf{C}(M \sqcup J)](\mathbf{meet}') \Leftrightarrow \mathbf{meet}'(\{\mathbf{m}'\}) \vee \mathbf{meet}'(\{\mathbf{j}'\})$
    b. $[\mathbf{C}(M) \sqcup \mathbf{C}(J)](\mathbf{meet}') \Leftrightarrow \mathbf{meet}'(\{\mathbf{m}'\}) \vee \mathbf{meet}'(\{\mathbf{j}'\})$
    c. $(\mathbf{meet}'(\{\mathbf{m}'\}) \vee \mathbf{meet}'(\{\mathbf{j}'\})) \wedge \forall A[\mathbf{meet}'(A) \rightarrow |A| \geq 2] \Leftrightarrow \perp$

Although the complete formalization of pragmatic considerations as outlined above is not straightforward, they are nevertheless useful. This kind of reasoning can be used to test whether the predictions of the semantic component are acceptable or not. In all the above cases application of the **C** operator led to propositions that are analyzed as pragmatically deviant. Thus, the semantic mechanism allows an account of these sentences' marked status. However, this is not the whole picture. For example, the marked status of sentence (86) below is not explained by considerations of contradiction and tautology alone.

(86) *(Either) [Mary and John] or Sue met.
    a. $[\mathbf{C}((M \sqcap J) \sqcup S)](\mathbf{meet}') \Leftrightarrow \mathbf{meet}'(\{\mathbf{m}', \mathbf{j}'\}) \vee \mathbf{meet}'(\{\mathbf{s}'\})$
    b. $\mathbf{meet}'(\{\mathbf{m}', \mathbf{j}'\}) \vee \mathbf{meet}'(\{\mathbf{s}'\}) \wedge \forall A[\mathbf{meet}'(A) \rightarrow |A| \geq 2]$
       $\Leftrightarrow \mathbf{meet}'(\{\mathbf{m}', \mathbf{j}'\}) \wedge \forall A[\mathbf{meet}'(A) \rightarrow |A| \geq 2]$

The proposition in (86a) that is generated by the semantic mechanism is independent of the SDR postulate. A conjunction of (86a) with the SDR postulate for *meet* derives the proposition in (86b), which conjoins the SDR postulate and the possible claim that Mary and John met. Hence it is neither contradictory, nor is it entailed by the SDR postulate. A similar situation is observed in the *sentential* coordination (87).

(87) *Mary and John met or Sue met.

Why are (86) and (87) nevertheless unacceptable? A simple answer is still available if we take pragmatic Gricean principles into account, as well as their implications for the analysis of disjunctive propositions.[21] The SDR entails that both (86) and (87) are synonymous to the shorter sentence *Mary and John met*. According to Grice's Quantity principle, the sentence *Mary and John met* should be strongly preferred over (86) and (87), and these latter sentences are therefore unacceptable.

Theoretically, this pragmatic account seems to me satisfactory, since it rests on some solid linguistic assumptions concerning selectional restrictions and the pragmatics of disjunction.

Although in the appeal to selectional restrictions and pragmatics we lose a great deal of rigor, this is probably because questions about the formal nature of these domains may need to wait some time before they can be properly answered. However, in the meantime some comfort for the formally minded can be found in what follows. The restriction *ccl* predicates impose on their arguments can be stated in a way that semantically mimics the relevant pragmatic considerations.

The intuition underlying this characterization is the requirement embodied in the SDR postulate: *ccl* predicates require an argument that is a "plural" set, one with two or more members. But more generality is needed in order to treat also NP arguments that are interpreted in the $((et)t)t$ domain, such as the subjects in (79a) and (86). We define the notion of a *completely plural* denotation, which is relevant to plural individuals, collective predicates and quantifiers over them, and recursively defined as follows:

(88) Let us call a type $\tau = \sigma t$ *plural-based* iff $\sigma = e$ or σ is plural-based. The set of
      completely plural objects of a plural-based type τ is defined as follows:

$$cpl_{\tau t} \stackrel{\text{def}}{=} \begin{cases} \lambda X_\tau.|X| \geq 2 & \text{if } \tau = et \\ \lambda X_\tau.\forall Y_\tau \in \min(X)\,[cpl(Y)] & \text{otherwise} \end{cases}$$

Examples
1. A plural individual A_{et} is *cpl* iff $|A| \geq 2$.
2. A collective predicate $\mathcal{P}_{(et)t}$ is *cpl* iff $\forall A \in \min(\mathcal{P})\,[|A| \geq 2]$ (this holds iff $\forall A \in \mathcal{P}\,[|A| \geq 2]$).
3. A collective quantifier $\mathcal{Q}_{((et)t)t}$ is *cpl* iff $\forall \mathcal{P} \in \min(\mathcal{Q})\,\forall A \in \mathcal{P}\,[|A| \geq 2]$.

Put in these terms, the SDR postulate says that the denotation of any *ccl* predicate in natural language must be *cpl*.

Observe that instead of the above pragmatic analysis, the following semantic stipulation can be used as a rule of thumb:

(89) An NP argument of a *ccl* predicate must denote a *cpl* object.

This correctly describes the facts noted above. In (83) the subject denotation is $C(J) = \lambda \mathcal{P}.\mathcal{P}(\{\mathbf{j'}\})$. The minimum of this collective quantifier is $\{\{\{\mathbf{j'}\}\}\}$, which is not *cpl*. In (79a) the subject denotes the function $\lambda \mathcal{P}.\mathcal{P}(\{\mathbf{m'}\}) \vee \mathcal{P}(\{\mathbf{j'}\})$. The minimum of this denotation is $\{\{\{\mathbf{m'}\}\}, \{\{\mathbf{j'}\}\}\}$, which is not a *cpl* object. In (86) the relevant minimum is $\{\{\{\mathbf{m'}, \mathbf{j'}\}\}, \{\{\mathbf{j'}\}\}\}$. This is not a *cpl* object either because $\{\{\mathbf{j'}\}\}$ is not *cpl*. By contrast, the subjects of sentences (61), (66) and (68) do denote *cpl* objects in every model where none of the proper names involved corefer. In models where, for instance, *Mary* denotes the same object as *John*, also $C(M \sqcap J)$ is not *cpl* and sentences like (61) are unacceptable, as expected. For example, consider sentence (90). Provided that *Dr. Jekyll* and *Mr. Hyde* are names of the same person the sentence is unacceptable.

(90) *Dr. Jekyll and Mr. Hyde met in the park.

Descriptively adequate though generalization (89) may be, it has to be emphasized again that it should not be considered as the "real explanation" of the problem. The *cpl* condition in (89) is only a handy empirical generalization that will henceforth be used in the analysis.

2.3.7   Elementary syntax-semantics of coordination and collectivity

A noun phrase like *Mary and John* has three denotations in the proposed system. These denotations are given below.

i. $M \sqcap J$

ii. $C(M \sqcap J)$

iii. $C(M) \sqcap C(J)$.

All of these are useful. Given the above typology of plural predicates, there are three kinds of predicates that need to be considered: distributive, completely collective and mixed predicates. An example of each group is given in (91).

(91) a. Mary and John slept.
     b. Mary and John met.
     c. Mary and John weigh (exactly) 140 kg.

The quantifier in (i), the standard denotation of the subject, is the only one available in (91a). This is due to type considerations: the distributive predicate *sleep* is of type et and therefore the subject can only denote the $(et)t$ quantifier in (i).[22] In (91b), which has a *ccl* predicate of type $(et)t$, only (ii) is relevant. Denotation (i) is ruled out because of its type and (iii) for selectional reasons: it is not *cpl*. The mixed predicate in (91c) is also of type $(et)t$. Consequently, (i) is ruled out as in (91b). Denotation (ii) derives a collective reading of (91c): the claim that Mary and John *together* weigh 140 kg. Using the denotation in (iii) we get a distributive reading equivalent to *Mary weighs 140 kg. and John weighs 140 kg.* In this case the non-*cpl* denotation (iii) is acceptable because the predicate in (91c) is not *ccl*.

So far so good, but it should be noted that the subject of sentence (91) is syntactically rather simple. To consider more complex examples, let us review a few elements of existing syntactic theories of coordination. The analyses in Ross (1967: 89–91) and many other studies of coordination (e.g. Dik (1968), Gazdar (1981)) propose the following basic rule scheme:

(92) $\mathbf{X} \rightarrow \mathbf{X}_1, \ldots, \mathbf{X}_{n-1} \left\{ \begin{array}{c} \text{and} \\ \text{or} \end{array} \right\} \mathbf{X}_n$

Here $\mathbf{X}, \mathbf{X}_1, \ldots, \mathbf{X}_n$ are of the same category and $n \geq 2$. According to this natural rule, *and* and *or* are general n-ary coordinators: one occurrence of them can coordinate an arbitrary number of projections. This makes a crucial difference for the syntactic analysis of certain examples. For instance, the coordination *Mary and Sue and John* is syntactically ambiguous between the two nested structures in figure 2.1. By contrast, only the flat structure in figure 2.2 is assigned to the coordination *Mary, Sue and John*.

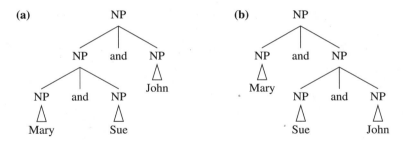

Figure 2.1
Mary and Sue and John

   Without getting into more complex syntactic questions concerning these structures,[23] we note that the expressions *both* and *either* are sensitive to the identity of the coordinator. This is shown by the contrasts in (93) and (94).

(93) *both* Mary *and/*or* Sue

(94) *either* Mary **and/or* Sue

The question how to account for such dependencies will not be discussed here either (see Larson (1985) for relevant discussion). However, note that they can enforce syntactic disambiguation of complex coordinations. For instance, while the coordination in figure 2.1 is ambiguous, the one in (95) is not. In this case only association to the right as in (95a) is grammatical whereas association to the left as in (95b) is of course ungrammatical.

(95) Mary and both Sue and John
    a.   Mary and [both Sue and John]
    b. *[Mary and both Sue] and John

Such simple syntactic distinctions are important for the analysis of the syntax-semantics interface of collectivity in NP coordinations. Consider first the conjunction *Mary and Sue and John*. In a compositional semantics the **C** operator must apply to full NP denotations. Consequently the structure in figure 2.1(a) = (96a) has the interpretations in

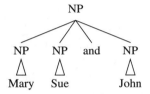

Figure 2.2
Mary, Sue and John

(i.a) to (iv.a) whereas the structure in figure 2.1(b) = (96b) has the interpretations (i.b) to (iv.b).

(96) a. [Mary and Sue] and John
      b. Mary and [Sue and John]

(i.a) $[M \sqcap S] \sqcap J$

(i.b) $M \sqcap [S \sqcap J]$

(ii.a) $C([M \sqcap S] \sqcap J)$

(ii.b) $C(M \sqcap [S \sqcap J])$

(iii.a) $C(M \sqcap S) \sqcap C(J)$

(iii.b) $C(M) \sqcap C(S \sqcap J)$

(iv.a) $[C(M) \sqcap C(S)] \sqcap C(J)$

(iv.b) $C(M) \sqcap [C(S) \sqcap C(J)]$

Other possibilities are ruled out. In general, compositionality implies the following principle: *semantic operations apply only to denotations of* CONSTITUENTS. Thus, the **C** operator can apply only to denotations of constituent NPs. Trivial as it is, this principle makes some non-trivial predictions, which are now to be discussed.

Phonological disambiguation   Phonological stress can contrinute to the disambiguation of syntactic structures. Consider for example the sentences (97) and (98) below.

(97) Mary and Sue, and John weigh 140kg.
      a. $[C(M \sqcap S) \sqcap C(J)](w140') \Leftrightarrow w140'(\{m', s'\}) \wedge w140'(\{j'\})$
      b. $[C(M) \sqcap C(S \sqcap J)](w140') \Leftrightarrow w140'(\{m'\}) \wedge w140'(\{s', j'\})$

(98) Mary and Sue and John weigh 140 kg.

In sentence (97) only the structure in figure 2.1(a) is possible due to the comma intonation. That this is the case can be attested semantically: sentence (97), just like (98) with "neutral" stress, can be true in case Mary and Sue weigh together 140 kg. and John alone weighs the same. However, (97), unlike (98), is false if Mary alone weighs 140 kg. and Sue and John weigh 140 kg. together (assuming, of course, that Sue is not weightless). This behaviour is expected under the present proposal: denotation (iii.a) leads to proposition (97a), which is true in the first situation. However, none of the denotations (ii.a) to (iv.a) leads to a true proposition in the latter situation. The facts reverse when we consider the denotations (ii.b) to (iv.b). Denotation (iii.b) leads to the proposition in (97b), which is true in the latter situation, and none of the denotations (ii.b) to (iv.b) derives a proposition that is verified by the former. Thus, the phonological disambiguation of (97) leads, together with the proposed collectivity mechanism, to the intuitively correct result.

No discontinuous collectivity   Note that sentence (98) is not true in case Mary and John weigh 140 kg. together, and Sue has the same weight on her own. This is of course expected, because the NPs *Mary* and *John* in (98) do not form a constituent in any of its parses. As a result no application of the **C** operator can "separate" the subject denotation in this way.

Flat conjunctions   Compare (98) with (99) below.

(99) Mary, Sue and John weigh 140 kg.

In (99), by contrast to (98), distributivity is a matter of "all or nothing": either the total weight of the three people is 140 kg. or the individual weight of each of them is 140 kg. Sentence (99) is not true in situations like the ones that verify propositions (97a/b) above, where two of the people weigh 140 kg. together, and so does the third one, but on his own. This is predicted by the compositional application of the **C** operator. The only possible interpretations of the subject of (99) are the following:

i. $\mathbf{C}(M) \sqcap \mathbf{C}(S) \sqcap \mathbf{C}(J)$
ii. $\mathbf{C}(M \sqcap S \sqcap J)$

Other possibilities (e.g. like the ones in the analysis of (98)) are ruled out. For example, *Sue and John* is not a constituent in (99) and therefore a denotation like $\mathbf{C}(M) \sqcap \mathbf{C}(S \sqcap J)$ is unavailable. As will be discussed in chapter 6, the fact that sentences like (99) have only an all-distributive and an all-collective interpretation is not accounted for by some other theories of plurals, for reasons to be reviewed there.

Syntactic disambiguation   Reconsider sentence (66), restated below:

(100) Mary and Sue or John met.

Only the constituency in (101b) is predicted to lead to an acceptable reading. In order to see that, observe first that for the structures (101a–b) the below interpretations are generated, analogous to (96) above.

(101) a. [Mary and Sue] or John
       b. Mary and [Sue or John]

(i.a) $[M \sqcap S] \sqcup J$

(i.b) $M \sqcap [S \sqcup J]$

(ii.a) $\mathbf{C}([M \sqcap S] \sqcup J)$

(ii.b) $\mathbf{C}(M \sqcap [S \sqcup J])$

(iii.a) $\mathbf{C}(M \sqcap S) \sqcup \mathbf{C}(J)$

(iii.b) $\mathbf{C}(M) \sqcap \mathbf{C}(S \sqcup J)$

(iv.a) $[\mathbf{C}(M) \sqcap \mathbf{C}(S)] \sqcup \mathbf{C}(J)$

(iv.b) $\mathbf{C}(M) \sqcap [\mathbf{C}(S) \sqcup \mathbf{C}(J)]$

Among these readings only (ii.b) is both *cpl* and of the appropriate type. Consequently, the system generates only the correct interpretation that is derived in (66a). Sentence (100) is predicted to be equivalent to the sentence *Mary and Sue met or Mary and John met*. That this analysis is linguistically realistic can be further verified by using the disjunction marker *either* in order to syntactically disambiguate the coordination.

(102) a. *Either [Mary and Sue] or Bill met.
      b.   Mary and [either John or Bill] met.

The unacceptable sentence (102a) can only have the underlined structure. As a result, the subject can be assigned only one of the readings in (ii.a) to (iv.a), which are all non-*cpl*. Thus, the oddness of the sentence is explained. By contrast, disambiguating the coordination as in (102b) leads to an acceptable sentence, which is intuitively equivalent to (100). The fact that the *cpl* denotation (ii.b) is among the readings of the coordination accounts for this.

2.3.8   Recapitulation

The main claims made in this section are the following:

• There is a boolean property of *and* conjunctions, called the *principal filter property*, that can serve as a basis for the explanation of apparent "non-boolean" effects with *and* without imposing any lexical ambiguity on top of its boolean analysis.

• A natural way of exploiting the principal filter property is using a type shifting operator that generates collectivity effects from standard Montagovian individuals in the boolean generalized quantifier domain. This mechanism is defined by composing an *existential raising* operator to a *minimum sort* operator.

• The collectivity type shifting operator is freely introduced in the examples that were addressed above and is not controlled by Partee and Rooth's "mismatch resolution" strategy of type fitting.

• The unacceptability of sentences such as *Mary met* follows from selectional violations and not from type mismatch considerations *à la* Bennett.

• A semantic account that uses a collectivity operator combines well with simple assumptions about the syntax of various types of NP coordination.

A central distinction between the present approach and previous work concerns the cross-linguistically attested difference between *and* and *or* in NP coordinations. As mentioned in subsection 2.2.1 above, this point remains mysterious in previous proposals that simply assign non-boolean interpretation to *and* in English. In the present approach, by contrast, the only differences between the two coordinators are those predicted by their standard boolean definitions. The fact that there are no cases of "non-boolean *or*" directly follows from the principal filter property: in cases of *and* conjunction such as (61) the PFP is effective so that application of the **C** operator generates a collective reading. By contrast, in cases of "pure" *or* coordinations such as (85), the **C** operator preserves the classical distributivity equivalence.

In localizing "non-boolean" effects of *and* within coordinations of noun phrases, the proposal in this chapter is similar to Hoeksema's accounts. Furthermore, also the use of minimal sets of quantifiers to model collectivity already appears in Hoeksema (1983). However, there are some important differences between the two proposals. While Hoeksema's use of minimal sets is in the *lexical* definition of non-boolean *and*, here min is a flexibility operator. Hoeksema's definition of *and* is further complicated by the assignment of set union, whereas in the present proposal the "union" effect is captured by the principal filter property without any withdrawal from the boolean assumption about *and*. This desirable situation is made possible by the "combinatorical freedom" of type-shifting principles allows this desirable move, but it has a certain cost: the use of the minimum operator gives rise to the empirical problems that also challenge the account in Hoeksema (1983) (cf. (21) above), as well as other problems. These problems will be treated in the next chapters (see the survey in subsection 2.3.9 below).

As for the debate on the nature of plural individuals, the proposal in this chapter clearly sides with Schwarzschild's approach but avoids its discussed problems. Consider example (103), a variation on (37a), and its two analyses in (103a–b).

(103) [The animals 1, 2, 3 and 4] and [the animals a, b, c and d] were separated.
   a. $[\mathbf{C}((A_1 \sqcap A_2 \sqcap A_3 \sqcap A_4) \sqcap (A_a \sqcap A_b \sqcap A_c \sqcap A_d))](\mathbf{separated'})$
       $\Leftrightarrow \mathbf{separated'}(\{1, 2, 3, 4, a, b, c, d\})$
   b. $[\mathbf{C}(A_1 \sqcap A_2 \sqcap A_3 \sqcap A_4) \sqcap \mathbf{C}(A_a \sqcap A_b \sqcap A_c \sqcap A_d)](\mathbf{separated'})$
       $\Leftrightarrow \mathbf{separated'}(\{1, 2, 3, 4\}) \wedge \mathbf{separated'}(\{a, b, c, d\})$

The "separation between groups" situations, which motivate a nested ontology in Hoeksema's and Landman's proposals, are captured following Schwarzschild by the general reading (103a). In addition, the "distribution to groups" effect, in which each of two groups is separated, was shown to be problematic for Schwarzschild's approach (cf. (40) above). This effect is captured by (103b): a simple non-collectivized boolean conjunction of two collectivized boolean conjunctions.

This discussion by no means settles the debate between nested ontologies and flat ontologies. In chapter 5 we will find reasons to adopt a variation of Landman's proposal that maps plural individuals to singular individuals of some sort. However, the *motivation* for this move, which creates a sort of nesting in the ontology of plurals, will not be cases like sentence (103), and the ontological implications of such a mapping from plural individuals to "impure atoms" will be argued to be less dramatic than in Landman's theory.

2.3.9   A road-map to the treatment of remaining problems

The present chapter has presented some basic principles for this book but it has left many questions unanswered. Not the least important among them is a conceptual one.

The flexible interpretation complicates the architecture of traditional Boolean Semantics as sketched in figure 1.3 (page 14), where function application is the only part in the derivation of the sentence's meaning that does not come from lexical meanings of phonologically overt morphemes. In a flexible interpretation process described in figure 1.3 there are additional operations in the analysis of the sentence. Is there any further motivation for introducing this complicating factor? More specifically, is there a way to motivate the **C** operator on independent grounds? Both questions will be answered affirmatively in chapter 4, while the more general idea of flexibility will be substantiated throughout this book. Some empirical problems with pointers to their treatment in this book are listed below.

Restrictions on flexibility   As mentioned above, the application of the minimum operator within **C** is problematic for many NPs. In addition to the aforementioned problems for NP coordinations like (21), the flexible approach gives bad results for some *simple* NP structures. For instance, the non-upward-monotone quantifier in (104) is not analyzed correctly.

(104) Less than five men met.

And worse, there is no explanation for the unacceptability of sentence (105) below.

(105) *Every child met.

Nothing in the present analysis rules out application of **C** to the denotation of the subject *every child*, which would yield a statement equivalent to *the children met*.

Further, the distributivity of *both . . . and* NP coordinations like (16) or (106) is not accounted for.

(106) *Both Mary and John are a nice couple.

Clearly, the proposed mechanism should be restricted. The principles that impose such restrictions are studied in section 4.3.

Note that cases like (104) exemplify a further complication. Even if the **C** operator is properly restricted, this will not lead to a treatment of such hard-to-paraphrase collective sentences. Such cases of "plural quantification" will be treated in chapter 5.

Indefinites and conjunction   Simple NP conjunctions with singular indefinites and proper names give rise to collectivity effects, similar to the collectivity effects with proper names that were discussed in this chapter. For example, sentence (107) has the interpretation given in (107a). Application of the **C** operator to the generalized quantifier conjunction in the manner employed above generates the statement in (107b).

(107) John and some man met.
         a. $\exists x[\mathbf{man}'(x) \wedge \mathbf{meet}'(\{\mathbf{j}', x\})]$

b. $[\mathbf{C}(\llbracket \text{John} \rrbracket \sqcap \llbracket \text{some man} \rrbracket)](\mathbf{meet'})$

  $\Leftrightarrow \exists B \in \min(\{A : \mathbf{j} \in A \wedge A \cap \mathbf{man'} \neq \emptyset\})[\mathbf{meet'}(B)]$

  $\Leftrightarrow [\neg[\mathbf{man'}(\mathbf{j'}) \wedge \exists x[\mathbf{man'}(x) \wedge \mathbf{meet'}(\{\mathbf{j'}, x\})]] \vee [\mathbf{man'}(\mathbf{j'}) \wedge \mathbf{meet'}(\{\mathbf{j'}\})]$

The statements in (107a) and (107b) are not equivalent. For example, consider a (likely) situation where John is a man. In such a situation, the quantifier conjunction that basically denotes the subject of (107) is coreferential with the quantifier for the proper name *John*. The reason is that every set that contains John trivially contains John and some man (namely, John himself), and that every set that contains John and some man thereby trivially contains John. This means that if John is a man then (107b) becomes tantamount to the funny sentence *John met*. However, sentence (107) is completely coherent in such a situation. A better formalization of (107) is given in (107a), which is true in case John and some *other* man met.[24]

The problem lies in the combination of the existential generalized quantifier analysis of indefinites and the present treatment of collectivity. Chapter 3 will argue for a revision of the generalized quantifier approach to indefinites that overcomes this problem.

General distributivity   In the present chapter only coordinations of *singular* NPs have been treated. As mentioned, however, distributivity and collectivity are general phenomena related to plurality. A treatment of simple plural NPs like *the teachers* or *five girls* will be provided in chapters 3 and 4.

A complicating factor is that even with simple proper name conjunction distributivity may be more complex than what we have assumed in this chapter. A well-known example from Gillon (1987: 212) is sentence (108) below.

(108)   Rodgers, Hammerstein and Hart wrote musicals.

(109)   Rodgers and Hammerstein wrote musicals together, and Rodgers and Hart wrote musicals together.

(110)   Rodgers wrote musicals, Hammerstein wrote musicals and Hart wrote musicals.

Gillon and others point that the sentence in (108) can be true due to the truth of (109), while the "completely distributive" sentence (110) may still be false. The immediate conclusion drawn by these works is that sentence (108) should have an analysis equivalent to (109), and not only a "purely distributive" reading as paraphrased in (110). In chapter 6 I will argue against this conclusion.

2.4   On Predicate Conjunction within the Boolean Framework

So far, this chapter has concentrated on apparent "non-boolean" effects in the interpretation of noun phrase coordination. However, as mentioned in subsection 2.2.2, there are also interesting challenges for the boolean assumption in certain cases of *predicate* conjunction.

In this section I briefly discuss these problems and summarize the solution proposed in Winter (1996, 1998: ch. 7).

Reconsider sentences (111a) and (112a), discussed above.

(111) a. The flag is green and white.
      b. #The flag is green and the flag is white.

(112) a. The books are old and new.
      b. #The books are old and the books are new.

Both (111a) and (112a) are clearly not equivalent to the respective sentential coordinations in (111b) and (112b). This is a problem for any straightforward boolean treatment of predicate conjunction. Krifka (1990) attempts to account for such effects of predicate conjunction using a cross-categorial generalization of the non-boolean denotation of *and* that is commonly used for NP coordinations like *Mary and John*. However, this section argues that the effects discussed above with predicate conjunction do not in fact pose a substantial challenge for the boolean analysis and can be explained as epiphenomena of independently known effects. Moreover, it will be claimed that the similarity between singular predicate conjunction as in (111a) and plural predicate conjunction as in (112a) is only apparent. I propose that the "non-boolean" interpretation of predicate conjunction in (111a) stems from the special semantics of color predicates, which function also as nominals. By contrast, cases like (112a) exemplify a general principle which is operative (only) in the interpretation of *plural* predicates. This is the *strongest meaning hypothesis* introduced by Dalrymple et al. (1994, 1998) for the interpretation of reciprocated predicates.

Let us start with singular predicate conjunction as in (111a). Lasersohn (1995) points out that the apparent non-boolean effect is strongly connected to the double function of color words as both adjectives and nouns (cf. *green is my favorite color*). A similar behaviour is observed in sentence (113) below, due to Krifka (1990), with the mass nouns *beer* and *lemonade*.

(113) This is beer and lemonade
     ⇔ #this is beer and this is lemonade.

By contrast, Lasersohn shows that with adjectives that do not have a nominal use, conjunction behaves as expected by the boolean analysis. For instance, the examples in (114) to (115) are all equivalent to their sentential correlates.

(114) a. #The house is big and small.
      b. #The board is long and short.
      c. #Mary is fat and thin.

(115) a. The house is comfortable and small.
      b. The board is short and useful.
      c. John is short and fat.

Sentence (114a) is just as contradictory as the sentence *The house is big and the house is small*. Sentence (115a) is equivalent to the sentential conjunction *The house is comfortable and the house is small*. Like the latter sentence, (115a) cannot be asserted of a big house that consists of a comfortable part and another part that is uncomfortable but small. These facts speak strongly against any general non-boolean analysis of *and* in singular predicate conjunctions.

Why does singular predicate conjunction nevertheless show non-boolean effects when the predicates involved have a nominal use? The answer is straightforward under the natural assumption that words like *green* or *beer* can function as "names" not only when they are in argument positions, but also when they are in predicate positions. If this is the case, the "non-boolean" interpretation of such conjunctions in (111a) and (113) would not be more surprising than their "non-boolean" interpretation in argument position as in (116) below, or, conversely, the "non-boolean" behaviour of conjunctions of more typical noun phrases when they appear in predicative positions as in (117).

(116) a. Green and white is my favorite combination of colors.
       b. Beer and lemonade is my favorite combination of drinks.

(117) These people are Mary and John.

Conjunction in predicative constructions as in (117) will be analyzed in chapter 4 using the same boolean analysis of NP conjunction in argument position that was developed in this chapter. Given the nominal behaviour of color predicates and mass terms, their appearances in predicative positions should be amenable to the same treatment. Of course, to give a full account of the interpretation process, we still have to analyze the semantic relationship between the "nominal" and "adjectival" uses of these expressions. This is the task of theories of mass terms and nominalization, and not a challenge for the boolean theory of coordination. I therefore leave this problem aside.

The "non-boolean" effects in the interpretation of *plural* predicate conjunction are quite different in being unrelated to nominalization processes. Contrast for instance the unacceptable singular predicate conjunction in (114a) with the following, minimally different, conjunction of predicates in the plural.

(118) The houses are big and small.

Sentence (118), unlike (114a), has a non-contradictory interpretation. Under this interpretation, the sentence can be true if some of the houses are big and the others are small. Sentence (118) is not equivalent to the sentential conjunction *The houses are big and the houses are small*. This shows that "non-boolean" effects can appear with plural predicate conjunction even when the conjoined predicates do not have any nominal use. The appearance of these effects is sensitive, however, to the lexical choice of the predicates. Consider for instance the following examples.

Figure 2.3
Ducks

(119) a. The ducks are swimming and flying.
       b. The ducks are swimming and quacking.

Sentence (119a) can be interpreted as true in the situation depicted in figure 2.3. This means that the sentence is not equivalent to the sentence *the ducks are swimming and the ducks are flying*, which is contradictory given common knowledge. Sentence (119b), by contrast, cannot be true under the same situation, although the quacking ducks are precisely the ones that are flying. This means that (119b) *is* equivalent to the sentence *the ducks are swimming and the ducks are quacking*, which is not contradictory. We see that a "non-boolean" effect appears when the two predicates are incompatible as in (119a), but not when they are compatible as in (119b). A similar generalization holds of the following (non-)equivalences.

(120) a. The books are old and new
           ⇎ #The books are old and the books are new.
       b. The books are old and interesting
           ⇔ The books are old and the books are interesting.

(121) a. The birds are below the cloud and above the cloud
           ⇎ #The birds are below the cloud and the birds are above the cloud.
       b. The birds are below the cloud and above the house
           ⇔ The birds are below the cloud and the birds are above the house.

This kind of sensitivity to lexical content is highly reminiscent of the *strongest meaning hypothesis* of Dalrymple et al. (1994, 1998), who propose this principle in order to deal with reciprocal expressions as in the sentences below.

(122) a.   The girls are standing on each other.
       b. #Every girl is standing on every other girl.

(123) a. The girls know each other.

   b. Every girl knows every other girl.

Sentence (123a) is close in its meaning to (123b). By contrast, the meaning of sentence (122a) is not even remotely similar to the meaning of sentence (122b), which cannot be true given the anti-symmetric properties of the relation *stand on*. Observing such contrasts, Dalrymple et al. propose that the interpretation of a reciprocal expression is always the strongest meaning (relative to some specified set of its possible meanings) that is compatible with lexical semantic knowledge on the reciprocated predicate. This is the essence of what they call *the strongest meaning hypothesis* (SMH).

The observations made above concerning the interpretation of plural predicate conjunction are parallel to this observation of Dalrymple et al. on reciprocal expressions. In both cases, when a "strong" proposition, obtained using universal quantification or boolean conjunction, is compatible with common knowledge about the predicates, it is also the attested reading of the sentence. This is the case in (123a) as well as in (119b), (120b) and (121b). By contrast, when such a strong reading is incoherent, it is not attested and the actual reading of the sentence is weaker. In Winter (1996, 1998: ch. 7) I propose that Dalrymple et al.'s SMH should therefore be extended into a general principle regulating the intervention of lexical knowledge in the interpretation process of *all* plural predicates. According to this principle conjunction is unambiguously boolean and reciprocals are unambiguously "universal." Consequently the "basic" interpretation of both sentences (119a) and (119b) is as formalized below.

(124) a. $\forall x \in \mathbf{duck}'[\mathbf{swim}'(x) \wedge \mathbf{fly}'(x)]$

   $\Leftrightarrow \forall x \in \mathbf{duck}' \forall P \in \{\mathbf{swim}', \mathbf{fly}'\}[P(x)]$

   b. $\forall x \in \mathbf{duck}'[\mathbf{swim}'(x) \wedge \mathbf{quack}'(x)]$

   $\Leftrightarrow \forall x \in \mathbf{duck}' \forall P \in \{\mathbf{swim}', \mathbf{fly}'\}[P(x)]$

In a similar way, the basic meanings of sentences (122a) and (123a) are both "strong" as in the following formulae.

(125) a. $\forall x \in \mathbf{girl}' \forall y \in \mathbf{girl}'[x \neq y \rightarrow \mathbf{stand\_on}'(y)(x)]$

   b. $\forall x \in \mathbf{girl}' \forall y \in \mathbf{girl}'[x \neq y \rightarrow \mathbf{know}'(y)(x)]$

After the uniform derivation of the basic meaning, which is independent of the lexical identity of the predicates involved, the SMH comes into play. In its extended formulation, the SMH requires the maximal number of relations between members of the sets involved that does not conflict with the lexical properties of the predicates. For instance, in the case of reciprocals, an analysis like (125b) for sentence (123a) is fully compatible with the lexical properties of the verb *know*. Therefore, a "complete graph" situation like the one described in figure 2.4a is needed in order for the sentence to be true. By contrast, the basic analysis of (122a) in (125a) is incompatible with the properties of the *stand on* relation. Consequently,

(a)   (b)

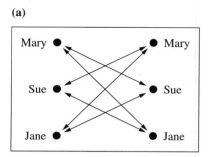
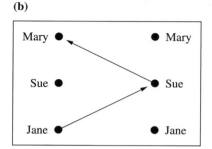

Figure 2.4
Situations verifying (123a) and (122a)

the SMH allows the sentence to be true also in situations like the one described in figure 2.4b, where only two *stand on* relations hold between the girls. This is a maximal number since obviously, there is no possibility to add another *stand on* relation to this picture without violating the lexical knowledge on the properties of this predicate.

A similar analysis is given to conjunctions of plural predicates. Thus, for instance, sentence (119b) (= *The ducks are swimming and quacking*) is assigned its basic meaning in (124b) because a situation as depicted in figure 2.5a satisfies this proposition and is fully compatible with the possibility that ducks swim and quack at the same time. By contrast, such a situation that verifies the basic meaning (124a) of (119a) (= *The ducks are swimming and* FLYING) is incompatible with our knowledge that ducks cannot swim and fly at the same time. Consequently, the SMH weakens the actual meaning of the sentence and allows it to be true also in situations as in figure 2.5b, where there is a maximal number of arcs connecting ducks and a property in the set {**swim′, fly′**} that is still compatible with the lexical meaning of these predicates.

(a)   (b)

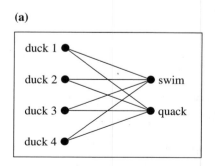
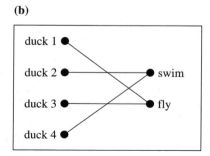

Figure 2.5
Situations verifying (119b) and (119a)

To summarize, this section has made two central claims on the apparent "non-boolean" effects in the interpretation of predicate conjunction:

1. When singular predicates are conjoined, "non-boolean" conjunction is only a manifestation of the flexible boolean interpretation of *nominal* expressions proposed in this chapter.
2. With plural predicates, "non-boolean" effects can also come from the operation of the SMH, which is proposed to be a general principle of plural predication.

These two independently motivated assumptions not only allow us to keep to the simple boolean analysis of conjunction, they also give a more fine-grained analysis of the conditions that regulate "non-boolean" effects with predicate conjunction.

Chapter 3
The Choice-Function Treatment of Indefinites

Indefinite noun phrases have been subject to recurrent controversies in the logical-semantic literature. One of the main sources of disagreement is a pre-theoretical one. Many works adopt, in some form or another, Hilbert and Bernays' intuition that the meaning of indefinite noun phrases like *some man* should be kept close to that of proper names like *John* and definite descriptions like *the man*. Roughly, it is claimed that while proper names and definites refer to contextually specified individuals, indefinites involve "arbitrary" individuals or some sort of variables over them. This conception wishes to distinguish between "referential" proper names and descriptions on the one hand and "quantificational" noun phrases like *every man* on the other. Russell (1919: 168), however, puts indefinites in the group of "quantificational" noun phrases and attacks their classification as "referential," maintaining that "the great majority of logicians who have dealt with this question" were "misled by grammar." In Montague semantics, where natural language syntax is taken more seriously, *all* NPs—including proper names and definites—refer to generalized quantifiers. The Montague grammarian may reasonably contend that both Russell and his opponents were misled by traditional formal logic, which obscures the semantic uniformity in the syntactic class of noun phrases. The appearance of Discourse Representation Theory, however, marked a withdrawal from this uniform treatment and revived a (discourse) "referential" approach to indefinites and other noun phrases, based on a consideration of their special anaphoric properties across sentences. This move towards discourse analysis, however motivated by its own theoretical goals, remains controversial. For the purposes of traditional truth-conditional semantics the uniform treatment of all NPs as generalized quantifiers still has a strong appeal.

Yet in this chapter some well-known truth-conditional facts concerning the scopal semantics of indefinites will motivate a significant departure from the generalized quantifier approach. Following Reinhart (1997), indefinites are treated using *choice functions*. Unlike Reinhart, however, choice functions are proposed as the *uniform* mechanism for interpreting indefinites. The semantic properties of plural indefinites motivate the use of a *distributivity operator* and show further advantages of the choice function treatment over an analysis of indefinites as existential quantifiers. On the other hand, the proposed formalization of choice functions is shown to be closely related to the standard quantificational analysis of indefinites.

Section 3.1 overviews some background of the general problem of NP scope and the scope problem of indefinites in particular. Section 3.2 surveys the general problem of distributive interpretations of plurals and, in more detail, the problem of interpreting plural numeral indefinites. Section 3.3 introduces the present choice function account and more facts pertinent to its linguistic evaluation. Section 3.4 discusses a central problem in the formal semantics of choice functions—the treatment of indefinites with an empty restriction set, and presents a formalization of choice functions that solves this problem. Section 3.5 concerns the overall organization of the system and points to some formal relations with generalized quantifier theory. Section 3.6 summarizes this chapter. An appendix in section 3.7 brings a preliminary compositional formulation of choice functions without appeal to representations with free variables.

3.1   The Scopal Semantics of Indefinites: Background

3.1.1   On scopal semantics

The problem of noun phrase scopal interpretation, or "NP scope" in short, starts from the failure of some simple assumptions about syntax and compositionality. Consider first a non-problematic example:

(1) Every referee read some abstract.

Assume that the syntax of sentence (1) involves the bracketing given in (2).

(2) $[_{NP_1}$ every referee] $[_{VP}$ read $[_{NP_2}$ some abstract]]

Assume further that the meanings of the NPs in (1) are compositionally derived using the standard treatment of generalized quantifier theory. This leads to a derivation of the constituent denotations in figure 3.1, where the structure in (2) determines the order of meaning composition.[1]

The sentence meaning that is derived in this way can be expressed in more popular logical notation by the formula in (3).

(3) $\forall x[\mathbf{referee}'(x) \rightarrow \exists y[\mathbf{abstract}'(y) \wedge \mathbf{read}'(y)(x)]]$

The assumptions sketched above are syntactically well-founded and can be incorporated into a compositional procedure. Moreover, the derived proposition (3) captures all known truth-conditional facts about sentence (1). For instance, the fact that sentence (4) entails (1) can be easily accounted for: proposition (5), which is derived for (4) in a similar compositional process, formally entails (3).

(4) Some abstract is one that was read by every referee.

(5) $\exists y[\mathbf{abstract}'(y) \wedge \forall x[\mathbf{refree}'(x) \rightarrow \mathbf{read}'(y)(x)]]$

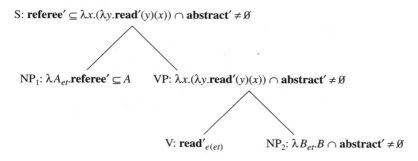

Figure 3.1
Meaning derivation

Some speakers experience what is called "scope ambiguity" upon exposure to sentences like (1). The intuition is sometimes described by saying that in certain circumstances the sentence can be *used* as if it were equivalent to (4). For instance, sentence (1) can allegedly be falsified when there is no single abstract that was read by all referees. This judgment, however authentic, is not simply truth-conditional: sentences (1) and (4) are of course not equivalent, because (1) does not entail (4). In general, the possible existence of *intuitions* about "scope ambiguity" is irrelevant for the objectives of the present discussion.[2]

While a simple compositional treatment of sentence (1) is possible, this no longer holds for sentence (6). The meaning of this sentence derived by the above process is (7).

(6) Some referee read every abstract.

(7) $\exists x[\mathbf{referee}'(x) \wedge \forall y[\mathbf{abstract}'(y) \to \mathbf{read}'(y)(x)]]$

Proposition (7) is not sufficient for an account of all the entailments that involve sentence (6). Intuitively, sentence (6) can be used to convey the meaning of (8), as formalized in (9).

(8) Every abstract is one that was read by some referee.

(9) $\forall y[\mathbf{abstract}'(y) \to \exists x[\mathbf{referee}'(x) \wedge \mathbf{read}'(y)(x)]]$

To see this, consider a situation where there is no single referee who read all the abstracts. However, every abstract was read by some referee or other. Sentence (6) is then intuitively true, or has a true reading, whereas (7) is formally false. In terms of entailments this insufficiency of (7) can be exemplified as follows. Sentence (8) intuitively entails (6) (at least under one of the readings of (6), if it has more than one). However, proposition (9) does not formally entail (7), as the situation just described shows.

The truth-conditional judgments of the previous paragraph are somewhat subtle and are not shared by all English speakers. However, the situation becomes much clearer in examples like the following.

(10) Some guard is standing in front of every building.

(11) Some cat is sitting inside every box.

(12) Some honest man was killed in every war.

In these cases, the above interpretative procedure will derive meanings which are pragmatically strange. For instance, (10) gets the meaning in (13) below, which oddly implies that one and the same guard is capable of standing in front of many buildings at the same time. Sentence (10) does not make this unlikely assertion. Its truth conditions are better captured by proposition (14).

(13) $\exists x[\textbf{guard}'(x) \wedge \forall y[\textbf{building}'(y) \rightarrow \textbf{stand\_in\_front}'(y)(x)]]$

(14) $\forall y[\textbf{building}'(y) \rightarrow \exists x[\textbf{guard}'(x) \wedge \textbf{stand\_in\_front}'(y)(x)]]$

We conclude that the simple compositional mechanism sketched above systematically fails to account for the semantics of sentences like (6) or (10) to (12). This problem has led to a theoretical verdict: these sentences are declared *ambiguous*. This means that we now expect any adequate grammar to generate two readings for each of these sentences. In (6), for instance, the easily derived reading (7) is the one where the object is interpreted as having *narrow scope* (NS) with respect to the subject. Alternatively, the sentence can also be read as (9), the object *wide scope* (WS) reading. In cases where the element that takes wide or narrow scope is obvious from the context or irrelevant, I sloppily refer to the "WS/NS reading" of a sentence without specifying the scope bearing element. Now, once scope ambiguity is assumed in cases like (6) and (10) to (12), it becomes natural to expect that also sentence (1) is ambiguous in this way. Let us adopt this assumption as well, for reasons of theoretical consistency.

This liberal attitude is justified because scope ambiguity can be viewed as a *theoretical* assumption. It is not necessarily a "naive" linguistic *judgment*, which is arguably quite insecure. A theory of ambiguity assumes that some sentences can denote both *true* and *false* in the same situation. This imposes a modification of the truth-conditionality criterion of section 1.2. An ambiguous modeltheoretic semantics is considered descriptively adequate only if it satisfies the following. Assume that $S_1, \ldots, S_n$ and S are natural language sentences and that the entailment $S_1, \ldots, S_n \Rightarrow S$ is accepted by speakers of the language. The theory has to make sure that whenever all the sentences $S_1, \ldots, S_n$ are taken to have a *true* reading, also S has a *true* reading. Conversely, when this relation between the sentence denotations holds in the theory then sentences $S_1, \ldots, S_n$ should intuitively entail sentence S. For instance, it may be proposed that sentence (4) intuitively entails (1), because the unique reading (5) of the first sentence is also a reading of the second. Thus, in any situation where (4) has a true reading also (1) has a true reading. Ambiguity is conceived of as "meta-level disjunction" of the different readings that are assigned to the sentence.[3]

The main question is of course how to account for WS readings of noun phrases in different positions. Before getting to the theoretical problem, let us observe two methodological principles that underly the discussion so far. First, as pointed out by Reinhart (1983: 195), sentences like (1), where the object WS reading entails the object NS reading, are not optimal cases for checking hypotheses about scopal semantics, since the object WS reading is truth-conditionally unnecessary. Sentences like (6) or (10) to (12) are sounder evidence for the necessity of WS readings.

(15) **Scope methodology 1**

A WS reading of an element in the sentence is easier to attest when it does not entail its NS reading.

A second point has to do with the status of the WS reading of sentences like (6), which is not completely clear. By contrast, the adequacy of the WS analysis is well-established in cases like (10) to (12). One reason may be that in the latter cases the NS reading is pragmatically unlikely. In (6), however, it is quite possible that one and the same referee read all the abstracts. When the NS reading is probable, it may be pragmatically preferred and speakers may find it harder to observe that the sentence also has a WS reading. This point is stated as follows.

(16) **Scope methodology 2**

A WS reading is easier to attest when it is pragmatically "more likely" than the NS reading.

Similar effects appear with other kinds of ambiguity as well. For instance, consider the following sentences.

(17) a. John read that Mary published an article in the newspaper.
     b. John read that Mary published a book in the newspaper.

It is easy to be misled into the conclusion that (17a) (uttered with "neutral" intonation) entails that John read somewhere that Mary published an article in the newspaper. Speakers may fail to observe that this "preferred reading" is not the only reading of the sentence. Upon some reflection, however, most people will agree that (17a) is true also if John read in the newspaper about an article that Mary published in a scientific journal, for instance. In contrast to (17a), sentence (17b) (using the same stress pattern) may seem to entail, at least for all practical purposes, that John read in the newspaper about Mary's book. This reading is preferred now, plausibly because most newspapers do not contain books. Despite this difference both (17a) and (17b) are reasonably classified as syntactically ambiguous. For similar considerations, both sentences like (6) and sentences like (10) are classified as scopally ambiguous.

The availability of wide scope readings for sentences like (6) and (10) to (12) is a major challenge for the compositional picture of natural language interpretation. If NS readings like (7) are not the only ones available for sentences like (6), then the aforementioned simple assumptions about syntax and compositional interpretation must be (at best) incomplete. The variety of existing proposals to deal with this problem is remarkable. Most accounts, however, can be naturally classified as belonging to one of two groups. The *syntactic* approach, as embodied in Montague (1973) and May (1977) among others, assumes that simple sentences like (6) are structurally or derivationally ambiguous. Roughly, in addition to a standard structure like (18a), the sentence also has a non-standard structure like (18b) that is responsible for the WS reading.

(18) a. [some referee] [read [every abstract]]
      b. [every abstract] [[some referee] read]

With a considerable amount of assumptions about the nature of the compositional process and the actual structures for which the bracketings stand, these representations can lead to the desired NS/WS ambiguity. In most accounts, (18a) and (18b) are related to a separate syntactic level, known as *Logical Form* (LF). Thus sentence (6) is unambiguously assigned the "surface structure" (18a), but the sentence has both (18a) and (18b) as possible LFs. The ambiguity arises because semantic interpretation is assumed to apply to LFs. The syntactic operation that can map one surface structure to many LFs is known as *Quantifier Raising* (QR).

The *semantic* approach to scopal semantics, initiated by Cooper (1975), wants to keep to the simple syntax of (18a). To do that, some operations are added to the semantic mechanism in order to directly derive multiple readings from this structure. A strictly compositional implementation of a semantic scope mechanism was given in Hendriks (1993).

It is hard to decide between the syntactic and semantic methods on the basis of simple examples like the ones given above. Importantly, however, the rich empirical study of scope phenomena in the literature since Lakoff (1970) and Rodman (1976) has revealed systematic *restrictions* on the availability of WS readings. Compare for example the sentences in (19).

(19) a.   John knows a girl from every country.
      b.   #John knows a girl who is from every country.

While sentence (19a) is coherent and stresses the internationality of John's circle of acquaintances, sentence (19b) strangely entails the existence of an "international girl." Therefore, clearly, the two sentences are not equivalent. It is assumed that this is because sentence (19a) has the WS reading (20), which is absent in sentence (19b).

(20) $\forall x[\mathbf{country'}(x) \rightarrow \exists y[\mathbf{girl'}(y) \wedge \mathbf{from'}(x)(y) \wedge \mathbf{know'}(y)(\mathbf{j'})]]$

A priori, this contrast is unexpected: replacing the noun phrase *every country* in (19a) and (19b) by a proper name like *France*, which does not give rise to scope ambiguities, restores equivalence between the two sentences. Thus it must be the scopal behavior of the universal NP that distinguishes (19a) from (19b).

The contrast in (19) has a striking resemblance to well-known restrictions on "extraction" phenomena, known as *island constraints* since Ross (1967). For instance, in parallel to (19), the question forms in (21) contrast in their grammaticality.

(21) a.   Which country does John know a girl from?

   b.   *Which country does John know a girl who is from?

The ungrammaticality of sentences like (21b) is described in terms of a syntactic restriction known as the *Complex NP Constraint* (CNPC). Intuitively speaking, the interrogative *which country* cannot escape its "deep" position in the complex NP *a girl who is from which country*. Consequently, the question in (21b) is ill-formed.

   Also some other constraints on extraction have been shown to be relevant for restrictions on scope. For instance, sentence (22a) is coherent and (in its WS reading) makes a true statement about the world. Sentence (22b), by contrast, is strange and unlikely to be true. As opposed to (22a) it entails that there is a woman who gave birth to every man.

(22) a.   Some woman gave birth to every man.

   b.   #Some woman gave birth to every man and will eventually die.

Apparently, sentence (22a) has the WS reading (23a), while sentence (22b) does not have the parallel reading (23b).

(23) a. $\forall x[\mathbf{man'}(x) \to \exists y[\mathbf{woman'}(y) \wedge \mathbf{give\_birth\_to'}(x)(y)]]$

   b. $\forall x[\mathbf{man'}(x) \to \exists y[\mathbf{woman'}(y) \wedge \mathbf{give\_birth\_to'}(x)(y) \wedge \mathbf{will\_die'}(y)]]$

Intuitively speaking, the object *every man* can take scope over the subject in (22a), but in (22b) it is "locked" inside the coordination. This scope island, known as the *Coordinate Structure Constraint* (CSC), was originally discovered by Ross as an island for extraction. The following extraction contrast is parallel to the contrast in (22). While the embedded question in (24a) is grammatical, the one in (24b) is not.

(24) a.   I wonder whom Mary gave birth to.

   b.   *I wonder whom Mary gave birth to and will eventually die.

   Yet another kind of island is the *Adjunct island*. For instance, sentence (25a) below is highly unlikely to have (25b) as a reading. This is because (25a) is a strange thing to say, as it *implies* (but not necessarily entails) that more than one woman could give birth to the same person. However, if (25b) were to be a reading of (25a), then (25a) would be expected to be as coherent as the natural expression of (25b) in (25c). This is not the case. We thus sloppily say that the NP *every woman in the room* cannot take scope over the conditional. A similar extraction effect is illustrated by the ungrammaticality of (26).

(25) a.   #If every woman in the room gave birth to John then he has a nice mother.

   b. $\forall x[\mathbf{woman'}(x) \to [\mathbf{give\_birth\_to'}(\mathbf{j'})(x) \to \mathbf{have\_nice\_mother'}(\mathbf{j'})]]$

   c.   For every woman in the room, if she gave birth to John then he has a nice mother.

(26) *Which woman did if give birth to John then he has a nice mother?

Note that the argument against (25b) as a reading of (25a) does not strictly follow the methodological principle 1 in (15). Therefore, it is a plausibility argument rather than a truth-conditional one. Moreover, any truth-conditional argument that involves conditionals must draw on their complex semantic/pragmatic behavior.[4] I will not be engaged with this notorious problem and assume in a simplifying manner that conditionals are interpreted as material implication. Despite these qualms, I think the marked status of sentences like (25a) is a clear evidence for the claim that NP scope cannot violate adjunct islands.[5]

Examples like the ones given above show systematic relations between constraints on NP scope and islands for extraction. The correlation is still incomplete. Contemporary research also strives to achieve a better understanding of cases where scopal semantics seems to be restricted in constructions that do not constrain extraction phenomena.[6] However, in the other direction the correlation does hold: restrictions that a language puts on NP extraction constrain NP scopal semantics as well. Let us refer to this empirical claim as the *extraction-scope generalization.*

This rule of thumb speaks in favor of a mechanism that treats scope and extraction on a par, and it is therefore an argument for syntactic approaches to scope over semantic approaches. In most syntactic accounts, a rule like QR is considered an instance of a general grammatical rule that governs extraction (among other phenomena). Thus, whatever the explanation of islands may be—a hard question to be sure—according to the syntactic approach it should automatically cover scope islands. By contrast, the semantic approach uses rules that are especially assumed in order to account for scopal effects and therefore it does not by itself offer an elegant explanation of the extraction-scope generalization.[7] Indeed, according to the non-representationalist view adopted here, a model-theoretic account is a priori preferable for describing truth-conditional phenomena like NP scope.[8] But the extraction-scope generalization changes the picture: if some complication of the syntax can handle both extraction and scope, then it is to be preferred over a comparably complicated scopal semantic mechanism that cannot account for extraction. This is not to say that a satisfying unified theory of extraction and scope actually exists. At the present stage an attempt to make a conclusive choice between competing accounts may be too hasty. However, Montague's work did offer a notation using lambdas and free variables that can describe the expected *results* of the scope mechanism, be it syntactic or semantic. For instance, the derivation of proposition (9) as the WS reading of (6) is commonly described using an enrichment of the syntax in (18b), which can be denoted as follows.

(27) [every abstract] $\lambda y.[[$some referee$] \lambda x.[x$ read $y]$

Replacement of the NP expressions in this representation by their generalized quantifier denotations then leads to the expected meaning. I use this notation for the sake of exposition alone, without any commitment to a theoretical claim. Representations like (27) are only used to describe the outcomes of some putative grammatical mechanism that I henceforth call the *standard scope mechanism.* This mechanism, like all "movement" rules in natural language, is assumed to be restricted by islands. The latter assumption should account for the extraction-scope generalization.

3.1.2 The scope problem of indefinites

A surprising exception to the extraction-scope generalization is the case of indefinite NPs. Consider the following sentence:

(28) If some building in Washington is attacked by terrorists then US security will be threatened.

The extraction-scope generalization expects (28) to have only reading (29): the narrow scope reading of the indefinite with respect to the conditional (cf. (25) and (26)).

(29) $[\exists x [\textbf{building}'(x) \wedge \textbf{attacked}'(x)]] \rightarrow \textbf{threatened}'(\textbf{security}')$

In the case of (28), this NS reading is quite unlikely to be true in the actual world: it claims that *any* attack on *any* building in Washington should threaten US security. However, one does not expect an attack on some deserted factory in the suburbs of Washington to make too much difference for the "world's only super-power." A more likely interpretation of (28) is as paraphrased in (30a) and formalized in (30b). In fact, (30a) entails (28), which cannot be the case if (28) is only interpreted using the NS reading (29).

(30) a. There is some building in Washington an attack of which may threaten US security.
      b. $\exists x [\textbf{building}'(x) \wedge [\textbf{attacked}'(x) \rightarrow \textbf{threatened}'(\textbf{security}')]]$

Reading (30b) is the WS reading of the indefinite over the conditional in (28). Its prominence can be increased by a continuation like *and I'm talking about the White House*. This shows that, unlike other NPs (cf. (25)), indefinites do not respect the extraction-scope generalization. As we shall see, many singular and plural indefinites show the same free scopal behavior with respect to various islands.[9] A question of fine-grainedness poses itself: how can we explain the exceptional scopal semantics of indefinites while respecting the extraction-scope generalization for other NPs? This question was suggestively introduced in Fodor and Sag (1982) and it poses a serious challenge for any theory of NP scopal semantics, be it syntactic or semantic. The puzzle will henceforth be referred to as the *scope problem* of indefinites.

3.1.3 Previous proposals

A straightforward approach to the scope problem of indefinites is what I will henceforth call the *free scope* approach. No work known to me is seriously committed to this line but many authors (e.g. Fodor and Sag) use it as a possible idea, comparing it to their own proposals. "Free scope" simply means that indefinites are traditionally treated as existential *quantifiers* and that it is the standard scope mechanism that derives their wide scope effects, also beyond islands. Thus it is stipulated that indefinites have some (possibly syntactic) feature that distinguishes them from other quantificational NPs.

Fodor and Sag (1982) argue against this approach. Instead, they propose that indefinites are *ambiguous*. On its standard quantificational reading, an indefinite NP behaves like any other quantificational NP. Especially, its scope is restricted by islands. However, Fodor and Sag propose that indefinites also have a *referential* (specific) reading: the indefinite can function as "a 'private' pointing gesture within the mind of the speaker" (Fodor and Sag (1982: 381)). In this reading a singular indefinite is supposed to behave semantically like a proper name or a singular demonstrative. For such NPs all scope construals are equivalent (see Zimmermann (1986, 1991)). Fodor and Sag argue that this is indeed the case with the "island-escaping" effect of the scope of indefinites: it results in *only one* reading.

This claim has been challenged in Farkas (1981), Rooth and Partee (1982: fn. 6) and, more recently, in Ruys (1992) and Abusch (1994). These works all adduce cases where Fodor and Sag's claim is argued to be incorrect. The empirical debate will be reviewed later in this chapter (subsection 3.3.4). Ruys and Abusch conclude that Fodor and Sag's "referential" approach is inadequate. Ruys gives a preliminary formulation of rules that apply to an LF representation of indefinites that crucially includes indices. These structural operations on such LFs are used to generate a semantic level of representation where the wide scope reading of indefinites beyond islands can be represented. Ruys does not officially propose this mechanism as a semantic theory, but rather as an illustration of the possibility that indefinites do not violate islands at LF but still get wide scope interpretations. This general point will be accepted below, though the proposed semantic mechanism will be very different from Ruys's. Abusch proposes to enrich Discourse Representation Theory (DRT, see Kamp and Reyle (1993)) with a storage mechanism that changes the syntactic position of the indefinite's representation. Abusch therefore heavily draws on the assumption of a distinct syntactic representational level for meaning. Importantly, this level, which is sometimes called *LF prime* (LF′), is an additional level beyond the syntactic level of LF that resolves scope ambiguities in syntactic theories of scope. Representational treatments of the scope problem that are similar in some respects to Ruys and Abusch's proposals appear in Farkas (1997) (using evaluation indices) and in Szabolcsi (1997) (using witness sets). To keep the discussion manageable I do not consider these alternatives, which have, however, similar presuppositions and empirical predictions as Ruys and Abusch. All these works are henceforth classified as adopting a *representational* approach to the scope problem of indefinites.

Another alternative, proposed in Reinhart (1992) for *wh* elements, is further developed in Reinhart (1997) to include non-interrogative indefinites as well. Reinhart proposes to use quantification over *choice functions* as the basic mechanism that generates the wide scope of indefinites beyond islands. This idea shares with the representational approach the intuition that indefinites are not ordinary quantificational expressions. However, like Fodor and Sag, Reinhart claims that also traditional existential quantifiers are among the readings of an indefinite.

Kratzer (1998) agrees with Reinhart about the need to distinguish a choice function analysis of indefinites that does not involve standard quantification. However, Kratzer does not accept the existential quantification over choice functions that is proposed by

Reinhart. For Kratzer, choice functions are *referential* entities, responsible for Fodor and Sag's "specific" reading of indefinites. Kratzer develops a counter-argument to the above mentioned arguments against Fodor and Sag (see section 3.3.4 below).

Some remarks on these proposals are in place. The free scope approach is certainly a sound description of some facts about the scope of indefinites. Its explanatory value, however, is rather limited. Besides stating that indefinites are not subject to syntactic restrictions on scope, this approach says nothing about what independent properties of indefinites can relate to this fact. Given this arbitrariness, it is to be expected that cross-linguistic variation should appear with respect to the kinds of NPs of which the scope is not sensitive to constraints on extraction. For instance, we expect languages in which the translation of an indefinite like *some composer* is scopally restricted while a universal NP like *every composer* is scopally free. This is not confirmed: as far as we know, every language allows free scope for indefinites even if it respects the extraction-scope generalization. This goes against the free scope approach. Nevertheless, despite its weakness, the free scope description is a convenient point of departure for comparison with other proposals. In fact, one of the main points of this chapter is to show that the free scope approach has to face some serious empirical difficulties.

Like the free scope approach, the specificity idea of Fodor and Sag is rather arbitrary. It is not clear why other NPs besides indefinites cannot activate a "pointing gesture in the mind of the speaker." For instance, why cannot an NP like *every composer* mean *Schubert* in a putative "specific" reading? Another disturbing aspect of the specificity idea is its approach to truth conditions. The specific reading of a sentence like *some woman smiled* is taken to be equivalent for certain speakers in certain contexts to the sentence *Princess Diana smiled*. However, the alleged "pointing gesture" is supposed to be a "private" one, so how can we *falsify* this idea? In simple sentences like this one it seems impossible. Technically speaking, the sentence is assumed to be n-way ambiguous, where n is the number of women plus one (the standard existential reading). While this ambiguity is truth-conditionally unattestable, Fodor and Sag do show a case where their proposal can be falsified. This point will be discussed in detail in subsection 3.3.4. In agreement with other work on the scope of indefinites, it will be shown that Fodor and Sag's prediction is not borne out, so that according to their own criterion, their theory is falsified.[10]

The representational approach does not offer a significant improvement over the other approaches. The additional rules designed to lead to the WS readings of indefinites are quite arbitrary: similar rules could have been assigned to other NPs with equal plausibility. If the liberal theoretical standpoint of representational proposals is seriously adopted it would allow us to account for *any* possible fact about scopal semantics by adding new rules in the mapping from LF to LF$'$ or by modifying existing ones.[11] In this situation, scientific argumentation is almost impossible because virtually *any* empirical argument against the system can be refuted by simply postulating a new rule. A concrete example of this general criticism will be given in subsection 3.3.2.

Reinhart's choice function account marks a significant advance in the analysis of the problem. Since it will be the basis for the developments below, I will now discuss the general idea in more detail.

3.1.4   The choice-function approach

Intuitively speaking, a choice function (CF) is a function that maps any non-empty set to one of its members. The treatment of indefinites using choice functions is based upon the following general assumptions:

A1. Indefinites lack quantificational force of their own. An indefinite basically denotes a *predicate*, henceforth the *restriction* predicate.

A2. An indefinite NP in an argument position, however, can end up denoting an *individual*. This is because its semantics involves a free function variable that assigns an individual to the restriction predicate.

A3. This function variable is "closed" using an existential quantifier, together with the requirement that it is a choice function. This *quantificational* procedure can apply at any compositional level.

Assumption (A1) is adopted from DRT. Familiar motivations for it are threefold: (i) The natural appearance of indefinites in predicative positions. Contrast, for instance, *John is a man* with **John is every man*. More on this point will be said in chapter 4. (ii) The fact that many languages lack an overt indefinite article. This suggests that some phonologically invisible mechanism handles function application when the indefinite is in argument position. The idea is that the same happens in languages like English, where the overt indefinite article lacks a denotational contribution. (iii) The well-known discourse-anaphoric properties of indefinites.

Once assumption (A1) is made, the other assumptions are one of the (few) possible ways to complete the compositional picture. Assumption (A2) is a specific proposal to deal with the type mismatch that (A1) creates. When the indefinite is in an argument position, the restriction predicate can either be lifted to a quantifier (the usual strategy) or lowered to an individual. It is the latter strategy that is assumed for indefinites. This idea can be traced back to Hilbert and Bernays's (1939) ϵ-logic, which treats existentials as *terms*.[12]

Assumption (A3) is necessary in order for sentences to be interpreted as propositions, as opposed to open formulae with free CF variables. This "existential closure" assumption is also borrowed from DRT, without the concomitant "unselective binding" strategy, but with the additional restriction of existential closure to choice functions. On the general justification for this technique see section 3.5 below.

Let us consider a simple concrete example:

(31) Some woman smiled.

By (A1) to (A3), what (31) is understood to assert is a statement about the existence of a choice function, such that the individual it picks from the predicate denoted by the noun *woman* is in the denotation of the predicate *smiled*. This intuition is given a formula in (32) below, where $\mathrm{CH}(f)$ means that f is a choice function.

(32) $\exists f[\mathrm{CH}(f) \wedge \mathbf{smile}'(f(\mathbf{woman}'))]$

Of course, in order for (32) to be meaningful, the set CH of $(et)e$ functions should be defined explicitly. The classical definition of choice functions reads as follows.

Definition 16 (choice functions)   Let E be a non-empty set. A function $f : \wp(E) \to E$ is a *choice function* iff for every $A \subseteq E$: if A is not empty then $f(A) \in A$.

In typed frameworks this means that the set CH of choice functions over τ-type individuals is defined as follows:

(33) $\mathrm{CH}_{((\tau t)\tau)t} \stackrel{\mathrm{def}}{=} \lambda f_{(\tau t)\tau}.\forall P_{\tau t} \neq \emptyset[P(f(P))]$

Let us provisionally assume that given this definition formula (32) can express the existential proposition $\mathbf{woman}' \cap \mathbf{smile}' \neq \emptyset$, which is the standard meaning assigned to sentence (31). In section 3.4 it will be shown that (32) in fact does *not* express this proposition and a more adequate alternative formalization of CFs will be proposed. Keeping this in mind, we note here that formula (32) is both sufficiently intuitive and adequate to serve the purposes of the informal discussion that will follow in sections 3.2 and 3.3.

What Reinhart has shown is that an analysis along these lines intuitively accounts for the scope problem of indefinites. For example, sentence (28) has now two readings, depending on the stage at which existential closure is performed:

(34) $[\exists f[\mathrm{CH}(f) \wedge \mathbf{attacked}'(f(\mathbf{building}'))]] \to \mathbf{threatened}'(\mathbf{security}')$

(35) $\exists f[\mathrm{CH}(f) \wedge [\mathbf{attacked}'(f(\mathbf{building}')) \to \mathbf{threatened}'(\mathbf{security}')]]$

In (34), existential closure takes place within the antecedent of the conditional. Consequently we get the "narrow scope" reading paraphrased in (36) below. In (35) existential closure takes scope over the conditional and this results in a "wide scope" reading, paraphrased in (37).

(36) US security will be threatened if there is *any* function choosing from the set of buildings in Washington one that was attacked by terrorists.

(37) There is a choice function such that US security will be threatened if the building it picks is attacked by terrorists.

The innovative aspect of Reinhart's idea is that in both readings no mechanism "pulls" the representation of the indefinite out of the island: in both cases the relevant predication is analyzed as $\mathbf{attacked}'(f(\mathbf{building}'))$. The non-trivial connection made between the predicative nature of indefinites and their exceptional scopal behavior makes this approach more attractive than competing ones. The idea will be further substantiated in the rest of this chapter.

The road is long and winding. Besides the empirical questions, there are also many technical obstacles standing in the way of an elegant implementation of choice functions in formal semantics. In addition to the aforementioned inadequacy in the standard use of choice functions, the above discussion also includes at least two departures from the theoretical framework of this book. First, the individual denoted by an indefinite NP is now an e type object, which is not a boolean entity. This withdrawal from the boolean assumption will be shown in section 3.4 to be strongly related to the problems in the standard use of choice functions. Its revision will lead to an easy solution. Second, in using procedures that involve free variables, the mechanism is no longer purely model-theoretic. Symbols like f and $\exists f$ do not have straightforward model-theoretic correlates. Furthermore, the way in which variable names are kept track of is not compositionally specified. This representationalism makes it hard to implement the mechanism in an elegant way. The proposal in section 3.7 is a preliminary attempt to improve this situation.

Important though they are for the overall objectives of this book, let us ignore these qualms for a while. Before any formal inquiry can start, the linguistic implications of the choice function mechanism should be further explored. Informal discussion of these implications is the subject of section 3.3, which addresses central questions about the distributivity of plural indefinites. The next section provides some background to this problem.

3.2   Indefinites and the Plurality Problem

Chapter 2 discussed the coordination-plurality problem and accounted for distributive and collective effects with simple conjunctive noun phrases like *Mary and John*. The problem is more general, however, and applies to all plural NPs. This section briefly presents some necessary background and terminology as regards the general puzzle, which will be especially relevant to the plurality problem of indefinites. Much more on the general plurality problem will be said in subsequent chapters.

Consider first the following simple sentences, containing a plural definite.

(38)   a. The girls met.
      b. The girls slept.

Most semantic accounts of plurality assign sentence (38a) a reading as in (39a), where the predicate denotation **meet**$'$ applies to the plural individual G denoted by *the girls*.[13] Scha (1981) proposes that also sentences like (38b) should get a similar "collective" analysis as in (39b) below.

(39)   a. **meet**$'(G)$
      b. **sleep**$'(G)$

We say that both (38a) and (38b) have a *C reading* according to the Scha analysis. This term deliberately avoids the impression that a C reading implies a "collective" achievement. Of course, the proposition in (39b) does not formally capture the "distributivity" impression that speakers may have with sentences like (38b): proposition (39b) claims nothing about individual girls. Scha argues that this is correct, since sentences like (38b) are vague in this respect: the sentence does not claim that *every* girl slept. Whatever claim (38b) makes about individual girls will result from lexical semantic properties of the predicate. Without getting any further into this point at this stage, I follow Dowty (1987) and refer to any implication that C readings of sentences like (38b) may have for singular individuals as *subentailed distributivity*. These implications are not necessarily truth-conditional entailments: they may also be a reflection of vague implications of the verb. In other words, the predicate denoted by the verb *sleep* might fail to have any logical implications for the singularities belonging to plural individuals in its extension. Hence a C reading is assigned to both sentences in (38), which is by definition vague with respect to the singularities that make up the plural individual. This may be all we need for truth-conditional purposes.

This simple account, although sensible for elementary sentences like (38b), is problematic for more complex sentences like the following.

(40) The girls are wearing a dress.

If we assume that the denotation of the predicate *wear a dress* directly applies to a plural individual, as in (41) below, then sentence (40) is incorrectly expected to be equivalent to the incoherent sentence in (42).

(41) $[\![\text{are wearing a dress}]\!] = \lambda x.\exists y \in \mathbf{dress}'[\mathbf{wear}'(y)(x)]$
    $[\![\text{the girls are wearing a dress}]\!] = [\![\text{are wearing a dress}]\!](G)$
    $\Leftrightarrow \exists y \in \mathbf{dress}'[\mathbf{wear}'(y)(G)]$

(42) #There is a dress that the girls are wearing.

Intuitively, the plural definite *the girls* in sentence (40) takes scope over the existential quantifier triggered by the indefinite subject *a dress*. This allows sentence (40) to be true in any situation where every girl is wearing a *different* dress. Let us use the term *Q-distributivity* for referring to such quantificational effects with plurals. It is very hard to model the Q-distributivity effect in (40) with a C reading as in (41), because (41) is also the reading of sentence (42), where no Q-distributivity effect is observed. A way to overcome this problem is to return to the traditional assumption that plural definites contribute a universal quantifier over singularities as in proposition (43) below. Let us refer to such an analysis of (40) as a *D reading* of the sentence.

(43) $\forall x \in G \exists y \in \mathbf{dress}'[\mathbf{wear}'(y)(x)]$

The C reading strategy is still needed, of course, for sentences like (38a). Thus sentences with plural definites are often analyzed as ambiguous between the D/C readings of the definite.

There are two common ways to derive this ambiguity:

1. *Ambiguity of determiners.* Bennett (1974), among others, proposes that plural definites are ambiguous between plural individuals and universal quantifiers due to a lexical ambiguity of the plural definite article.

2. *A distributivity operator.* Link (1983), among others, proposes that plural definites unambiguously denote plural individuals but that a covert *distributivity operator* may map a plural individual to a universal quantifier over the singular individuals it contains.

The common definition of a distributivity operator is based on the function that maps any plural individual to the universal quantifier over the singularities it contains. A simple way to define such an operator in set-theoretical format employs the subset relation, which is expressed by the determiners *every* or *each*. This distributivity/subset operator is defined in (44) below. This definition is for expository purposes of this chapter alone. The technical implementation of distributivity operators will be substantially revised in the next chapters. Using the D operator, the D reading derived for sentence (40) in (45) is equivalent to (43). This simple analysis will be assumed for the sake of the informal discussion in this chapter. It will be substantially modified in subsequent chapters.

(44) $D(A)(B)$ iff $A \subseteq B$

(45) $D(G)(\lambda x.\exists y \in \textbf{dress}'[\textbf{wear}'(y)(x)])$

Moving on to plural *in*definites, consider the large class of numeral noun phrases like *exactly six boys*, *less than five shops*, etc. The present chapter, however, concentrates on the subclass of *simple* numeral indefinites like *six boys* and *five shops*.[14] Sentence (46) requires a C reading for similar reasons as sentence (38a). A plausible candidate for the C reading of sentence (46) is given in (46a). By contrast, sentence (47), like (40), shows a Q-distributivity effect that cannot be modeled using the C reading but requires the D reading in (47a).

(46) Three girls met.
      a. $\exists A \subseteq G[|A| = 3 \wedge \textbf{meet}'(A)]$

(47) Three girls are wearing a dress.
      a. $\exists A \subseteq G[|A| = 3 \wedge \forall x \in A \exists y \in \textbf{dress}'[\textbf{wear}'(y)(x)]]$

As with definites, there are two main strategies for generating the D/C ambiguity for simple numeral indefinites. One way, following Bennett (1974), is to take numerals like *three* as lexically ambiguous *determiners*.[15] I defer a more detailed presentation of this analysis to chapter 5. An alternative route is to let bare numerals denote *predicate cardinality modifiers*. For instance, the modificational denotation of *three* maps the denotation of *girls* to the set of plural individuals consisting of three singular girls. The resulting "predicative" denotation of the noun phrase is given below.

(48) $[\![\text{three girls}]\!] = \{A \subseteq G : |A| = 3\}$

Although this is technically a set of sets, it should not be thought of as a generalized quantifier: the sets in this denotation are not treated as denotations of linguistic predicates, but as plural individuals. Hence, the denotation in (48) is a predicate over pluralities. It was mentioned above that if an indefinite denotes such a "restriction predicate" it cannot directly compose with the main predicate in the sentence as in Bennett's proposal. As in the case of singular indefinites, this mismatch can be solved by introducing a covert existential mechanism that quantifies over (plural) individuals in the restriction predicate. This can be a phonologically null determiner that lifts the restriction predicate into an existential quantifier over plural individuals, as proposed in Link (1987), Verkuyl (1993: ch. 5) and Carpenter (1997: ch. 8), among others. Other theories, which do not analyze indefinites as ordinary existential quantifiers, use for this purpose the existential mechanism that they independently assume for singular indefinites. Such an implementation is proposed by Kamp and Reyle (1993: ch. 4), for example, among others working within the DRT tradition.

Summarizing, we can divide the approaches to plural numeral indefinites into two classes according to their analysis of the NP denotation:

1. Numeral indefinites denote existential *quantifiers*. The numeral itself denotes either a determiner (Bennett and Scha) or a cardinality modifier with an additional null existential determiner within the NP (Link et al.).

2. Numeral indefinites basically denote *predicates*. The numeral denotes a cardinality modifier and the additional existential mechanism is not simply due to a null determiner but relies on a more complex general existential process for the interpretation of indefinites.

Section 3.3 will argue for the second line, where choice functions will supply the general existential mechanism.

A note on "exactness" with bare numerals   A classical problem that is highly relevant for the interpretation of numerals should be mentioned. While in many contexts a sentence like *three girls slept* seems to be equivalent to *exactly three girls slept*, this is not always the case. In fact, it is well-known that there are contexts where speakers accept the former sentence as true and the latter as false. For instance, consider the contrast between the following examples.

(49) a.   Three girls slept, I can assure you. But there were probably many more who did.
     b.   #Exactly three girls slept, I can assure you. But there were probably many more who did.

While the two assertions in (49a) are consistent, those in (49b) give contradictory information. Because of such facts it has been proposed by scholars of the Gricean tradition (e.g. Horn (1972: 37–47)) that bare numerals like *three* do not contribute an "exactness" assertion and are interpreted as equivalent to *at least three*. Pragmatic principles are held responsible for the similarity between *three* and *exactly three* in many other contexts.

To reach a principled theoretical decision on this problem is a hard semantic-pragmatic task that I will not undertake. The Gricean assumption of the equivalence of *n* and *at least n* has become quite standard in semantic theory and is crucial for the present proposal as well. It is adopted here without further argumentation.[16]

3.3   The Scope and Distributivity of Numeral Indefinites: A Choice Function Account

Plural numeral indefinites are a natural test case for theories of scope and plurality. Like singular indefinites they clearly show island-free scopal behavior. As plurals, they also give rise to distributivity/collectivity effects. The present section focuses on the implications of the interactions between these phenomena for a semantic theory of indefinites.

3.3.1   The Ruys observation

Both Ruys (1992) and Abusch (1994) observe that the scopal semantics of plural numeral indefinites can violate islands, quite like that of singular indefinites. This is to be expected. However, Ruys observes a surprising fact about the scopal behavior of plural numerals. To see the point, consider one of Ruys's simpler examples:[17]

(50) If three relatives of mine die I will inherit a house.

The WS reading of the plural indefinite over the conditional in (50) can be attested in the following situation. Suppose I have three old uncles: Paul, George and Ringo, who together own a beautiful house in England. Each of them owns one third of the house and plans to bequeath it to me. Now (50) may well be true even though I also have many poor relatives who will not bequeath me anything when they pass away. Thus, not *any* three relatives of mine will bequeath me a house, so (50) is false on the NS reading for *three relatives of mine*. That (50) is still true in this situation suggests that the sentence has a reading where the plural "takes scope" over the conditional. But what exactly is this reading? The two plausible candidates are paraphrased in (51) and (52).

(51) I have three relatives such that if they (all) die I will inherit a house.

(52) I have three relatives such that for *each* of them, if he dies I will inherit a house.

Ruys's point is that (51) captures the wide scope reading of (50) whereas (52) does not. Consider the situation in which uncle Paul is dead and uncle George and uncle Ringo are alive and well. I go to the court and claim the house. The court rejects my request: I will not inherit the house as long as my uncles George and Ringo are alive. Does this situation falsify (50)? Certainly not. It does not falsify (51) either. However, (52) is falsified. Conclusion: (51) is the correct paraphrase of the wide scope reading of (50).

What does this mean? The difference between (51) and (52) is a difference of Q-distributivity scope. Paraphrase (51) is either a case of predication over the collection of relatives plus subentailed distributivity or a case where Q-distributivity scope is within the conditional. Which possibility among the two is the correct analysis does not matter for us at this stage because they both lead to the same truth conditions. However, in sentence (52) Q-distributivity takes scope over the conditional and therefore it is inadequate as a paraphrase of sentence (50). Tentatively then, we can say that with respect to *existential scope*, the plural numeral in (50) behaves quite like the singular indefinite *some building* in sentence (28) and escapes the adjunct island. However, with respect to *Q-distributivity scope*, the plural behaves more like the non-indefinite noun phrase *every man* in sentence (25): both disallow a scope position beyond the island.

These distinctions involve semantic intuitions that might seem subtle. However, the fact that Q-distributivity cannot obtain with island-escaping scope is highly robust. According to methodological principle 2 in (16), we can test this by constructing an example in which the only pragmatically plausible reading would be one in which Q-distributivity takes scope beyond island boundaries. If the sentence turns out to be odd this must mean that the reading in question is not there. A relevant test is the following variation on Ruys's example.[18]

(53) #If three women gave birth to John then he has a nice mother.

This odd sentence is a priori expected to have three possible interpretations:

(54) a. Existential NS + subentailed distributivity (or NS Q-distributivity):
      If (each member of) any set of three women gave birth to John, then he has a nice mother.
   b. Existential WS + subentailed distributivity (or NS Q-distributivity):
      There is a set A of three women such that if (each member of) A gave birth to John, then he has a nice mother.
   c. Existential WS + WS Q-distributivity:
      There is a set A of three women such that for each member x of A, if x gave birth to John, then he has a nice mother.

If Q-distributivity beyond island boundaries were possible, (53) would have been expected to have the reading paraphrased in (54c), which expresses a contingent and completely reasonable proposition given common world knowledge about the predicate *to give birth*. However, we can be sure that (54c) is not a reading of (53), because (53) is clearly a strange thing to say: it implies the possibility that three women (all) gave birth to John. The existential narrow scope construal for (53) in (54a) is pragmatically odd in the same way. The same holds for the WS existential reading in (54b). Therefore, the fact that the sentence sounds so odd is to be expected if Q-distributivity beyond islands is not an available option.

Similar effects appear also with other islands, as shown in the following examples.

(55) #Every artist who was born in three cities became famous.
   a. There is a set A of three cities such that for each member x of A, every artist who was born in x became famous.

(56) #A baby was adopted by John or was born to three women.

    a. There is a set A of three women such that for each member x of A, a baby was adopted by John or was born to x.

An a priori possible reading for (55) with Q-distributivity having scope over the Complex NP island is paraphrased in (55a). If this reading existed it would have eliminated the oddness effect in (55). For similar reasons, (56a) is surely not a reading of (56), where the plural indefinite is within a Coordinate Structure island.

    Let us summarize the empirical conclusion:

The Ruys observation   While the *existential* scopal semantics of indefinites can violate island constraints, the scope of *Q-distributivity* is restricted to islands.[19]

This observation holds also of plural indefinites with the articles *some* or *several*. For instance, sentence (57) is as odd as (53), which means that it cannot be interpreted as in (57a).

(57) #If some/several women gave birth to John then he has a nice mother.

    a. There is a set A of some women such that for each member x of A, if x gave birth to John then he has a nice mother.

What is the theoretical significance of the Ruys observation? Ruys suggests that it necessitates a serious complication in the "free scope" approach to indefinites. The LF representation of (50) according to this approach is as in (58). Any analysis of (58) must block the D reading of the "island escaping" indefinite. However, a C reading must still be allowed in order to capture the WS effect.

(58) [three relatives] [λx.[if x die I will inherit a house]]

How can we block the D reading in a free scope mechanism? As far as I know, in all approaches to the plurality problem of numerals this can be done only by means of stipulation. Bennett traces the C/D ambiguity to the two-way lexical ambiguity of the numeral. Thus the indefinite NP has to have some feature that disallows a D reading for the determiner whenever the standard scope mechanism assigns the NP wide scope beyond an island. Such an unattractive assumption is additional to the stipulation inherent to the "free scope" approach to indefinites: apparently we also have a subclass of readings for indefinites that *are* sensitive to island constraints. Namely, D readings. In the next subsection we will see that even this additional stipulation cannot save the combination of the free scope approach with the determiner ambiguity analysis.

    Other approaches to the plurality problem hold a distributivity operator responsible for the D reading of indefinites. In order to prevent a Q-distributive reading in the process of interpreting (58), the distributivity operator should be blocked somehow. To do that, the class of plural predications in natural language should be divided in an arbitrary way: when an NP is interpreted *in situ* or within island boundaries a distributivity operator can apply (see subsection 3.3.3). However, when an NP escapes an island this is not possible. Again, the free scope approach makes a solution to the plurality problem look like a statement of the facts.

Reinhart's approach to the scope problem shows some improvement. According to Reinhart the standard scope mechanism of QR does not assign indefinites syntactic scope beyond islands. Consequently, Reinhart does not need to block any reading of (58), because in her proposal this is not an available LF of (50). The "island-escaping" effect is treated by Reinhart's CF reading of the indefinite *in situ* with wide scope existential closure:

(59) $\exists f[\mathrm{CH}(f) \wedge [\mathbf{die}'(f(\llbracket\text{three relatives}\rrbracket)) \rightarrow \mathbf{inherit\_house}']]$

"There is a choice of a plural individual, A, consisting of three relatives of mine, such that if A dies I will inherit a house."

By definition, choice functions apply only to predicates. Therefore, crucially, in order for (59) to be meaningful, the denotation $\llbracket\textit{three relatives}\rrbracket$ must be a predicate over plural individuals: the set of all plural individuals consisting of exactly three relatives (cf. (48)). The choice function picks one plural individual from this set. This requires the modificational analysis of numerals. Note that (59) does not involve any overt distribution of the plural individual chosen, and for this reason it generates a wide scope *existential* reading without Q-distributivity. Rather, Reinhart assumes that distributive effects in such cases are due to subentailments of the predicate. This is sufficient to capture the Ruys observation. Let us consider another example, not discussed by Reinhart, which shows another effect discovered in Ruys (1992:107, ex.(36)):

(60) #Some artist who was born in two small villages in Holland is a genius.

The curious effect in such examples with two indefinites is that a "wide scope" reading for the plural indefinite does not appear at all: the sentence is odd and cannot mean that two small villages in Holland are the birth place of a genius artist. This is of course completely unexpected in the free scope approach without the further stipulations mentioned. However, nothing about (60) is surprising for the CF approach, since the sentence gets the following CF analysis:[20]

(61) $\exists g \exists f[\mathrm{CH}(f) \wedge \mathrm{CH}(g) \wedge \mathbf{genius}'(f(\mathbf{artist}' \cap \lambda x.\mathbf{born\_in}'((g(\llbracket\text{two villages}\rrbracket)))(x)))]$

The order of the existential quantifications over choice functions ($\exists g \exists f$ or $\exists f \exists g$) is immaterial for the proposition expressed by (61). Essentially for this reason, this proposition correctly reflects the strangeness of (60): the noun phrase *some artist* cannot be understood within the scope of a Q-distributive reading of the noun phrase *two small villages*. The latter indefinite gets only *collective* wide scope (+ subentailed distributivity), which in this case is not distinguished from collective narrow scope.

These predictions of Reinhart's mechanism yield an insightful account of the Ruys observation. However, the question of how to derive Q-distributivity must be answered now, in order to make sure that the mechanism will indeed work. We are up to discover another surprising fact.

3.3.2   The double scope observation

Reinhart assumes that indefinites can be interpreted in two ways. One way is the classical "distributive" analysis of generalized quantifier (GQ) theory with numerals as determiners. The other way is the CF interpretation, which treats plural numerals as modifiers. There is no distributivity operator in Reinhart's system.[21] The need to assume a double strategy for the interpretation of indefinites is a less attractive aspect of Reinhart's proposal. The only semantic motivation for the GQ construal of the indefinite is the need to generate Q-distributivity with numeral indefinites. Moreover, it is not clear how to account for Q-distributivity with non-indefinite plurals (cf. *the girls* in (40)).

The problems are not only conceptual. Reinhart's proposal is still empirically insufficient. Consider the following example:[22]

(62) If three workers in our staff have a baby soon we will have to face some hard organizational problems.

This sentence certainly has a narrow scope reading for the indefinite. In this reading it claims that *any* three workers who will have a baby soon will cause problems to the organization. However, there is also a wide scope reading here, which can be paraphrased as follows:

(63) There are three workers such that if *each* of them has a baby soon we will have to face some hard organizational problems.

It is important to note is that this is *the only* reasonable reading of (62) where the plural indefinite "takes scope" over the adjunct island conditional. To see this, consider the following alternatives:

(64) There are three workers such that for *each* of them, if he/she has a baby soon we will have to face some hard organizational problems.

(65) #There are three workers such that if there is a baby that they *all* have soon, we will have to face some hard organizational problems.

The Ruys observation tells us that (64) is not a reading of (62). To verify that, one has to go through the considerations that were mentioned in the analysis of (50) and (53). As for the analysis paraphrased in (65), this is perhaps a grammatical reading of (62), but it is pragmatically implausible: it implies that three people can have one and the same baby, a situation most of us cannot imagine. In more theoretical terms, (62) is an example where the plural indefinite can take existential wide scope *over* the island, whereas a Q-distributivity effect appears, but its scope is *within* the island. Note that with respect to distributivity this is the same effect as we discussed concerning (40), so subentailed distributivity can be excluded here.

Let us describe this effect as follows:

The double scope observation   The existential and the Q-distributivity imports of numeral indefinites can have two distinct scopes.

Another example of this phenomenon is the following sentence.

(66) Every teacher who gave a lecture to three excellent classes in our school was very satisfied afterwards.

    a. There are three excellent classes in our school, such that every teacher who gave a (potentially different) lecture to them was very satisfied afterwards.

Also in (66), the existential scope of the plural indefinite can escape the island as indicated by the (66a) paraphrase, where the possibility that each of the three classes was given a different lecture indicates that this is a case of Q-distributivity having scope *within* the complex NP island.

The Ruys observation states that Q-distributivity scope is restricted when the indefinite is within an island. Therefore, double scope is easily attestable. Reasonably, however, numeral indefinites should be able to show "double scope" behavior in any syntactic environment, independently of the Ruys observation. This can be seen in the following sentences, where the plural indefinites are not within islands.

(67) Exactly one teacher gave a lecture to three excellent classes in our school.

(68) Every teacher of three excellent classes in our school that were given a lecture was satisfied.

Consider for example the two existential-WS readings of the plural in (67), with the following two possible scopes for Q-distributivity ($\exists!x$ stands for "exactly one x"):

(69) $\exists A[\textbf{classes}'(A) \wedge \textbf{three}'(A)$
$\wedge \exists!x[\textbf{teacher}'(x) \wedge \forall z \in A \ \exists y[\textbf{lecture}'(y) \wedge \textbf{gave}'(y)(z)(x)]]]$

(70) $\exists A[\textbf{classes}'(A) \wedge \textbf{three}'(A)$
$\wedge \forall z \in A \ \exists!x[\textbf{teacher}'(x) \wedge \exists y[\textbf{lecture}'(y) \wedge \textbf{gave}'(y)(z)(x)]]]$

Assume there are only three classes: c_1, c_2 and c_3. Teacher t_1 is the only teacher who gave a lecture to the three of them. Teacher t_2 also gave a lecture, but only to c_1. In this situation, (67) can intuitively be interpreted as true, like (69), whereas (70) is false. Thus the "double scope" reading (69) is available for (67). An analogous story applies to (68).

The double scope observation is a major problem for any free scope approach that employs a purely quantificational treatment of indefinites like Bennett's. On this approach, (62) can have only one LF that derives existential wide scope readings:

(71) [three workers] [λx.[[if x have a baby] we will face problems]]

If the indefinite in (71) is analyzed using the D reading of the determiner, we overgenerate the non-reading (64). If we use the C reading, we get the pragmatically implausible reading (65). On the Bennett/Scha approach we have only one position for both existential and Q-distributivity scope, so that the reading (63) cannot be generated at all.

Reinhart's original proposal is faced with a similar problem. The CF representation can capture only (65). Reinhart does not allow any Q-distributivity effect in the CF "island-escaping" reading and consequently a double scope effect as in (63) is not generated. But is it really the case that such an effect cannot be generated given the CF approach to the scope problem?

My proposal is as follows. Let us readopt the common assumption about a grammatical operation of distributivity. Now, instead of adopting Reinhart's CF/GQ double strategy, let us make choice functions be the *only* mechanism for interpreting indefinites: GQs are no longer necessary for modeling Q-distributivity. Simple numerals can unambiguously denote modifiers. The separation between existential scope, derived by the CF mechanism, and Q-distributivity scope, derived by the D operator (see (44)), allows us to capture the double scope effect in (62) in the following way:

(72) $\exists f[\text{CH}(f) \wedge [D(f(\llbracket\text{three workers}\rrbracket))(\llbracket\text{have a baby}\rrbracket) \rightarrow \textbf{problems}']]$

Let us examine this analysis in detail. The numeral *three* is analyzed as a modifier. The indefinite *three workers* therefore basically denotes a predicate: the set of plural individuals consisting of exactly three singular workers. The CF variable f picks one plural individual from this set. The distributivity operator D applies to this individual, and generates a universal quantifier over singular individuals. This quantifier takes scope over the complex predicate *have a baby*, like any other quantifier.[23] However, the scope of this quantifier is restricted to the adjunct island, so that it does not take scope over the conditional. The indefinite *a baby* is analyzed using a narrow scope existential closure of a CF, assumed above in (A3). Thus, writing out the denotation of the complex predicate *have a baby* in (72) gives the following formula.

(73) $\exists f[\text{CH}(f)$
$\wedge [D(f(\llbracket\text{three workers}\rrbracket))(\lambda x.\exists g(\text{CH}(g) \wedge \textbf{have}'(g(\textbf{baby}'))(x))) \rightarrow \textbf{problems}']]$

Even without spelling out all the necessary details, this representation seems to capture reading (63) of sentence (62). As will be shown in subsection 4.2.5, this is indeed formally true.

The second general hypothesis of this book can now be officially stated.

Hypothesis 2 (the CF/D hypothesis)   Choice functions are the *uniform* mechanism for interpreting indefinites. An independent distributivity operator is responsible for their Q-distributive interpretation.

After capturing the double scope observation we must be careful to guarantee that the proposed CF and distributivity mechanism also respects the Ruys observation. That is: Q-distributivity scope must remain restricted to islands. In fact, this holds due to a basic property of Reinhart's approach, which is independent of the implementation of Q-distributivity. In Reinhart's CF treatment the restriction of the indefinite is never "pulled out" of a syntactic island. The universal quantifier derived by a distributivity operation is generated at the position where the restriction is. Hence the scope of Q-distributivity cannot violate islands. To get a feeling of how strong this prediction is, the reader is urged to challenge Reinhart's "don't pull restrictions out of islands" strategy by supplementing his/her preferred mechanism of distributivity to Reinhart's system in such a way that Q-distributivity scope beyond islands *is* generated. I know of no way to achieve that without further stipulations.

This robustness is a beautiful property of Reinhart's proposal. In case the Ruys observation turns out to be wrong it would be very hard to save the CF approach! This is in contrast to the free scope stipulation or Ruys' and Abusch' representational approaches to the scope problem. These lines simply propose to "pull" the indefinite or its restriction out of the island. The distributivity operator can be restricted to islands (as in Kamp and Reyle's system[24]), but it can also be designed to violate islands (as Abusch (1994: 117–123) proposes). This means that free scope and representational systems are less restrictive than Reinhart's with respect to the scope of Q-distributivity: whatever the facts are, these strategies can deal with them.

3.3.3 Standard scope within island boundaries

We have seen that the proposed treatment of numeral indefinites by means of CFs and a distributivity operator has certain advantages over Reinhart's CF/GQ proposal. However, in one respect both strategies are too weak, at least on the explicit assumptions mentioned above. Consider for example the following sentence from Reinhart (1997):[25]

(74) An American flag was hanging in front of two buildings.

     a. In front of two buildings there was a (potentially different) American flag hanging.

In order to get the prominent reading (74a) of (74), both approaches must assume that the standard scope mechanism applies to the indefinite NP object. In the GQ approach this is well-known. As regards the CF treatment, we have seen in the analysis of (60) that a plural indefinite cannot Q-distribute over a singular indefinite that is not within its syntactic scope. The same applies to (74).

Reinhart (1997) allows indefinites, like other NPs, to take standard island-restricted. In an LF analysis this means that after QR applies, (74) has roughly the structure in (75), to which both Reinhart's approach and the present one assign the desired Q-distributive reading.

(75) [two buildings] λy.[[an American flag] λx.[x is hanging in front of y]]

Such Q-distributive WS readings of plural indefinites appear in many cases where world knowledge makes the NS reading incoherent. This also occurs when the subject is not a simple singular indefinite. For example:

(76) Exactly one cat is sitting in five baskets.

(77) The mayor was disqualified in nine cities.

(78) Two guards are standing in front of twenty buildings in this town.

These facts suggest that indefinites should indeed be able to take standard scope within island boundaries. Theoretically, this is of course highly plausible. Once a standard scope mechanism is used for other NPs there is no a priori reason to let indefinites be exempt from the operation of this mechanism. However, this is in conflict with some proposals (e.g. Ruys (1992: 105–108), Beghelli (1993), Ben-Shalom (1993)) that suggest that indefinites (among other NPs) do not get standard wide scope. The factual motivation for the "no-standard-scope" approach is that plural indefinites are much less easily interpreted as having wide Q-distributivity scope than the classical case of singular *every/each* NPs. Consider for example a paradigm case of WS interpretation, known as "inverse linking":

(79)   Some girl from every city is happy.

(80) #Some girl from three cities is happy.

While a WS reading for (79) is prominent, a parallel reading for (80) is marginal, if existent at all. However, it may be observed that the plural indefinite in (80) behaves just like any other plural in that respect. Consider for example the following sentence.

(81) #Some girl from all/these/most cities is happy.

There is no particular difference between (80) and (81) as regards the availability of the WS reading for the plural NPs. Thus, if the lack of a WS reading for the indefinite in (80) is to be accounted for in terms of its being "weak" (which also accounts for its grammaticality in *there* sentences, among other phenomena) for instance, then it is unclear why also the "strong" NPs in (81) lack a WS reading.

Moreover, we cannot describe the data by simply saying that inverse linking contexts never allow WS for plural NPs. Availability of the WS reading for the plural is significantly more obvious in cases like (82) and (83).

(82) A principal actor in ninety movies in the festival was American.

(83) A principal actor in all movies in the festival was American.

Therefore, the question to ask is not: why do plural *indefinites* refuse to get standard WS readings? Rather, the question is: why is it so *hard* for NPs other than *every/each* NPs—that is, for indefinites and other NPs alike—to get a Q-distributive WS reading? I have no answer to this question.[26] The only point that should be stressed is that a theory that wishes to account for cases like (74) to (78) and (82) to (83) had better assume a standard scope mechanism for indefinites, restricted by island constraints. The nature of further constraints on the scope of NPs is left for further research.

3.3.4 Narrow and intermediate scope

Assumption (A3) of the CF proposal, which states that existential quantification over CFs can take place at any stage of the compositional analysis, is crucial for the present approach. If choice functions, as I propose, are the only strategy for interpreting indefinites, then they must also be responsible for scopes narrower than the widest one. Conceptually, this is the null hypothesis once we assume existential closure: an operation that "looks at the syntactic structure" and applies existential closure only at certain compositional stages would have to be superimposed on the CF mechanism. However, the "specificity" proposal of Kratzer (1998) disagrees with this strategy of free existential closure. In Kratzer's approach choice functions are conceived of as deictic entities, which are supplied by the context of utterance and need not be existentially closed at all. Therefore, the analysis amounts to postulation of existential closure at the highest matrix level.

Facts that bear upon this question have been the center of extensive debate in the literature. This section first reassesses some familiar data concerning the "intermediate" scope of indefinites outside syntactic islands. Then, coming back to the plurality-coordination problem of chapter 2, we will see that in accounting for the collective interpretation of NP coordinations with indefinites, the present treatment provides further evidence for non-maximal existential scope using choice functions.

Intermediate scope   Consider sentence (84) from Kratzer (1998), a variation on an example by Fodor and Sag (1982).

(84) Every professor will rejoice if a student of mine cheats on the exam.

    a. NS: $\forall x[\mathbf{prof}'(x) \rightarrow [\exists y[\mathbf{student}'(y) \wedge \mathbf{cheat}'(y)] \rightarrow \mathbf{rejoice}'(x)]]$

    b. IS: $\forall x[\mathbf{prof}'(x) \rightarrow \exists y[\mathbf{student}'(y) \wedge [\mathbf{cheat}'(y) \rightarrow \mathbf{rejoice}'(x)]]]$

    c. WS: $\exists y[\mathbf{student}'(y) \wedge \forall x[\mathbf{prof}'(x) \rightarrow [\mathbf{cheat}'(y) \rightarrow \mathbf{rejoice}'(x)]]]$

According to a well-known claim by Fodor and Sag (henceforth F&S) this sentence has only two readings. One reading is the NS reading of the indefinite, given in (84a). The other is the WS reading of the indefinite over both the conditional and the matrix subject, as formalized in (84c). Crucially, F&S argue that such sentences have no reading like (84b), where the scope of the indefinite escapes the adjunct island of the conditional but remains narrower than the scope of the subject *every professor*. Let us refer to this candidate reading as an *intermediate scope* (IS) interpretation of the indefinite. F&S's claim is interesting because it makes an empirical distinction between their and Kratzer's "specificity" approach and the other approaches to the scope problem, including Reinhart's and the one defended here. However, it is very hard to decide whether the claim is true or not on the basis of examples like (84). All three statements in question are pragmatically plausible. As methodological principle 2 in (16) asserts, this is not a solid basis for deciding on scopal possibilities, since in this situation even the status of a unique non-NS reading as in simple sentences like (6) is not clear to all speakers. A judgment concerning the availability of two potential non-NS readings in (84) cannot be expected to be more well-founded.

Indeed, F&S's judgments were already doubted in Farkas (1981) and Rooth and Partee (1982: fn. 6). More recently, Ruys (1992) and Abusch (1994) gave further examples that seriously challenge F&S's claim. Consider the following example from Ruys (1992: 101).

(85) *Every professor* will rejoice if a student of *his* cheats on the exam.

If the pronoun is understood as anaphoric to the NP *every professor* then the WS reading disappears. It is much easier now to attest the IS reading paraphrased in (86b) below.

(86) a. NS: For every professor: if there is a student of the professor who cheats on the exam then the professor will rejoice.
      b. IS: For every professor there is a student of his such that if this student cheats on the exam the professor will rejoice.

To see this, consider a situation where Prof. Smith will rejoice if a student of him, named John, will cheat on the exam. Smith, however, does not want his other students to cheat. Such a situation falsifies the NS reading paraphrased in (86a), but it does not necessarily falsify sentence (85). This indicates that the IS reading is present.

Although Kratzer (1998) accepts this conclusion, she argues that the interpretation of the anaphor is responsible for the effect. Anticipating an argument along these lines, Reinhart (1997) decisively shows that the pronoun is not necessary for an IS reading. Reinhart's example (slightly changed) is as follows.

(87) Every linguist has looked at every analysis that solves some problem.
      a. IS: For every linguist x there is a problem y such that x has looked at every analysis that solves y.
      b. NS: Every linguist has looked at every analysis.
      c. WS: There is a problem x, such that every linguist has looked at every analysis of x.

Note that (87a) is an available reading for (87): in a situation where every linguist has her preferred problem and she has looked at every analysis that solves it, sentence (87) is true. In fact, (87a) is the pragmatically *prominent* reading of (87): assuming (somewhat optimistically) that every analysis solves some problem, the NS reading of (87) reduces to (87b), and the WS reading is (87c). Both readings are presumably false, as most readers can personally verify.

Unlike the original examples of F&S, Reinhart's strategy for testing the existence of the IS reading is in agreement with methodological principle 2 in (16): world knowledge makes the IS reading of (87) the only likely one. Once the reasoning behind the construal of the example is identified, we can duplicate the IS effect with other sentences. For example:

(88) Every movie director is happy to direct every film that features some actor.

    a. IS: For every director x there is an actor y such that x is happy to direct every film featuring y.

(89) Every country's security will be threatened if some building is attacked by terrorists.

    a. IS: For every country there is a (potentially different) building, an attack on it might threaten the country's security.

Also in these cases, the IS reading is the prominent one. The theoretical implication is that, contrary to what follows from F&S's claim, a CF account with free introduction of existential closure is empirically motivated.

NP coordinations with indefinites   In subsection 2.3.9 above (on page 68) a problem with the interpretation of indefinites in NP coordinations was mentioned. Provided that John is a man, the boolean treatment of coordination seems to wrongly predict that the following sentences are equivalent:

(90)   John and some man met.

(91)   #John met.

The problem stems from the combination of the boolean approach to coordination and collectivity with the standard treatment of the indefinite as an existential quantifier. In this standard analysis, the conjunction *John and some man* and the proper name *John* are coreferential under the assumption that John is a man. The reason is that if John is a man then any set containing John trivially contains a man, namely John himself. Conversely: any set containing John and a man trivially contains John. Because of this equivalence we cannot explain the semantic difference between sentence (90) and sentence (91) under the boolean analysis of *and* and the treatment of indefinites as existential generalized quantifiers. The CF mechanism for the interpretation of the indefinite overcomes this problem. Sentence (90) is roughly analyzed as follows:

(92) $\exists f[\mathbf{CH}(f) \land \mathbf{C}(\{A : \mathbf{j} \in A\} \cap \{A : f(\mathbf{man'}) \in A\})(\mathbf{meet'})]$
       $\Leftrightarrow \exists f[\mathbf{CH}(f) \land \mathbf{meet'}(\{\mathbf{j'}, f(\mathbf{man'})\})]$

The coordination *John and some man* is interpreted in (92) as intersection of two principal ultrafilters. One is the standard boolean denotation of *John*, the other is the principal ultrafilter generated by the entity $f(\mathbf{man'})$ for the "chosen man."[27] Consequently, (92) can be true due to values of f that choose a man who is different than John. If, for instance, John and Bill met, then the existence of a CF picking up Bill from the set of men guarantees that (92) turns out true. In subsection 4.2.2 (page 149) we will see that this makes (92) equivalent to (93a), which is desirable, in view of the fact that (93b) is equivalent to (90).

(93) a. $\exists x[\mathbf{man'}(x) \land \mathbf{meet'}(\{\mathbf{j'}, x\})]$

    b. There is some man whom John met.

The crucial point for our discussion here is that adopting the analysis of (90) sketched in (92), we can construct a direct argument in favor of existential closure of CF variables at lower levels than the matrix sentence level. Consider the following example.

(94) Every piano was lifted by John and some man.

Sentence (94) can be true in the following situation S: piano p_1 was lifted by John and Bill *together*, piano p_2 was lifted by John and George together, and so on, for all pianos. This means that the NP *John and some man* should have an interpretation as a plural individual, similar to its interpretation in the analysis of (90). However, it was shown above that under the adopted analysis of conjunction this is not possible with a GQ representation for the indefinite; we must use the CF interpretation. On the other hand, (94) is true in S, where different pianos are lifted by John with *different* men. Thus, the existential import of the indefinite *some man* in (94) should be assigned narrower scope than the scope of the universally quantified subject of the sentence. That is, we should allow (94) to have the reading in (95), where $\{\mathbf{j}', f(\mathbf{man}')\}$ is derived using the $\mathbf{C}$ operator and boolean coordination, as in (92).

(95) $\forall x[\mathbf{piano}'(x) \rightarrow \exists f[\mathrm{CH}(f) \wedge \mathbf{lifted\_by}'(\{\mathbf{j}, f(\mathbf{man}')\})(x)]]$

The same point can be exemplified with any transitive verb that allows a collective interpretation of its object argument. Consider for example:

(96) Every girl defeated John and some boy.

(97) Every group surrounded this skyscraper and some building.

(98) Every dish was eaten by Mary and some girl.

Chapter 4 will go further into the integration of CFs and the boolean approach to collectivity.

3.3.5   Scope and collectivity of complex numerals

The discussion above has concentrated on singular and plural indefinites with the articles *a* and *some*, and on indefinites with the simple plural numerals *two*, *three*, etc. There are of course more indefinites that potentially show scope and plurality problems. The ones that are most related to the subject of this chapter are the *complex numerals*. These are indefinites headed by expressions as in (99).

(99) a. exactly three
      b. more/less than five
      c. at least/most seven
      d. no less/more than nine
      e. between two and eight

The plurality problems and the scope problems of such complex numerals are even more complicated than the problems in the domain of simple indefinites. Liu (1990), Kamp and

Reyle (1993: ch. 4), Beghelli (1995) and Corblin (1997) among others, mention some differences between the scope and plurality behavior of the two kinds of indefinites. Two distinctions that these authors discuss are especially relevant to our present purposes: the ability of these NPs to appear in collective environments and the availability of island escaping scope.

Consider first the collectivity distinction by way of observing the following contrast:

(100) a.   Eleven/some students I know and respect constitute the team that won the cup yesterday.

b.   *At least eleven/at most eleven/between five and thirteen/more than ten/less than twelve students I know and respect constitute the team that won the cup yesterday.

We see that while the simple indefinites in (100a) show collectivity just like plural definites (e.g. *the students*) or proper noun conjunction (e.g. *Mary and John*), complex definites do not allow this interpretation in (100b). A central idea that occurs in the literature (e.g. in the aforementioned works) is that complex numerals, unlike simple indefinites, are "real distributive quantifiers" like *every student*. Of course, this idea is too raw, as plural complex numerals certainly do show some kind of collectivity. This is illustrated by the following sentence.

(101)   At least eleven/at most eleven/between five and thirteen/more than ten/less than twelve students I know and respect met.

Despite this difficulty, section 4.3 follows this line of thought and proposes that complex numerals are indeed unambiguously quantificational while simple indefinites "basically" denote predicates. Chapter 5 will substantiate this idea by explaining the conditions that regulate the collective interpretation of complex numerals (cf. (100b) vis-à-vis (101)) and other quantificational NPs.

Since it is proposed that complex numeral indefinites denote ordinary generalized quantifiers and not predicates, the CF approach predicts that they do not give rise to any violation of island constraints (recall that the CF analysis of simple indefinites draws on their basic analysis as predicative). Like Liu, Beghelli and Corblin, I believe this factual claim is correct. First, it is clear that the classical distributive quantifier readings of complex numerals, like simple ones, do not violate island constraints. For instance, like sentence (53), also sentence (102) is weird and cannot be paraphrased as in (103a) or (103b).

(102)   #If exactly three women gave birth to John then he has a nice mother.   ·

(103)   a.   There are exactly three women x such that if x gave birth to John then he has a nice mother.

b.   There is a set A of exactly three women such that for each member x of A, if x gave birth to John then he has a nice mother.

Of course, this does not show that *existential* wide scope beyond islands is impossible with complex numerals. Consider, however, the contrasts between the the (a) and (b) pairs of sentences in the following examples.

(104) a. If *some* woman I know gave birth to John then he has a nice mother.
      b. #If *exactly one* woman I know gave birth to John then he has a nice mother.

(105) a. If *two* people I know are John's parents then he is lucky.
      b. #If *exactly two* people I know are John's parents then he is lucky.

Sentence (104a) can be interpreted as in (106) below, with the *some* indefinite taking scope over the conditional. By contrast, sentence (104b) strangely implies that more than one woman I know could have possibly given birth to John.[28] A similar contrast arises between the bare numeral in sentence (105a), which can be paraphrased as in (107) below, and the complex numeral in sentence (105b), which cannot.

(106) There is some woman I know such that if she gave birth to John then he has a nice mother.

(107) There are two people I know such that if they are John's parents then he is lucky.

We conclude then, that the existential scope of complex numerals is island-restricted. This fact supports a determiner analysis of complex numerals as in Barwise and Cooper (1981). In order to deal with cases of collectivity such as sentence (101), a flexible system which is more complicated than Barwise and Cooper's will be proposed in chapter 5.

There are interesting scope and plurality problems with other kinds of indefinites besides numerals. On some scope problems of *bare plurals*, see Carlson (1977) and section 4.2.7. On the relevance of expressions like *a certain* to scope phenomena see Hintikka (1986), as well as Kratzer (1998).

3.3.6 Summary
The main claims made in this section are:

• The CF approach is a conceptually plausible method for analyzing the semantics of simple indefinites, which predicts their free scopal behavior.
• Simple plural numerals denote modifiers. Complemented with a distributivity operator, the CF approach correctly captures the contrast between the island-escaping existential scope of numeral indefinites and their island-restricted Q-distributivity scope. The GQ approach to distributivity of Bennett, Scha and Reinhart does not make this distinction. The free scope and representational approaches to indefinites can make the necessary distinctions only if a considerable amount of stipulations is made.
• The standard scope mechanism applies to indefinite NPs in the same way as it applies to non-indefinites. Further restrictions that apply to the scope of NPs other than the classical wide scope takers *every* and *each* might affect also the standard scope of indefinites.

- The CF mechanism is not only responsible for widest existential scope. It is the uniform method for interpreting indefinites.

The linguistic properties of the CF mechanism justify a deeper investigation of the formal system that is required for its explicit implementation. This is the topic of the next section.

3.4 The Formal Semantics of Choice Functions

This section concerns the way in which choice functions are to be properly used in a formal semantics of indefinites. The main difficulty is the interpretation of indefinites with an empty restriction predicate. A negative result will be shown, which seriously challenges the non-boolean e-type treatment of individuals that has been employed so far in our choice function analysis. The problem is solved by readopting the Boolean-Montagovian treatment of individuals as quantifiers. This treatment is argued to provide a correct account of scopal effects with indefinites.

3.4.1 The empty restriction problem

The simplest attempt at using CFs in the analysis of indefinites, which was tentatively employed above, tries to model sentences like (108) using existential quantification over functions as in (109).

(108) Some cow is red.

(109) $\exists f [\text{CH}(f) \wedge \textbf{red}'(f(\textbf{cow}'))]$

This straightforward treatment is problematic. Consider a situation where there are no cows but some red entities. Thus, $\textbf{cow}' = \emptyset$ and $\textbf{red}' \neq \emptyset$. Note that any CF that maps the empty set to a red entity satisfies (109). Since such CFs obviously exist in the described situation, sentence (108) is non-standardly evaluated as *true*. Generally, formula (109) is equivalent to the following formula.

(110) $\exists x [\textbf{red}'(x) \wedge \textbf{cow}'(x)] \vee [\exists x (\textbf{red}'(x)) \wedge \neg \exists x (\textbf{cow}'(x))]$

This particular departure from the standard existential analysis of indefinites is clearly undesired. For instance, while sentence (111a) intuitively entails sentence (111b), proposition (112a) does not formally entail proposition (112b). For instance, if John milks some brown cow and there are no red cows, then (112a) is true whereas (112b) is false.

(111) a. John milks some red cow.
       b. Some cow that John milks is red.

(112) a. $\exists f [\text{CH}(f) \wedge \textbf{milk}'(f(\textbf{red}' \cap \textbf{cow}'))(\textbf{j}')]$
       b. $\exists f [\text{CH}(f) \wedge \textbf{red}'(f(\textbf{cow}' \cap \lambda x.\textbf{milk}'(x)(\textbf{j}')))]$

One might think that the problem can be fixed by somehow changing the definition of choice functions in (33). However, there is no straightforward way to do that: without significant changes of the standard ontology or of the interpretation of logical constants, formula (109) cannot convey the desired existential statement **cow**$'$ $\cap$ **red**$'$ $\neq \emptyset$. To see why this is so, assume that CH is replaced by an arbitrary predicate C of the same type. Then the proposition that a sentence *Some A is B* denotes is the following.

(113) $\exists f[C(f) \wedge B(f(A))]$

As shown below, for no definition of C can (113) mean that $A \cap B$ is not empty. Moreover, the only "conservative proposition" that (113) can convey is a contradiction. To establish that, note that any set C in (113) naturally defines a determiner D^C as given in (114): a relation between the sets A and B.

(114) $D^C \overset{\text{def}}{=} \lambda A.\lambda B.\exists f[C(f) \wedge B(f(A))]$

The claim is in proposition 4 below. We use the notation $\emptyset_{et}$ for $\lambda x.\bot$ and $\mathbf{U}_{et}$ for $\lambda x.\top$.

Proposition 4   For every $C_{((et)e)t}$: if D^C is conservative then $D^C = \lambda A.\lambda B.\bot$.

Proof   By definition of D^C: $D^C(\emptyset)(\emptyset) \Leftrightarrow \exists f[C(f) \wedge \emptyset(f(\emptyset))]$.
By definition of $\emptyset$: $\exists f[C(f) \wedge \emptyset(f(\emptyset))] \Leftrightarrow \bot$.
For every B: $D^C(\emptyset)(B) \Leftrightarrow D^C(\emptyset)(\emptyset)$ (by conservativity).
Therefore, for every B: $D^C(\emptyset)(B) \Leftrightarrow \bot$. (i)
By definition of D^C: $D^C(\emptyset)(\mathbf{U}) \Leftrightarrow \exists f[C(f) \wedge \mathbf{U}(f(\emptyset))]$.
By (i): $D^C(\emptyset)(\mathbf{U}) \Leftrightarrow \bot$.
Conclusion: $\neg\exists f[C(f) \wedge \mathbf{U}(f(\emptyset))]$.
But by definition of $\mathbf{U}$: $\forall f_{(et)e}\mathbf{U}(f(\emptyset))$.
Therefore: $\neg\exists f[C(f)]$.
Conclusion: $D^C = \lambda A.\lambda B.\bot$.

Some is a conservative determiner, which has of course a non-empty interpretation in many models. Hence the above fact entails that proposition (113) is different from $A \cap B \neq \emptyset$, no matter what C is. We may therefore conclude that it is not definition (33) that is to blame: something is wrong with the assumption that the proposition scheme in (113) can reflect standard existential quantification.

3.4.2   Back to Montagovian individuals

In fact, the non-boolean treatment of individuals in formula (113) is the most suspicious aspect of this formula. In a sentence like *Some A is B*, this scheme analyzes the subject as an *e-type* individual $f(A)$. Consequently, when A is empty, it becomes hard to guarantee that $B(f(A))$ is false, since as far as definition (33) is concerned, the function f may map A to an element of B. The Montague treatment of NPs offers the key to the solution: let us restore the quantificational $(et)t$ type for the indefinite. With this typing, the problem can be overcome as follows:

1. When the restriction set A is empty, the indefinite denotes the *empty quantifier* ($0_{(et)t}$). This will guarantee falsity, because B is trivially not in the empty quantifier.

2. When A is not empty, the indefinite denotes the standard Montagovian individual that corresponds to $f(A)$. Namely: the principal ultrafilter $\lambda X.X(f(A))$.

Note that the idea of letting an indefinite with an empty restriction denote the empty quantifier is not at all arbitrary. The empty quantifier is the standard GQ denotation of indefinites with an empty restriction. In boolean terms: **some**$'(0_{et}) = 0_{(et)t}$.

There are various ways in which a quantificational treatment of indefinites along these lines can be implemented in CF theory. The technique adopted here involves lifting a choice function f into a determiner $\langle f \rangle$. This determiner maps the empty set to the empty quantifier and any other set A to the principal ultrafilter generated by $f(A)$. Thus, formally, we define the following lifting operator of $(et)e$ functions to determiners:

(115) $\langle\ \rangle_{((et)e)((et)((et)t))} \overset{\text{def}}{=} \lambda g_{(et)e}.\lambda X_{et}.\lambda Y_{et}.X \neq \emptyset \wedge Y(g(X))$

We write $\langle f \rangle$ instead of $\langle\ \rangle(f)$.

In general, a sentence *Some A is B* is now modeled as in (116). It is easy to establish that this is equivalent to $A \cap B \neq \emptyset$.

(116) $\exists f[\text{CH}(f) \wedge \langle f \rangle(A)(B)]$

More concretely, this means that sentence (108) is modeled as follows.

(117) $\exists f[\text{CH}(f) \wedge \langle f \rangle(\textbf{cow}')(\textbf{red}')]$
 $\Leftrightarrow \exists f[\text{CH}(f) \wedge \textbf{cow}' \neq \emptyset \wedge \textbf{red}'(f(\textbf{cow}'))]$
 $\Leftrightarrow \exists x[\textbf{cow}'(x) \wedge \textbf{red}'(x)]$

Given this treatment, we can study the implication of the CF mechanism for more complex cases.

3.4.3 Examples

An important feature of the CF approach is its special treatment of scope effects with indefinites. From the large literature on NP "scope" one is sometimes led to think schematically of a "wide scope" interpretation for an indefinite as an existential quantification with the restriction predicate "pulled out." The CF approach, however, treats the indefinite "locally," without moving the restriction syntactically. This is roughly illustrated below.

(118) . . . some cow . . .
 a. $\exists x[\textbf{cow}'(x) \wedge \ldots]$
 b. $\exists f[\ldots \langle f \rangle(\textbf{cow}') \ldots]$

While discussing sentence (108) above, we saw that under the formalization in (117) there is no undesired semantic difference between the two approaches. However, when potential scope relations between the indefinite and other elements in the sentence exist, differences show up. Consider first (119).

(119) Every artist who was born in some small village in Holland became famous.

(120) $\exists x[\textbf{village}'(x) \land \forall y[(\textbf{artist}'(y) \land \textbf{born\_in}'(x)(y)) \rightarrow \textbf{famous}'(y)]]$

(121) $\exists f[\text{CH}(f) \land \forall x[(\textbf{artist}'(x) \land \langle f \rangle(\textbf{village}')(\lambda y.\textbf{born\_in}'(y)(x))) \rightarrow \textbf{famous}'(x)]]$
  $\Leftrightarrow [\exists x[\textbf{village}'(x) \land \forall y[(\textbf{artist}'(y) \land \textbf{born\_in}'(x)(y)) \rightarrow \textbf{famous}'(y)]]]$
  $\lor [\neg\exists x(\textbf{village}'(x)) \land \exists x(\top)]$

Proposition (120) is usually assumed to express the wide scope reading of the indefinite in sentence (119). The statement in (121) is the corresponding CF representation. These two formulae do not reflect the same proposition. Consider the restriction predicate **village**′, which stands for *small village in Holland*. In a situation where this predicate denotes a non-empty set, formula (121) gets the same value as formula (120). However, when its denotation is empty, (120) is *false* whereas (121) is *true* whenever something exists. Formula (121) gets this value because $\langle f \rangle(\textbf{village}')$ is the empty quantifier for every choice function f. Therefore the restriction of the universal quantifier in (121) is false, so any choice function can satisfy (121). Choice functions exist iff the universe is not empty, hence (121) is true if small villages in Holland do not exist but something else does. The question is of course: is it reasonable to model (119) as *true* when there are no small villages in Holland?

The answer is positive. As far as the *narrow scope* reading of (119) is concerned, this is the standard truth value assigned to the sentence. Indeed, the *wide scope* reading standardly assigned to the sentence is *false* in this situation but, in practice, direct linguistic facts do not easily provide evidence for this outcome. The reason is that effects coming from the empty restriction of the indefinite interact here with effects of the empty restriction of the universal NP. To exemplify the problem, let us contrast sentence (122) with (123), which is a minimal lexical variation on (119).

(122) Every artist who was born in Antarctica became famous.

(123) Every artist who was born in some big city in Antarctica became famous.

Assuming that no artist was born in Antarctica and that there is no big city in Antarctica, there is no semantic contrast between (123) and (122): both seem equally "odd." However, standardly, (122) is treated as true. I would like to claim that this is why it is hard to determine what truth value a reading of (123)/(119) should get when the restriction of the indefinite is empty. It seems to me impossible to decide whether the oddness of (123) comes with a scope ambiguity where the readings involved are true and false, as the standard account has it, or whether it is odd but unambiguously true, like sentence (122). The scope methodology principle 1 in (15) expects such decisions to be very hard because the existence of a true NS reading for the indefinite (also in the standard analysis) makes it hard to find out whether the sentence should have an additional, false, reading.[29] Semantically, there is a difference between the CF treatment and the standard analysis, but in practice, it is very hard to decide which treatment predicts better results here.

Given this, it is desirable to look for examples that provide more robust evidence. One possible case is the following.

(124) John feeds some brave rabbit or milks some red cow.
    a. $\exists x \exists y [\mathbf{brave\_rabbit}'(x) \wedge \mathbf{red\_cow}'(y) \wedge [\mathbf{feed}'(x)(\mathbf{j}') \vee \mathbf{milk}'(y)(\mathbf{j}')]]$
    b. $\exists f \exists g [\mathrm{CH}(f) \wedge \mathrm{CH}(g)$
        $\wedge \, [f(\mathbf{brave\_rabbit}')(\lambda x.\mathbf{feed}'(x)(\mathbf{j}')) \vee f(\mathbf{red\_cow}')(\lambda y.\mathbf{milk}'(y)(\mathbf{j}'))]]$
      $\Leftrightarrow \exists x[\mathbf{brave\_rabbit}'(x) \wedge \mathbf{feed}'(x)(\mathbf{j}')] \vee \exists y[\mathbf{red\_cow}'(x) \wedge \mathbf{milk}'(y)(\mathbf{j}')]$

The "free scope" assumption about indefinites implies that (124) has the WS reading (124a), where the scope of both indefinites violates the coordinate structure island. According to the CF mechanism, (124b) is the correct WS interpretation. The crucial point is that (124) does not seem to assert the existence of *both* brave rabbits and red cows as (124a) does. Existence of only one of these rare kinds of animals should be sufficient for the truth of (124), in case John takes care of the creature in the indicated manner. Here the CF formula (124b) is preferable: it is the reading of the sentential disjunction in (125), which is intuitively equivalent to (124).

(125) John feeds some brave rabbit or John milks some red cow.

Reinhart (1997) mentions another example that may support the CF treatment of the empty restriction case. Contrast sentence (126a) with (126b), assuming, as usually, that there are no French kings.

(126) a. The organizers did not invite two French kings to the party.
    b. There are two French kings that the organizers did not invite to the party.

While it is easy to judge (126b) as false, this is much harder for (126a), contra the standard assumption. By contrast, consider the sentences (127), where the restriction set of French directors is known to be non-empty.

(127) a. The organizers did not invite two French directors to the party.
    b. There are two French directors that the organizers did not invite to the party.

In this case it becomes easy to judge both (127a) and (127b) as true, provided, for instance, that the organizers did not invite Jean-Luc Godard and Eric Rohmer to the party but did invite many other French directors. Thus, when the NS and WS readings differ in their truth values according to the CF approach, the judgment that proves the existence of a WS reading becomes much easier. Consider further the following sentences.

(128) a. Every organizer who did not invite two French kings to the party got the sack.
    b. Every organizer got the sack.

The two sentences are intuitively equivalent, provided again that there are no French kings. This is what the CF mechanism leads us to expect, once we consider the three readings generated for (128a):

(129) a. NS: $\forall x[[\mathbf{organizer'}(x)$
$\wedge \neg\exists f[\mathrm{CH}(f) \wedge \langle f\rangle(\mathbf{two'}(\mathbf{F\_kings'}))(\lambda y.\mathbf{invite'}(y)(x))]] \rightarrow \mathbf{sack'}(x)]$
   b. IS: $\forall x[[\mathbf{organizer'}(x)$
$\wedge \exists f[\mathrm{CH}(f) \wedge \neg\langle f\rangle(\mathbf{two'}(\mathbf{F\_kings'}))(\lambda y.\mathbf{invite'}(y)(x))]] \rightarrow \mathbf{sack'}(x)]$
   c. WS: $\exists f[\mathrm{CH}(f)$
$\wedge \forall x[[\mathbf{organizer'}(x) \wedge \neg\langle f\rangle(\mathbf{two'}(\mathbf{F\_kings'}))(\lambda y.\mathbf{invite'}(y)(x))]$
$\rightarrow \mathbf{sack'}(x)]]$

These readings are all equivalent to sentence (128b), assuming that the universe is not empty.[30] However, the standard "free scope" analysis of (128a) assumes a *patently true* reading for (128a); viz. the following IS interpretation.

(130) $\forall x[[\mathbf{organizer'}(x) \wedge \exists 2y[\mathbf{french\_king'}(y) \wedge \neg\mathbf{invite'}(y)(x)]]$
$\rightarrow \mathbf{get\_the\_sack'}(x)]$

This putative reading is vacuously true because there is no organizer for whom there are two French kings that he invited. Thus, the standard treatment does not respect the intuitive equivalence in (128).

These pieces of evidence, while admittedly inconclusive, do support a modest assertion: it is not clear at all that the standard way of obtaining scopal readings of indefinites is superior to the CF treatment proposed in this section. In other cases studied, the predictions of definition of the CF treatment are very close to the standard WS reading, and only differ from the standard analysis in ways similar to the differences discussed with respect to (119). Below two further examples are given, with the calculation of the sound interpretation assigned by the CF mechanism.

(131) If some building in Washington is attacked by terrorists then US security will be threatened. ((28) repeated)
   a. WS reading:
$\exists f[\mathrm{CH}(f) \wedge [\langle f\rangle(\mathbf{building'})(\mathbf{attacked'}) \rightarrow \mathbf{threatened'}(\mathbf{security'})]]$
$\Leftrightarrow \exists x[\mathbf{building'}(x) \wedge [\mathbf{attacked'}(x) \rightarrow \mathbf{threatened'}(\mathbf{security'})]]]$
$\vee \neg\exists x\ \mathbf{building'}(x)$

(132) Every linguist has looked at every analysis that solves some problem. ((87) repeated)
   a. IS reading:
$\forall x[\mathbf{linguist'}(x) \rightarrow \exists f[\mathrm{CH}(f)$
$\wedge \forall y[(\mathbf{analysis'}(y) \wedge \langle f\rangle(\mathbf{problem'})(\lambda z.\mathbf{solve'}(z)(y)))$
$\rightarrow \mathbf{look\_at'}(y)(x)]]] \Leftrightarrow \forall x[\mathbf{linguist'}(x)$
$\rightarrow [\exists z[\mathbf{problem'}(z) \wedge \forall y[(\mathbf{analysis'}(y) \wedge \mathbf{solve'}(z)(y)) \rightarrow \mathbf{look\_at'}(y)(x)]]]$
$\vee \neg\exists z\ \mathbf{problem'}(z)$

The analysis of examples with plural indefinites requires an integration with the treatment of plurals, and it is therefore deferred to chapter 4.

3.4.4 Notes on anaphora and Skolem functions

Consider the following sentence.

(133) Every child loves a woman he knows.

The classical analysis of scope and anaphora in Montague (1973) expects the pronoun in (133) to be able to get "bound" by the subject *every child* only when the indefinite object containing the pronoun is interpreted as having narrow scope with respect to the binding subject. This is an immediate prediction of any analysis that reflects noun phrase scope syntactically and treats "bound" readings of pronouns like bound variables in formal logic.

The CF analysis, by contrast, separates the existential scope of indefinites from their c-command relations. Consequently, (133) gets two semantic representations with a bound pronoun: (134) and (135). The interesting one is of course the latter, where the indefinite "takes scope" over the subject although it contains a pronoun which is bound by it. For the sake of exposition, I simplify the representations and use $(et)e$ type CFs without the necessary $\langle \ \rangle$ lifting operator.

(134) $\forall x[\textbf{child}'(x) \rightarrow \exists f[\text{CH}(f) \wedge \textbf{love}'(f(\lambda y.\textbf{woman}'(y) \wedge \textbf{know}'(y)(x)))(x)]]$

(135) $\exists f[\text{CH}(f) \wedge \forall x[\textbf{child}'(x) \rightarrow \textbf{love}'(f(\lambda y.\textbf{woman}'(y) \wedge \textbf{know}'(y)(x)))(x)]]$

Ignoring the empty restriction problem, the proposition in (134) correctly reflects the standard narrow scope interpretation of the indefinite in (133). The proposition in (135), however, is unlikely to reflect any reading of (133). To see why consider a situation where two children, say John and Bill, know precisely the same (non-empty) set of women. For instance, suppose that both John and Bill know Mary and Sue but no other woman. The proposition in (135) then requires that John and Bill love the *same* woman. For, suppose that f_0 is a function that satisfies (135). Then f_0 is a choice function, hence it maps the set consisting of Mary and Sue to one of its members, say Mary. By (135) this means that every child must love Mary if the set of women he knows are just Mary and Sue. Specifically, both John and Bill will have to love Mary. This is of course stronger than what (133) asserts in this situation. Intuitively, (133) does not require that John and Bill love the same woman, even though the set of women they know is the same.

It is possible to criticize this argument against (135) as a reading of (133). After all, we have only shown that (135) is stronger than what the sentence intuitively means. However, (135) entails the standard reading (134), which is also generated. Thus, it might be claimed, following the scope methodological principle 1 in (15), that (135) is in fact a reading of (133), but it is not very prominent due to the entailment relation. I do not think such an argument is very appealing. Something seems foundationally wrong with the assumption that (133) can express the kind of complicated statement (135) makes. Assuming that every child knows some woman this proposition can be paraphrased by: "for every child there is a woman he knows and loves and for any two children who know the same women there is a woman they both know and love." It is hard to figure out how sentences like (133) could ever mean that. However, let us leave this question aside for the time being and move on to another example, which reveals another aspect of the problem.

I will show now that both the classical approach to scope and anaphora and the CF analysis as described above cannot generate all the readings associated with sentences containing indefinites with bound pronouns. However, a natural extension of the choice function mechanism into a mechanism of *Skolem functions* handles this problem correctly. This will give further support for the central argument of this chapter concerning the insufficiency of ordinary quantification for the analysis of indefinites. An example that illustrates this claim is the following.

(136) Every child who hates a certain woman he knows will develop a serious complex.

The "specificity" marker *a certain* in (136) favors a "wide scope" reading of the indefinite. For instance, the sentence can be true if every child who hates *his mother* will develop a serious complex, but children who hate other women they know will not suffer from anything. To see this, suppose that John is a child who hates a certain woman he knows, say Margaret Thatcher. Now, (136) does not necessarily mean that John will develop a serious complex: hating Thatcher might even be a relief for John. Under the relevant reading, sentence (136) only requires that there *is* some woman John knows such that if he hates her he will develop a serious complex. Many psychologists would say that one's mother is a plausible candidate for being such a woman. Thus the situation just described, where John hates Thatcher but does not suffer from any complex, does not necessarily falsify (136). Importantly, however, this kind of situation does falsify the standard narrow scope reading of the indefinite in (137) or its CF version in (138). Hence we conclude that these analyses are insufficient for (136).[31]

(137) $\forall x[[\textbf{child}'(x) \wedge \exists y[\textbf{woman}'(y) \wedge \textbf{hate}'(y)(x) \wedge \textbf{know}'(y)(x)]]$
           $\rightarrow \textbf{complex}'(x)]$

(138) $\forall x[[\textbf{child}'(x) \wedge \exists f[\text{CH}(f) \wedge \textbf{hate}'(f(\lambda y.\textbf{woman}'(y) \wedge \textbf{know}'(y)(x)))(x)]]$
           $\rightarrow \textbf{complex}'(x)]$

In the classical analysis, there is no alternative bound pronoun reading for (136). In the CF analysis there is: the proposition in (139) with widest scope to the existential closure operator.

(139) $\exists f[\text{CH}(f) \wedge \forall x[\textbf{child}'(x) \wedge \textbf{hate}'(f(\lambda y.\textbf{woman}'(y) \wedge \textbf{know}'(y)(x)))(x)]$
           $\rightarrow \textbf{complex}'(x)]$

However, (139) is not the correct wide scope reading of (136). To see this, consider again the situation where John and Bill are the children, who both know Mary and Sue but no other women. Suppose that Mary is John's mother and that Sue is Bill's mother. Suppose further that both John and Bill hate *each other*'s mother, but each of them loves his own mother very much and will not suffer from any complex. Intuitively, sentence (136) can still be true: under the relevant reading the sentence only requires that the existence of a *particular woman* hated by the child will cause him a severe complex. However, for considerations analogous to the ones above, the proposition in (139) is falsified in this situation: any choice function f_0 that maps the set $\{\mathbf{m'},\mathbf{s'}\}$ to $\mathbf{m'}$ will falsify (139), for Bill hates Mary and will not suffer from any complex. Symmetrically, if f_0 maps the set to $\mathbf{s'}$ then the sentence is falsified as well, for John hates Sue and will not develop any complex.

We see again that choice functions do not cope successfully with indefinites that contain bound pronouns. Here the failure is clearer than in (133), since now we have detected a situation where the sentence is *true* which is not allowed by the proposed semantics. This point does not show, however, that the general strategy of quantifying over function variables is wrong. To the contrary: the problem we are facing is very much reminiscent of the well-known puzzle of so-called *functional questions*, illustrated in (140).[32]

(140) Which woman does everyone love? His mother.

One of the prominent proposals in the literature on functional questions indeed uses quantification over functions. See Engdahl (1980:ch.3), Groenendijk and Stokhof (1984:ch.3), Chierchia (1993), Jacobson (1999), and Sharvit (1997), among others. This approach models a question like (140) as asking about the function that maps every person to a woman he loves. The answer specifies this function as the *mother* function: the function that maps any person to his mother. I will not elaborate here on the complex phenomenon of functional questions. Suffice it to say that this effect is undoubtedly related to the problems considered above.

What is relevant for our immediate purposes is to note that the readings commonly attributed to functional questions involve the well-known concept of *Skolem functions*, which are a straightforward generalization of choice functions. Skolem functions provide a solution of the problems observed for choice functions with sentences (133) and (136). The definition of this concept is given below.[33]

Definition 17 (Skolem functions)   Let $E, E_1, \ldots, E_n$ be non-empty sets where $n \geq 0$. A function $f : (E_1 \to (\ldots \to (E_n \to (E \to \mathbf{2})) \ldots)) \to (E_1 \to (\ldots \to (E_n \to E) \ldots))$ is a *Skolem function of arity* n iff for every function $g : E_1 \to (\ldots \to (E_n \to (E \to \mathbf{2})) \ldots))$, for all $x_1 \in E_1, \ldots, x_n \in E_n$: if $g(x_1) \ldots (x_n)$ characterizes a non-empty set $A \subseteq E$, then $(f(g))(x_1) \ldots (x_n) \in A$.

In type-theoretical terms we define a Skolem function of arity n as an object of the following type:

$$(\tau_1(\ldots (\tau_n(\tau t)) \ldots))(\tau_1(\ldots (\tau_n \tau) \ldots)).$$

The definition of Skolem functions using this type is given below.

(141) $SK^n \overset{\text{def}}{=} \lambda f. \forall g_{\tau_1(\ldots(\tau_n(\tau t))\ldots)} \forall x_{\tau_1} \ldots \forall x_{\tau_n}$
$[g(x_{\tau_1}) \ldots (x_{\tau_n}) \neq \emptyset \to (g(x_{\tau_1}) \ldots (x_{\tau_n}))((f(g))(x_{\tau_1}) \ldots (x_{\tau_n}))]$

With this notation it is clear that choice functions are simply the Skolem functions of arity 0: $\text{CH} = SK^0$.

The relevant reading of sentence (136) can be generated using Skolem functions. Instead of letting a Skolem function of arity zero (= CF) apply to the restriction *woman he knows*, we use a Skolem function of arity *one* in correspondence to the single pronoun within the restriction. Instead of viewing the restriction as a set, we interpret it as a function from entities to sets: the function that maps every entity to the set of women he knows.[34] This function can be represented by the lambda term $\lambda u. \lambda v. \mathbf{woman}'(v) \wedge \mathbf{know}'(v)(u)$. We therefore assign the following proposition to (136).

(142) $\exists f_{(e(et))(ee)}[SK^1(f)$
$\wedge \forall x[[\mathbf{child}'(x) \wedge \mathbf{hate}'(f(\lambda u. \lambda v. \mathbf{woman}'(v) \wedge \mathbf{know}'(v)(u))(x))(x)]$
$\to \mathbf{suffer}'(x)]]$

In words: there is a Skolem function f such that for every child x: f assigns to the function from entities to the set of women they know a function g from entities to entities such that x hates $g(x)$. Since f is a Skolem function, we know that if the set of women x knows is not empty then $g(x)$ is in this set. Consequently, if every child knows a woman, then (142) is equivalent to:

(143) $\forall x[\mathbf{child}'(x) \to \exists y[\mathbf{woman}'(y) \wedge \mathbf{know}'(y)(x) \wedge [\mathbf{hate}'(y)(x) \to \mathbf{suffer}'(x)]]]$

This analysis provides a very plausible "wide scope" interpretation of the indefinite in (136). Under this reading, the sentence does not require that if a child hates *any* woman he knows then he will suffer from a complex. Rather, this reading requires that for every child *there is* a woman he knows such that if he hates her he will develop a complex.

We may now return to sentence (133). Using Skolem functions of arity 1 we obtain two interpretations of this sentence:

(144) $\forall x[\mathbf{child}'(x)$
$\to \exists f[SK^1(f) \wedge \mathbf{love}'(f(\lambda u. \lambda v. \mathbf{woman}'(v) \wedge \mathbf{know}'(v)(u))(x))(x)]]$

(145) $\exists f[SK^1(f)$
$\wedge \forall x[\mathbf{child}'(x) \to \mathbf{love}'(f(\lambda u. \lambda v. \mathbf{woman}'(v) \wedge \mathbf{know}'(v)(u))(x))(x)]]$

Incidentally, in this case (144) is equivalent to (145) (provided, as usual, that every child knows at least one woman). This explains why it is hard to recognize any ambiguity in (133), in contrast to (136).

A point that deserves more attention than what I can give here concerns the *compositional analysis* of sentences using Skolem functions. Without argument, let me express the following hypothesis.

(146) The arity of a Skolem function in the analysis of an indefinite is equal to the number of "free variables" in its restriction.

Thus, simple indefinites like *some woman* are analyzed, as done throughout this chapter, using Skolem functions of arity zero (= choice functions). Indefinites like *some woman he likes* are analyzed using Skolem functions of arity one. Indefinites like *some woman he showed her* is to be analyzed using Skolem functions of arity two, and so on.

3.4.5 A note on intensionality

So far we have concentrated on the scope of indefinites in extensional contexts. A traditional problem that has not been addressed here concerns the behavior of indefinites in intensional environments. In such contexts, indefinites are notorious for showing *de dicto/de re* ambiguities, which are classically treated as scopal phenomena.[35] For instance, sentence (147) is standardly analyzed as having reading (148a), which is paraphrased in (148b).

(147) John believes that some cat snored.

(148) a. $\exists x[\textbf{cat}'(x) \wedge \textbf{bel}'_{(st)(et)}(\check{}[\textbf{snore}'(x)])(\textbf{j}')]$
       b. There is some cat whom John believes to have snored.

It is expected that wide scope existential closure of CF variables should be able to derive such *de re* readings like this one without giving the indefinite syntactic scope over the verb *believe*. Sentence (149) below exemplifies the urgency of the matter more clearly, since normally, the standard scope mechanism is used for the derivation of the *de re* reading equivalent to: *There is some cat such that if John believes that it snored then he is probably mistaken.* If, however, as was claimed above, any reading of the indefinite in (149) with scope over the conditional should not be generated by the standard scope mechanism, then it must be guaranteed that the CF mechanism correctly derives this reading.

(149) If John believes that some cat snored then he is probably mistaken.

Let us concentrate on (147). A correct CF treatment of this sentence should naturally extend to more complicated cases such as (149). Reinhart (1997) proposes an analysis that employs intensional choice functions. Her definition relies on letting the CF apply to the *property* denoted by the restriction and yield an individual in the *extension* of this property. Thus an *intensional choice function* (ICF) is of type $(s(et))e$ and the set of ICFs is defined as follows:

(150) $\text{ICH} \overset{\text{def}}{=} \lambda f_{(s(et))e}.\forall P_{s(et)}[\check{}P \neq \emptyset_{et} \to [\check{}P](f(P))]$

Using this definition, a "wide scope" reading of (147) is generated by the representation in (151) below.

(151) $\exists f[\text{ICH}(f) \wedge \textbf{bel}'_{(st)(et)}(\check{}[\textbf{snore}'(f(\hat{}\textbf{cat}'))])(\textbf{j}')]$

In case the extension of **cat'** is not empty, this means that there is a function that assigns to the property $\hat{}\textbf{cat}'$ a member x of its extension such that John believes that x snored. This is the intended *de re* reading (148a) if the extension of the property ˆ**cat**′ is non-empty. The question of how to deal with the empty set problem in intensional contexts will be left open here.

3.5   On the Conceptual Organization of the Theory

In order to be an explanatory scientific theory, any formal system for the description of an empirical domain must be founded on a small number of conceptually simple principles. When it comes to choice function theory, maybe its most promising conceptual feature is the fact that it attempts to derive the scopal behavior of indefinites from one simple postulate: assumption (A1) that concerns their predicative denotation (see subsection 3.1.4). At the present stage of the theory, unfortunately, it is impossible to motivate the whole CF mechanism by this assumption alone. However, it is possible to give at least a partial justification of the other assumptions besides (A1). These assumptions—the general assumptions (A2) and (A3) and the more technical additions of the previous sections—are listed below.

1. The restriction predicate of an indefinite can be *lowered* to an individual.
2. The lowering mechanism involves a *free variable*.
3. This variable is *existentially closed*.
4. Existential closure is restricted to *choice functions*.
5. Some lifting mechanism (e.g. the ⟨ ⟩ operator) is responsible for the *quantificational type* of indefinite NPs.

Let us examine these assumptions and their interactions more closely.

Assumption 1 is one of the two straightforward options for resolving the type mismatch that (A1) creates. The other strategy—standard *lifting* of the restriction predicate into an existential quantifier—is a possibility that is consistent with the present approach, because the CF mechanism is an *extension* of standard existential quantification as shown in the appendix 3.7.

Assumption 2 is the heaviest assumption in the whole CF mechanism: as the complexity of the mechanism in appendix 3.7 shows, this assumption may dictate a significant departure from any known simple version of non-representational semantics. The compositional mechanism proposed there is still too cumbersome and stipulative. However, it is important to note that assumption 2 in fact follows from assumption 1 under some solid assumptions regarding quantification in natural language. If the $(et)e$ lowering mechanism of assumption 1 were a denotation and not a "free variable," then it would have led to illogical statements that contradict universals from generalized quantifier theory. This point will become clear from the discussion below.

Assumption 3 will be discussed in subsection 3.5.2 below.

Assumption 4, which is the subject of subsection 3.5.1, will be shown to be unnecessary. It follows from the other assumptions, together with some principles of generalized quantifier theory.

Assumption 5 is necessary for avoiding trivial or non-conservative treatments of indefinites, as shown by proposition 4. However, the ⟨ ⟩ operator, the specific solution to the empty restriction problem, is a stipulation that brings welcome results, but which cannot at present be motivated on independent grounds.

3.5.1   What makes choice natural?

Given that the semantics of indefinites involves functions from predicates to individuals, it still does not follow that these have to be *choice* functions. Suppose that this is not the case, and that only the assumptions (A1), (1) to (3) and (5) above are adopted. Thus, instead of the analysis in (116), repeated below as (152), we would have (153) as the analysis of a sentence of the scheme *some A is B*, with the arbitrary restriction C replacing the choice function predicate CH.

(152) $\exists f[\text{CH}(f) \wedge \langle f \rangle(A)(B)]$

(153) $\exists f[C(f) \wedge \langle f \rangle(A)(B)]$

There are in principle many alternative predicates C that could replace CH in proposition (152). Consider for example the following definitions and the ways in which they would contribute to the analysis of the simple sentence *Some cow is red*.

$C_1 = 1_{((et)e)t}$ (all $(et)e$ functions)

This would model the sentence as equivalent to *Something is red and something is a cow*.

$C_2 = 0_{((et)e)t}$ (no $(et)e$ functions)

The sentence would be analyzed as contradictory.

$C_3 = \lambda g.\forall A[g(A) = \textbf{lenin}']$ (the function that maps *Lenin* to each set)

This would take the sentence as equivalent to *Cows exist and Lenin is red*.

   Of course, none of these possibilities is realized as the actual meaning of indefinites. But *why* is it so? What makes *choice* functions the natural choice for human languages?

   Generalized quantifier theory can offer an answer to this question. Given the other assumptions as regards the interpretation of indefinites, a predicate $C_{((et)e)t}$ naturally defines the determiner D^C indicated in (154) below (note that (154) is different from (114)).[36]

(154) $D^C \stackrel{\text{def}}{=} \lambda A.\lambda B.\exists f[C(f) \wedge \langle f \rangle(A)(B)]$

The determiners corresponding to C_1, C_2 and C_3 are the following ones:

$D^{C_1} = \lambda A.\lambda B.A \neq \emptyset \wedge B \neq \emptyset$

$D^{C_2} = 0$

$D^{C_3} = \lambda A.\lambda B.A \neq \emptyset \wedge B(\textbf{lenin}')$

It is easy to verify that D^{C_1} is not conservative, that D^{C_2} is trivial (in the sense to be defined below) and that D^{C_3} is not isomorphism invariant (the notions of conservativity and isomorphism invariance were defined in section 1.5). GQ theory rules out such functions as (lexical) denotations of determiners in natural language. Thus, if the restriction CH in (152) were replaced by one of those predicates then a sentence of the form *Some A is B* would end up violating systematic restrictions on the meaning of sentences of this form.

Let us state the relevant universals of GQ theory in more detail. The conservativity universal of Barwise and Cooper (1981) is well-known:

(U1) All natural language determiners are conservative.

One remarkable property of conservativity is that it also holds of *complex* determiners like *four or five*, *all but one*, *more than three*, etc. Consequently, the following equivalence pattern holds for any determiner D.

(155) D dogs barked ⇔ D dogs are dogs that barked

As for isomorphism invariance, we assume the following universal.

(U2) All *simple* natural language determiners are isomorphism invariant.

This universal is not as general as (U1): it holds only of simple (that is, lexical) determiners. A well-known potential counter-example is constituted by possessive constructions such as *John's*, which do not satisfy isomorphism invariance. Note, however, that this construction is not lexical and, arguably, even not a syntactic determiner. Other candidates for determiners that are not isomorphism invariant are possesives like *my* or *your* and demonstratives like *this* and *that*. However, in chapter 4 it is proposed that these items, like the articles *the* and *a*, should not be treated as semantic determiners but as *predicate modifiers*.

A less familiar, yet not less sound, universal on determiners is *non-triviality*. Barwise and Cooper (1981: 181) consider the logically possible determiners that map any set either to the empty quantifier or to the power set quantifier $\wp(E)$. Let us call this property *right triviality*, which is formally defined as follows.

(156) A determiner D is *right trivial* iff
        for all $A, B, C \subseteq E$: $D_E(A)(B) \Leftrightarrow D_E(A)(C)$.

Barwise and Cooper claim that no (simple) determiner in natural language is right trivial, but consider this universal itself trivial. Thijsse (1983: fn.12) disagrees with this contention. Without contradiction, I would like to agree with both claims. Barwise and Cooper certainly have a point, since right triviality of a determiner D would result in highly uninformative sentences. For instance, with a right trivial determiner D, the truth of the sentence *D dogs barked* can be assessed without regard to who the barkers are. Given that languages syntactically require sentential predicates, it would have been highly surprising if there existed lexical determiners that would make them semantically redundant in this way. In this sense, then, right triviality is *linguistically* trivial. However, Thijsse's remark is also warranted: non-triviality is not *logically* trivial. After all, languages *could* have been more uninformative than they in fact are. For instance, it is remarkable that *lexical* trivial determiners are ruled out, whereas trivialities of *complex* expressions—such as sentences with tauto-logical/contradictory meanings, or right trivial complex determiners (see below)—are not syntactically ruled out. This may be a relevant fact about the difference between the "semantic autonomy of the lexicon" and the "semantic autonomy of syntax." Concluding, the non-triviality universal (U3) is not linguistically void.

(U3) No simple natural language determiner is right trivial.

Like (U2), this universal does not necessarily hold of complex determiners. For instance, the determiner *less than zero* is right trivial. It is moreover also left trivial (in the natural sense defined below). A sentence like *less than zero dogs barked* is a logical contradiction.

Left triviality, the counterpart of right triviality is defined as follows.

(157) A determiner D is *left trivial* iff
       for all $A, B, C \subseteq E$: $D_E(A)(B) \Leftrightarrow D_E(C)(B)$.

Note that a universal about the left triviality of simple determiners would be redundant, as it follows from (U1) and (U3): a conservative non-right-trivial determiner is not left trivial either. However, a determiner can be conservative and not left trivial, while being right trivial. The determiner D such that $D_E(A)(B)$ holds if and only if $A \neq \emptyset$ is an example. This means that non-right-triviality, as opposed to non-left-triviality, is a significant restriction on conservative determiners.

We now return to the question of how possible values for the restriction C can be deduced from these universals. Consider first the following fact.

Lemma 5   If D^C is conservative then $C \subseteq$ CH.

Proof   Assume contrary to what we want to prove that $C \setminus$ CH $\neq \emptyset$. Let $f_0 \in C \setminus$ CH. By definition of CH, there is a set $A_0 \neq \emptyset$ such that $f_0(A_0) = a \notin A_0$. By definition of D^C: $D^C(A_0)(\{a\}) \Leftrightarrow \exists f[C(f) \land \langle f \rangle (A_0)(\{a\})]$. The right-hand side of this biimplication is true by the assumption regarding f_0. Conclusion: $D^C(A_0)(\{a\})$. By conservativity of D^C: $D^C(A_0)(A_0 \cap \{a\})$. Because $a \notin A_0$ we have $D^C(A_0)(\emptyset)$.   (i) But by definition of D^C: $D^C(A_0)(\emptyset) \Leftrightarrow \exists f[C(f) \land \langle f \rangle (A_0)(\emptyset)]$. By definition $\neg \langle f \rangle (A_0)(\emptyset)$ for every f. Hence $\neg D^C(A_0)(\emptyset)$, in contradiction to (i). Conclusion: $C \subseteq$ CH.

The above fact means that if D^C is to be a conservative determiner then only choice functions can be quantified over in the semantic process. However, this does not yet uniquely determine D^C as the existential determiner. For instance, consider the following restriction:

$$C_4 = \lambda g.\text{CH}(g) \land \forall A[A(\textbf{lenin}') \rightarrow g(A) = \textbf{lenin}']$$

(These are the CFs that assign *Lenin* to each set that contains him.) This definition would make the sentence *Some cow is red* mean *Some cow is red and Lenin is red if he is a cow.* However unlikely this analysis is, D^{C_4} is conservative. On the other hand, this determiner is not isomorphism invariant, just like D^{C_3}. A more simple example for a conservative determiner D^C that is different than the existential determiner is the determiner $D^{C_2} = 0$. This determiner is moreover isomorphism invariant. However, it is a trivial determiner. Isomorphism invariance and non-triviality, in addition to conservativity, are indeed sufficient to guarantee that D^C is the existential determiner $\mathbf{some}' = \lambda A.\lambda B.\exists x[A(x) \wedge B(x)]$. This is established in the following proposition.

Proposition 6 If D^C is conservative, isomorphism invariant and non-trivial then $D^C = \mathbf{some}'$.

Proof [37] $D^C \subseteq \mathbf{some}'$ simply by lemma 5: D^C is conservative and therefore $C \subseteq$ CH. Using this, we conclude from the definition of D^C that $D^C(A)(B)$ entails $\exists f[\mathrm{CH}(f) \wedge \langle f \rangle(A)(B)]$. By definition this entails $\mathbf{some}'(A)(B)$.

Let us show now $\mathbf{some}' \subseteq D^C$.

Note first that by definition of $\langle f \rangle$:

$D^C(A)(B) \Leftrightarrow \exists f[C(f) \wedge A \neq \emptyset \wedge B(f(A))]$.   (*)

Assume $\mathbf{some}'(A)(B)$ holds and assume d is some element of the (non-empty) set $A \cap B$.

Since D^C is non-trivial, there are A' and B' s.t. $D^C(A')(B')$.

By (*) we conclude that there is $f' \in C$.

This f' trivially witnesses the proposition $\exists f[C(f) \wedge A \neq \emptyset \wedge f(A) = f'(A)]$.

Hence, by (*), we conclude $D^C(A)(\{f'(A)\})$.   (i)

By conservativity of D^C: $D^C(A)(A \cap \{f'(A)\})$.

By (*): $\exists f[C(f) \wedge f(A) \in A \cap \{f'(A)\}]$.

Hence $f'(A) \in A$.

Let π be a permutation of the E domain that permutes d and $f'(A)$ but maps every other element to itself.

Since $f'(A) \in A$ and $d \in A$ we get $\pi(A) = A$.

By (i) and permutation invariance of D^C: $D^C(\pi(A))(\pi(\{f'(A)\}))$.

Equivalently: $D^C(A)(\{d\})$.

By (*) we conclude $\exists f[C(f) \wedge A \neq \emptyset \wedge f(A) = d]$.

But $d \in B$, therefore $\exists f[C(f) \wedge A \neq \emptyset \wedge B(f(A))]$.

We conclude that $D^C(A)(B)$ holds, as needed to be proved.

This result shows that the "semantic structure" (152) and universals (U1) to (U3) ensure that indefinites express classical existential quantification. However, this still underdetermines C itself. There are certain logical possibilities besides CH that are not ruled out by proposition 6. For instance, consider the following definition:

$C_5 = \lambda g.\mathrm{CH}(g) \wedge g(\emptyset) = g(\mathbf{U})$

(These are the CFs that map both the empty set and its complement to the same entity) Obviously $C_5 \neq$ CH. On the other hand, it is easy to establish that $D^{C_5} = \mathbf{some}'$, hence there is no principle in GQ theory that rules out C_5 in (152).

This underspecification of C is linguistically harmless. Proposition 6 shows that (U1) to (U3) do specify D^C as the existential determiner. Thus, meanings of sentences with existential quantification over functions *are* determined, so variation among speakers with respect to C's value is in principle possible, but it would be hard to detect it.

3.5.2 On existential closure

Various semantic frameworks assume some "free" mechanism of existential quantifica- tion.[38] The status of existential closure (EC) of CF variables within semantic theory can be viewed in different ways. One way is to regard EC of CFs as an instance of a general grammatical operation that applies to free variables. The main problem for this view is to explain why certain kinds of variables are subject to existential closure, while others are not. For instance, assume, as customary, that the pronoun in (158) is treated as a free vari- able y. It is conceivable that wide scope EC of this variable applies in the analysis of this sentence as in (159a). The reason is that (158) entails (160), hence a reading like (159a) for (158) would not be too disastrous. However, if EC is a free procedure, then it is also to be expected that (159b), with a narrow scope EC, is a reading of the sentence. But (159b) is, of course, weaker than what (158) asserts and hence unsuitable to model its meaning.

(158) Everything proves it.

(159) a. $\exists y \forall x [\mathbf{prove}'(y)(x)]$
       b. $\forall x \exists y [\mathbf{prove}'(y)(x)]$

(160) There is something that everything proves.

In order to avoid EC of pronoun variables in this way, one might propose that the grammar closes only variables that are grammatically—that is: non-lexically—introduced, such as for instance, CF variables or (perhaps) event variables in a Davidsonian setting. Pronouns are *lexical* entities and hence are not subject to EC. It remains to be seen if and how this idea can be substantiated.

An alternative line, which is fundamental to Kratzer's approach to CFs, is to deny the need for EC to begin with. Instead, Kratzer treats CFs as indexical items, similar to demonstratives or other deictic expressions like *here*, *now* and *I*. This idea goes back to Fodor and Sag's "specificity" intuition. In addition to the empirical problems mentioned in subsection 3.3.4, there is the complication that adoption of this line makes it hard for Kratzer to give a uniform analysis of indefinites using CFs: narrow scope indefinites require the standard existential quantifier analysis in her proposal.

As always, one way is to maintain that EC of CF variables is a theoretical primitive that cannot be further explained. Of course, it would be somewhat disappointing if this turns out to be the case, but I think that at the present stage there is no justification for such pessimism.

3.6 Summary of Chapter 3

This chapter has concentrated on the scope problem of indefinites and studied the *choice function* mechanism as an alternative general semantics of indefinites that solves this problem. We started by discussing the notion of *scopal semantics* in natural language. I suggested that scope ambiguity is not necessarily a linguistic *phenomenon*. Rather, it can be viewed as a *theoretical product* of mechanisms we use in order to deal with complex truth-conditional phenomena that systematically challenge standard theories of syntax and semantics. These phenomena are sometimes extremely hard to detect. Two methodological principles were used in order to overcome this "experimental" difficulty: one should (i) eliminate entailments from a candidate wide scope reading to the narrow scope reading; and (ii) increase the "pragmatic likelihood" of readings in question over alternative readings. I discussed the *extraction-scope generalization* with respect to the parallelism between scope islands and the Ross islands for extraction. The remarkable scopal behavior of indefinites constitutes a systematic exception to this generalization, which any theory of scope should explain. Some further problems in the analysis of *plural* indefinites were discussed and the notion of *Q-distributivity*, which is relevant for the scope problem of plural indefinites, was introduced. I reviewed previous accounts of the scope of indefinites and argued that Reinhart's choice function proposal is the most promising. It was shown, however, that Reinhart's treatment of plural indefinites does not capture all the complex interactions between their existential scope and the scope of Q-distributivity. In addition to the *Ruys observation* of the island-restricted nature of the scope of Q-distributivity, a *double scope* effect was observed, which requires an additional distinction between the Q-distributivity scope and the island escaping existential scope of indefinites. Reinhart's proposal was modified by eliminating the ambiguity of indefinites in her mechanism. Instead, it was proposed that indefinites are *uniformly* interpreted using CFs, but that their double scope behavior motivates a *distributivity operator*. This operator will be further studied in chapters 5 and 6 below.

   After the linguistic motivation for choice functions had been established, their precise formulation was investigated. Standard application of the choice function to the restriction set of the indefinite generates non-boolean *e*-type individuals. It was proved that no treatment of this kind can derive the desired existential interpretation of indefinites without using some non-standard logical techniques. To solve this problem, the *boolean* Montagovian treatment of individuals as generalized quantifiers was reinstalled and it was shown that this treatment accounts for the scopal semantics of indefinites. A preliminary generalization of choice functions to *Skolem functions* was introduced, which deals with some problematic interactions between the scope of indefinites and anaphora. Finally, the conceptual organization of the theory was reviewed and it was shown how one of the main stipulations of the mechanism—the restriction that functional quantification ranges over *choice* functions—can be eliminated and reduced to universal considerations from generalized quantifier theory.

3.7 Appendix: A Variable-Free Implementation

The use of free variables in the above exposition of the proposed choice function semantics marks a withdrawal from the basic assumptions made in chapter 1. The function variables that are employed in this semantics do not straightforwardly denote modeltheoretic objects, and their introduction is a representational step that complicates the syntax-semantics interface considerably. Although many researchers do not share this criticism against free variables in semantics, I think it should be taken seriously. See Jacobson (1999), Hepple (1991) and Szabolcsi (1987), among others, for discussion and alternatives.

As an example of the complications that free variables introduce, consider the following simple sentence.

(161) Some author admires some teacher.

There is no principle in our assumptions so far that prevents the proposition in (162) from being generated as a reading of (161).

(162) $\exists f[\mathrm{CH}(f) \wedge \langle f \rangle(\mathbf{author}')(\lambda x.\langle f \rangle(\mathbf{teacher}')(\lambda y.\mathbf{admire}'(y)(x)))]$

In this representation one existential operator binds two CF variables. The proposition it expresses is a highly unlikely analysis of sentence (161). Consider a situation where the set of authors is the same set as the set of teachers, that is: $\mathbf{author}' = \mathbf{teacher}'$. Denote this set by $\mathbf{at}'$. In this situation (162) reduces to (163).

(163) $\exists f[\mathrm{CH}(f) \wedge \langle f \rangle(\mathbf{at}')(\lambda x.\langle f \rangle(\mathbf{at}')(\lambda y.\mathbf{admire}'(y)(x)))]$
     $\Leftrightarrow \exists x[\mathbf{at}'(x) \wedge \mathbf{admire}'(x)(x)]$

This means that when the authors and the teachers are the same set, (162) claims that some author (who is also a teacher) admires herself. It is hard to see how sentence (161) could possibly mean that: the sentence only requires that some author admires a (potentially different) teacher.

The purpose of this appendix is to give a preliminary outline of a theory of indefinites and choice functions without free variables. We will provide a compositional mechanism that replaces the informal translation process to higher-order formulae employed so far. Following the works that were mentioned above, and, ultimately, Quine (1966), one can mimic free variables by applying the following strategy. Suppose that φ is a logical expression of type σ containing one free variable of type τ. A denotation that corresponds to this representation could be a function of type $\tau\sigma$ that for every entity of type τ gives the value of φ when this entity is substituted for the free variable. For instance, so far we have translated the indefinite *some woman* into the *(et)t representation* in (164a), but from now on the indefinite will directly *denote* the $((et)e)((et)t)$ function described by the lambda-term in (164b).

(164) a. $\langle f_{(et)e} \rangle(\mathbf{woman}')$
      b. $\lambda f_{(et)e}.\langle f \rangle(\mathbf{woman}')$

The main problem that ensues is how to let function "variable substitutes" as in (164b) reach the site where they get "bound" by the existential operator.[39] For instance, when the denotation of the indefinite *some woman* composes with the denotation of the verb *smile* we want to get the function in (165b) of type $(e(et))t$, which mimics the free variable f in (165a).

(165) a. $\langle f_{(et)e}\rangle(\mathbf{woman'})(\mathbf{smile'})$
       b. $\lambda f_{(et)e}.(\langle f\rangle(\mathbf{woman'})(\mathbf{smile'}))$

Note that we need the following type transition, in order to reach (165b) from (164a) and the *et* denotation of $\mathbf{smile'}$:

(166) $((et)e)((et)t),\ et\ \vdash\ ((et)e)t$

Intuitively, the semantics of this rule should allow a function that takes CFs as argument to abstract over this argument and apply to its second argument first: an *et* predicate. In order to obtain this result, we can use the general rule of *Conditionalization*. Van Benthem (1991: ch. 4–5) introduces Conditionalization within a non-directional version of the Lambek calculus (Lambek (1958)), an extension of the Ajdukiewicz calculus defined in chapter 1. In natural deduction format the conditionalization rule has the following formulation and semantics.

This rule derives the type transition in (166) with the required "percolation" of the CF variable in the semantics. The relevant composition process is derived as follows.[40]

$$
\begin{array}{cc}
\dfrac{\dfrac{((et)e)((et)t)\quad [(et)e]^1}{(et)t}\ \mathrm{APP}\quad et}{\dfrac{t}{((et)e)t}\ \mathrm{COND}^1}\ \mathrm{APP}
&
\dfrac{\dfrac{\dfrac{\lambda f.\langle f\rangle(\mathbf{woman'})\quad [g]^1}{\langle g\rangle(\mathbf{woman'})}\quad \mathbf{smile'}}{\langle g\rangle(\mathbf{woman'})(\mathbf{smile'})}}{\lambda g.\langle g\rangle(\mathbf{woman'})(\mathbf{smile'})}
\end{array}
$$

Note that the free variable in this derivation is only a meta-level variable that is used in the proof. It is not assumed as a part of the semantic representation.

As Van Benthem shows, this rule can be used to solve another problem for compositional semantics: the composition of object denotations of type $(et)t$ with transitive verb denotations of type $e(et)$. This is illustrated below, in the derivation of the meaning of the verb phrase *see every woman*.

$$\dfrac{\dfrac{e(et)\quad [e]^1}{et}\,\text{APP}\quad [e]^2}{\dfrac{\dfrac{t}{et}\,\text{COND}^1}{\dfrac{t}{et}\,\text{COND}^2}\qquad (et)t}\,\text{APP}\qquad \dfrac{\dfrac{\dfrac{\dfrac{\mathbf{see}'\quad [y]^1}{\mathbf{see}'(y)\qquad [x]^2}}{\mathbf{see}'(y)(x)}}{\dfrac{\lambda y.\mathbf{see}'(y)(x)\qquad \mathbf{every}'(\mathbf{woman}')}{\mathbf{every}'(\mathbf{woman}')(\lambda y.\mathbf{see}'(y)(x))}}}{\lambda x.\mathbf{every}'(\mathbf{woman}')(\lambda y.\mathbf{see}'(y)(x))}$$

Unfortunately, as pointed out in Van Benthem (1991: 124) and Hendriks (1993: 69–70), the COND rule is too general: many undesired derivations are generated as well. For instance, nothing blocks the following derivation of the meaning of *see every woman*.

$$\dfrac{\dfrac{e(et)\quad [e]^1}{et}\,\text{APP}\quad (et)t}{\dfrac{t}{et}\,\text{COND}^1}\,\text{APP}\qquad \dfrac{\dfrac{\dfrac{\mathbf{see}'\quad [y]^1}{\mathbf{see}'(y)\qquad \mathbf{every}'(\mathbf{woman}')}}{\mathbf{every}'(\mathbf{woman}')(\mathbf{see}'(y))}}{\lambda y.\mathbf{every}'(\mathbf{woman}')(\mathbf{see}'(y))}$$

This second possibility to derive the meaning of *see every woman* using COND has the false prediction that the verb phrase has the reading *was seen by every woman*. This is, of course, absurd, and means that the COND rule should be restricted. The system proposed below offers no elegant restriction on Conditionalization. Rather, in this system the two desired aspects of the COND rule exemplified above will be achieved by two more stipulative rules, which, however, do not give rise to the overgeneration that results from full conditionalization.

The system is introduced using a *sequent format*, which is often more convenient than the natural deduction format used so far. A rule $\Gamma \vdash \tau$ with semantics $X \Rightarrow x$ indicates that a non-empty sequent Γ of types derives the type τ and that sequent X of denotations of the corresponding types in Γ derives a denotation x of type τ. The system contains the following trivial type transition as an axiom:

(A) $\tau \vdash \tau$, with semantics $x \Rightarrow x$.

The *application* and *permutation* rules of the Ajdukiewicz calculus have the following sequent format:[41]

$(R_1)\quad \dfrac{\Gamma \vdash \tau\sigma \quad \Delta \vdash \tau}{\Gamma, \Delta \vdash \sigma}\,\text{APP}\qquad \dfrac{X \Rightarrow x \quad Y \Rightarrow y}{X, Y \Rightarrow x(y)}$

$(R_2)\quad \dfrac{\Gamma \vdash \tau}{\Pi(\Gamma) \vdash \tau}\,\text{PERM}\qquad \dfrac{X \Rightarrow x}{\Pi(X) \Rightarrow x}$

Here Π is any permutation.

For reasons to be explained below, there are two functional type constructors in the system. One constructor is defined as before, by concatenating types τ and σ into $\tau\sigma$. The second constructor maps τ and σ to $\tau \to \sigma$. Formally, then, we redefine the set of types as the smallest set TYPE that satisfies the following two conditions:

1. $e \in$ TYPE and $t \in$ TYPE
2. if $\tau \in$ TYPE and $\sigma \in$ TYPE then $(\tau\sigma) \in$ TYPE and $(\tau \to \sigma) \in$ TYPE.

The semantics of these two type constructors is the same. That is, for all types τ, σ: $D_{\tau\sigma} = D_{\tau \to \sigma} = D_\sigma^{D_\tau}$. The difference between the two constructors is not in the denotations they encode but rather in their *composition potentials*. For instance, a denotation of type $((et)e) \to ((et)t)$ will be able to "percolate" its CF argument to the site of existential closure as illustrated in the transition from (164b) to (165b). By contrast, an identical denotation of type $((et)e)((et)t)$ cannot perform this feat. The rule that is responsible for the "percolation potential" of the argument of functions of type $\tau \to \sigma$ is the following *Argument Conditionalization* rule.

$$(R_3) \quad \frac{\Gamma, \sigma_1 \vdash \sigma_2}{\Gamma, \tau \to \sigma_1 \vdash \tau \to \sigma_2} \text{ ACOND} \qquad \frac{X, y_1(x_\tau) \Rightarrow y_2(x_\tau)}{X, y_1 \Rightarrow y_2}$$

Here, X is a sequent of denotations and $y_1(x)$ and $y_2(x)$ are function denotations applied to x. The semantics of this rule should be read as follows: if for *any* x we can derive $y_2(x)$ from X and $y_1(x)$, then from X and y_1 we can derive y_2. We conventionally assume that the choice of x does not affect for the validity of the derivation of the premise. In other words: x does not have any occurrence within any of the members of the sequent X (this could happen due to recursive application of ACOND).

The ACOND rule lets a function of type $\tau \to \sigma_1$ "abstract over" its τ type argument and derive any function of type $\tau \to \sigma_2$ if σ_2 can be derived from σ_1 in the same context. Note that the ACOND rule differs from the COND rule in that a $\to$ constructor cannot be introduced "for free." ACOND only applies to $\to$ types that are already present. For instance, a "lifting" rule like $e \vdash (e \to t) \to t$, which is derivable using COND, is not derivable by means of ACOND.

As a simple example for the use of ACOND as a replacement for COND, consider again the desired transition from (164b) to (165b). It is obtained as follows.

$$\frac{et, \ (et)t \vdash t}{et, \ ((et)e) \to ((et)t) \vdash ((et)e) \to t} \text{ ACOND}$$

$$\frac{\textbf{smile}', \ (\lambda f.\langle f \rangle(\textbf{woman}'))(g) \ \Rightarrow \ (\lambda f.\langle f \rangle(\textbf{woman}')(\textbf{smile}'))(g)}{\textbf{smile}', \ \lambda f.\langle f \rangle(\textbf{woman}') \ \Rightarrow \ \lambda f.\langle f \rangle(\textbf{woman}')(\textbf{smile}')}$$

The premise is just a different presentation of the derivation $\textbf{smile}', \ Q_{(et)t} \Rightarrow Q(\textbf{smile}')$, which holds due to function application and permutation, where Q is instantiated as the object $\langle g \rangle(\textbf{woman}')$, for an arbitrary $(et)e$ variable g.

Note that we have to distinguish two functional constructors because a general ACOND rule for one constructor would not do. It would generate the problems that also encumber the COND rule. For instance, consider how a wrong meaning of the verb phrase *see every man* could have been derived using ACOND if the constructor $\to$ were the only functional type constructor.

$$\frac{(e \to t) \to t, \; e \to t \vdash t}{(e \to t) \to t, \; e \to (e \to t) \vdash e \to t} \; \text{ACOND}$$

$$\frac{\textbf{every}'(\textbf{man}'), \; \textbf{see}'(x) \; \Rightarrow \; (\lambda y.\textbf{every}'(\textbf{man}')(\textbf{see}'(y)))(x)}{\textbf{every}'(\textbf{man}'), \; \textbf{see}' \; \Rightarrow \; \lambda y.\textbf{every}'(\textbf{man}')(\textbf{see}'(y))}$$

Thus, the verb phrase *see every man* could have again received the inadequate analysis equivalent to *was seen by every man*. This is precluded in the present system, since lexical items that do not involve a CF interpretation are assigned the standard typing that does not contain the $\to$ constructor. For instance, the verb *see* gets the type $e(et)$, which is not subject to wrong applications of ACOND such as the one illustrated above.

To obtain composition of quantifiers and transitive verbs, the system uses a *Saturation* rule, following Nam (1991). This rule allows a quantifier of type $(\tau t)t$ to compose with an n-ary relation whose first argument is of type τ. Thus, since the Conditionalization rule is not available for it, a quantifier and a relation always have only one composition possibility. The semantics of the rule is defined using the function SAT, which maps a quantifier and an n-ary relation to an $(n-1)$-ary relation. In the definition of this function it is convenient to use the fact that boolean types can be viewed as encoding n-ary relations, where $n \geq 0$. This arity of boolean types is recursively defined below. We call a type $(\tau \to \sigma)$ boolean iff the corresponding type $(\tau\sigma)$ is boolean.

(167) **Arity of boolean types**

Type t is of arity 0. Let σ be a boolean type of arity n. Then any boolean type $\tau\sigma$ or $\tau \to \sigma$ is of arity $n + 1$.

(168) **Saturation**

For $Q \in D_{(\tau t)t}$ and $R \in D_{\tau\sigma}$, where σ is a boolean type of arity $n \geq 0$:
$$\text{SAT}(Q, R) \stackrel{\text{def}}{=} \lambda x_1 \ldots \lambda x_n.Q(\lambda x.R(x)(x_1) \ldots (x_n))$$

The saturation rule is defined using this operator:

$$(\text{R}_4) \quad \frac{\Gamma \vdash (\tau t)t \quad \Delta \vdash \tau \; op \; \sigma}{\Gamma, \Delta \vdash \sigma} \; \text{SAT} \qquad \frac{X \Rightarrow Q \quad Y \Rightarrow R}{X, Y \Rightarrow \text{SAT}(Q, R)}$$

Here *op* is the null constructor or the $\to$ constructor and σ is a boolean type of arity $n \geq 0$.

The axiom (A) and the rules (R_1) to (R_4) allow us to percolate an arbitrary number of arguments of functions of type $\tau \to \sigma$ to their binding site. Of course, if we want to bind CF variables we need to introduce the existential closure operator. Compositionally, this is an existential quantifier over the domain of $(et)e$ functions, restricted by the set of choice functions CH. Formally:

(169) **Existential Choice Closure**

$$\text{ECC}_{(((et)e)t)t} \stackrel{\text{def}}{=} \lambda A_{((et)e)t}.A \cap \text{CH} \neq \emptyset$$

We assume that the ECC operator can be introduced freely at any step in the translation process.

By way of illustration of this system, consider the following sentence.

(170) If some woman admires some man then everything's OK.

We assume the following lexical items with the corresponding types and denotations.

if	$t(tt)$	$\mathbf{if}' = \lambda\varphi_t.\lambda\psi_t.\varphi \to \psi$
some	$(et)e \to ((et)((et)t))$	$\mathbf{some}' = \lambda f_{(et)e}.\lambda A_{et}.\lambda B_{et}.\langle f\rangle(A)(B)$
woman	et	$\mathbf{woman}'$
admires	$e(et)$	$\mathbf{admire}'$
man	et	$\mathbf{man}'$
then	tt	$\mathbf{then}' = \lambda\varphi_t.\varphi$
everything's OK	t	$\mathbf{ok}'$

Note that the denotation of the article *some* is a function from CFs to the corresponding determiner. The type of this function employs the arrow, which guarantees that the CF argument is able to percolate.

Consider first the derivation of the NS reading for both indefinites in (170). First note that saturating **some**$'$ using ECC simply gives the existential determiner **E**:

$$\text{SAT}(\text{ECC}, \mathbf{some}')$$
$$= \lambda A_{et}.\lambda B_{et}.\text{ECC}(\lambda g_{(et)e}.\mathbf{some}'(g)(A)(B))$$
$$= \lambda A.\lambda B.(\lambda X_{((et)e)t}.X \cap \text{CH} \neq \emptyset)(\lambda g.\mathbf{some}'(g)(A)(B))$$
$$= \lambda A.\lambda B.\exists f[\text{CH}(f) \wedge \mathbf{some}'(f)(A)(B)]$$
$$= \lambda A.\lambda B.\exists f[\text{CH}(f) \wedge \langle f\rangle(A)(B)]$$
$$= \lambda A.\lambda B.A \cap B \neq \emptyset$$
$$= \mathbf{E}$$

This equation means that any reading that can be achieved with standard existential quantifiers can also be achieved in the CF approach.

The above entails that when the two indefinite articles in (170) are immediately saturated by ECC, we obtain the NS reading of both indefinites. The proof of this fact is summarized in the following derivation:

With some simplifications, one can verify that the derived proposition is the same as the one expressed by the following formula:

$$[\exists x \exists y [\mathbf{woman}'(x) \wedge \mathbf{man}'(y) \wedge \mathbf{admire}'(y)(x)]] \rightarrow \mathbf{ok}'$$

A more interesting reading of (170) is the one where both indefinites take scope over the conditional. The following derivation of this reading makes substantial use of the ACOND rule. Two steps in the derivation, which are marked with numbers, are explicated below. First, we derive the meaning of the sub-sentence *some woman admires some man* with both CFs "percolated" (remarks for this derivation are given below).

$$\cfrac{\cfrac{\begin{array}{c}\mathbf{some}'\\=\lambda f.\lambda A.\lambda B.\langle f\rangle(A)(B)\end{array} \quad \mathbf{woman}'}{\lambda f.\lambda B.\langle f\rangle(\mathbf{woman}')(B)}\ {}_{\text{ACOND}} \quad \cfrac{\mathbf{admire}' \quad \cfrac{\mathbf{some}' \quad \mathbf{man}'}{\lambda f.\lambda B.\langle f\rangle(\mathbf{man}')(B)}\ {}_{\text{ACOND}}}{\lambda f.\text{SAT}(\lambda B.\langle f\rangle(\mathbf{man}')(B), \mathbf{admire}')}\ {}_{\text{ACOND + SAT}^*}}{\lambda g.\lambda f.(\lambda B.\langle f\rangle(\mathbf{woman}')(B))(\text{SAT}(\lambda B.\langle g\rangle(\mathbf{man}')(B), \mathbf{admire}'))}\ {}_{\text{ACOND} \times 2^{\dagger}}$$

(Note: $*$ See remark 1 below. $\dagger$ See remark 2 below.) Let us denote the derived meaning by φ, which is of type $((et)e) \rightarrow (((et)e) \rightarrow t)$. Using φ we derive the meaning of the matrix sentence with widest scope for both indefinites as given below.

$$\cfrac{\cfrac{\cfrac{\cfrac{\begin{array}{c}\mathbf{if}' \quad \varphi\end{array}}{\begin{array}{c}\lambda g.\lambda f.\mathbf{if}'((\lambda B.\langle f\rangle(\mathbf{woman}')(B))\\(\text{SAT}(\lambda B.\langle g\rangle(\mathbf{man}')(B), \mathbf{admire}')))\end{array}}\ {}_{\text{ACOND} \times 2} \quad \cfrac{\mathbf{then}' \quad \mathbf{ok}'}{\mathbf{then}'(\mathbf{ok}')}\ {}_{\text{APP}}}{\begin{array}{c}\lambda g.\lambda f.\mathbf{if}'((\lambda B.\langle f\rangle(\mathbf{woman}')(B))\\(\text{SAT}(\lambda B.\langle g\rangle(\mathbf{man}')(B), \mathbf{admire}')))(\mathbf{then}'(\mathbf{ok}'))\end{array}}\ {}_{\text{ACOND} \times 2}}{\begin{array}{c}\text{SAT}(\text{ECC}, \lambda g.\lambda f.\mathbf{if}'((\lambda B.\langle f\rangle(\mathbf{woman}')(B))\\(\text{SAT}(\lambda B.\langle g\rangle(\mathbf{man}')(B), \mathbf{admire}')))(\mathbf{then}'(\mathbf{ok}')))\end{array}}\ \substack{\text{ECC} \\ \text{SAT}}}{\begin{array}{c}\text{SAT}(\text{ECC}, \text{SAT}(\text{ECC}, \lambda g.\lambda f.\mathbf{if}'((\lambda B.\langle f\rangle(\mathbf{woman}')(B))\\(\text{SAT}(\lambda B.\langle g\rangle(\mathbf{man}')(B), \mathbf{admire}')))(\mathbf{then}'(\mathbf{ok}'))))\end{array}}\ \substack{\text{ECC} \\ \text{SAT}}$$

The application of a number of (laborious) simplifications reveals that the derived meaning can be expressed by a more readable formula using CFs:

$$\exists f \exists g [\text{CH}(f) \wedge \text{CH}(g) \wedge [\langle f\rangle(\mathbf{woman}')(\lambda x.\langle g\rangle(\mathbf{man}')(\lambda y.\mathbf{admire}'(y)(x))) \rightarrow \mathbf{ok}']]$$

Remark 1 In more detail and using the sequent format, this stage involves the following type and meaning derivations.

$$\cfrac{\cfrac{(et)t \vdash (et)t \quad e(et) \vdash e(et)}{e(et), (et)t \vdash et}\ {}_{\text{SAT}}}{e(et), ((et)e) \rightarrow ((et)t) \vdash ((et)e) \rightarrow (et)}\ {}_{\text{ACOND}}$$

$$\cfrac{\cfrac{\mathbf{admire}' \Rightarrow \mathbf{admire}' \quad \lambda B.\langle g\rangle(\mathbf{man}')(B) \Rightarrow \lambda B.\langle g\rangle(\mathbf{man}')(B)}{\mathbf{admire}', (\lambda f.\lambda B.\langle f\rangle(\mathbf{man}')(B))(g) \Rightarrow (\lambda f.\text{SAT}(\lambda B.\langle f\rangle(\mathbf{man}')(B), \mathbf{admire}'))(g)}}{\mathbf{admire}', \lambda f, \lambda B.\langle f\rangle(\mathbf{man}')(B) \Rightarrow \lambda f.\text{SAT}(\lambda B.\langle f\rangle(\mathbf{man}')(B), \mathbf{admire}')}$$

Remark 2   This is a situation where two denotations containing (bound) CF variables are composed. Successive application of ACOND "percolates" both CF slots to the composed denotation. More concretely, the subject *some woman* denotes a quantifier Q with a CF slot, of type $((et)e) \rightarrow ((et)t)$, and the verb phrase *admires some man* denotes a predicate P with another CF slot, i.e. it is of type $((et)e) \rightarrow (et)$. The type of the sentence reflects the presence of two CF slots: $((et)e) \rightarrow (((et)e) \rightarrow t)$. The composition using ACOND looks as follows.

$$
\cfrac{\cfrac{\cfrac{(et)t,\ et \vdash t}{((et)e) \rightarrow ((et)t),\ et \vdash ((et)e) \rightarrow t}\ \text{ACOND}}{((et)e) \rightarrow ((et)t),\ ((et)e) \rightarrow (et) \vdash ((et)e) \rightarrow (((et)e) \rightarrow t)}\ \text{ACOND}}{\cfrac{Q(h'),\ P(h)\ \Rightarrow\ ((\lambda g.\lambda f.(Q(f))(P(g)))(h))(h')}{\cfrac{Q,\ P(h)\ \Rightarrow\ (\lambda g.\lambda f.(Q(f))(P(g)))(h)}{Q,\ P\ \Rightarrow\ \lambda g.\lambda f.(Q(f))(P(g))}}}
$$

Chapter 4

Predicate-Quantifier Flexibility

The flexibility of noun phrase interpretation is one of the main principles that underly the analyses in the previous chapters, and in this book in general. Chapter 2 employed a type-shifting operation for the derivation of the collective interpretation of NP coordination. Chapter 3 proposed a choice function mechanism that shifts predicative denotations of simple indefinites to Montagovian individuals—a simple kind of generalized quantifiers. The present chapter unifies the two mechanisms by adopting a more general conception of semantic flexibility. Following Partee's 1987 article "Noun Phrase Interpretation and Type Shifting Principles," I propose that noun phrases can have different semantic functions: while all noun phrases can be interpreted as generalized quantifiers, some NPs can also function as predicates. Partee's system is revised at two major points: the definition of the flexibility principles involved in the interpretation of the noun phrase and the nature of the restrictions on their application. Instead of Partee's operators, the *minimum* operator of chapter 2 and the *choice function* mechanism of chapter 3 are proposed as the core engine for flexible NP interpretation. The restrictions on these operators are argued to follow from the commonly assumed syntactic analysis of nominals as *determiner phrases* (DPs).

An important motivation for Partee's flexible strategy is the appearance of certain nominals in positions following the copula *be* and in other so-called "predicative" positions. Partee's proposal, as well as some other semantic approaches to this phenomenon, are reviewed in section 4.1. Section 4.2 proposes an implementation of Partee's flexibility strategy that uses the two mechanisms from the previous chapters as general semantic *category-shifting* procedures between predicates and quantifiers. This proposed flexibility of semantic categories is significantly different from Partee and Rooth's (1983) *type-fitting* strategy described in chapter 2, which changes only the *type* of linguistic expressions but not their semantic *category* in the sentence. Category shifting principles, by contrast to type fitting, do not necessarily change the type of an expression and are driven by the syntax, not by type mismatch. The proposed category shifting mechanism generalizes Partee's account of argument and predicate singular NPs to a treatment which also deals with plural and coordinate NPs. The generalization crucially involves a distributivity operator at the NP level.

Section 4.3 proposes that syntactic differences between nominals restrict the application of category shifting principles. According to the *DP hypothesis* of Abney (1987), it is assumed that nominals have two phrasal levels: a noun phrase (NP) and a determiner phrase (DP). It is proposed that the NP level is unambiguously predicative and the DP level is unambiguously quantificational. Category shifting principles apply at the intermediate D′ level, which is therefore flexible between the two semantic categories. This syntactic division accounts for the restrictions on the application of category shifting principles and for a number of intricate facts about the syntax and semantics of nominals in general. Section 4.4 studies some remaining problems in the definition of the type system in flexible semantics and section 4.5 introduces a simple grammar that illustrates some of the main principles of this chapter.

4.1 Flexibility and Predicative Nominals: The Problem and Previous Proposals

This section reviews Partee's approach to flexible NP interpretation and predicative NPs in particular, with some discussion of alternative treatments of these constructions.[1] Partee's general semantic program will be adopted, but we will also point out some problems in her usage of Montague's treatment of *be* as a general flexibility operator.

4.1.1 The Partee Triangle

Partee and Rooth (1983) used semantic operators with no morphological realization in order to lift the type of certain expressions when they are coordinated with expressions of a higher type. One well-known example that was mentioned in chapter 2 is the "Montague Raising" operator that lifts a noun phrase denotation of type e into a quantifier of type $(et)t$. In Partee (1987) the flexibility approach is extended to other problems of NP interpretation. Partee proposes that in addition to the e and $(et)t$ types of entities and quantifiers, noun phrases can also have the predicative type et as a "marked" option. NP denotations of the three types are connected to each other using *type-shifting operators*. These operators are arranged in the diagram of figure 4.1, which, following Van Benthem (1991: 348), will be referred to as the *Partee Triangle*.[2]

The definitions of the six operators in figure 4.1 are given below:

$$\mathbf{M} = \lambda x.\lambda A.A(x)$$

$$\mathbf{M}^{-1} = \lambda Q. \begin{cases} x & \text{if } Q = \mathbf{M}(x) \\ \text{undefined} & \text{otherwise} \end{cases}$$

$$\mathbf{Q} = \lambda x.\lambda y.x = y$$

$$\iota = \lambda A. \begin{cases} x & \text{if } A = \mathbf{Q}(x) \\ \text{undefined} & \text{otherwise} \end{cases}$$

$$\mathbf{E} = \lambda A.\lambda B.A \cap B \neq \emptyset$$

$$\mathrm{BE} = \lambda Q.\lambda x.Q(\{x\})$$

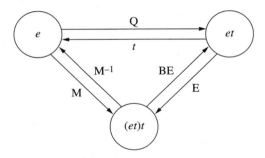

Figure 4.1
The Partee Triangle

The *Montague Raising* operator **M** mentioned in chapter 2 (page 52) maps any entity to the corresponding principal ultrafilter (see page 50). The *Montague lowering* operator $\mathbf{M}^{-1}$ is the partial inverse function mapping any principal ultrafilter to the entity that generates it. The *Quine* operator **Q** maps an entity to the singleton set it constitutes. The *iota* operator ι is the partial inverse function mapping singletons to their constituting entity. The operator **E** of *Existential raising* maps a set A to the corresponding existential quantifier: the set of sets whose intersection with A is not empty. The BE operator was proposed by Montague as a mapping from a quantifier to the set of entities that constitute singletons in its extension.

Let us now briefly review the processes of NP interpretation that these operations are supposed to model. As in the earlier proposal of Partee and Rooth (1983), Partee assumes that proper names and pronouns are basically of type e. In Partee's proposal also definite NPs can get this primitive type using the *iota* operator (see below). As explained in chapter 2 (page 52), in a boolean framework this assumption necessitates a lifting operation that maps such NP denotations of type e into Montagovian generalized quantifiers of type $(et)t$. This is the role of the *Montague Raising* operator, which is illustrated by the analysis (2) of the disjunctive NP in sentence (1).

(1) Mary or John slept.

(2) $(\mathbf{M}(\mathbf{m}'_e) \sqcup \mathbf{M}(\mathbf{j}'_e))(\mathbf{sleep}'_{et})$
    $\quad \Leftrightarrow ((\lambda P.P(\mathbf{m}')) \sqcup (\lambda P.P(\mathbf{j}')))(\mathbf{sleep}')$
    $\quad \Leftrightarrow (\lambda P.P(\mathbf{m}') \vee P(\mathbf{j}'))(\mathbf{sleep}')$
    $\quad \Leftrightarrow \mathbf{sleep}'(\mathbf{m}') \vee \mathbf{sleep}'(\mathbf{j}')$

The *existential* operator **E** is useful for interpreting bare singular indefinites in languages that allow the omission of the indefinite article. Thus in the Hebrew sentence (3), the **E** operator is responsible for lifting the restriction predicate of the indefinite into a generalized quantifier. This is illustrated in (4).

(3) yeled ba

     child came

     "*A* child came"

(4) $\mathbf{E}(\mathbf{yeled}'_{et})(\mathbf{ba}'_{et})$

     $\Leftrightarrow$ $\mathbf{yeled}' \cap \mathbf{ba}' \neq \emptyset$

     $\Leftrightarrow$ $\exists x[\mathbf{yeled}'(x) \wedge \mathbf{ba}'(x)]$

The *iota* operator is one of the classical proposals to treat *definite* noun phrases. This function is defined only for singletons, which accounts for the intuition that sentences with singular definites are often semantically/pragmatically deviant when the restriction predicate does not determine a unique entity. More will be said on this in subsection 4.2.4. As an example of the application of the *iota* operator, consider the simple sentence (5) and its analysis in (6).

(5) The child came.

(6) Provided that $\mathbf{child}'_{et} = \{x\}$: $\mathbf{come}'_{et}(\iota(\mathbf{child}'_{et})) \Leftrightarrow \mathbf{come}'(x)$

Note that the requirement in the above definition of the *iota* operator that the set A equals $\mathbf{Q}(x)$ is equivalent in (6) to the requirement that the predicate $\mathbf{child}'$ characterizes a singleton set that consists of the element x. Hence, the truth value of (5) is defined if and only if the set $\mathbf{child}'$ includes only one element, and then the denotation $\iota(\mathbf{child}')$ is simply this element.

The *Quine* operator derives a predicative reading for e-type denoting NPs. A sentence like (7), where a proper name follows the copula *be*, may be handled as in (8), which supplies the correct identity statement.

(7) This man is John.

(8) $(\mathbf{Q}(\mathbf{j}'_e))(\mathbf{this\_man}'_e)$

     $\Leftrightarrow$ $(\lambda x.x = \mathbf{j}')(\mathbf{this\_man})$

     $\Leftrightarrow$ $\mathbf{this\_man}' = \mathbf{j}'$

The BE operator is also used for the interpretation of NPs in predicative positions. However, unlike the $\mathbf{Q}$ shift, BE is a general operator that maps any $(et)t$ quantifier to an et predicate. Operators from quantifiers to predicates make up one of the main topics of this chapter. The motivation for introducing general procedures, as well as the merits and demerits of the specific BE operator, will be discussed in detail in the following subsections of this section. As for the $\mathbf{M}^{-1}$ operator, Partee mentions only theory-internal motivation: it may open possibilities for analyzing indefinites in Discourse Representation Theory using free variables of type e. I ignore this point here and refer the reader to Partee (1987: 129) and the references listed there.

Partee also shows some symmetries between the six operators. Generally, composition of a lowering operation with the corresponding lift leads to an identity function: $\iota \circ \mathbf{Q}$, BE $\circ$ $\mathbf{E}$

and $\mathbf{M}^{-1} \circ \mathbf{M}$ are the identity functions on entities, predicates and quantifiers respectively. Other closure properties are these:

$$\mathbf{E} \circ \mathbf{Q} = \mathbf{M}$$

$$\mathrm{BE} \circ \mathbf{M} = \mathbf{Q}$$

$$\mathbf{M}^{-1} \circ \mathbf{E} = \iota$$

Partee (1987) and Van Benthem (1986: 68–70, 1991: 67) address some further properties of this array of operators.

The Partee triangle is not officially proposed as a theory of flexible NP interpretation. Rather, the objective of Partee's paper is to provide a systematic study of the semantic connections between some operators for NP interpretation that have been proposed in the semantic literature. However, there are some natural expectations with respect to any theory that purports to substantiate Partee's approach in linguistic theory. First, of course, the proposed operators should have sufficient empirical motivation, and second, the theory must provide general principles that govern the application of these procedures and clarify whether they have morphological/syntactic manifestations. For instance, the theory has to determine if the $\mathbf{E}$ operator has any syntactic correlate: the indefinite article (when it is morphologically realized) or a null element (when the indefinite lacks an article).

The present study will first try to substantiate the need for a procedure like the BE operator that shifts quantifiers to predicates. The following subsection provides some background to the problem.

4.1.2 Three approaches to *be* and predicative NPs
An old puzzle concerning noun phrase interpretation is the ability of some nominals to appear in positions which are typically reserved for adjectival or prepositional phrases. Most notably, some English NPs follow the copula *be* as naturally as APs or PPs. This is illustrated by the sentences (10a–c), in comparison to (9).

(9) a. Mary is *tall*.
   b. Mary is *in the classroom*.

(10) a. Mary is *a teacher*.
    b. John is *the teacher*.
    c. This woman is *Sue*.

Occurrences of NPs in such positions are often referred to as *predicative*. Some other predicative NP constructions will be exemplified as we go along.

The semantic question is how to let structures of the form NP_1 *be* NP_2 denote a truth-value. Of course, this question cannot be separated from the issue of the interpretation of *be* constructions in general. The latter problem, in turn, relates to the semantics of APs and PPs. I will not go into all the details of existing analyses, but rather characterize three influential semantic approaches that will serve as a background for further developments.

A traditional approach assumes that the copula is ambiguous between *be of predication* and *be of identity*.[3] Roughly speaking, the first *be* is held responsible for the application of a predicate to its subject argument. This *be* of predication is assumed to occur with APs and PPs as in (9) and with indefinites as in (10a). All these expressions are traditionally assigned predicative denotations. In type theoretical notation, *be* of predication denotes the function mapping any predicate to itself, in (11) below.[4] Since the contribution of such a function to the semantics is trivial, it is sometimes proposed that *be* of predication has no meaning at all. By contrast, *be* of identity is assumed to denote a transitive predicate that imposes an equality relation between its two arguments. This function is formalized in (12). Proper names in predicative positions as in (10c) are assumed to be arguments of such a relation, which would explain the "identity" reading.

(11) $BE^{pred}_{(et)(et)} \stackrel{\mathrm{def}}{=} \lambda A_{et}.A$

(12) $BE^{id}_{e(et)} \stackrel{\mathrm{def}}{=} \lambda x.\lambda y.x = y$

Within traditional approaches to *be* there is no consensus with respect to the analysis of predicative definites as in (10b). Some authors (e.g. Higginbotham (1987: 49)) assume that definites have a predicative denotation and hence require *be* of predication. Others take definites to be "referential" only, and consequently assume that such cases involve *be* of identity. More will be said on this question in the following sections.

An alternative to this traditional view is proposed by Montague in his 1970 (EFL) and 1973 (PTQ) articles. Montague's approach was followed by (among others) Keenan and Faltz (1985). These authors assign APs and PPs the type of predicate modifiers, which amounts to $(et)(et)$ in extensional terms. One motivation for this move is compositional: constructions like *the* BLUE *chair* or *the chair* IN THE ROOM are easily analyzed if the predicate modifier type is assigned to the underlined AP or PP. Another reason is the so-called *non-intersective* interpretation of certain adjectives, discussed, among others, in Kamp (1975) and Keenan and Faltz (1985: 118–134). For example, there is a difference between the interpretation of the sentence *Jumbo is a small elephant* and the interpretation of the conjunction *Jumbo is small and Jumbo is an elephant*. The first sentence does not entail the second, because Jumbo may be a small elephant but still fail to be small, at least under the common interpretation of the word. Kamp and Keenan and Faltz show that such facts can be accounted for by assuming the $(et)(et)$ type for the adjective *small*.[5] If APs and PPs are assigned the general type $(et)(et)$, then the analysis of cases like (9) becomes problematic for the traditional approach: *be* of predication of type $(et)(et)$ cannot combine with an AP or a PP of the same type via function application. To solve this problem, both Montague (in EFL) and Keenan and Faltz use *be* of predication of a higher type: a function from predicate modifiers to predicates. Keenan and Faltz's definition is repeated in (13) below in type theoretical notation. This definition ensures that a sentence like *Jumbo is small* is true iff for some predicate P, Jumbo is a small P.[6]

In order to treat the predicative NPs in (10), a different strategy is used. In the PTQ/Keenan and Faltz systems all NPs are treated as quantifiers. Montague proposes, and Keenan and Faltz adopt, a second denotation of *be* as a function from quantifiers to predicates. This is the BE function of the Partee triangle and it is repeated in (14).

(13) $\text{BE}^{\text{kf}}_{((et)(et))(et)} \overset{\text{def}}{=} \lambda M_{(et)(et)}.\lambda x.\exists P_{et}[(M(P))(x)]$

(14) $\text{BE}_{((et)t)(et)} \overset{\text{def}}{=} \lambda Q_{(et)t}.\lambda x.Q(\{x\})$

This definition of BE has the effect of taking only the singletons from a quantifier and constructing the predicate that holds precisely of the entities in these singletons. For instance, in sentence (10a) Montague lets the indefinite *a teacher* denote the existential generalized quantifier: $\{A : A \cap \textbf{teacher}' \neq \emptyset\}$. The set of singletons in this quantifier is the set of singletons $\{x\}$ such that $\{x\} \cap \textbf{teacher}' \neq \emptyset$. The predicate we get by inspecting the entities in these singletons is just the predicate **teacher**′ itself. Thus, the denotation of the expression *be a teacher* is the same as the denotation of the noun *teacher*. Consequently (10a) is analyzed correctly. In (10c) the denotation of *be Sue* is the singleton $\{\textbf{s}'\}$, as the entity **s**′ constitutes the only singleton in the quantifier denotation of the proper name. This leads to a correct analysis of the sentence as a statement of identity between **s**′ and the entity generating the principal ultrafilter denoted by the subject *this woman*. Also the combination of BE with definite NPs as in (10b) yields a correct interpretation, given Montague's quantificational analysis of definites.

Partee (1987) proposes a variation on Montague's analysis of *be* constructions. For Partee APs and PPs have *et* as one of their possible types.[7] This allows her either to adopt a traditional *be* of predication for sentences like (9) or to assume that *be* makes no semantic contribution in these circumstances (Partee is inconclusive about this point). As for cases such as (10), with predicative NPs, Partee (1987: 122) uses Montague's definition of BE but proposes to "treat this operator not as the meaning of the word *be* but as a type-shifting functor that we apply to the generalized quantifier meaning of an NP whenever we find the NP in an *et* position." Partee shows that this idea eliminates the need to assume lexical ambiguity of *be*, as well as other items that give rise to predicative interpretations of NPs. For instance, the sentences in (15) demonstrate that the verb *consider* is like *be* in that it can have both adjectives and noun phrases as arguments.

(15) a. Mary considers John competent in semantics.

b. Mary considers John an authority on unicorns.

Montague's strategy would imply that the verb *consider* must be analyzed as ambiguous between an interpretation that takes $(et)(et)$ arguments (for adjectives) and an entry that takes $(et)t$ arguments (for NPs). Partee's use of the BE operator gives NPs an adjectival denotation, so that there is no need for verbs like *consider* to select arguments of the (*et*)*t* type: the adjective-taking denotation of the verb is sufficient. This approach is more attractive than the ambiguity strategy, and not only for conceptual reasons: Partee notes that her approach allows an analysis of cases like (16) below, where an indefinite is conjoined with an adjective.

(16) Mary considers John competent in semantics and an authority on unicorns.

In Montague's approach such constructions do not get any straightforward analysis, as noun phrases and adjectives are of different types. More examples of this sort are given in (17) and (18), reproduced from Sag et al. (1985), which provides a syntactic account of such coordinations of "unlike" categories.

(17) Pat has become a banker and very conservative.

(18) Pat is either stupid or a liar.

The following sentence shows that even proper nouns can appear in coordinations with "predicative" categories.

(19) The place we're looking for is either Oslo or in the north of Norway.

These English examples support Partee's argument that the predicative function of NPs cannot simply result from the copula denotation, as in the Montague/Keenan and Faltz analysis. Moreover, sentence (19) shows that also the traditional assumption on the ambiguity of *be* is not a complete solution. In this sentence the proper name *Oslo* would motivate *be* of identity but the PP would require *be* of predication, hence the traditional assumption that *be* is ambiguous is problematic here.

   Cross-linguistically, the point is even more general. As Keenan and Faltz (1985: 187) note, many languages can convey the meaning of *be* constructions in English without employing any overt copula. Such verbless constructions are exemplified by the following Hebrew sentences.

(20) dana gvoha / ba-xeder
      Dana tall   / in-the-room
      "Dana *is* tall/in the room"

(21) dana mora   / ha-mora
      Dana teacher / the-teacher
      "Dana *is a* teacher/the teacher"

   Doron (1983) is an extensive study of these phenomena, which will be addressed in section 4.3 below. Sentences like (21) are problematic for Montague's analysis for the same reason as the English example (15b).[8] Since Montague holds the copula responsible for predicative occurrences of NPs, it is unclear how a predicative denotation can be obtained when no copula appears.[9] Partee allows the necessary "semantic glue" to be introduced also covertly, which provides a preliminary account of the Hebrew data as well.

4.1.3   Problems with Partee's use of BE

Despite the advantages of Partee's analysis of *be* over Montague's analysis, and even over the (stipulative) ambiguity analysis of *be*, there are also some problems with Partee's proposal. One problem with the use of the BE operator in Partee's paper is that it is under-motivated given the other operators she proposes: the typical cases where singular NPs appear in predicative positions are covered by the Partee triangle without requiring any application of the BE operator. For instance, proper names are assumed to be basically of type *e* and hence their denotation can be lifted by the *Quine* operator as in (7) into the correct *et* denotation. A similar point holds for definites, because these can also be interpreted as being of type *e* using the *iota* operator. Simple singular indefinites as in the Hebrew sentence (21) may come with no overt determiner. In such languages there is no reason to use a covert **E** operator in order to lift the noun denotation to a quantifier and then postulate a covert BE operator in order to lower it back to the original predicate. If the traditional predicative treatment of these indefinites is retained, then both the BE operator and the **E** operator are redundant here.

To my knowledge, the only situations where Partee's strategy strictly requires the usage of BE are the examples she gives in which the determiner *no* occurs in predicative nominal constructions, as in (22) below. Here, the standard generalized quantifier denotation of the post-copula noun phrase can be lowered using BE, which leads to the correct analysis in (22a).

(22) John is no friend of mine.
   a. $\text{BE}(\textbf{no}'(\textbf{friend}'))(\textbf{j}')$
      $\Leftrightarrow (\text{BE}(\lambda P.P \cap \textbf{friend}' = \emptyset))(\textbf{j}')$
      $\Leftrightarrow (\lambda x.\{x\} \cap \textbf{friend}' = \emptyset)(\textbf{j}')$
      $\Leftrightarrow \{\textbf{j}'\} \cap \textbf{friend}' = \emptyset$
      $\Leftrightarrow \neg\textbf{friend}'(\textbf{j}')$

There are reasons for doubting, however, whether this single construction provides sufficient motivation for introducing a general BE strategy. As Partee remarks, cases like (22) are stylistically "marked" in English, as opposed to the natural examples of (10). More importantly, if Partee's analysis is correct, we should expect a similar analysis in cases like (23) below, where the determiner *no* appears in its plural form. However, if *no* in (23) has the determiner denotation that generalized quantifier theory assigns to it, which is equivalent to the denotation of *exactly zero*, sentence (24) should be just as good as (23), contrary to fact.

(23) John and Mary are no friends of mine.

(24) *John and Mary are exactly zero friends of mine.

Furthermore, if the analysis of (22) is given in terms of a lowered generalized quantifier, we may expect it to apply also to such a generalized quantifier when it is modified by an exception phrase as in (25). Using standard analyses of exceptive constructions in generalized quantifier theory,[10] Partee's BE analysis generates the coherent reading (25a): "this person is a friend of mine and he is John." However, (25) is uninterpretable.

(25) *This person is no friend of mine except John.
  a. $\mathbf{BE}(\lambda P.P \cap \mathbf{friend'} = \{\mathbf{j'}\})(\mathbf{this\_person'})$
  $\Leftrightarrow (\lambda x.\{x\} \cap \mathbf{friend'} = \{\mathbf{j'}\})(\mathbf{this\_person'})$
  $\Leftrightarrow \mathbf{friend'}(\mathbf{this\_person'}) \wedge \mathbf{this\_person'} = \mathbf{j'}$

A similar problem appears with the following plural variation of (25).

(26) *These people are no friends of mine except John and Mary.

There is an additional complication in Partee's approach. In general, since BE is assumed to be available for all NPs, Partee has to resort to pragmatics in order to account for the unacceptability of certain NPs in predicative positions. For instance, Partee's account predicts that sentence (27) below will be true in case there is only one teacher. Partee proposes that this situation is ruled out due to pragmatic factors. However, this line of reasoning predicts that also other sentences with *every* such as (28) below, are just as bad as (27) in a situation with exactly one teacher. It is quite clear that this is not the case. For example, the continuation in (27a) does not make sentence (27) any better. By contrast, the discourse (28)-(28a) is perfectly coherent.[11]

(27) *John is every teacher in this school.
  a. #This is because John is the *only* teacher in this school.

(28) Every teacher in this school is here.
  a. This is because there is only one teacher in this school, and he is here.

To conclude, I think that Partee's use of the BE operator has more disadvantages than advantages. Partee needs BE in her system only for cases like (22). However, even for such cases which have *no* in predicative constructions, the BE operator does not provide a sufficiently general analysis. Given Partee's other assumptions, it seems advantageous to do away with the BE operator altogether. In agreement with this conclusion, the proposal in the next sections (especially section 4.3) is to use only a *restricted* mapping from quantifiers to predicates, rather than a general procedure. Consequently, cases of predicative NPs headed by *no* as in (22) and (23) are not accounted for. Like Doron (1983: 160–161), I believe that a correct treatment of such examples should involve an analysis of *no* as invoking predicate or sentence negation, rather than the standard determiner analysis of *no* that Partee adopts.[12]

However, since any analysis of these constructions would require a detailed study of English negation in general, I do not attempt to provide one here.

4.2 Category-Shifting Principles

The aim of the flexible mechanism proposed in this section is to integrate Partee's approach with the treatment of coordinate and indefinite NPs of the previous chapters. Subsection 4.2.1 introduces the general paradigm of category shifting. Subsection 4.2.2 illustrates the use of this system for the treatment of singular NPs and their coordinations, in argument and predicate positions. Subsection 4.2.3 discusses a major challenge for the extension of this system for dealing with *plural* NP coordinations. This problem is handled using a predicative analysis of definites in subsection 4.2.4, which will be further motivated later in this chapter, and application of a distributivity operator at the NP level, defined in subsection 4.2.5. Subsection 4.2.6 shows some consequences of the proposed system for the analysis of wide scope disjunction and collectivity. Subsection 4.2.7 deals briefly with the problem of bare plurals, and the overall proposal is summarized in subsection 4.2.8.

4.2.1 The basic proposal

Let us first introduce some terminology. Section 4.1 has discussed the common claim that in addition to their well-motivated semantic role as quantifiers, some NPs can have a predicative contribution to sentence meaning. We will say that these NPs have two *semantic categories*, which we can label $+Q$ (quantifier) and $-Q$ (predicate). As for the *type* of NPs, I reject the Partee/Roth assumption that some NPs can denote non-boolean e-type individuals. Adopting Bennett's typing of plurals we therefore have the following three types for singular and plural NPs of the two semantic categories:

et   singular predicates

(et)t   singular quantifiers and plural predicates

((et)t)t   plural quantifiers

I will henceforth omit parentheses when referring to these types. Note that the informal terms "singular" and "plural" indicate the kind of individuals that denotations range over and they do not necessarily pertain to morphological number. The complex relations between the "semantic number" feature and morphological number will be studied in chapter 5. In this system the *ett* type can be used for both predicative and quantificational noun phrases. This creates some problems, because we can no longer count on the type system to rule out semantically ill-formed operations like the conjunction of an *ett* predicate and an *ett* quantifier or the application of an *ett* predicate to another predicate of type *et*. For the time being, I use the informal labels "singular quantifier" and "plural quantifier" in order to distinguish between the two uses of the *ett* type. In section 4.4 this distinction will be addressed more formally.

Having adopted these notions, we may now move on to the basic semantic assumptions of the system. The following three assumptions concern the lexical meaning of some of the main items analyzed in this chapter.

(A1)   Proper names are lexically quantificational: they denote *ett* type principal ultrafilters.

(A2)   The articles *a* and *the*, and the simple numerals *two, three*, etc., denote predicate modifiers.

(A3)   The copula *be* does not have any denotation, or denotes the identity function on predicates.

Assumption (A1), re-adopted from chapter 2, has by now become a habit. Assumption (A2) follows chapter 3. It implies that simple indefinite NPs, as well as definites, initially denote predicative functions. The article *some* will be given a slightly different analysis in section 4.3. Assumption (A3) concerns the trivial semantics of the copula *be*, which reflects the traditional assumption regarding *be* of predication. Like Partee's proposal and unlike traditional approaches, the present account avoids the postulation of a separate "*be* of identity*." Section 4.4 will show some evidence that the identity function denotation of *be* is preferable to the assumption that *be* is meaningless.

The major basic assumption to be made is that the semantic system includes *category shifting principles* that map NP denotations of one semantic category (quantifier or predicate) to denotations of the other semantic category available for that NP. As argued in chapter 2, the coordination-plurality problem motivates a *minimum* sort operator that maps quantifiers to predicates. Chapter 3 argued for an analysis of simple indefinites which uses a *choice function* mechanism that shifts predicates to quantifiers: a predicate P is mapped to the quantifier $\langle f \rangle(P)$, where f is a choice function that is existentially closed in the compositional interpretation of the sentence and $\langle \ \rangle$ is a mapping from choice functions to determiners. The main assumption of the present chapter, listed below as hypothesis 3, is that these two category-shifting principles should be used instead of the flexibility operators of the Partee triangle.

Hypothesis 3 (the category shifting hypothesis)   The category shifting principles of the min operator and the CF mechanism are the general procedures for predicate-quantifier flexibility in the analysis of the NP.

For ease of reference, the definitions of the minimum operator and choice functions are repeated below.

(29) **Minimum Sort**

$$\min_{(\tau t)(\tau t)} \stackrel{\text{def}}{=} \lambda Q_{\tau t}.\lambda A_\tau.Q(A) \wedge \forall B \in Q[B \sqsubseteq A \to B = A]$$
(min(X) is the set of minimal objects in X)

(30) **Choice Functions**

$$CH_{((\tau t)\tau)t} \overset{def}{=} \lambda f_{(\tau t)\tau}.\forall P_{\tau t} \neq \emptyset[P(f(P))]$$

(the set of choice functions of type $(\tau t)\tau$)

$$\langle \ \rangle_{((\tau t)\tau)((\tau t)((\tau t)t))} \overset{def}{=} \lambda g_{(\tau t)\tau}.\lambda X_{\tau t}.\lambda Y_{\tau t}.X \neq \emptyset \wedge Y(g(X))$$

(lifting τ-based choice functions to τ-based determiners)

In section 3.7 it was shown that the CF mechanism, in its variable free implementation, is in fact a generalization of the existential **E** operator, defined below.[13]

(31) $\mathbf{E} \overset{def}{=} \lambda A.\lambda B.\exists x[A(x) \wedge B(x)]$
$= \lambda A.\lambda B.\exists f[CH(f) \wedge \langle f \rangle(A)(B)]$

For the sake of presentation it is in many cases notationally convenient to mention only the **E** operator without the CF derivation that leads to it. Since **E** is in fact an elaboration of a CF derivation, I will often refer to the category shift from predicates to quantifiers as the *E/CF* mechanism.

4.2.2 Examples: singular NPs and their coordinations

The **C** operator of chapter 2 is the composition of existential raising and the minimum sort operator. It follows from this that the above assumptions account for the analysis of the coordination-plurality problem with singular conjuncts that was given in chapter 2. This is illustrated below for our prototypical example *Mary and John met*.

(32) $\exists f[CH(f) \wedge \langle f \rangle(\min(M \sqcap J))(\mathbf{meet'})]$
   $\Leftrightarrow \mathbf{E}(\min(M \sqcap J))(\mathbf{meet'})$
   $\Leftrightarrow (\mathbf{C}(M \sqcap J))(\mathbf{meet'})$
   $\Leftrightarrow \mathbf{meet'}(\{\mathbf{m'}, \mathbf{j'}\})$

Hypothesis 3 also contains a restatement of the assumptions of chapter 3 that were designed to account for the scope problem of indefinites. In addition, the introduction of the min operator as a separate category shift can be shown to allow a preliminary analysis of predicative NPs as well. Consider sentence (10c), reproduced below as (33). The min operator maps the denotation of *Sue*, $S = \{A : s' \in A\}$, to the *ett* predicate that holds only of the singleton $\{s'\}$. This necessitates some adjustment of the type of the subject NP in order to derive a truth-value for the sentence. One way to do that is to apply the category shifts min and the **E** (i.e. the CF mechanism) successively. This analysis is given in (33a).

(33) This woman is Sue.
   a. $(\mathbf{E}(\min(\llbracket\text{this woman}\rrbracket)))(\min(S))$
      On the assumption that $\llbracket\text{this woman}\rrbracket = \lambda P.P(a_c)$, where $a_c \in \mathbf{woman'}$ is determined by the context of utterance:
      $\Leftrightarrow (\mathbf{E}(\min(\lambda P.P(a_c))))(\min(S))$
      $\Leftrightarrow \{\{a_c\}\} \cap \{\{s'\}\} \neq \emptyset$
      $\Leftrightarrow a_c = s'$

This analysis of predicative NPs does not involve operations of type lowering: even min is only a type sort operator. This means that the subject of (33) must be of type *ettt*. More on this necessary lifting from *ett* to *ettt* will be said in chapter 5 (see the operator *qfit* on page 235). This higher-type analysis may seem too complicated for simple singular sentences, but the same assumptions can also be profitably exploited for the analysis of plural predicative NPs. The analysis of sentence (34) in (34a) is parallel to the analysis of sentence (33). The only difference is that in sentence (34) the subject denotation need not be lifted, as it is basically of type *ettt*.

(34) These women are Sue and Mary.
   a. $[\![$these women$]\!](\min(S \sqcap M))$
      On the assumption that $[\![$these women$]\!] = \lambda \mathcal{P}.\mathcal{P}(A_c)$, where $\emptyset \neq A_c \subseteq$ **woman**$'$:
      $\Leftrightarrow (\lambda \mathcal{P}.\mathcal{P}(A_c))(\{\{\mathbf{s}', \mathbf{m}'\}\})$
      $\Leftrightarrow A_c = \{\mathbf{s}', \mathbf{m}'\}$

We see that the category shift min, which was used in chapter 2 for collectivizing simple NP coordinations in argument positions, is now used for analyzing "collective conjunctions" as in (34), where the predicative character of the coordination is more evident.

A similar method can be used for treating predicates that result from conjoining indefinites in predicative positions. Note first that coordinations with indefinites can give rise to singular predicates, as illustrated in (35). The analysis in (35a) is straightforward, due to assumption (A2) on the predicative nature of *a* indefinites.

(35) Mary is an author and a teacher.
   a. M(**author**$' \sqcap$ **teacher**$'$)
      $\Leftrightarrow$ **author**$'(\mathbf{m}') \wedge$ **teacher**$'(\mathbf{m}')$

However, coordinations of indefinites also give rise to plural collective predicates, as exemplified in sentence (36) below.[14] This phenomenon is dealt with using the CF reading of the indefinites and subsequent application of the min operator, as in (36a).

(36) These (two) women are an author and a teacher.
   a. $\exists f \exists g[\mathrm{CH}(f) \wedge \mathrm{CH}(g) \wedge [\![$these women$]\!](\min(\langle f \rangle(\mathbf{author}') \sqcap \langle g \rangle(\mathbf{teacher}')))]$
      On the assumption that $[\![$these women$]\!] = \lambda \mathcal{P}.\mathcal{P}(A_c)$, where $\emptyset \neq A_c \subseteq$ **woman**$'$:
      $\Leftrightarrow \exists f \exists g[\mathrm{CH}(f) \wedge \mathrm{CH}(g) \wedge (\lambda \mathcal{P}.\mathcal{P}(A_c))(\min(\langle f \rangle(\mathbf{author}') \sqcap \langle g \rangle(\mathbf{teacher}')))]$
      $\Leftrightarrow \exists x \exists y[\mathbf{author}'(x) \wedge \mathbf{teacher}'(y) \wedge (\lambda \mathcal{P}.\mathcal{P}(A_c))(\min(\lambda P_1.P_1(x) \sqcap \lambda P_2.P_2(y)))]$
      $\Leftrightarrow \exists x \exists y[\mathbf{author}'(x) \wedge \mathbf{teacher}'(y) \wedge (\lambda \mathcal{P}.\mathcal{P}(A_c))(\{\{x, y\}\})]$
      $\Leftrightarrow \exists x \exists y[\mathbf{author}'(x) \wedge \mathbf{teacher}'(y) \wedge A_c = \{x, y\}]$

In cases like (36) it might seem desirable not to treat the indefinites using the CF category shift but rather to let them remain predicative. However, if we want to exploit the principal filter property of chapter 2 in order to get the collective interpretation of the conjunction then its analysis must involve quantificational denotations. A surprising argument in favor of this CF analysis of (36) will be given in section 4.3.

Note again the parallelism in the derivation of collectivity in argument and in predicate positions. For instance, when the coordination *an author and a teacher* appears in an argument position as in sentence (37) below, its collective analysis in (37a) is identical to the analysis in (36a), except that in argument positions we need further existential raising to arrive at its quantificational reading. This also holds for sentence (38) from subsection 3.3.4, which is analyzed in (38a).

(37) An author and a teacher met.
    a. $\exists f \exists g [\text{CH}(f) \wedge \text{CH}(g) \wedge \text{E}(\min(\langle f \rangle(\textbf{author}') \sqcap \langle g \rangle(\textbf{teacher}')))(\textbf{meet}')]$
        $\Leftrightarrow \exists x \exists y [\textbf{author}'(x) \wedge \textbf{teacher}(y) \wedge \textbf{meet}'(\{x, y\})]$

(38) John and some man met.
    a. $\exists f [\text{CH}(f) \wedge \text{E}(\min(\text{J} \sqcap \langle f \rangle(\textbf{man}')))(\textbf{meet}')]$
        $\Leftrightarrow \exists x [\textbf{man}'(x) \wedge \textbf{meet}'(\{\textbf{j}', x\})]$

4.2.3   The problem of plural NP coordination

The considerations above suggest that a flexibility mechanism that involves only the min and E/CF category shifts can account for the semantics of singular, plural and coordinate NPs in both argument and predicate positions. As far as singular NPs and their coordinations concern, I believe the assumptions above are indeed sufficient. However, for the analysis of simple plural definites and indefinites the mechanism sketched above fails to generate some desired interpretations. To see that, consider the following example from chapter 2.

(39) Two Americans and three Russians made an excellent basketball team.

The prominent reading of this sentence asserts the existence of two Americans and three Russians who *together* made an excellent team. However, the two predicates that the conjoined plurals denote are of type *ett*. Applying the minimum operator to (one of) these predicates would generate undesired interpretations, and would go against the use of this operator as applying to quantifiers.[15] The only readings that are generated by the system so far are the ones where the E/CF mechanism applies, either to each predicative conjunct separately, or to the conjunction as a whole. These two possibilities are given below.

(40) a. $((\text{E}(\textbf{two}'(\textbf{americans}'))) \sqcap (\text{E}(\textbf{three}'(\textbf{russians}'))))(\textbf{excellent\_team}')$
    b. $(\text{E}((\textbf{two}'(\textbf{americans}')) \sqcap (\textbf{three}'(\textbf{russians}'))))(\textbf{excellent\_team}')$

Proposition (40a) reflects the unlikely (though reasonably existing) interpretation of sentence (39) that claims that there were two basketball teams of non-standard sizes. The analysis in (40b) is contradictory, because the intersection of predicates with plural individuals of different cardinality (two and three respectively) is necessarily empty. Each of these two strategies is useful for the analysis of other sentences, as will become evident later in this chapter.[16] But the prominent reading of sentence (39) above is not generated by the above assumptions. It is easy to see what the missing part in the analysis may be once we compare sentence (39) to the following sentence.

(41) [Jim and Bob] and [Vitaly, Boris and Yvgeny] made an excellent basketball team.

The conjunction in (41) is correctly analyzed by intersecting two "distributive" *ett* quantifiers, similar to the familiar analysis in (32) above. What we need in order to mimic this analysis also in the case of sentence (39) is to allow the indefinites to have a *quantificational ett* denotation as well. In fact, the (uncontroversial) need to have a distributive analysis of sentences with plural indefinites was recognized already in section 3.3.2, when we observed the double scope behavior of indefinites. Now, quite surprisingly, we observe a need for a distributive reading of coming from the *collective* behavior of plural indefinites in coordinations. Moreover, in order to obtain this collective reading using the proposed flexible mechanism we need to commit now to the *location* of this distributive reading, which has to be the noun phrase itself.[17] A similar point also holds for plural *definites*, in both argument and predicate positions, as illustrated by the following sentences.

(42) The Americans and the Russians made an excellent basketball team.

(43) These women are the authors and the teachers.

In sentence (42) the problem is similar to the problem in analyzing sentence (39). In sentence (43) the problematic reading is the one under which the sentence claims that the group of women is composed out of two sub-groups: the group of (contextually relevant) authors and the group of (contextually relevant) teachers.

In these cases involving coordinations of plural in/definites, the proposed analysis will derive the distributive reading by assuming that the relevant plurals are initially predicative and that the CF mechanism mapping them to quantifiers is also responsible for their (optional) distributivity. As mentioned in chapter 3, the assumption concerning the predicative nature of simple indefinites was adopted by a number of previous works. The proposed predicative analysis of definites is introduced in some detail in the following subsection, as a preparation for the treatment of distributivity as part if the CF mechanism.

4.2.4   The predicative analysis of definites

So far it was assumed, for reasons that will be clarified in section 4.3, that the reading of definites is initially predicative. This section introduces more formal details about this assumption, which allows a unified treatment using CFs of both indefinites and definite NPs.

Singular definites: two traditional approaches   A traditional logical representation of the singular definite article employs the aforementioned *iota* operator, which maps the restriction predicate of the definite into a logical argument of the main predicate. The operator is given a Strawsonian semantic interpretation along the lines sketched above, which is designed to capture the intuition that singular definites can be felicitously used only when the restriction predicate uniquely determines an entity, that is: when it denotes a singleton. If this is the case, the *iota* operator returns the entity that constitutes the singleton. If the restriction set is empty or contains more than one element, the result of applying the *iota* operator is undefined. Strawson's view of definite descriptions has been developed in various directions, but its *iota* implementation is sufficient for our purposes here.

An alternative approach is Russell's analysis of the definite as an ordinary quantifier which *truth-conditionally* requires uniqueness. According to this analysis, the celebrated sentence *The king of France is bald* is simply false in the present state of things.[18] Montague's implementation of Russell's view lets singular definite NPs denote the empty quantifier when the restriction set is not a singleton, which results in the falsity of this sentence. When the uniqueness requirement is met, the definite denotes the principal ultrafilter generated by the unique entity in the restriction set. An extensional determiner version of Montague's definition is given in (44).

(44) $\mathbf{the}^m_{(et)((et)t)} \stackrel{\text{def}}{=} \lambda A.\lambda B.|A| = 1 \wedge A \subseteq B$

The main difference between the *iota* operator and the Russell/Montague analysis involves the case where the noun fails to denote a singleton. This issue has been discussed extensively in the literature on definites and presupposition. I will not contribute to the debate, taking it that any theory of definites should decide on this matter. The present account can be easily adopted to any of these views.

Plural definites   Sharvy (1980) extends the *iota* analysis of singular definites to plural definites. A similar proposal appears in Link (1983). The first step of this extension is to define the denotation of the plural noun. In set-theoretical terminology, a plural noun denotation includes all the non-empty subsets of the denotation of its singular form.[19] For instance, the denotation of the plural noun *wolves* is defined in terms of the denotation of *wolf* as follows.

$\mathbf{wolves}'_{ett} = \lambda A_{et}.\emptyset \neq A \subseteq \mathbf{wolf}'$

Sharvy and Link propose that a definite noun phrase like *the wolves* refers to the "largest" element in the denotation of the plural noun, if there is such an element. Set-theoretically, this is the unique set in the denotation $\mathbf{wolves}'$ that is a superset of all other sets in this denotation. Such an element exists whenever the set of wolves is not empty, and then the set $\mathbf{wolf}'$ itself is the maximal element of $\mathbf{wolves}'$. Formally we arrive at the maximal elements by means of the operator of *maximum sort*, the opposite of the minimum sort operator of chapter 2 that was repeated above in (29). The polymorphic definition of the maximum operator is the following, for any boolean type τ.

(45) **Maximum Sort**

$$\max_{(\tau t)(\tau t)} = \lambda P_{\tau t}.\lambda x_\tau.P(x) \wedge \forall y \in P[x \sqsubseteq y \to x = y]$$

(max(X) is the set of maximal objects in X)

The set max(**wolves'**) is either the singleton {**wolf'**} (when the set **wolf'** is not empty) or the empty set (when **wolf'** is empty). Under Bennett's typing, both the *iota* operator and the Russell/Montague method allow a correct treatment of this maximized plural noun interpretation, as can be seen in (46) and (47), respectively.

(46) $\iota_{(\tau t)\tau} = \lambda A_{\tau t}. \begin{cases} x_\tau & \text{if } A = \{x\} \\ \text{undefined} & \text{otherwise} \end{cases}$

(47) $\mathbf{the}^{m}_{(\tau t)((\tau t)t)} = \lambda A_{\tau t}.\lambda B_{\tau t}.|A| = 1 \wedge A \subseteq B$

When wolves exist, a sentence like *The wolves gathered* is analyzed by both methods as stating that the set **wolf'** is in the extension of the predicate *gather*. When there is no wolf, the Russellian-Montagovian analysis takes the sentence to be false whereas the *iota* analysis takes it to be meaningless. The analyses are formalized in (48) and (49) below.

(48) $\mathbf{gather'}_{ett}(\iota(\max(\mathbf{wolves'}))) = \begin{cases} \mathbf{gather'}(\mathbf{wolf'}) & \text{if } \mathbf{wolf'} \neq \emptyset \\ \text{undefined} & \text{otherwise} \end{cases}$

(49) $\mathbf{the}^{m}(\max(\mathbf{wolves'}))(\mathbf{gather'})$

$\Leftrightarrow |\max(\mathbf{wolves'})| = 1 \wedge \max(\mathbf{wolves'}) \subseteq \mathbf{gather'}$

$\Leftrightarrow |\mathbf{wolf'}| \geq 1 \wedge \mathbf{gather'}(\mathbf{wolf'})$

In the *iota* analysis it is assumed that a function yields an undefined value when it applies to an undefined argument, in which case the truth value in (48) is undefined. This "percolation" of undefined values is to be obtained by a *partial* evaluation procedure, which the *iota* analysis should supply. Following Sharvy and Link, both the *iota* analysis in (48) and the Russellian/Montagovian analysis in (49) exploit the fact that the maximal collection of sets in the denotation **wolves'** contains exactly one set if and only if the set of wolves **wolf'** is not empty. When this condition holds, the maximal set of **wolves'** is the set **wolf'** itself. Both treatments detect no anomaly when the set **wolf'** contains only one member. Then *the wolves* denotes the singleton containing the unique wolf in the *iota* treatment, and the principal ultrafilter generated by this singleton (in the Russellian/Montagovian treatment). As will be suggested in section 5.4.1, the "semantic plurality" impression with plural nouns may be an effect which is not purely semantic.

Note the similarity between the ways in which the max and the min operators are used. While min maps a quantifier to a predicate, max maps a predicate to an individual. Rullmann (1995), for various reasons, proposes that maximization is a general principle in natural language. This may put flexibility and maximization/minimization operators in a broader perspective, which I will not study here. See subsection 5.5.2 for more motivation for a maximality operator.

Observe that after application of the max operator to the plural noun, the semantics that is used for singular definites applies to plural definites as well. Sharvy and Link use this observation in order to argue for a unified semantics of the definite article that holds for singulars and plurals alike. This is possible because, although the max operator is not strictly required in the analysis of singular definites, it may be used there with no particular harm. For Sharvy and Link the domain for both singular and plural individuals is the *e* domain which is assumed to be ordered by the *part-of* relation between *e* type individuals, so that max can also be used for singular definites. A similar move is possible also in Scha's (1981) boolean framework, where both singular and plural individuals are interpreted in the *et* domain. For instance, a singular noun like *wolf* is modeled by an *ett* set of singletons in the Scha system, so that max(**wolf′**) is non-empty if and only if there is exactly one singleton in the denotation of the noun. The definite article can therefore apply to this maximized set in the usual way, deriving the same results as the analysis without max. In the Scha framework we may formalize the unified denotation for the singular article as either ι ∘ max or **the**^{m} ∘ max. This unification is not so easily obtained in the Bennett typing we have adopted here, because there is no order assumed on the primitive domain of singular individuals. However, Van Benthem (1986: 62) proposes to extend the boolean order relation also to non-boolean domains. According to Van Benthem's definition, the relation $\sqsubseteq$ reduces to identity on all the non-boolean domains. Consequently, max$_{(et)(et)}$ reduces to the identity function on *et* predicates, which means that it could apply to singular definites in the Bennett framework as well. For simplicity I will not pursue Van Benthem's generalization here, assuming instead, like Bennett, that plural and singular definite articles have different meanings: the plural definite article involves maximization of the noun denotation whereas the singular article does not.

The definite article as a predicate modifier   I both the *iota* and the Russell/Montague approaches to definites, the definite article maps the restriction predicate to an "argument" denotation: in the *iota* analysis a definite denotes an entity, whereas Russell and Montague take definites to denote quantifiers. At this point I would like to propose a slight modification that is independent of the debate between the two approaches. I will treat definites as basically predicate-denoting, similar to simple indefinite descriptions. In this reformulation the definite article only modifies the noun denotation by introducing the appropriate uniqueness presupposition or truth-condition. Consider first the modificational definitions for the singular definite article in (50).

(50) Presuppositional: $\mathbf{the}^{\text{sg}}_{(et)(et)} = \lambda P. \begin{cases} P & \text{if } |P| = 1 \\ \text{undefined} & \text{otherwise} \end{cases}$

   Truth-conditional: $\mathbf{the}^{\text{sg}}_{(et)(et)} = \lambda P. \lambda x. P(x) \wedge |P| = 1$

The presuppositional denotation maps any singleton to itself and is undefined for non-singletons. The truth-conditional article also maps singletons to themselves, but non-singletons are mapped to the empty set.

As a result, a definite NP now basically denotes a predicate, so that we can apply the general E/CF category shift to definites that appear in argument position. For instance, the simple sentence (51) is analyzed using E/CF as in (51a).

(51) The wolf arrived.

   a. $\mathbf{E}(\mathbf{the}^{sg}(\mathbf{wolf}'))(\mathbf{arrive}')$
      $\Leftrightarrow \exists f[\mathrm{CH}(f) \wedge \langle f \rangle(\mathbf{the}^{sg}(\mathbf{wolf}'))(\mathbf{arrive}')]$

In the truth-conditional analysis of $\mathbf{the}^{sg}$, the analysis in (51a) states that there is a unique wolf, and that this wolf arrived. When there is a unique wolf, the definite article has no effect, and existential quantification using $\mathbf{E}$ amounts to the claim that this wolf arrived. When uniqueness is not satisfied, $\mathbf{the}^{sg}(\mathbf{wolf}')$ is the empty set in the truth-conditional analysis of $\mathbf{the}^{sg}$, and existential quantification amounts to falsity. The presuppositional denotation of $\mathbf{the}^{sg}$ should guarantee that we then get undefined truth-conditions instead of falsity. In order to avoid the partial semantics that is involved in this treatment, I will henceforth use only the Russellian analysis, without being specifically committed to it.

The modificational analysis of the plural article is analogous to the singular case, with the addition of maximization. The two versions are given below.

(52) Presuppositional: $\mathbf{the}^{pl}_{(ett)(ett)} = \lambda \mathcal{P}. \begin{cases} \max(\mathcal{P}) & \text{if } |\max(\mathcal{P})| = 1 \\ \text{undefined} & \text{otherwise} \end{cases}$

   Truth-conditional: $\mathbf{the}^{pl}_{(ett)(ett)} = \lambda \mathcal{P}.\lambda A.\max(\mathcal{P})(A) \wedge |\max(\mathcal{P})| = 1$

As an illustration of the application of the truth-conditional definition, reconsider the simple sentence in (53) below. The E/CF analysis of this sentence is given in (53a). Some simplifications show that both formulas are equivalent to the Russellian-Montagovian analysis in (49), asserting that the set of wolves is not empty and that it gathered.

(53) The wolves gathered.

   a. $\exists f_{(ett)(et)}[\mathrm{CH}(f) \wedge \langle f \rangle(\mathbf{the}^{pl}(\mathbf{wolves}'))(\mathbf{gather}')]$
      $\Leftrightarrow \mathbf{E}(\mathbf{the}^{pl}(\mathbf{wolves}'))(\mathbf{gather}')$

Given that we have anyway assumed an E/CF category shift, this modificational treatment of definites is a rather innocent variation on the previously mentioned approaches.[20] The reason for our revision will be clarified in section 4.3, where I will argue that some facts discovered by Doron (1983) call for a predicative analysis of definites.

A predicative treatment of definites simplifies their analysis in predicative positions such as in (10b). There is now no need to use the min category shift, since the denotation of definites is basically predicative. This is illustrated by the following analyses.

(54) This woman is the teacher.

   a. $[\![\text{this woman}]\!](\mathbf{the}^{sg}(\mathbf{teacher}'))$
      On the assumption that $[\![\text{this woman}]\!] = \lambda P.P(a_c)$, where $a_c \in \mathbf{woman}'$:
      $\Leftrightarrow (\lambda P.P(a_c))(\mathbf{the}^{sg}(\mathbf{teacher}'))$

$\Leftrightarrow$ $(\mathbf{the}^{\mathrm{sg}}(\mathbf{teacher}'))(a_{\mathrm{c}})$

$\Leftrightarrow$ $\mathbf{teacher}'(a_{\mathrm{c}}) \wedge |\mathbf{teacher}'| = 1$

(55) These women are the teachers.

    a. $[\![\text{these women}]\!](\mathbf{the}^{\mathrm{pl}}(\mathbf{teachers}'))$

       On the assumption that $[\![\text{these women}]\!] = \lambda \mathcal{P}.\mathcal{P}(A_{\mathrm{c}})$, where $\emptyset \neq A_{\mathrm{c}} \subseteq \mathbf{woman}'$:

       $\Leftrightarrow$ $(\lambda \mathcal{P}.\mathcal{P}(A_{\mathrm{c}}))(\mathbf{the}^{\mathrm{pl}}(\mathbf{teachers}'))$

       $\Leftrightarrow$ $(\mathbf{the}^{\mathrm{pl}}(\mathbf{teachers}'))(A_{\mathrm{c}})$

       $\Leftrightarrow$ $\max(\mathbf{teachers}')(A_{\mathrm{c}}) \wedge |\max(\mathbf{teachers}')| = 1$

       $\Leftrightarrow$ $A_{\mathrm{c}} = \mathbf{teacher}' \wedge |\mathbf{teacher}'| \geq 1$

Collectivity effects with conjunctions of singular definite NPs in predicative positions can now also be analyzed. This is illustrated in (56) below.

(56) These women are the author and the teacher.

    a. $\exists f \exists g [\mathrm{CH}(f) \wedge \mathrm{CH}(g)$

       $\wedge [\![\text{these women}]\!](\min(\langle f \rangle(\mathbf{the}^{\mathrm{sg}}(\mathbf{author}')) \sqcap \langle g \rangle(\mathbf{the}^{\mathrm{sg}}(\mathbf{teacher}'))))]$

       On the assumption that $[\![\text{these women}]\!] = \lambda \mathcal{P}.\mathcal{P}(A_{\mathrm{c}})$, where $\emptyset \neq A_{\mathrm{c}} \subseteq \mathbf{woman}'$:

       $\Leftrightarrow$ $\exists x \exists y [\mathbf{author}'(x) \wedge \mathbf{teacher}'(y) \wedge A_{\mathrm{c}} = \{x, y\}]$

       $\wedge |\mathbf{teacher}'| = 1 \wedge |\mathbf{author}'| = 1$

The statement in (56a) is similar to (36a), the formalization of the parallel case with indefinite predicative NPs, except for the additional requirement that there be a unique author and a unique teacher.

4.2.5 Deriving NP distributivity

Now that a fuller treatment of definite NPs has been introduced we can address the question of how to derive the distributive reading of plural definites and indefinites. The predicative analysis of definites as illustrated in (51b) and (53b) involves the choice function mechanism as the necessary category shift from a predicate to a quantifier. Recall that the $\langle \rangle$ operator is used to lift CFs to the determiner type in a way that avoids the empty restriction problem. I would like to propose that it is this lifting which is responsible for NP distributivity. I will use *two* lifts from CFs to determiners with plural NPs. One lift is simply the higher-type version of the $\langle \rangle$ operator defined in (30) above. That is, for any choice function f from *ett* predicates to *et* plural individuals, $\langle f \rangle$ is the determiner that maps any non-empty *ett* predicate $\mathcal{A}$ to the *ettt* principal ultrafilter generated by $f(\mathcal{A})$. Empty predicates are mapped to empty quantifiers, as before. The other CF lift, denoted $\langle \rangle^{d}$, maps f to a determiner that for a non-empty *ett* predicate $\mathcal{A}$ returns an *ett* principal *filter* generated by $f(\mathcal{A})$. The two definitions are given below.

(57) $\langle \rangle \overset{\text{def}}{=} \lambda g_{(ett)(et)}.\lambda \mathcal{A}_{ett}.\lambda \mathcal{B}_{ett}. \mathcal{A} \neq \emptyset \wedge g(\mathcal{A}) \in \mathcal{B}$

     $\langle \rangle^{d} \overset{\text{def}}{=} \lambda g_{(ett)(et)}.\lambda \mathcal{A}_{ett}.\lambda B_{et}. \mathcal{A} \neq \emptyset \wedge g(\mathcal{A}) \subseteq B$

The $\langle\,\rangle$ operator was illustrated above. To exemplify the use of the $\langle\,\rangle^d$ operator, consider sentence (58), which was used in chapter 3 as an argument for the existence of a distributive reading for sentences with plural definites. Its analysis using the $\langle\,\rangle^d$ lift is given in (58a).

(58) The girls are wearing a dress.
$$\text{a. } \exists f[\text{CH}(f) \wedge \langle f\rangle^d(\textbf{the}^{\text{pl}}(\textbf{girls}'))(\lambda x.\textbf{E}(\textbf{dress}')(\lambda y.\textbf{wear}'(y)(x)))]$$
$$\Leftrightarrow \exists f[\text{CH}(f) \wedge \textbf{the}^{\text{pl}}(\textbf{girls}') \neq \emptyset$$
$$\wedge f(\textbf{the}^{\text{pl}}(\textbf{girls}')) \subseteq \lambda x.\textbf{E}(\textbf{dress}')(\lambda y.\textbf{wear}'(y)(x))]$$
$$\Leftrightarrow \textbf{the}^{\text{pl}}(\textbf{girls}') \neq \emptyset \wedge \exists A \in \textbf{the}^{\text{pl}}(\textbf{girls}')[A \subseteq \lambda x.\textbf{E}(\textbf{dress}')(\lambda y.\textbf{wear}'(y)(x))]$$
$$\Leftrightarrow \textbf{girl}' \neq \emptyset \wedge \forall y \in \textbf{girl}' \exists x \in \textbf{dress}'[\textbf{wear}'(x)(y)]$$

A similar analysis is used for the analogous case with plural indefinites:

(59) Three girls are wearing a dress.
$$\text{a. } \exists f[\text{CH}(f) \wedge \langle f\rangle^d(\textbf{three}'(\textbf{girls}'))(\lambda x.\textbf{E}(\textbf{dress}')(\lambda y.\textbf{wear}'(y)(x)))]$$
$$\Leftrightarrow \exists f[\text{CH}(f) \wedge \textbf{three}'(\textbf{girls}') \neq \emptyset \wedge f(\textbf{the}^{\text{pl}}(\textbf{girls}'))$$
$$\subseteq \lambda x.\textbf{E}(\textbf{dress}')(\lambda y.\textbf{wear}'(y)(x))]$$
$$\Leftrightarrow \exists A \in \textbf{three}'(\textbf{girls}')[A \subseteq \lambda x.\textbf{E}(\textbf{dress}')(\lambda y.\textbf{wear}'(y)(x))]$$
$$\Leftrightarrow \exists A \subseteq \textbf{girl}'[|A| = 3 \wedge \forall y \in A \exists x \in \textbf{dress}'[\textbf{wear}'(x)(y)]]$$

The $\langle\,\rangle^d$ operator completes the formal account of plural in/definites and their distributivity. As anticipated above, this allows to derive the *collective* readings for such NPs using the minimum and the modified E/CF category shifting mechanisms. Consider first sentence (39), which is restated and analyzed below.

(60) Two Americans and three Russians made an excellent basketball team.
$$\text{a. } \exists f \exists g[\textbf{E}(\text{min}(\langle f\rangle^d(\textbf{two}'(\textbf{americans}'))$$
$$\sqcap \langle g\rangle^d(\textbf{three}'(\textbf{russians}')))) (\textbf{basketball\_team}'_{ett})]$$
$$\Leftrightarrow \exists A \subseteq \textbf{american}' \exists B \subseteq \textbf{russian}'[|A| = 2 \wedge |B| = 3$$
$$\wedge (\textbf{E}(\text{min}((\lambda P_1.A \subseteq P_1) \sqcap (\lambda P_2.B \subseteq P_2))))(\textbf{basketball\_team}')]$$
$$\Leftrightarrow \exists A \subseteq \textbf{russian}' \exists B \subseteq \textbf{american}'[|A| = 2 \wedge |B| = 3$$
$$\wedge \textbf{basketball\_team}'(A \sqcup B)]$$

In a similar fashion, sentences (42) and (43), with plural definites, get the collective interpretation of the coordination.

(61) The Americans and the Russians made an excellent basketball team.
$$\text{a. } \exists f \exists g[\textbf{E}(\text{min}(\langle f\rangle^d(\textbf{the}^{\text{pl}}(\textbf{americans}')) \sqcap \langle g\rangle^d(\textbf{the}^{\text{pl}}(\textbf{russians}'))))$$
$$(\textbf{basketball\_team}'_{ett})]$$
$$\Leftrightarrow \textbf{american}' \neq \emptyset \wedge \textbf{russian}' \neq \emptyset \wedge \textbf{basketball\_team}'(\textbf{american}' \sqcup \textbf{russian}')]$$

(62) These women are the authors and the teachers.
$$\text{a. } \exists f \exists g[\text{CH}(f) \wedge \text{CH}(g) \wedge [\![\text{these women}]\!](\text{min}(\langle f\rangle^d(\textbf{the}^{\text{pl}}(\textbf{authors}'))$$
$$\sqcap \langle g\rangle^d(\textbf{the}^{\text{pl}}(\textbf{teachers}')))))]$$

On the assumption that $[\![$these women$]\!] = \lambda \mathcal{P}.\mathcal{P}(A_c)$, where $\emptyset \neq A_c \subseteq$ **woman**$'$:

$\Leftrightarrow$ **author**$' \neq \emptyset \wedge$ **teacher**$' \neq \emptyset \wedge A_c =$ **author**$' \sqcup$ **teacher**$'$

We can now also formalize the double scope effects in sentence (63) below, which is reproduced from chapter 3. The analysis is given in (64).

(63) If three workers in our staff have a baby soon we will have to face some hard organizational problems.

(64) $\exists f[\mathrm{CH}(f) \wedge [\langle f \rangle^d (\textbf{three}'(\textbf{workers}'))(\lambda x. \exists y(\textbf{baby}'(y) \wedge \textbf{have}'(y)(x)))$
$\quad \rightarrow$ **problems**$']]$

$\Leftrightarrow$ **three**$'(\textbf{workers}') = \emptyset \vee \exists A \in \textbf{three}'(\textbf{workers}')$
$\quad [(\lambda P.A \subseteq P)(\lambda x. \exists y(\textbf{baby}'(y) \wedge \textbf{have}'(y)(x))) \rightarrow \textbf{problems}']$

$\Leftrightarrow |\textbf{worker}| < 3 \vee \exists A \subseteq \textbf{worker}'$
$\quad [|A| = 3 \wedge \forall x \in A[\exists y(\textbf{baby}'(y) \wedge \textbf{have}'(y)(x)) \rightarrow \textbf{problems}']]$

4.2.6   The generalized E/CF mechanism: consequences for collectivity and wide scope disjunction

The main difference between the way in which choice functions are used in this chapter and the mechanism of chapter 3 is that CFs apply now not only to simple indefinites but also to other predicative NP denotations. Especially, CFs can apply to predicative NP denotations that are obtained using the min operator. This has some consequences for the analysis of *or* coordinations. Consider the following sentence.

(65) Mary and [John or [John and Bill]] earned $5000 together.

The sentence can of course be true in case Mary, John and Bill earned $5000 together. However, this cannot be captured by the **C** operator of chapter 2, which is a composition of the **E** and min category shifts. The problem is the same as the complication we noted for conjunctions of indefinites in subsection 3.3.4. This can be seen as follows. The analysis of (65) that collectivizes the conjunct *Mary* with the other conjunct is the one given in (66) below.

(66) $\textbf{E} \circ \min(\mathrm{M} \sqcap (\mathrm{J} \sqcup (\mathrm{J} \sqcap \mathrm{B})))(\textbf{earn\_5000}')$

$\Leftrightarrow \textbf{E} \circ \min(\{A : \textbf{m}' \in A \wedge (\textbf{j}' \in A \vee (\textbf{j}' \in A \wedge \textbf{b}' \in A))\})(\textbf{earn\_5000}')$

$\Leftrightarrow \textbf{E} \circ \min(\{A : \textbf{m}' \in A \wedge \textbf{j}' \in A\})(\textbf{earn\_5000}')$

$\Leftrightarrow \textbf{earn\_5000}'(\{\textbf{m}', \textbf{j}'\})$

In this analysis the minimum operator applies to the standard generalized quantifier reading of the whole subject. However, this denotation "ignores" the conjunct *Bill*: it is easy to verify that the quantifier $\mathrm{M} \sqcap (\mathrm{J} \sqcup (\mathrm{J} \sqcap \mathrm{B}))$ equals $\mathrm{M} \sqcap \mathrm{J}$. This holds due to the simple boolean fact that $\mathrm{J} \sqcup (\mathrm{J} \sqcap \mathrm{B}) = \mathrm{J}$. The resulting statement in (66) claims that Mary and John collectively earned $5000. While this statement certainly entails sentence (65), it does not cover the kind of situations we are after where the three people together earned $5000 and Mary and John alone did not earn this amount.

The problem is solved once we adopt the proposal of the present chapter that the existential CF mechanism should be separated from the min operator. Then sentence (65) can also be analyzed as follows.

(67) $\exists f[\mathrm{CH}(f) \wedge \mathbf{E} \circ \min(\mathrm{M} \sqcap \langle f \rangle^d (\min(\mathrm{J}) \sqcup \min(\mathrm{J} \sqcap B)))(\mathbf{earn\_5000}')]$

$\Leftrightarrow \exists f[\mathrm{CH}(f) \wedge \mathbf{E} \circ \min(\mathrm{M} \sqcap \langle f \rangle^d(\{\{\mathbf{j}'\}\} \sqcup \{\{\mathbf{j}', \mathbf{b}'\}\}))(\mathbf{earn\_5000}')]$

$\Leftrightarrow \exists f[\mathrm{CH}(f) \wedge \mathbf{E} \circ \min(\mathrm{M} \sqcap \langle f \rangle^d(\{\{\mathbf{j}'\}, \{\mathbf{j}', \mathbf{b}'\}\}))(\mathbf{earn\_5000}')]$

$\Leftrightarrow \exists A \in \{\{\mathbf{j}'\}, \{\mathbf{j}', \mathbf{b}'\}\}[\mathbf{E} \circ \min(\mathrm{M} \sqcap \{B : A \subseteq B\})(\mathbf{earn\_5000}')]$

$\Leftrightarrow \exists A \in \{\{\mathbf{j}'\}, \{\mathbf{j}', \mathbf{b}'\}\}[\mathbf{E} \circ \min(\{B : \mathbf{m}' \in B \wedge A \subseteq B\})(\mathbf{earn\_5000}')]$

$\Leftrightarrow \exists A \in \{\{\mathbf{j}'\}, \{\mathbf{j}', \mathbf{b}'\}\}[\mathbf{earn\_5000}'(\{\mathbf{m}'\} \sqcup A)]$

$\Leftrightarrow \mathbf{earn\_5000}'(\{\mathbf{m}', \mathbf{j}'\}) \vee \mathbf{earn\_5000}'(\{\mathbf{m}', \mathbf{j}', \mathbf{b}'\})$

In this analysis, both quantificational conjuncts in the disjunction *John or* [*John and Bill*] are minimized *before* they are disjoined. These two minimizations lead to the sets $\{\{\mathbf{j}'\}\}$ and $\{\{\mathbf{j}', \mathbf{b}'\}\}$, the union of which is the set $\{\{\mathbf{j}'\}, \{\mathbf{j}', \mathbf{b}'\}\}$. Application of $\mathbf{E}$ at this stage would not help: $\mathbf{E}$ leads to an *ettt* quantifier, which excludes further collectivization with *Mary*, since the min operator applies only to *ett* denotations.[21] However, application of a distributed choice function $\langle f \rangle^d$ picks up one of the members in the set $\{\{\mathbf{j}'\}, \{\mathbf{j}', \mathbf{b}'\}\}$ and returns the corresponding principal filter it generates. This denotation is what we need, as it is conjoined with the denotation of *Mary* and can further be collectivized to get to the desired reading.

This interpretation of sentence (65) can be informally described as a case where disjunction "takes scope" over the collective interpretation of the conjunction. This is made possible by our decision to define the CF mechanism as a general category-shifting principle. The same mechanism can contribute to the solution of other scope puzzles with *or*, which were first addressed by Rooth and Partee (1982). Consider the following sentence (68). The paraphrase that reflects the standard "narrow scope" reading of the disjunctive NP is formalized in (69).

(68) If Bill praises Mary or Sue then John will be happy.

(69) $[\mathbf{praise}'(\mathbf{m}')(\mathbf{b}') \vee \mathbf{praise}'(\mathbf{s}')(\mathbf{b}')] \rightarrow \mathbf{happy}'(\mathbf{j}')$

The reading in (69) is true in case John does not care which of the two girls Bill praises: he will be happy if Mary is praised and he will also be happy if Sue is praised. However, this reading does not capture all the situations in which sentence (68) can be true. Suppose John likes one of the two girls and wants Bill to praise that girl. Then the sentence is not falsified if Bill praises the other girl and John remains unhappy: under the WS *or* reading it is a *particular* girl that John wants Bill to praise. This kind of interpretation of (68) can be highlighted by adding to the sentence a statement like *but I don't know which one of the two girls John wants Bill to praise*. The reading of (68) that could capture this effect, the so-called "wide scope *or*" reading of the sentence, is paraphrased below.

(70) If Bill praises Mary then John will be happy or if Bill praises Sue then John will be happy.

This phenomenon resembles the wide scope of indefinites that was treated in chapter 3. Since the NP disjunction in (68) is inside a scope island (the *if* clause), its "wide scope" interpretation over the conditional island is not explained by the standard scope mechanism. However, the CF mechanism can capture this phenomenon when it is used as a general existential category shift. As in (67), the disjunction is minimized and a choice function that is existentially closed from outside the scope island picks one of the members in the resulting set. This is illustrated in (71) below, which accurately mimics the paraphrase of (68) in (70).

(71) $\exists f[\text{CH}(f) \wedge [\langle f \rangle^d(\min(M \sqcup S))(\lambda x.\mathbf{praise}'(x)(\mathbf{b}')) \rightarrow \mathbf{happy}'(\mathbf{j}')]]$

$\Leftrightarrow \exists f[\text{CH}(f) \wedge [\langle f \rangle^d(\{\{\mathbf{m}'\}, \{\mathbf{s}'\}\})(\lambda x.\mathbf{praise}'(x)(\mathbf{b}')) \rightarrow \mathbf{happy}'(\mathbf{j}')]]$

$\Leftrightarrow \exists A \in \{\{\mathbf{m}'\}, \{\mathbf{s}'\}\}[(\lambda P.A \subseteq P)(\lambda x.\mathbf{praise}'(x)(\mathbf{b}')) \rightarrow \mathbf{happy}'(\mathbf{j}')]$

$\Leftrightarrow [\mathbf{praise}'(\mathbf{m}')(\mathbf{b}') \rightarrow \mathbf{happy}'(\mathbf{j}')] \vee [\mathbf{praise}'(\mathbf{s}')(\mathbf{b}') \rightarrow \mathbf{happy}'(\mathbf{j}')]$

These facts point out that the replacement of the **E** operator in the Partee triangle by the CF mechanism is not just motivated by conceptual elegance. Some cases require CFs also when no indefinites are involved.

4.2.7 A note on bare plurals

As mentioned above, in the proposed system it is natural to assign a basically predicative denotation to bare plurals, as they easily appear in predicative positions (see (72) below) and have an existential reading (see (73)). Bare plurals also get collectivized in coordinations, both in argument positions and in predicate positions. This is illustrated in (74).

(72) These women are teachers.

(73) Teachers arrived early yesterday.

(74) a. Women and men gathered in the room yesterday.
　　 b. These people are women and men.

This is the same behavior as has been observed above for singular indefinites headed by *a*. It might, therefore, seem reasonable to treat bare plurals simply as the plural counterpart of singular indefinites with the *a* article. Carlson (1977: ch. 2), however, is a bold and suggestive attack on this very idea. Two of Carlson's objections are especially important in the context of the present book. First, Carlson argues that bare plurals do not take wide scope as easily as singular indefinites. Moreover, Carlson claims that there are cases where bare plurals take scope *narrower* than items they c-command while singular indefinites do not.

One of Carlson's examples for the first claim is the contrast between (75a) and (75b), where only the first sentence gets the wide scope interpretation.

(75) a. John didn't see a spot on the floor.
          WS (available): "There was a spot on the floor that John didn't see."
      b. John didn't see spots on the floor.
          WS (unavailable): "There were spots on the floor that John didn't see."

An example for Carlson's second claim is the contrast between the infelicity of (76a), which "means that there is some omnipresent dog" vis-à-vis the felicity of (76b), the preferred reading of which has the bare plural in the scope of the quantificational adverb.

(76) a. #A dog was everywhere.
      b. Dogs were everywhere.

Such differences in scopal behavior between bare plurals and singular indefinites are of course problematic for any extension of the present account to bare plurals: a CF mechanism that does not distinguish between the two kinds of indefinites would generate a non-existent reading in (75b) and would not account for the contrast in (76). Such a CF treatment would predict that bare plurals have the same existential scope possibilities as plural *some* indefinites. As Carlson argues, this is inadequate.

Carlson's account of these differences between bare plurals and singular indefinites involves his well-known *kind* reading of bare plurals, which allows a unified account of their existential and generic uses. This proposal has led to an on-going debate about the nature of genericity, as reflected in, for instance, the volume Carlson and Pelletier (1995). See also Chierchia (1998a), which includes a neo-Carlsonian analysis of bare plurals within a flexible view on noun phrase interpretation. The generic interpretation of bare plurals and its relations with their existential reading are of course major problems for semantic theory. I will not be able to contribute here to the solution of these problems.

4.2.8 Summary

In the proposed system there are two "semantic features" relevant for NP interpretation. An NP denotation is either predicational or quantificational, and in both guises it ranges over singular or plural individuals. Type et is the type of predicates over singular entities. Type ett serves for both singular quantifiers and plural predicates. Type $ettt$ is the type of plural quantifiers. A predicational type can be lifted to a quantificational type of the same "semantic number" using a lifted choice function $\langle f \rangle$. Denotations of the double-purpose type ett can move from singular-quantificational to plural-predicative via the min category shift and they can move in the reverse direction via a distributed choice function $\langle f \rangle^d$. This array of category shifting operators, as graphically illustrated in figure 4.2, is proposed as an alternative of the Partee triangle in figure 4.1. This new configuration accounts for effects of collectivity and distributivity with singular and plural NPs and their coordinations, in both argument and predicate positions.

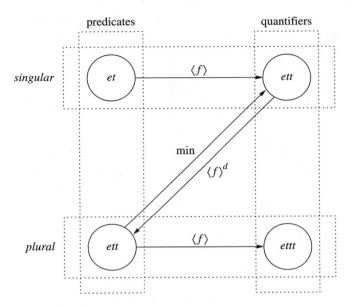

Figure 4.2
The Category Shifts

4.3   Syntactic Restrictions on Category Shifting

Any theory that employs phonologically invisible operations—like the flexibility mechanisms employed throughout this book—should provide a principled account of the conditions under which these operations apply. As far as semantic type shifting concerns, there
are two existing approaches to the restrictions on their application.

1. A "liberal" approach: type shifting is allowed when possible.
2. A "lazy" approach: type shifting is allowed (only) when inevitable.

The liberal technique is used by Groenendijk and Stokhof (1989) and Hendriks (1993),
where a type shifting operator may be introduced anywhere in the compositional analysis
of the sentence, provided that its type matches the types of the elements it combines with. In
the "lazy" *type fitting* strategy of Partee and Rooth (1983), which was discussed in subsection
2.3.5, type shifting only applies when this is strictly necessary for the meaning composition
process. These situations where the type calculus alone cannot apply are referred to as *type
mismatch*. In subsection 2.3.5 we have seen some problems for a lazy application of the **C**
operator, which is the composition of the min operator and the E/CF mechanism. For this
reason type fitting is not the right approach to constraining the application of these category
shifting operators.

In this section it is shown that also the liberal approach to type shifting is problematic when it comes to the application of category shifting. It is proposed that category shifting principles are *syntax driven* and that their application is governed by the internal structure of nominals. Using Abney's (1987) analysis of nominals as *Determiner Phrases* (DPs), it is proposed that category shifting applies within the DP only at the D′ level. The phrasal NP and DP levels are semantically "rigid": they inherit their semantic categories from the denotations of their immediate constituents, with no application of covert flexibility operators. Consequently, the NP level is unambiguously predicative whereas the DP level is unambiguously quantificational. This proposal is referred to as the *Flexible DP Hypothesis*.

After introducing the motivations for restricting category shifts in subsection 4.3.1, the Flexible DP Hypothesis is presented in subsection 4.3.2. Its implications are further discussed in subsections 4.3.3 and 4.3.4, where evidence is brought from accusative marking in Hebrew, verbless predication, and appositional uses of conjunction. Subsection 4.3.5 studies further the interpretation of plural predicative nominals.

4.3.1   Motivation for restricting category shifts

Three central phenomena have been treated in this book using category shifting principles: collectivity of NP coordination, wide scope beyond syntactic islands and predicative readings of nominals. Let us consider some reasons for restricting category shifting in the treatment of these phenomena.

Predicate nominals   In subsection 4.1.3 some problems for Partee's (1987) treatment of predicative nominals were pointed out. The problematic aspect of Partee's proposal is the assumption that the meanings of all nominals can be shifted into predicates using Montague's BE operator. Some of the problematic examples for this proposal are reproduced below.

(77) *These people are no friends of mine except John and Mary.

(78) *John and Mary are exactly zero friends of mine.

(79) *John is every teacher in this room.

In these unacceptable examples the predicative nominal basically denotes a quantifier, but its lowering into a predicate using the BE operator results in an acceptable statement. The principles for ruling out such interpretations are not explained in Partee's paper. Similar problems appear if the category shifting mechanism proposed above freely applies to these nominals. For instance, assume sentence (77) were to be analyzed using category shifting principles. Application of the min operator to the standard generalized quantifier denotation of the predicative nominal would derive the following predicate.

(80) $\min(\lambda P.P \cap \mathbf{friend}' = \{\mathbf{j}', \mathbf{m}'\})$
      $= \{\{\mathbf{j}', \mathbf{m}'\}\}$

The only minimal set in the denotation of the nominal *no friends of mine except John and Mary* is the set consisting of John and Mary themselves. Composition of the resulting predicate with the denotation of the subject *these people* would derive a perfectly acceptable statement, equivalent to the sentence *These people are John and Mary*. However, this cannot be the meaning of example (77), which is furthermore unacceptable. Similar problems would appear if category shifting principles applied in (78) or (79). Example (78) would be analyzed as a contradiction. In (79), application of min to the predicate nominal would require applying category shifting to the subject as well, generating a non-existent reading equivalent to *John is the only teacher in this room*.

Collective interpretations   The following pairs of sentences show some contrasts in the availability of collective interpretations.[22]

(81) a.   Eleven students I know are the team that won the cup yesterday.
     b.   *Exactly eleven students I know are the team that won the cup yesterday.

(82) a.   Mary and John are a nice couple.
     b.   *Both Mary and John are a nice couple.

(83) a.   The teachers are numerous.
     b.   *All the teachers are numerous.

In the *a* examples a collective interpretation is possible (and prominent). The *b* examples are unacceptable, but application of category shifting operators to them may generate collective analyses equivalent to the collective readings of the *a* sentences. For instance, consider the following analysis of the subject in (81b).

(84) $\mathbf{E}(\min(\lambda P.|P \cap \mathbf{teacher'}| = 11))(\mathbf{team\_that\_won\_the\_cup'}_{ett})$
     $\Leftrightarrow \mathbf{E}(\lambda P.P \subseteq \mathbf{teacher'} \wedge |P| = 11)(\mathbf{team\_that\_won\_the\_cup'})$
     $\Leftrightarrow \exists P \subseteq \mathbf{teacher'}[|P| = 11 \wedge \mathbf{team\_that\_won\_the\_cup'}(P)]$

This analysis generates a non-existent interpretation of (81b), which is incidentally the (only) coherent reading of (81a). We conclude that the system should disallow category shifting in (81b) but allow it to apply in (81a). Note that such contrasts do not appear with all collective predicates. For instance, the subjects of *both* (81a) and (81b) get a coherent interpretation in the following examples.

(85) (Exactly) eleven students I know $\left\{\begin{array}{l} \text{a. met in a coffee shop.} \\ \text{b. gathered in the hall.} \\ \text{c. built a raft together.} \end{array}\right\}$

The difference between the predicates in (81) to (83) and the predicates in (85), which was first observed in Dowty (1987), will be one of the main topics of chapter 5. In chapter 5 it will also become clear that existential readings like the ones generated by the E/CF mechanism for the phrase *eleven students* in these sentences, are inappropriate for *exactly eleven students* even in examples (85a–c). For the time being, we are interested in the general principles that block the application of category shifting with complex numeral DPs (*exactly eleven*, *more than two*, etc.), but let them to apply to simple numeral DPs (*eleven, two* etc.). Similarly, the theory should capture the difference between the subjects in the pairs like (82a–b) and (83a–b).

Wide scope beyond islands   In section 3.3.5 it was noted that not all indefinites exhibit wide scope behavior beyond syntactic islands. Let us reconsider the following examples.

(86) a.   If *some* woman I know gave birth to John then he has a nice mother.
       b.   #If *exactly one* woman I know gave birth to John then he has a nice mother.

(87) a.   If *two* people I know are John's parents then he is lucky.
       b.   #If *exactly two* people I know are John's parents then he is lucky.

Once more, we see that the complex numerals in the *b* cases resist an interpretation that is admitted by the simple indefinites in the *a* cases. Likewise, if we allow category shifting principles to apply to those complex numerals, undesired interpretations are generated. In (87b), for example, the following analysis is equivalent to the (prominent) wide scope reading of (87a), but this analysis represents a reading that is non-existent in (87b).

(88) $\exists f[\text{CH}(f) \wedge [\langle f \rangle(\min(\lambda P.|P \cap \textbf{people\_i\_know}'| = 2))(\textbf{john's\_parents}')$
        $\rightarrow \textbf{he\_lucky}']]$
     $\Leftrightarrow |\textbf{people\_i\_know}'| < 2$
        $\vee \exists A \subseteq \textbf{people\_i\_know}'[|A| = 2 \wedge [\textbf{john's\_parents}'(A) \rightarrow \textbf{he\_lucky}']]$

The facts that were surveyed above lead to the conclusion that the category shifting system is not freely applicable and that its operators should be applied in a highly controlled manner. On the other hand, subsection 2.3.5 has already shown cases where Partee and Rooth's "lazy" restriction on type shifting (the "type fitting" strategy) is too strong a constraint on the application of the **C** (collectivity) operator. Hence in these cases, the type mismatch requirement is also a too strong restriction on the application of the more general category shifting paradigm. Moreover, in other cases the type fitting strategy is also too permissive. This can be observed from unacceptable examples like (77) to (79) and (81b) to (83b). In the Bennett typing these examples all involve type mismatch, but as we have seen, applying category shifting principles in these cases leads to unacceptable analyses.

Since both the liberal approach to flexibility and the type driven approach of Partee and Rooth do not yield the right results for category shifting principles, we are left with the question concerning the nature of the required restrictions on their application. The following subsection proposes a *syntax driven* approach to this problem.

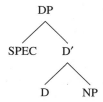

Figure 4.3
X-bar DP structure

4.3.2   The Flexible DP Hypothesis

It has been observed for a long time that nominals have an internal structure that is much more complex than the one that is expected in the standard X-bar theory of the noun phrase.[23] Furthermore, the classical semantic treatment of determiners in generalized quantifier theory is certainly too crude. For instance, nested structures as in (89) cannot simply be treated by successive application of the standard determiner functions for the words *the, three, all* and *every*.

(89) a. the three students
     b. all the students
     c. every three students

Since Abney (1987), a popular approach to the phrase structure of nominals is the *DP hypothesis*. According to this general line, what had been previously called a noun phrase has in fact the X-bar structure of a *determiner phrase*. A simple version of this proposal is given in figure 4.3.

In this phrase the D word is the *head*, complemented by a *noun phrase* (in the technical sense of X-bar theory). The specifier of the DP, whose categorial identity is debatable, is labeled here simply by SPEC. I do not adopt any further assumptions about the internal structure of the DP, as the structure in figure 4.3 is sufficient for the present purposes. For the sake of the discussion in the rest of this chapter let us adopt the terminology that this structure dictates and refer to the general syntactic category as "determiner phrase" rather than the traditional term "noun phrase." The term "nominals" is used pre-theoretically to refer to strings in natural language that are used as subjects, objects etc.[24] Note that a nominal that is analyzed as a DP missing a SPEC position can also be analyzed as a D′. Moreover, such a nominal whose DP structure includes an empty D position can in addition be analyzed as an NP.

As a working hypothesis for the study of the restrictions on category shifting, I propose the following syntactic-semantic hypothesis based on the assumed DP structure.[25]

Hypothesis 4 (the flexible DP hypothesis)   Category shifting applies only at the D′ level. The semantic categories of the phrasal NP and DP levels are fixed: NP is predicative whereas DP is quantificational.

According to this hypothesis, we classify the following kinds of nominals:

1. *Rigid nominals*: Nominals whose only possible syntactic analysis is as DPs. These nominals are unambiguously quantificational.[26]
2. *Flexible nominals*: Nominals that can be analyzed both as DPs and as D's. Since category shifting applies at the D' level, all these nominals are ambiguous between quantifiers and predicates. The class of flexible nominals is further subdivided into two syntactic classes:
   a. Nominals that can be analyzed as NPs. These nominals are initially predicative.
   b. Nominals that cannot be analyzed as NPs and their structure must therefore include a D' level. These nominals are initially quantificational.

Whenever no confusion should arise, let us refer to the two sub-classes of flexible nominals as **D'**s and **NP**s respectively.

This a priori division of nominals into three classes, with their different semantic properties, follows quite directly from the flexible DP hypothesis. The actual classification of various nominals as rigid, D's or NPs is a complex syntactic-semantic decision that should be empirically motivated. The two main questions we have to answer in order to substantiate the proposed classification of nominals are the following.

i. What are the criteria that distinguish between flexible nominals (= NPs and D's) and rigid nominals?

ii. What are the criteria that distinguish between NPs and D's?

In this book I am only able to address a small part of the numerous ramifications of these questions for syntax and semantics. The rest of this section shows the assumptions about DP structure of various nominals that are needed to account for the semantic data above, as well as more evidence for some of these syntactic assumptions.

4.3.3 Flexible nominals versus rigid nominals

The distinction between rigid nominals and flexible nominals is designed to capture the contrasts between nominals that were summarized in subsection 4.3.1. Flexible nominals are intended to be those nominals that appear naturally in predicative positions, exhibit collective interpretations (with predicates as in (81) to (83)) and show wide scope effects beyond islands. Application of category shifting allows flexible nominals to be interpreted in these contexts. Rigid nominals are expected to be unacceptable in such contexts because their DP analysis is purely quantificational. Thus assume the following typology of nominals.

(90) Flexible nominals
    a. Proper names: *Mary, John*
    b. Singular and plural definites: *the woman, this man, their children*
    c. Simple singular and plural indefinites: *a woman, some man, three women, some men, several children*
    d. Bare plurals(?): *women, men*

  e. Simple *and/or* coordinations of flexible nominals: *Mary and John, three women or five men*, etc.

(91) Rigid nominals
  a. Singular "quantified" nominals: *every woman, each man, no student*
  b. Plural "quantified" nominals: *all (the) women, most men, no students, many students, few students*
  c. Complex numerals: *at least/most three women, more/less than seven men, exactly one teacher, between four and ten cats*
  d. Complex coordinations: *both Mary and John, either Sue or exactly one teacher, neither Jane nor George, one woman but no men, Linda as well as Jim, Ruth and Dan as well/too*
  e. Simple *and/or* coordinations including at least one rigid nominal: *John and every woman, some woman or both John and Bill*

The following DP structures illustrate this distinction.

(92) a. [$_{DP}$ [$_{D'}$ Mary]]
  b. [$_{DP}$ [$_{D'}$ the women]]
  c. [$_{DP}$ [$_{D'}$ John] or [$_{D'}$ three women]]
  d. [$_{DP}$ [$_{D'}$ John]] or [$_{DP}$ [$_{D'}$ three women]]

(93) a. [$_{DP}$ [$_{SPEC}$ every][$_{D'}$ woman]]
  b. [$_{DP}$ [$_{SPEC}$ at least three][$_{D'}$ men]]
  c. [$_{DP}$ both [$_{DP}$[$_{D'}$ Mary]] and [$_{DP}$[$_{D'}$ John]]]
     alternatively:
     [$_{DP}$ [$_{SPEC}$ both] [$_{D'}$[$_{D'}$Mary] and [$_{D'}$ John]]]
  d. [$_{DP}$[$_{DP}$[$_{D'}$ John]] and [$_{DP}$ [$_{SPEC}$ every] [$_{D'}$ woman]]]

The distinction between the two groups follows from the possibility to analyze the nominals in (90) as D's and the unavailability of this analysis for the nominals in (91). This unavailability is based on three independent syntactic assumptions:

1. The nominals in (91a–c) all involve a SPEC-DP position filled by elements like *every*, *all*, *at least three* etc. as in (93a–b).
2. Coordination requires categorial identity of the conjuncts. Therefore, nominals as in (91e), which include at least one rigid nominal conjunct, have only a DP analysis as in (93d) and are hence rigid.[27]
3. Complex coordinations like *both . . . and* apply at the DP level as in (93c), but not at lower levels within the DP, hence the unavailability of the D' analysis for the nominals in (91d).

As far as complex numerals as in (91c) concern, the first assumption follows quite straightforwardly from X-bar theory. *Complex* numerals like *more than three, between two and four, fewer than five* cannot occupy the lexical head position and must sit in SPEC-DP, while simple numerals like *three* can sit lower within the DP.[28] Consequently, the semantic differences between complex numerals and simple numerals are directly accounted for under the flexible DP hypothesis. The assumption that like complex numerals, also items like *every* and *all* as in (91a–b) must sit in SPEC-DP is more stipulative at this stage, and I cannot syntactically substantiate it here.[29]

The second assumption, concerning the categorial identity of D′/DP conjuncts, predicts that a simple coordination of flexible nominals is flexible, whereas one rigid nominal in a coordination makes the whole coordination rigid. This prediction is borne out in the following contrast.

(94) a.   Mary and four other students I know are the team that won the cup.
      b.   *Mary and exactly four other students I know are the team that won the cup.

In sentence (94a), two flexible nominals are conjoined. The conjunction is syntactically classified as flexible, and indeed, it gets a collective interpretation characteristic of such nominals. By contrast, the second conjunct in (94b) is rigid, and consequently the whole conjunctive subject is also classified as rigid. This is supported by the fact that (94b) does not get any collective reading.

The third assumption, which distinguishes "simple" coordinations (e.g. with *and*) from "complex" coordinations (e.g. with *both . . . and*), is based on an observation by Neijt (1979: 1–7). As Neijt points out, the syntactic distribution of *both . . . and* and *either . . . or* constructions is more restricted than the corresponding "bare" *and/or* coordinations. For example, compare the acceptability of the nominals in (95) below to the unacceptability of the nominals in (96). Similar contrasts appear with other cases of complex nominal coordinations as in (97), and also with other categories as in (98).

(95) a. every man and/or woman
      b. three men and/or women
      c. most men and/or women

(96) a. *every both man and woman
      b. *three/most either men or women

(97) a. *most neither men nor women
      b. *every tall man but short woman
      c. *one man as well as woman
      d. *each man and woman as well/too

(98) a.   very [tall and thin]
            ten meters [above the house and below the cloud]
      b. *very both tall and thin
           *ten meters both above the house and below the cloud

According to Neijt, examples such as these indicate that complex coordinations do not apply at the X′ level whereas simple coordinations do.[30] It is not clear to me how this general proposal can be elegantly integrated with the version of the DP hypothesis assumed above, since unacceptable coordinations as in (96) and (97) can be analyzed as involving coordinations at the NP level, which is expected to be OK under Neijt's hypothesis.

However, after observing the syntactic unacceptabilities above it is not at all surprising that there is also a *semantic* difference between simple and complex coordinations of nominals, as the examples below again illustrate.

(99) (*Both) Mary and Sue are a nice couple.

(100) These women are (*both) Mary and Sue.

As the examples in (96) and (97) show, complex coordinations are not allowed inside the DP. Given our assumption that category shifts apply only at the D′ level, they simply cannot apply to the complex coordinations in (99) and (100) since these must be DP coordinations. When *both* is omitted, these examples can be analyzed as involving D′ coordination, where category shifting freely applies. Note that in this approach the coordinator *and* and its complex counterparts *both . . . and*, *and . . . too* etc. are synonyms. The same is true for *or* and *either . . . or*. The semantic differences between simple and complex coordinations appear only due to the different DP structures they induce.

Further support for this idea comes from the Hebrew accusative marker *et*. This particle obligatorily precedes proper names and other definite DPs in object positions, as in the following sentences.

(101) dan makir et   rina / ha-mora
       Dan knows ACC Rina / the-teacher
       "Dan knows Rina/the teacher."

When the object is a simple *and*/*or* coordination, there are two options: either *et* precedes the whole coordination or there is a separate *et* for each conjunct. This is illustrated below.

(102) dan makir et   rina ve/o   sara
       Dan knows ACC Rina and/or Sara
       "Dan knows Rina and/or Sara."

(103) dan makir et   rina ve/o   et   sara
       Dan knows ACC Rina and/or ACC Sara
       "Dan knows Rina and/or Sara."

However, when the coordination is the Hebrew parallel to *both . . . and* (*gam . . . ve-gam*) or the parallel to *either . . . or* (*o . . . o*), the accusative marker *et* MUST precede each conjunct separately. This is shown by the following examples.

(104) a. *dan makir et   gam rina ve gam sara
          Dan knows ACC too   Rina and too   Sara

      b. dan makir gam et   rina ve gam et   sara
         Dan knows too   ACC Rina and too   ACC Sara

      "Dan knows both Rina and Sara."

(105) a. *dan makir et   o rina o sara
          Dan knows ACC or Rina or Sara

      b. dan makir o et   rina o et   sara
         Dan knows or ACC Rina or ACC Sara

      "Dan knows either Rina or Sara."

In a similar fashion, also other complex coordinations in Hebrew require a separate *et* marker in front of each conjunct. This is illustrated below.

(106) a. *dan makir et   lo rina ve lo sara
          Dan knows ACC not Rina and not Sara

      b. dan makir lo et   rina ve lo et   sara
         Dan knows not ACC Rina and not ACC Sara

      "Dan knows neither Rina nor Sara."

(107) a. *dan makir et   rina ve kmo xen sara[31]
          Dan knows ACC Rina and as   well Sara

      b. dan makir et   rina ve kmo xen et   sara
         Dan knows ACC Rina and as   well ACC Sara

      "Dan knows Rina and Dan knows Sara as well."

(108) a. *ha-va'ada   baxara et ha-mu'amad   ha-naxon
          the-committee selected ACC the-candidate-MASC the-right
          aval ha-mu'amedet   ha-lo-nexona
          but   the-candidate-FEM the-not-right

      b. ha-va'ada   baxara et ha-mu'amad   ha-naxon aval
         the-committee selected ACC the-candidate-MASC the-right but
         et   ha-mu'amedet   ha-lo-nexona
         ACC the-candidate-FEM the-not-right

      "The committee selected the right male candidate but the wrong female candidate."

If we naturally assume that DPs, but not D's, are assigned accusative case using Hebrew *et*, then these contrasts follow from our previous assumptions. When the coordination is a simple *velo* ("*and/or*") coordination, each conjunct can be analyzed as a D′ and then only the complex DP need to be assigned case using *et*. However, when the coordination is using the more complex constructions *gam . . . ve-gam* and *o . . . o*, we must have two separate DPs, which require two separate *et*'s.[32]

A closely related fact was noticed in an unpublished work by Dorit Ben-Shalom and Ziva Wijler, who argue that DP conjunctions with double *et* can be interpreted only distributively. The following examples support this claim.

(109) dilan avar   be-mispar ha-širim še katav et simon ve garfunkel
      Dylan exceeded in-number the-songs that wrote ACC Simon and Garfunkel
      "Dylan wrote more songs than Simon and Garfunkel."

(110) dilan avar   be-mispar ha-širim še katav et simon ve et garfunkel
      Dylan exceeded in-number the-songs that wrote ACC Simon and ACC Garfunkel
      "Dylan wrote more songs than both Simon and Garfunkel."

As the English translations indicate, there is a semantic difference between the two sentences. Suppose that Dylan wrote more songs than what the couple Simon and Garfunkel wrote *together*, but suppose further (unrealistically) that Dylan wrote less songs than Simon and also less songs than Garfunkel. In this situation sentence (109) can be interpreted as true but (110) is univocally false. Thus, the doubly accusative marked conjunction *et simon ve et garfunkel* in (110) must be read distributively. This is what we expect if, as assumed above, *et* applies only at the DP level and DP conjunctions are rigid, hence unambiguously distributive.

An open problem   In section 4.2.6 the following examples of "wide scope *or*" were accounted for using the category shifting mechanism.

(111) Mary and [John or [John and Bill]] earned $5000 together. (= (65))

(112) If Bill praises Mary or Sue then John will be happy. (= (68))

However, the relevant interpretation can also appear with *either . . . or*:

(113) Mary and [either John or [John and Bill]] earned $5000 together.

(114) If Bill praises either Mary or Sue then John will be happy.

In this section application of category shifting is ruled out for coordinations like *either John or John and Bill* and *either Mary or Sue*. Consequently, it becomes unclear how the "WS *either . . . or*" interpretation of sentences like (113) and (114) is to be derived. Matters are complicated here by syntactic differences between *either . . . or* and *both . . . and*. Larson (1985) points out some differences in English. In Hebrew, contrasts between *gam . . . ve-gam* and *o . . . o* appear with respect to the distribution of the accusative marker *et*, as illustrated by the ungrammaticality of sentence (115) below as opposed to the grammatical (though perhaps marginal) status of (116) (cf. (104) and (105) above).

(115) *kol   mi   she-makir   et   gam rina ve-gam sara muzman la-mesiba
        every who that-knows ACC too   Rina and-too Sara invited   to-the-party

(116) ?kol   mi   she-makir   et   o rina o sara muzman la-mesiba
        every who that-knows ACC or Rina or Sara invited   to-the-party
        "Everyone who knows either Rina or Sara is invited to the party."

These differences may still leave open the possibility that category shifting applies to (some) *either . . . or* coordinations, while being ruled out with *both . . . and*.

4.3.4   NPs versus D's

So far, we have concentrated on the distinction between rigid nominals and flexible nominals. Now it is time to address question (ii) above about the distinction between the two kinds of flexible nominals: D's and NPs. Recall that the label "D's" refers to flexible nominals whose structure must include a D' level, whereas "NPs" is the name we use for flexible nominals that can also be analyzed as NPs. From the flexible DP hypothesis it follows that D's are initially quantificational whereas NPs are initially predicative. The semantic category of both kinds of flexible nominals can be shifted of course, but only at the D' level. This means that although both kinds of flexible nominals should in principle show the same range of meanings, this will not necessarily happen in all syntactic environments: a syntactic environment that selects for NP would disallow D' nominals altogether and will allow NPs, but only under their predicative interpretation with no category shifting. This section shows two manifestations of this distinction between nominals: the phenomenon of *verbless predication* and the so-called *appositional* use of conjunction. It is proposed that NPs can appear with no overt copula in predicative constructions and allow appositional conjunction, while D's require an overt copula and rule out appositional uses of conjunction. These syntactic differences cause some unexpected contrasts in the interpretation of the two kinds of nominals.

Verbless predicate nominals and Doron's observation   Many works on predicate nominals use the traditional distinction between *be* of identity and *be* of predication. Montague's analysis challenges this traditional distinction by showing that most nominals in predicative positions can be handled uniformly using the BE operator that maps generalized quantifiers to predicates. There are, however, well known distributional facts distinguishing between different nominals in predicative positions, and these phenomena are problematic for Montague's uniform strategy. Doron (1983) extensively studies such effects in Hebrew and English, relating them to the semantics of predicate nominals. In this section I will show

how some of Doron's central observations can be treated in the present framework although, following Montague and Partee, no ambiguity of the copula is assumed.

In English, Doron (1983) illustrates the contrast between predicative nominals using "small clause" constructions like the following.

(117) a. John considers this woman to be *a good teacher/the best teacher/Mary/some good teacher I know/you.*

b. John considers this woman *a good teacher/the best teacher/*Mary/ *some good teacher I know/*you.*

While all the italicized DPs in (117a) appear with an overt *be* copula, only two of them are allowed in (117b) where the copula is missing. A similar contrast, also due to Doron (p.c.), is between (119) and (118) below.

(118) a. I found John my strongest supporter.

b. I found John to be my strongest supporter.

(119) a. *I found my strongest supporter John.

b. I found my strongest supporter to be John.

In (119), the definite *my strongest supporter* is allowed without a preceding copula. By contrast, in (118), the proper noun *John* is not allowed to appear without the copula under the same interpretation.[33]

As Doron points out, in Hebrew this kind of contrasts is more easily visible than in English. This is because in Hebrew also matrix sentences are allowed to appear with no overt copula, similarly to English small clauses. The following example illustrates this fact for predicative adjectives and prepositional phrases.

(120) dana (hi) xaxama/ ba-bayit
Dana(is) smart/ in-the-house
"Dana is smart/in the house."

When it comes to simple sentences with predicative nominals, examples (121) and (122) below illustrate that Hebrew definites and bare indefinites behave similarly to the English definite and *a* indefinite in the small clause of example (117) above. These nominals do not require an overt copula.[34]

(121) ha-xavera haxi tova šeli (hi) mora
the-friend most good of-I (is) teacher
"My best friend is a teacher."

(122) dana (hi) ha-mora,   lo at!
Dana (is) the-teacher, not you
"Dana is the teacher, not you!"

By contrast, the Hebrew copula is obligatory with proper names, pronouns and *eize* ("*some*") indefinites, as illustrated by the pairs of sentences below.

(123) a. *ha-xavera haxi tova šeli dana
          the-friend most good of-I Dana

       b. ha-xavera haxi tova šeli *hi* dana
          the-friend most good of-I is Dana

           "My best friend is Dana."

(124) a. *ha-mora   at, lo dana!
          the-teacher you, not Dana

       b. ha-mora   hi at, lo dana!
          the-teacher is you, not Dana!

           "The teacher is you, not Dana!"

(125) a. *dana eizo mora   še-ani makir
          Dana some teacher that-I know

       b. dana hi eizo mora   še-ani makir
          Dana is some teacher that-I know

           "Dana is some teacher I know."

As Doron (1983: 114) further observes, the presence/absence of the copula corresponds to the presence/absence of a wide scope reading for a bare indefinite in the predicate position. Thus, while the sentence in (126a) is scopally ambiguous, as indicated by the translation, this is not the case in (126b), where the copula is missing.

(126) a. rina ša'ala im dani *hu* psantran še-šaxaxti   et   šmo
          Rina asked if Dani *is* pianist   that-forgot-I ACC name-his
          Ambiguous: "Rina asked whether Dani was a pianist whose name I had forgotten"
          or "There is a pianist whose name I forgot and Rina asked whether Dani was that
          pianist"
       b. rina ša'ala im dani psantran še-šaxaxti   et   šmo
          Rina asked if Dani pianist   that-forgot-I ACC name-his
          Unambiguous: "Rina asked whether Dani was a pianist whose name I had
          forgotten."

Summarizing, there are two kinds of nominals with respect to the status of the copula in predicative constructions:

(127) Optional copula
   a. definites
   b. *a*/bare indefinites interpreted narrowest scope

(128) Obligatory copula
   a. proper names and pronouns
   b. *some*/*eize* indefinites (all scopes)
   c. *a*/bare indefinites interpreted wide scope

Let us assume that the nominals in (127) are all NPs (= have an NP analysis), whereas the nominals in (128) are all D's (= have no NP analysis). Assume the following syntactic rule concerning the distribution of the copula.

(129) **The BE rule**: Verbless predicative constructions select for NP while overt copula requires D'.

The classification of "wide scope indefinites" as D's, and hence the scope effect observed by Doron in (126), gets a straightforward account in this system. Since choice functions apply only at the D' level, their introduction requires an overt copula as in (126a). This is the origin of the wide scope reading in this case. When the copula is missing as in (126b), the only possible analysis of the predicative nominal is as an NP, where CFs cannot apply. Hence, the sentence does not have any wide scope interpretation for the predicative indefinite.

The analysis of proper nouns deserves some elaboration. According to the copula test, proper nouns are D's since they require an overt copula. However, this is not always the case. As pointed out by Partee (1987) and Zwarts (1992), among others, proper nouns often behave like "ordinary" nouns, as in examples like *He is a real Einstein*, *The Vermeer she bought is beautiful*, etc. I propose that proper nouns are in fact "ordinary" nouns that come from the lexicon with a D' structure that semantically imposes uniqueness on the noun denotation.[35] Syntactically, let us assume the following (possibly lexical) structure for English proper nouns, with an empty definite article ϕ_{the} and an empty determiner ϕ_{cf} with the meaning of a choice function variable.

(130) $[_{D'} \phi_{cf} [_{NP} \phi_{the} N]]$

Semantically, as in the case of regular definites (cf. subsection 4.2.4 above), the empty definite article imposes uniqueness and the choice function has no alternative but to "choose" the unique element from the noun's denotation. The noun can also appear without the additional D' structure and then it behaves like any other "ordinary" noun. In Hebrew, Doron points out that it is precisely those situations where the uniqueness requirement of proper nouns is relaxed that allow them to appear without a copula. Doron's example is along the lines of the following.

(131) ha-yom dana trocki   ve-sara   lenin
       today   Dana Trotsky and-Sara Lenin
       "Today Dana is Trotsky and Sara is Lenin."

In the context of a play about the Russian revolution, where Dana plays Trotsky and Sara plays Lenin, (131) is perfectly acceptable. In such a context, however, the proper nouns *Trotsky* and *Lenin* lose their uniqueness requirement, as there may be many Trotskys and Lenins in such plays. Thus, these proper nouns in (131) behave more like ordinary Hebrew bare indefinites. We may assume that the D′ analysis of "proper nouns" is in principle available for all nouns, and that the question of which nouns prominently appear as "proper" (with a D′ structure) and which nouns tend to function as "bare" Ns is primarily an extra-grammatical matter of language use. This line of reasoning expects a third kind of nouns: ones with only an NP structure without the additional D' level. Such bare nouns would behave like the English/Hebrew definite, allowing verbless predication, but imposing uniqueness without any overt definite article. Possibly relevant examples may include the English noun *president* (as in *John is president*, cf. Partee, 1987: 125) or languages like Polish and Russian, which express uniqueness without definite articles.

Interactions between predicative DPs and collectivity give further support to the present mechanism. First let us reconsider sentences (35) and (36), repeated below with their semantic analysis.

(132) Mary is an author and a teacher.
       a. M(**author′** ⊓ **teacher′**)
          ⇔ **author′(m′)** ∧ **teacher′(m′)**

(133) These (two) women are an author and a teacher.
       a. $\exists f \exists g[CH(f) \wedge CH(g) \wedge \; [\![\text{these women}]\!](\min(\langle f \rangle(\textbf{author}') \sqcap \langle g \rangle(\textbf{teacher}')))]$

The meaning of the predicative nominal *an author and a teacher* in (132) can be analyzed as in (132a) with no application of any category shift: the two indefinites are NPs, hence initially predicative. The BE rule expects the copula to be only optional in the Hebrew translation of (132). This is corroborated by the grammaticality of sentence (134) below.

(134) dana (hi) soferet ve-mora
       Dana (is) author and-teacher
       "Dana is an author and a teacher."

By contrast, the prominent "collective" reading of the plural predicate nominal in (133) can be derived in the present system only by successive application of CF and min, as given in (133a). In order to exploit the principal filter property and get the collective reading of the conjunction we must first have two quantificational denotations that are obtained using the

CF shift. Since the only pragmatically plausible reading of (133) is this "collective" one, the BE rule predicts that in the Hebrew translation of this sentence, a copula is obligatory. This is indeed the case, as the sentences in (135) show.

(135) a. *(shtey) ha-našim   halalu soferet ve-mora
          (two)   the-women these author and-teacher

     b. (shtey) ha-našim   halalu *hen* soferet ve-mora
         (two)   the-women these *are* author and-teacher

       "These (two) women are an author and a teacher."

Incidentally, works that use vague terminology like "predicational" sentences and "identity" sentences would probably classify sentence (133) as belonging to the first category simply because the predicate nominals are *a* indefinites. Doron's clear syntactic criterion applied to the Hebrew translations in (135) points to the opposite classification, which is expected in the present system.

A similar contrast to the one between the Hebrew sentences in (135) can be demonstrated in English as in the following examples.[36]

(136) a. *To my delight, I found my two new students a first-rate pianist and a professional singer.
     b. To my delight, I found my two new students to be a first-rate pianist and a professional singer.

These contrasts suggest that the presence or absence of a copula with predicative nominals is not only a matter of the identity of the nominal. Even with nominals that allow the omission of the copula, its presence or absence affects the availability of collective readings (cf. (135) and (136)) and wide scope interpretations (cf. (126)). The possibility to account for such intricate effects is one of the main advantages of restricting category shifting using the syntactic strategy proposed in this section.

Appositional conjunction   Most English nominal conjunctions are in the plural. However, some cases are known to be an exception to this rule. Consider for instance the following examples from Hoeksema (1988: 36).

(137) a. A great man and a good father *has* passed away.
     b. My great opponent and the hero of my youth *has* passed away.
     c. A great man and the best magician in New Jersey *has* passed away.

This phenomenon is sometimes called *appositional conjunction*. In these examples the two conjoined nominals must be "coreferential" in the sense that sentence (137a), for instance, is interpreted as equivalent to the following formula.

(138) $\exists x[\textbf{great\_man}'(x) \wedge \textbf{good\_father}'(x) \wedge \textbf{passed\_away}'(x)]$

By contrast, when the singular *has* in (137) is replaced by plural *have*, the coreference entailment disappears. For instance, consider the following sentence.

(139) A great man and a good father *have* passed away.

In this case the coreference entailment disappears, and the two conjuncts furthermore refer to different people.[37]

However, not all nominals behave like the definites and *a* indefinites in (137). Hoeksema notes that with other nominals, as in the following examples, appositional conjunction (that is, conjunction in the singular number) is impossible even when the two nominals are known to be coreferential.

(140) a. *Dr. Jekyll and Mr. Hyde *has* passed away.
     b. *Charles Dodgson and Lewis Carroll *has* passed away.
     c. *Charles Dodgson and the author of *Alice has* passed away.
     d. *John and my best friend *has* passed away.
     e. *My hero and Houdini *has* passed away.
     f. *Amy and a long-time lover *has* passed away.

Note further that indefinites with the article *some*, by contrast to the *a* indefinites in (137), do not allow appositional conjunction. This is illustrated below.

(141) a. *Some great man and some good father *has* passed away.
     b. *Some great man and the best magician in New Jersey *has* passed away.

Importantly, what we observe here is that the nominals in (127), which can appear without a copula, also allow appositional conjunction. Conversely, the nominals in (128), which require a copula, also require plural number of conjunctions they appear in.[38] The theoretical intuition that accounts for this generalization is straightforward: since the nominals that require no copula are NPs, hence basically predicative, their conjunction, like the conjunction of other predicative categories (e.g. AP and PP) requires no change in the number feature. However, at the D′ level, which is not purely predicative like NP, conjunction must be in the plural. Let us state this rule as follows, parallel to the BE rule in (129).

(142) **The Number rule**: NP coordinations are singular while D′ coordinations are plural.

This rule immediately accounts for the "coreferential" interpretation in (137). The only structure it allows for the subjects in these examples is the following, involving NP coordination.

(143) $[_{DP} [_{D'} \phi_{cf} [_{NP} NP \text{ and } NP]]]$

Semantically, the CF variable, denoted by the empty ϕ_{cf} category, chooses one entity from the intersection of the two predicates. This is illustrated in the following semantic analysis of sentence (137a), equivalent to its paraphrase in (138).

(144) $\exists f[\mathrm{CH}(f) \wedge \langle f \rangle(\mathbf{great\_man}'_{et} \cap \mathbf{good\_gather}'_{et})(\mathbf{passed\_away}')]$

If however the two coordinated elements must be analyzed as D's, as it is the case in (140) and (141), then plural number becomes obligatory. Conversely, when the conjunction is in the plural as in (139), the conjunction must be a D' conjunction. Consequently these sentences get a "non-coreferential" reading where CFs apply to both conjuncts independently, as in the following analysis of (139).

(145) $\exists f \exists g[\mathrm{CH}(f) \wedge \mathrm{CH}(g) \wedge (\langle f \rangle(\mathbf{great\_man}') \sqcap \langle g \rangle(\mathbf{good\_father}'))(\mathbf{passed\_away}')$
$\quad \Leftrightarrow \exists x[\mathbf{great\_man}'(x) \wedge \mathbf{passed\_away}'(x)]$
$\quad \wedge \exists y[\mathbf{good\_father}'(y) \wedge \mathbf{passed\_away}'(y)]$

4.3.5 Remarks on plural predicate nominals and Mr. Fawlty's conception of doctors
The discussion so far has concentrated on singular nominals and their coordinations in predicate positions. Most English flexible nominals appear in predicate positions as naturally as their singular correlates, with the expected division between nominals that require an overt copula and nominals that do not require a copula (cf. (117)):

(146) a. John considers these women to be *good teachers/the best teachers/Mary and Sue/some good teachers I know/you*.
      b. John considers these women *good teachers/the best teachers/*Mary and Sue/*some good teachers I know/*you*.

Also in Hebrew, bare plural indefinites and plural definites headed with *ha* (*the*) behave like their singular counterparts in allowing for copula omission when appearing in predicate positions. Plural indefinites headed by *kama* (plural *some, several*) require an overt copula like their singular *eize/some* correlates. Compare for instance the sentences in (147), (148) and (149) to the respective sentences in (121), (122) and (125).

(147) ha-xaverot haxi tovot   šeli (hen) morot
      the-friends most good-plu of-I (are) teachers
      "My best friends are teachers."

(148) dana ve-rina   (hen) ha-morot,   lo aten!
      Dana and-Rina (are) the-teachers, not you-plu
      "Dana and Rina are the teachers, not you!"

(149) a. *ha-našim   halalu kama   morot   še-animakir
         the-women these some/several teachers that-I know

      b. ha-našim   halalu *hen* kama   morot   še-animakir
         the-women these *are* some/several teachers that-I know

         "These women are some/several teachers I know."

These facts are unsurprising if bare plurals and plural definites are basically predicative as suggested above, and if *some/several* plural indefinites lexically involve application of CFs, as proposed for singular *some*.

What is also unsurprising given the present analysis is the appearance of numeral indefinites in predicative positions, as illustrated by the Hebrew sentence (150) and the Italian sentence (151).

(150) ha-gvarim ha'ele (hem) šloša morim
      the-men   these (are) three teachers
      "These men are teachers and their number is three."

(151) Questi uomini sono tre insegnanti
      these men   are three teachers
      "These men are teachers and their number is three."

Since bare numerals are treated as predicative NPs, the BE rule correctly expects the copula in (150) to be only optional. Note that in such predicative positions, bare numerals like *three* semantically entail "exact counting," as opposed to their behavior in argument position (cf. remark in page 93). For instance, while the discourse in (152) is acceptable, (153) is contradictory.

(152) šloša morim nimca'im ba-xeder,   ve ulay   yoter
      three teachers are   in-the-room, and maybe more

(153) ha-gvarim ha'ele (hem) šloša morim, #ve ulay   yoter
      the-men   these (are) three teachers, #and maybe more

This behavior is expected by the present account because in (152) the existential quantification over CFs gives rise to a statement that is compatible with situations of more than three teachers in the room. By contrast, sentence (153) involves identity between the set of men and a set of three teachers. Even when existential quantification over CFs is involved (which is one of the derivational options), one set cannot be equal to a set of cardinality three without being itself of the same cardinality. This is the origin for the "exactness" effect in (153) under the proposed account.

English sentences similar to (150) and (151) are often judged marginal. However, they are not completely ungrammatical, as the following episode from the TV series *Fawlty Towers* (Cleese and Booth (1989: 191–192)) repeatedly proves. Basil Fawlty is the nervous hotel owner, very much worried about the decline in the dignity of his guests. Sybil is his practical wife. Dr. Abbott and his wife are new guests waiting at the reception.

Basil Good evening.
Mrs Abbott Good evening.
Basil (to Dr Abbott) Good evening.

Dr Abbott   Good evening.

Basil (beats his chest a few times, Tarzan style)   Ah . . . that felt better.

Sybil   Thank you, Mr Abbott. *(She takes another look at the card.)*

Oh, Doctor Abbott, I'm sorry.

Basil (freezes for a split second)   Doctor?

Dr Abbott   . . . Yes.

Basil   I'm terribly sorry, we hadn't been told. *(Dr Abbott looks at him questioningly.)* We hadn't been told that you were a doctor.

Dr Abbott   Oh.

Basil   How do you do, doctor. *(He offers his hand; Dr Abbott shakes it briefly.)* Very nice to have you with us, doctor.

Dr Abbott   Thank you.

Sybil   You're in room five, doctor.

Basil   And Mrs Abbott, how do you do. *(He shakes hands with her.)*

Dr Abbott   Dr Abbott, actually.

Basil   . . . I'm sorry?

Dr Abbott   Doctor Abbott.

Mrs Abbott   Two doctors.

Basil (to Dr Abbott)   You're two doctors?

Mrs Abbott   Yes.

Basil   Well, how did you become two doctors? That's most unusual . . . I mean, did you take the exams twice, or . . . ?

Dr Abbott   No, my wife's a doctor . . .

Mrs Abbott   . . . I'm a doctor.

Basil   You're a doctor too! So you're three doctors.

A potential problem is the (marginal) possibility of *complex* numerals to appear in predicative positions (at least in Hebrew):

(154)   ha-gvarim ha'ele hem paxot me-xamiša morim.

   the-men   these   are   less   than-five   teachers

   "These men are teachers and their number is less than five."

This is unexpected since, as will be stressed in chapter 5, the predicative analysis of complex numerals is highly unlikely for argument positions. Thus, to the extent that examples like (154) are acceptable, it is not clear how complex numerals can get their interpretation in predicative positions.

4.3.6   Summary of section 4.3

By way of summarizing this section, table 4.1 gives some examples of nominals and their proposed syntactic and semantic analysis. The feature $\pm F$ designates whether a nominal is

Table 4.1
DP syntax and semantics

Syntax	Semantic value	Semantic category
$[_{NP}$ a student]	**student**$'$	$-Q +F$
$[_{NP}$ the student]	**the**$'($**student**$')$	$-Q +F$
$[_{NP}$ three students]	**three**$'($**students**$')$	$-Q +F$
$[_{D'}$ some $[_{NP}$ student]]	$\langle f \rangle$(**student**$'$)	$+Q +F$
$[_{NP}[_{NP}$ a student] and $[_{NP}$ a teacher]] (singular)	**student**$'$ ⊓ **teacher**$'$	$-Q +F$
$[_{D'}[_{D'}$ ϕ_{cf} $[_{NP}$ a student]] and $[_{D'}$ ϕ_{cf} $[_{NP}$ a teacher]]] (plural)	$\langle f \rangle$(**student**$'$) ⊓ $\langle g \rangle$(**teacher**$'$)	$+Q +F$
$[_{D'}$ some $[_{NP}$ students]]	$\langle f \rangle$(**students**$'$)	$+Q +F$
$[_{D'}$ ϕ_{cf} $[_{NP}$ ϕ_{the} Mary]]	$\langle f \rangle$(**the**$'(\{$**m**$'\}))$	$+Q +F$
$[_{D'}[_{D'}$ ϕ_{cf} $[_{NP}$ ϕ_{the} Mary]] and $[_{D'}$ ϕ_{cf} $[_{NP}$ ϕ_{the} John]]]	$\langle f \rangle$(**the**$'(\{$**m**$'\}))$ ⊓ $\langle g \rangle$(**the**$'(\{$**j**$'\}))$	$+Q +F$
$[_{D'}[_{D'}$ ϕ_{cf} $[_{NP}$ ϕ_{the} Mary]] and $[_{D'}$ ϕ_{cf} $[_{NP}$ the student]]]	$\langle f \rangle$(**the**$'(\{$**m**$'\}))$ ⊓ $\langle g \rangle$(**the**$'($**student**$'))$	$+Q +F$
$[_{DP}$ every $[_{D'}[_{NP}$ student]]]	**every**$'($**student**$'$)	$+Q -F$
$[_{DP}$ no $[_{D'}[_{NP}$ student]]]	**no**$'($**student**$'$)	$+Q -F$
$[_{DP}$ exactly three $[_{D'}[_{NP}$ students]]]	**exactly_three**$'($**students**$'$)	$+Q -F$
$[_{DP}[_{DP}[_{D'}$ ϕ_{cf} $[_{NP}$ ϕ_{the} Mary]] and $[_{DP}$ every $[_{D'}[_{NP}$ student]]]]	$\langle f \rangle$(**the**$'(\{$**m**$'\}))$ ⊓ **every**$'($**student**$'$)	$+Q -F$
$[_{DP}$ both $[_{DP}[_{D'}$ ϕ_{cf} $[_{NP}$ ϕ_{the} Mary]] and $[_{DP}[_{D'}$ ϕ_{cf} $[_{NP}$ ϕ_{the} John]]]]	$\langle f \rangle$(**the**$'(\{$**m**$'\}))$ ⊓ $\langle g \rangle$(**the**$'(\{$**j**$'\}))$	$+Q -F$

flexible or rigid, while the feature $\pm Q$ designates whether it is initially quantificational (a D$'$) or predicative (an NP).

4.4   Problems of Typing Strategies

This chapter has followed Partee's flexibility paradigm and assumed that (some) nominals are ambiguous between predicates and quantifiers. As we have seen, this assumption has considerable linguistic advantages over Montague's "strict" assignment of semantic types (and categories) to syntactic categories. However, flexible interpretation also raises some technical problems for the mapping between categories and types. In order to study this question there is another point that we need to consider in addition to the Montague/Partee dichotomy: the type of plural individuals. In section 2.3.1 we have adopted Bennett's typing of plurals, which distinguishes between the types of singular individuals (type e) and plural individuals (type et). An alternative line, adopted in the influential works of Scha (1981)

Table 4.2
Different typing strategies

Typing strategy	DP	PRED
Montague-Link	ett $(+Q)$	et $(-Q)$
Montague-Bennett	ett $(+Q)$, $ettt$ $(+Q)$	et $(-Q)$, ett $(-Q)$
Partee-Link	et $(-Q)$, ett $(+Q)$	et $(-Q)$, ett $(+Q)$
Partee-Bennett	et $(-Q)$, ett $(\pm Q)$, $ettt$ $(+Q)$	et $(-Q)$, ett $(\pm Q)$, $ettt$ $(+Q)$

and Link (1983), is to use one domain of entities for both singularities and pluralities. In Scha's theory, all entities, singular and plural alike, are of type et. In Link's proposal, all entities are of type e, and the structure of their domain comes from outside the type hierarchy. For the sake of the present discussion, let us adopt Link's version for representing this uniform typing strategy. The four ways of combining the different approaches to the typing of singular and plural nominals are summarized in table 4.2. This table considers the sentence structure DP-PRED, where the predicate PRED can be a predicative nominal. As before, the $\pm Q$ feature designates whether a denotation of a given type can be predicative, quantificational, or both.

One of the attractive properties of Montague's strict assignment of types to categories is that it easily avoids semantically ill-formed operations. With Link's uniform typing of plurals this is obviously so: the Montague-Link typing allows no type mismatch to appear between a subjects and predicates, and a DP denotation can always safely apply to the predicate denotation. Consequently, types are not even necessary as a means to rule out improper semantic analyses. However, under Bennett's typing of plurals, Montague's strategy requires a type calculus (e.g. the calculus of chapter 1) to prevent ill-defined situations where a semantically singular quantifier (type ett) applies to a semantically plural predicate (type ett) or a plural quantifier (type $ettt$) applies to a singular predicate (type et).

In Partee's approach one problematic situation should be ruled out, even though type theoretically there is no principle that blocks it. This is the situation where the subject DP is analyzed as predicative while the linguistic predicate PRED is analyzed as quantificational. Consider the following example.

(155) Some woman is no teacher.

Under Partee's assumptions (and either Link's or Bennett's typing), the copular predicate in this example can in principle remain in its initial type ett while the subject is shifted to type et using the BE operator. This possibility would derive the following erroneous analysis.

(156) $(\mathbf{no}(\mathbf{teacher'}))(\mathbf{BE}(\mathbf{E}(\mathbf{woman'})))$
   $\Leftrightarrow (\mathbf{no}(\mathbf{teacher'}))(\mathbf{woman'})$
   $\Leftrightarrow \neg \exists x[\mathbf{teacher'}(x) \wedge \mathbf{woman'}(x)]$

This analysis expects sentence (155) to have a reading equivalent to the sentence *There is no woman teacher*. However, the expectation is clearly incorrect.[39] Note that the problem is not simply in Partee's treatment of *no* in sentences like (155), which was criticized above in section 4.1.3. Similar problems may appear also in the flexible system proposed above, which does not allow predicative analyses to nominals like *no teacher*. Consider for instance the following analog to sentence (155).

(157) This woman or that woman is neither Mary nor Sue.

This sentence incidentally shows that although complex coordinations like *neither Mary nor Sue* are analyzed here as rigid DPs, they need to get a predicative reading. This will be discussed further in section 4.5 below. However, we also need to prevent an analysis analogous to (156), which would interpret the predicative nominal as quantificational and the subject as predicative (using either Partee's BE operator or the present min operator). This analysis would be paraphrased as in (158) below, which is of course logically stronger than sentence (157).

(158) Mary is neither this woman nor that woman *and* Sue is neither this woman nor that woman.

This problem for Partee's flexible strategy is in the assumption that predicative constructions of the form *copula + nominal* can be interpreted as having a quantificational reading. If this situation is prevented, then linguistic predicates (VPs, copula constructions, etc.) would always be correctly analyzed as predicational (type *et*). Consequently, the type calculus would require that the subject DP is of type *ett* (or *e*). In fact, in the proposed flexible system it is easy to make sure that predicate nominals always have a predicative reading. Let us return to assumption (A3) from subsection 4.2.1:

(A3)   The copula *be* does not have any denotation, or denotes the identity function on predicates.

Let us adopt the second option in (A3), and (under the Partee-Link typing) assume that the copula denotes the identity function of type *(et)(et)*. This means that now a predicative nominal must be of type *et* and that type *ett* is ruled out. According to the theory of section 4.3, also when no copula appears (as in verbless Hebrew sentences or English small clauses), the nominal must anyway be of a predicative type, because in these situations the nominal is syntactically an NP, which only has a predicative analysis.

In the Partee-Bennett typing, which is the one adopted throughout this book, there is an additional problem that remains: the types of DP and PRED can match while their semantic categories do not match. Consider for instance the following sentence, whose correct analysis was given in (59) above.

(159) Three girls are wearing a dress.

A possible analysis that we should prevent in such sentences is the analysis obtained when both the subject and the verb phrase are analyzed as semantic predicates: a "plural" predicate of type ett for the subject and a "singular" et predicate for the VP. Such an analysis would lead to the wrong truth conditions in (160a) below, paraphrased in (160b).

(160) a. $(\lambda A_{et}.|A| = 3 \wedge A \subseteq \mathbf{girl'})(\mathbf{wear\_a\_dress'})$
           $\Leftrightarrow |\mathbf{wear\_a\_dress'}| = 3 \wedge \mathbf{wear\_a\_dress'} \subseteq \mathbf{girl'}$
       b. There are three girls who are the only entities that are wearing a dress.

Also some other similar problems may appear under the Partee-Bennett typing we have adopted. To avoid such problems, a simple though non-standard solution is to let the *primitive* types in our system encode the difference between "singular" entities and "plural" entities. Assume that the set TYPE$_0$ of primitive types (cf. definition 1 in chapter 1) includes, in addition to the e and t types, also a type e_2 for plural individuals. To avoid confusion, let us replace the standard notation e by e_1, for "singular" entities. Thus, now the set of types is the smallest set TYPE that satisfies the following:

1. $e_1 \in$ TYPE, $e_2 \in$ TYPE, and $t \in$ TYPE
2. If $\tau \in$ TYPE and $\sigma \in$ TYPE then $(\tau\sigma) \in$ TYPE

The domains for complex functional types are defined as usual, but the primitive domain for type e_2 is identified with the complex domain $D_{e_1 t}$. Formally:

1. D_{e_1} is an arbitrary non-empty set
   $D_t = \{0, 1\}$
   $D_{e_2} = D_t^{D_{e_1}}$
2. For any two types $\tau, \sigma \in$ TYPE: $D_{\tau\sigma} = D_\sigma^{D_\tau}$

With these types, the type of an expression determines again whether it is predicative or quantificational: type $e_i t$ is for predicates and $e_i tt$ is for quantifiers, where $i \in \{1, 2\}$. The syntactic predicative reading of the subject in sentence (159) is of type $e_2 t$, which does not match the $e_1 t$ type of the verb phrase. Therefore, problematic analyses such as (160) are ruled out.

   In this type system, unlike standard ones, the denotation of an expression does not uniquely determine its type. For instance, because $D_{e_2} = D_t^{D_{e_1}}$, an expression denoting a function f in this set may be specified to be of type e_2 or of type $e_1 t$, but not of both. Thus, the type of an expression is no longer just a reflection of the structure of the domain its denotations come from, but also a syntactic device for ruling out undesired interpretations. This use of types stands in opposition to the non-representationalist starting point of chapter 1, and I therefore consider it to be a weakness of the present proposal. Using the Partee-Link typing instead of the Partee-Bennett typing adopted here would not improve too much the situation, because then inelegant modifications of the present proposal would be required elsewhere in the system.

4.5   A Toy Grammar

The following toy grammar formally illustrates some of the main ideas of this chapter. This grammar treats a few singular and plural nominals and their coordinations using syntactic introduction of category shifts. The grammar consists of the following parts:

1. Sets of *categories* according to their bar level:
    $\text{CAT}_0 \stackrel{\text{def}}{=} \{D, N, V, \text{SPEC}_D, \text{SPEC}_N, \text{FLEX}, \text{BE}, \text{COOR}_{\pm\text{sim}}\}$
    $\text{CAT}_1 \stackrel{\text{def}}{=} \{D', N'\}$
    $\text{CAT}_2 \stackrel{\text{def}}{=} \{DP, NP, VP, S, \text{PREDP}_{\pm\text{cop}}\}$
    We denote $\text{CAT} = \text{CAT}_0 \cup \text{CAT}_1 \cup \text{CAT}_2$, the set of all categories.

2. A set LEX of *lexical entries*:

LEX $\stackrel{\text{def}}{=}$ {*Mary, John, woman, women, every, the, a, some, ϕ_{cf}, $\phi_{\min}$, tall, smiled, is, are, and, both . . . and*}.

The null elements $\phi_{\min}$ and ϕ_{cf} denote the corresponding category shifts.

3. Functions **cat** : LEX $\rightarrow$ CAT$_0$ from lexical items to lexical categories and **type** : LEX $\rightarrow$ TYPE from lexical items to types. These functions are defined in table 4.3.

Table 4.3
A toy lexicon

$x \in$ LEX	$\mathbf{cat}(x)$	$\mathbf{type}(x)$	
Mary	D'	$(e_1 t)t$	
John	D'	$(e_1 t)t$	
woman	N	$e_1 t$	
women	N	$e_2 t$	
every	SPEC$_D$	$(e_1 t)(e_1 tt)$	
the	SPEC$_N$	$(e_i t)(e_i t)$	$i \in \{1, 2\}$
a	SPEC$_N$	$(e_1 t)(e_1 t)$	
three	SPEC$_N$	$(e_2 t)(e_2 t)$	
some	D	$(e_i t)(e_j tt)$	$i, j \in \{1, 2\}, i \geq j$
ϕ_{cf}	FLEX	$(e_i t)(e_j tt)$	$i, j \in \{1, 2\}, i \geq j$
$\phi_{\min}$	FLEX	$(e_1 tt)(e_2 t)$	
tall	AP	$e_i t$	$i \in \{1, 2\}$
smiled	V	$e_i t$	$i \in \{1, 2\}$
is/are	BE	$(e_i t)(e_i t)$	$i \in \{1, 2\}$
and	COOR$_{+\text{sim}}$	$\tau(\tau\tau)$	τ is boolean
and	COOR$_{-\text{sim}}$	$\tau(\tau\tau)$	τ is boolean

4. A *phrase structure grammar* G over the set of lexical categories CAT_0 and the two syncategorematic particles {both, and} as terminals and using the categories in the set $CAT \setminus CAT_0$ as non-terminals:

$DP \rightarrow (SPEC_D) \, D'$

$D' \rightarrow (D) \, NP$

$D' \rightarrow FLEX \, D'$

$NP \rightarrow (SPEC_N) \, N'$

$N' \rightarrow N$

$N' \rightarrow AP \, N'$

$PREDP_{-cop} \rightarrow AP/NP$

$PREDP_{+cop} \rightarrow AP/NP/D'$

$VP \rightarrow V/ \, PREDP_{-cop}/ \, BE \, PREDP_{+cop}$

$S \rightarrow DP \, VP$

$X \rightarrow X \, COOR_{+sim}X, \quad$ where $X \in CAT_1 \cup CAT_2$

$X \rightarrow X \, COOR_{-sim}X, \quad$ where $X \in CAT_2 \setminus \{NP\}$

This grammar exemplifies the following properties of the above proposal:

• The denotation of definites, *a* indefinites and numerals is basically predicative and their basic category is NP, which does not require a copula in predicative positions.
• Proper names, *some* indefinites, and any other nominal whose structure involves category shifting are basically of category D', which requires an overt copula in predicative positions.
• "Quantified" nominals such as *every woman* are rigid and they do not have any predicative interpretation.
• "Complex" coordinations, as opposed to simple ones, are rigid and cannot undergo category shifts: *both . . . and*, as opposed to *and*, applies only to XPs (other than NP). Hence complex nominal coordinations must be DPs, where category shifting does not apply.
• A coordination that involves one or more rigid nominal cannot undergo category shifts: *every* and *both . . . and* create DPs and these can only coordinate with other DPs. Hence, no category shifts can apply to such coordinations.

Note that in this grammar one kind of rigid nominals is allowed to appear in predicative positions: complex coordinations (e.g. *both . . . and*) of flexible nominals are semantically rigid, but they inherit their semantic category from their conjuncts, hence they may interpreted as either predicates or quantifiers. This has been shown above, in examples similar to (161a) below.

(161) a. This woman is neither Mary nor Sue.

b. Neither Mary nor Sue arrived.

In sentence (161a), the only possible syntactic analysis of *neither Mary nor Sue* is as a coordination of two $PREDP_{+cop}$ categories. By contrast, in (161a), the only analysis of this nominal is as a coordination of two DPs. Correspondingly, in the first sentence this nominal has a predicative denotation whereas in the second sentence it has a quantificational denotation. Note that the syntactic category PREDP or DP uniquely determines the semantic category as predicate or quantifier, respectively.

In order to enrich this grammar with a treatment of appositional conjunction, it should be extended to deal with number agreement, which will not be done here. However, once this necessary ingredient is added to the grammar, appositional conjunction can be easily handled with a rule like the following:

$$X[\text{pl}] \rightarrow X[\text{sg}] \, COOR_{\pm\text{sim}} \, X[\text{sg}], \quad \text{where } X \in \{D, D', DP\}$$

This rule guarantees that a conjunction of two singular items can become plural only if it is a "D headed" category. Other coordinations require identity between their number feature and the number features of the conjuncts. Hence, conjunction of singular categories other than DP or D', especially a conjunction of singular NPs, cannot be plural.

4.6   Summary of Chapter 4

This chapter generalized the proposals of the previous chapters into a flexible system for the interpretation of nominals. The *minimum* operator is used as a general mapping from quantifiers to predicates and the *choice function* mechanism is used as a general existential operator from predicates to quantifiers. This semantic mechanism of *category shifting* is proposed instead of Partee's diagram for the flexible interpretation of nominals. We have seen that the proposed configuration of the theory requires introduction of a *distributivity operator* that applies to denotations of nominals. This operator was implemented as part of the choice function mapping from predicates to quantifiers. Some implications of the unified treatment of general existential shifting using choice functions were then shown to be correct.

It was proposed that the restrictions on category shifting follow from differences in the syntax of two groups of nominals. *Rigid nominals* are those nominals that must unambiguously be analyzed as *determiner phrases*. The group of *flexible nominals* consists of nominals that also have a *D-bar* (D') analysis. All category shifting principles within the DP apply at the D' level. These flexible nominals are further subclassified into nominals that are initially NPs and nominals that are initially D's. Because the NP level is unambiguously predicative, the former nominals naturally appear in predicative positions with no copula and in appositional conjunctions. The "D' level" nominals, although flexible, are initially quantificational and they are (therefore) more restricted in their semantic distribution: they require a copula in order to become predicative and they resist appositional uses of conjunction. Of special interest in this NP/D' dichotomy is the predicative analysis of *definites* and the treatment of *proper nouns*, which were analyzed as ordinary nouns with a covert D' structure that accounts for their initially quantificational reading. This theoretical connection between the syntax of nominals and their formal semantics is referred to as the *flexible DP hypothesis*, and it is supported by a variety of linguistic phenomena from English and Hebrew. The technical implications of this configuration for the structure of the *type system* for natural language were briefly addressed.

The role of category shifting principles in the proposed system can be summarized as follows:

- Category shifts change the *semantic category* of an expression.
- Category shifts do not necessarily *lift* the standard type of an expression. The min operator and the $\langle f \rangle^d$ operation of distributed choice functions are standardly viewed as type *sorts*.
- Category shifting principles are not driven by semantic type mismatch but by syntactic mechanisms like null elements or other syntactic triggers.

As anticipated in chapter 2, this conception of category shifting differs substantially from Partee and Rooth's (1983) type fitting strategy. However, in the next chapter we will find reason to use the type fitting strategy in other cases of plurality and quantification.

Chapter 5

Plural Quantification and the Atom/Set Distinction

Two problems of foundational importance to the study of plurality are in the focus of the investigations in this chapter. The first problem concerns the general parameters that determine whether a sentence gets a collective interpretation. The second problem is the formal semantic analysis of this collective interpretation when the nominal involved is a plural quantificational nominal such as *all dogs, no cats* and *exactly five mice*. The starting point for these investigations is a novel typology of predicates in natural language (nouns, verbs and adjectives) according to their behavior with quantificational nominals. Predicates that allow collectivity effects with such nominals are referred to as *set predicates*. Predicates with which collectivity is ruled out in these situations are called *atom predicates*. Following the descriptive work in Dowty's article "Collective Predicates, Distributive Predicates and *All*" (1987), it is shown that this typology substantially differs from the traditional distinction between distributive predicates and collective predicates. Unlike previous alternative typologies, the atom/set distinction between predicates is robustly defined using a simple truth-conditional criterion.

After establishing this distinction between predicates, two other factors that affect collective interpretations are identified and studied: the morphological number of predicates, and the *quantificational/non-quantificational* denotation of flexible and rigid nominals as defined in chapter 4. These three factors together are used to develop a general *type-fitting* system that accounts for collectivity effects in various circumstances. The atom/set classification of a predicate determines its *lexical* type: whether it ranges over atoms (*e* type entities) or over sets (*et* type individuals). The role of morphological number in the proposed type-fitting analysis is to determine the type of the *number inflected* predicate: singular predicates range over *e* type entities while plural predicates ambiguously range over *e* or *et* type entities. The quantificational/non-quantificational classification of the nominal determines whether it allows a mapping from sets to "impure atoms," following Landman's proposals in his "Groups" (1989) and "Plurality" (1996) articles. It is argued that this "impure atom" operation applies only to flexible (predicative) nominals.

The second major topic of this chapter concerns the implications of the "collectivity triggering" mechanism for the semantics of collectivity with quantificational plurals. As in the previous work by Scha and Van der Does, the theory of generalized quantifiers is used for dealing with plural nominals and their collectivity effects. Unlike these works, collectivity with generalized quantifiers is achieved by a *uniform* type-fitting strategy for determiners that is triggered by the *ett* type of plural nouns. This analysis of plural determiners is strongly based on the *conservativity* properties of quantification in natural language. The empirical consequences of this lifting strategy are studied, and, following Szabolcsi (1997), it is proposed that existential quantification over *witness sets* should be part of the interpretation of nominals.

The organization of the chapter is as follows. Section 5.1 describes the problems in general terms and section 5.2 reviews previous proposals. Section 5.3 establishes the new typology of atom predicates and set predicates. Section 5.4 characterizes the factors that affect collective interpretations and introduces the basic principles that will be used to account for them. Section 5.5 uses the proposed type-fitting system to study quantification over sets in a generalized quantifier setting. Section 5.6 is a less extensive study of the "impure atom" strategy in the interpretation of predicative flexible nominals. Section 5.7 recapitulates the chapter by way of analyzing the entailment relations between sentences with the determiners *every* and *all*, the plural article *the* and the expression *member of*.

5.1   The Problem: Plural Quantification and the Semantic Number of Predicates

Generalized quantifier theory was originally implemented in linguistics for the semantic analysis of sentences with distributive predicates such as *sleep*, *smile*, *be happy* and the like. Sentences of the form Det-N-VP are analyzed by letting the noun and the verb phrase refer to sets of atomic ("singular") individuals. The determiner denotes a relation between such sets. This analysis obtains a general treatment of nominals in singular sentences as in (1) below, as well as plural sentences as in (2).

(1) a. Every girl slept.
     b. Exactly one student smiled.
     c. No teacher is happy.

(2) a. All the girls slept.
     b. Exactly five students smiled.
     c. No teachers are happy.

Standard versions of generalized quantifier theory ignore collective predicates like *meet*, *gather* or *be similar*. Theories of plurality start from taking into account these predicates as well. Studies of plurals often concentrate on noun phrases like *the girls*, *Mary and John* or *three teachers* as in the following examples.

(3) a. The girls gathered in the hall.
     b. Mary and John met.
     c. Three teachers are similar.

These nominals are sometimes called "referential." A more appropriate term for describing these nominals according to the semantic treatment of chapter 4 is "flexible" or "potentially predicative." However, such nominals are not the only nominals that give rise to collectivity effects. Also the rigid "quantificational" plural nominals of (2) can felicitously appear in sentences with collective predicates, as illustrated in (4) below.

(4) a. All the girls gathered in the hall.
    b. Exactly five students met.
    c. No teachers are similar.

This combination is hard to crack. Classical generalized quantifier theory does not deal with collective predicates to begin with. Theories of plurality, on the other hand, usually assume that the subject denotes a plural individual (e.g. a set). This assumption is tenable in (3a–b) and can be generalized to (3c), assuming existential quantification over collections (e.g. as in the choice function account of chapter 3). However, such a "plural individual" analysis becomes much more problematic in (4a–b) and virtually impossible in (4c). Let us refer to this problem as the *plural quantification* problem: how do plural nominals in general combine with collective predicates?

This problem cannot be separated from another question: what are the factors that govern *whether* a sentence has a collective interpretation? There are some relevant factors, and certainly one of the most surprising among them was first pointed out by Dowty (1987). Dowty shows that the intuitively "collective" predicates do not behave in a uniform way when combined with nominals such as *all the girls*. For instance, the predicate *gather* appears felicitously in (3a) and (4a) alike. By contrast, Dowty notes that collective predicates such as *be a good team* or *be numerous* give rise to acceptable sentences with a plural definite as in (5a), but not with an *all* nominal as in (5b).[1]

(5) a. The girls are a good team/numerous.
    b. *All the girls are a good team/numerous.

More examples of collective predicates that behave in this way will be given later in this chapter. For the time being, note that the same kind of contrast between the predicates in (4) and the predicates in (5) reappears with subjects headed by other plural determiners besides *all*. Compare for instance the following sentences in (6) to the sentences in (4b–c) above.

(6) *Exactly five students/no teachers are a good team/are numerous.

These facts suggest that the pre-theoretical distinction between "distributive" and "collective" predicates is not fine-grained enough: both predicates like *gather* or *meet* and predicates like *be a good team* or *be numerous* are traditionally classified as collective. Why do only the former give rise to collectivity effects when combined with *all the students* or *exactly five students*? My answer to this question will be based on the assumption that unacceptable sentences as in (5b) and (6) are not simply grammatically ill-formed. Rather, as in examples such as *Mary met*, a selectional restriction of the predicate is violated. We say that sentences (5b) and (6), unlike sentences (4) and (5a), *lack a collective interpretation*. The advantage of this view on the data will become clear when we will see more collective predicates that behave like *be a good team* in lacking a collective reading, but without giving rise to unacceptabilities as in (5b) and (6).

In addition to this distinction between predicates there are other important, though perhaps less surprising, parameters that govern collectivity. An obvious factor is the *identity of the nominal*. For instance, as mentioned above, sentence (5a), containing a flexible plural nominal, has a collective interpretation. Sentence (5b), with the rigid "quantificational" nominal *all*, does not. Another important factor that affects collectivity is *morphological number*. For instance, while sentence (4a), repeated below as (7a), has a plural subject and gets a collective interpretation, sentence (7b), with a singular subject, does not.

(7) a.   All the girls gathered in the hall.
    b.   *Every girl gathered in the hall.

The general problem of classifying and accounting for the factors that affect the availability of collective readings, or in more general terms, the *semantic number* of the sentence, is the main subject of sections 5.3 and 5.4. Sections 5.5 and 5.6 formalize and develop this account.

5.2   Previous Proposals

5.2.1   Dowty (1987): *all* and the typology of predicates

Dowty's article follows the preliminary work in Link (1983) and tries to define the meaning of the determiner *all* when it combines with various predicates. An insightful observation of Dowty's is the aforementioned distinction he makes between the behavior of predicates like *meet* or *gather* and predicates like *be a good team* or *be numerous* when they combine with an *all* nominal. To describe this difference Dowty uses an informal notion of *distributive subentailments*. By this term he refers to implications a predicate has for the members of a plural individual in its extension. The following quote from Dowty (1987: 101) clarifies this notion a bit more.

Consider what is required of individual students for the sentence *the students gathered in the hall* to be true. Clearly, every student in the group referred to by *the students* (or "almost every student") must come into the hall and remain long enough that they are all there at a common time. Thus *gather* distributively [sub-]entails some property of members of its group subject (each undergoing a change of location), but *gathering* itself can only be true of the group *qua* group.

By contrast to *gather*, Dowty classifies predicates like *be a good team* and *be numerous* as being devoid of any distributive subentailments. Dowty then hypothesizes that what *all* adds to the truth conditions of a sentence is "to fully distribute the predicate's subentailments to every member of the group argument." For instance, a sentence like ALL *the girls gathered* in (4a) is interpreted like the sentence *The girls gathered* plus the information that *every girl contributed to the gathering* (= fulfilled a subentailment of the verb *gather*). Predicates like *be a good team* are assumed to have no distributive subentailments, hence Dowty concludes that in cases like (5b) the determiner *all* has nothing to distribute over and the sentence is ruled out.

As Dowty recognizes, one obvious drawback of his proposal is that the formal nature of subentailments is not clarified. This makes it hard to substantiate the idea. Moreover, even in this preliminary situation it is possible to observe a general empirical problem for the subentailment line. Dowty's paper deals only with *all*, but as we will see, the distinction that is made between collective predicates is far more general and applies to many other plural determiners. For instance, while the sentences in (8) below have coherent readings, the sentences in (9) do not.[2]

(8) $\left\{ \begin{array}{l} \text{Less than eleven} \\ \text{No} \end{array} \right\}$ students gathered in the hall.

(9) $\left\{ \begin{array}{l} \text{*Less than eleven} \\ \text{*No} \end{array} \right\}$ students are the team that won the cup yesterday.

Clearly, this is the same difference Dowty observes between the corresponding sentences with an *all* nominal as a subject. However, any simple attempt to extend Dowty's subentailment intuition to other determiners besides *all* runs into unpleasant problems. For instance, whatever the meanings of the sentences in (8) may be, they certainly cannot be paraphrased by sentences like the following.

(10) The students gathered in the hall and less than eleven/no students contributed to the gathering.

In situations where the entire set of students is sufficiently large, the sentences in (10) have a contradictory flavor, where this is surely not the case in (8). Thus, although Dowty's descriptive distinction between predicates is highly suggestive and furthermore extends to constructions he does not discuss, his account of the distinction does not.[3] What we need in order to start dealing with this problem is a *general* theory of quantificational nominals in collective environments. The works of Scha and Van der Does, to which we turn now, aim at extending generalized quantifier theory in precisely this direction.

5.2.2 Plural quantification: the lifting strategies of Scha and Van der Does

In a seminal paper, Scha (1981) proposes an extension of the standard theory of quantification to the treatment of plurality phenomena. Among the many problems that Scha addresses in an especially terse style, he also proposes a treatment of sentences as in (4) and (8) above. The works of Van der Does (1992, 1993) contain a systematic extension of Scha's approach within contemporary generalized quantifier theory. I will now briefly review the proposals by Scha and Van der Does (S&D), deferring more elaborate empirical discussion to later stages in this chapter.

All the predicates in the S&D systems get the "collective" *ett* type: they range over plural individuals. All determiners get the *(et)(ettt)* type: they denote functions from sets to generalized quantifiers that range over plural individuals. Thus, in a nominal such as *exactly five students*, the plural common noun denotes a set of individual students. However, the determiner *exactly five* maps this set to an *ettt* quantifier over *et* plural individuals. There are some readings that a plural determiner may have in S&D's systems. Van der Does follows Van Benthem (1991: 68) and shows that these readings can be obtained systematically from standard determiners of type *(et)(ett)*.

The first reading of plural determiners is only an adjustment of their standard "distributive" reading to their new type. Under this reading, a quantifier like *exactly five students* still ranges over singularities, but these singularities are singleton *et* sets rather than *e* type individuals. Thus, the distributive interpretation of a sentence like (11) below claims that the total number of students who lifted a piano *on their own* is exactly five. This statement is formalized in (12).

(11) Exactly five students lifted a piano.

(12) $|\{x \in \textbf{student}' : \textbf{lift\_piano}'(\{x\})\}| = 5$

The lifting operator **D** (= Van der Does's $\textbf{D}_1$) that generates this statement is defined below. The **D** function maps any standard determiner D of type *(et)(ett)* to a higher type determiner **D**(D) of type *(et)(ettt)*.

(13) $\textbf{D} \overset{\text{def}}{=} \lambda D_{(et)(ett)}.\lambda A_{et}.\lambda B_{ett}.D(A)(\{x_e : B(\{x\})\})$

There are two non-distributive analyses of sentences like (11) in S&D's proposals.[4] One collective analysis is "existential-modificational." For (11) this statement claims that there is a collection of exactly five students and that this collection lifted a piano. Thus, the numeral *exactly five* is treated as a predicate modifier that maps the set of students to the set of its subsets of cardinality five. An existential quantifier picks up one of the collections in this set. This reading is formalized in (14) and it is obtained using the $\textbf{C}_a$ lift on determiners that is defined in (15).[5]

(14) $\exists X[X \subseteq \textbf{student}' \wedge |X| = 5 \wedge \textbf{lift\_piano}'(X)]$

(15) $\textbf{C}_a \overset{\text{def}}{=} \lambda D.\lambda A.\lambda B.\exists X \subseteq A[D(A)(X) \wedge B(X)]$

Scha assumes another non-distributive reading of plural determiners, which Van der Does refers to as *neutral*. In sentence (11), for instance, this reading counts the individual students who participated in piano liftings that were performed by sets of students (including singleton sets). Thus, the sentence does not require that there is any set of five students that lifted a piano. Rather, it is required that the *total* number of students in the sets of students that lifted a piano is five. Formally, this reading is given in (16). The lifting operator **N** (= Van der Does's $\textbf{N}_2$) that generates it is defined in (17).

(16) $|\{x \in X : X \subseteq \mathbf{student}' \land \mathbf{lift\_piano}(X)\}| = 5$

(17) $\mathbf{N} \stackrel{\text{def}}{=} \lambda D.\lambda A.\lambda \mathcal{B}.D(A)(\cup(\mathcal{B} \cap \wp(A)))$

Note that the set $\cup(\mathcal{B} \cap \wp(A))$ contains x if and only if x is an element of a subset X of A such that X belongs to $\mathcal{B}$.

There are many intricate empirical problems for these lifting strategies. It would also not be too much to expect a more parsimonious configuration than three different lifts of the same type. I will address these qualms as we go along. Two of the central empirical problems for S&D's lifts should be mentioned at the outset, however. First, as Van Benthem (1986: 52–53) warns, a modificational reading like the one generated by the $\mathbf{C}_a$ lift is highly undesired with distributive predicates. For instance, assuming like Scha that all predicates have the *ett* type, sentence (18) gets the interpretation in (19).

(18) Less than five students arrived.

(19) $\mathbf{C}_a(\mathbf{less\_than\_5}')(\mathbf{student}')(\mathbf{arrive}')$
    $\Leftrightarrow \exists A \subseteq \mathbf{student}'[|A| < 5 \land \mathbf{arrive}'(A)]$

With such an analysis, sentence (18) would counter-intuitively be predicted to be consistent with the sentence *More than five students arrived*. The reason is that the statement in (19) is verified in a situation where some set of less than five students is in the extension of *arrive* while other sets of more than five students are also in this denotation. This problem is sometimes referred to in the literature as the *Van Benthem problem* for collective quantification. Note that the problem does not depend on Scha's assumption that distributive predicates like *arrive* can have sets in their lexical denotation. The problem appears also under more common techniques where *arrive* can indirectly take sets as arguments using a distributivity operator on predicates. The Van Benthem problem itself lies in the general existential strategy of the $\mathbf{C}_a$ operator.[6] A straightforward way to eliminate this problem is simply to avoid the existential-modificational strategy altogether. This is the line I adopt in subsection 5.5.2, arguing that this lift is under-motivated.

Another problem with the generality of the lifting operators appears when we consider the ways Scha and Van der Does use them for different determiners. For instance, the determiner *every* is lifted only by the $\mathbf{D}$ operator. The determiner *all*, by contrast, can be lifted by $\mathbf{C}_a$ as well. This distinction is necessary to account for the clear contrast between sentences like **Every student met* and *all the students met*. Similar assumptions have to rule out the application of $\mathbf{C}_a$ and $\mathbf{N}$ to the singular determiners *no* (as opposed to plural *no*) and *exactly one* (as opposed to *exactly five*). In Scha's paper, which uses the lifts only as lexical strategies that derive multiple readings for determiners, such distinctions are simply stipulated. Thus, if $\mathbf{every}'$ is standardly the subset relation, then for Scha *every* unambiguously denotes $\mathbf{D}(\mathbf{every}')$, whereas *all* is ambiguous between $\mathbf{D}(\mathbf{every}')$ and $\mathbf{C}_a(\mathbf{every}')$. Van der Does, whose lifting strategies are general, also resorts here to a mere description, stating that *every* is "intrinsically distributive" and ruling out unnecessary lifts using a feature system.

The principles that govern such restrictions on the lifts are left unexplained. The reason for this shortcoming is the lack of any semantic difference between singular nouns and plural nouns in the S&D systems: a singular noun like *student* and its plural form *students* denote the same *et* predicate. The semantic differences between singular and plural nominals must therefore come from unattractive assumptions about the lexical ambiguity of certain determiners (Scha) or ad hoc syntactic mechanisms (Van der Does).

In the system that is proposed below, differences in morphological number between nouns play a crucial role in their semantics. The system is planned in such a way that the single collective type shifting operator to be used can apply only with plural determiners, due to the $(et)t$ type of plural nouns. Consequently it will become clear why collective quantification requires morphological plurality.

5.3   Atom Predicates versus Set Predicates

This section proposes a new typology of natural language predicates according to their "semantic number." This typology is used in order to formulate a principle that distinguishes between predicates whose denotations range over *atoms* (*e* type individuals) and predicates whose denotations range over *sets of atoms* (*et* type objects). Subsection 5.3.1 reviews the traditional distinction between distributive predicates and collective predicates. It is argued that this typology is not useful as a criterion for making a distinction between predicates that range over atoms and predicates that range over sets. Subsection 5.3.2 develops Dowty's observations into a new general truth-conditional typology, which is proposed as the key for the model-theoretic definition of the semantic number of predicates.

5.3.1   Distributive predicates versus collective predicates

This subsection tries to clarify the notions of distributive predicates and collective predicates, which have so far been used in this book in a sloppy way. I will argue that such a clarification is hard to obtain, and in any case is not very useful for truth-conditional semantics, hence for the purposes of our present discussion.

Subsection 2.3.1 of chapter 2 introduced the traditional typology of natural language predicates according to their semantic number. This typology talks about three classes of predicates:

1. *Distributive* predicates such as *sleep*, *smile* and *sing*.
2. *Collective* predicates, which are subdivided into:
   a. *Mixed* predicates such as *lift a piano*, *write a book* and *weigh 140 kg*.
   b. *Completely collective* (*ccl*) predicates such as *meet*, *gather* and *be a good team*.

This three-way distinction is based on two typological tests. The first kind of typological distinction, the *distributive/collective* typology, checks whether predicates show a distributivity equivalence (see section 2.1) when combined with so called "referential" nominals like *Mary and John*. For instance, the predicate *sleep* is classified as "distributive" because sentence (20a) below is equivalent to sentence (20b).

(20) a. Mary and John slept.
 b. Mary slept and John slept.

By contrast, predicates like *lift a piano* and *meet* are classified as "collective" because the sentences in (21a)/(22a) are not equivalent to their (respective) counterparts in (21b)/(22b).

(21) a. Mary and John lifted a piano.
 b. Mary lifted a piano and John lifted a piano.

(22) a. Mary and John met.
 b. *Mary met and John met.

The second typology, the *ccl*/non-*ccl* typology, tests whether a predicate leads to an unacceptable sentence when it combines with a singular nominal like *Mary*. For instance, the predicates *sleep* and *lifted a piano* are classified as non-*ccl* because the sentences in (23) below are felicitous. By contrast, the predicate *meet* is classified as *ccl* because of unacceptabilities as in sentence (24).

(23) Mary slept/lifted a piano.

(24) *Mary met.

If the two criteria distributive/collective and *ccl*/non-*ccl* are general enough, then *mixed* predicates can simply be defined as collective predicates that are not *ccl*.[7] I therefore think that the discussion above restates quite adequately the three-way typology of predicates that has been (often implicitly) assumed in the literature on plurals.

So far so good. However, to make sense of such typological distinctions we have to check whether they generalize to more constructions than the ones that were given above. In this respect both typologies have to face some difficulties. The *ccl*/non-*ccl* typology has to explicate the notion of a "singular nominal." As mentioned in subsection 2.3.6, "singular" cannot mean "morphologically singular," for this would leave very few *ccl* predicates, if any. For instance, as mentioned there, the predicate *meet* can felicitously appear in its singular form with arguments such as *the committee*. Hence, the problem of generalizing the *ccl*/non-*ccl* typology is mainly in the explication of the difference between a morphological singular nominal such as *the committee* and other morphologically singular nominals such as *the woman*. As we will see in section 5.6 below, this task is anything but trivial. Of course, the unacceptability of sentences like *The woman met* or *Mary met* is a concrete fact that we should like to account for. As argued in subsection 2.3.6, I believe that the best strategy for obtaining such an account is by appealing to the general phenomenon of *selectional restrictions* (e.g. as in *?colorless green ideas*), rather than to any theory of entailment like the one this book strives to develop. Thus, as in subsection 2.3.6, I will have to leave this problem aside.

The distributive/collective typology also faces some problems concerning its generality. Dowty (1987) convincingly points out that plural definites, for instance, do not show the kind of distributivity equivalence that is expected with "distributive" predicates such as *sleep*, *smile* or *sing*. Dowty exemplifies the problem using the sentence in (25) and the discourse in (26).

(25) At the end of the press conference, the reporters asked the president questions.

(26) a. What was that noise?
      b. Oh, I'm sure it was only the children getting up to watch cartoons. Go back to sleep.

Sentence (25) does not assert that *all* the reporters asked questions. Similarly, sentence (26b) does not entail that all the children are getting up. Dowty (1987: 103) concludes:

(27) I argue that even with "true" distributive predicates, the question of how many members of the group referent of a definite nominal must have the distributive property is in part lexically determined and in part determined by the context, and only rarely is every member required to have these properties.

Similar points have occasionally been made in the literature concerning many other intuitively distributive predicates. For the example Dowty's point implies that sentence (28a) is *not* equivalent to sentence (28b).

(28) a. The students slept.
      b. Every student slept.

Thus, predicates like *sleep* start to behave as collective predicates when they combine with plural definites. What is the explanation of the lack of equivalence in this case vis à vis the distributivity equivalence in (20) above? I know of no truth-conditional theory that accounts for such differences, and in fact, I believe that this is as it should be. As will be shown in section 6.4, there are even cases of proper name conjunction where a distributivity equivalence as in (20) does not appear. Contrary to what might have been implied in section 2.1, this suggests that the strong equivalence impression in cases like (20) does not come from the formal semantics of these constructions alone. If this conclusion is correct, then there may be little sense in using the distributive/collective typology of predicates in formal semantics. To say the least, no existing theory known to me uses this distinction profitably. This is so because any theory that manages to account truth-conditionally for the equivalence in (20) (with proper name conjunction) fails to account for the lack of equivalence in (28) (with plural definites) and vice versa.

These negative remarks leave open the question whether there are any differences between natural language predicates that motivate a model-theoretic distinction between them according to their "semantic number." The following subsection gives a positive answer to this question, and proposes a new, truth-conditional classification of atom predicates and set predicates.

5.3.2   A truth-conditional typology

One of Dowty's central observations, reviewed above in subsection 5.2.1, shows that predicates like *be numerous* and *be a good team* differ from predicates like *meet* and *gather* in disallowing collective interpretations of nominals headed by *all*. Dowty observes that sentences as in (29a) below are coherent and meaningful, while the sentences in (29b) are unacceptable.

(29) a. All the students met/gathered in the hall.
     b. *All the students are numerous/a good team.

In this aspect a plural nominal such as *all the students* sharply contrasts with a singular nominal such as *every student*, which is unacceptable with *both* kinds of predicates, as the sentences below illustrate.

(30) a. *Every student met/gathered in the hall.
     b. *Every student is numerous/a good team.

We may thus describe the difference between the predicates *meet* and *gather* and the predicates *be numerous* and *be a good team* by saying that while the former predicates are sensitive to the replacement of *all* by *every*, the latter are not. While the sentences in (29a) and (30a) cannot possibly have the same grammatical status, the unacceptable sentences in (29b) and (30b) are equivalent for all purposes.

The same distinction between predicates can be made using other pairs of plural/singular determiners besides *all* and *every*. For instance, the contrast between predicates such as *meet* and *gather* and predicates such as *be numerous* and *be a good team* is preserved when *all* is replaced by the determiner *no* in its plural use and *every* is replaced by singular *no*. Likewise, we can use the plural/singular pairs of determiners *at least two/more than one* or *many/many a*, and observe a similar contrast between the two predicates. This is illustrated in the following examples.

$$(31) \quad \left\{ \begin{array}{l} \text{No} \\ \text{At least two} \\ \text{Many} \end{array} \right\} \text{students} \left\{ \begin{array}{l} \text{met} \\ *\text{are a good team} \end{array} \right\}$$

$$(32) \quad \left\{ \begin{array}{l} \text{No} \\ \text{More than one} \\ \text{Many a} \end{array} \right\} \text{student} \left\{ \begin{array}{l} *\text{met} \\ *\text{is a good team} \end{array} \right\}$$

Thus, we see that the contrast that Dowty observed between the predicates *meet* and *be a good team* is unlikely to appear only as a result of the semantics of *all*.[8] It is also a systematic difference between the behavior of these predicates with other morphologically plural nominals, compared to their behavior with corresponding singular nominals. The crucial point is that now, instead of concentrating on "referential" nominals like *Mary and John* and *the students* as in the distributive/collective classification of the former subsection, we turn our attention to the behavior of predicates with "quantificational" nominals. In general, we classify a predicate PRED according to its behavior in sentences like the following.

(33) a. all the/no/at least two/many students PRED
      b. every/no/more than one/many a student PRED

To have names for the two kinds of predicates we recognized, let us introduce the following terminology.

Terminology   Let PRED be a natural language predicate (verb, noun or adjective). Assume the sentences in (33a) and the corresponding sentences in (33b) are equally acceptable and, if acceptable, are furthermore semantically equivalent. Then PRED is called an *atom predicate*. If the respective sentences in (33a) and (33b) differ in either acceptability or truth-conditions then PRED is called a *set predicate*.[9]

Both predicates *meet* and *be a good team* are traditionally classified as "collective." However, according to the criterion above the predicate *meet* is classified as a set predicate whereas *be a good team* is called an atom predicate. The theoretical reason for this choice of terminology is that this is the proposed criterion for defining which predicates range over atoms and which ones range over sets. Let us however use these terms for the time being as purely descriptive terms for the two kinds of predicates we have identified.

Note that what matters for the atom/set criterion is not simply acceptability/non-acceptability judgments, but also truth-conditions. For instance, the predicate *meet* qualifies as a set predicate because it is sensitive to the replacement of *every* by *all*, singular *no* by plural *no*, and so on. This sensitivity may surface as a difference in acceptability as between the pairs (29a)/(30a) or the *meet* pairs in (31)/(32) above. However, when the compared sentences are both acceptable, the sensitivity of the predicate *meet* to morphological number may also surface as a truth-conditional distinction. For instance, consider the following sentences.

(34) a. All the committees met.
      b. Every committee met.

Here both sentences (34a) and (34b) are acceptable, yet they are not equivalent: while (34b) unambiguously reports on meetings of *individual* committees, sentence (34a) may be interpreted as reporting on a joint meeting of the committees *together*, with no respect to individual meetings each committee might have had. This judgment is quite robust for the speakers I consulted. I propose that the origin for the meaning difference in (34) is strongly connected to the acceptability differences we have observed above, where the noun *students(s)* is used instead of *committee(s)*.

Let us give a brief typological survey of atom predicates and set predicates according to the above criterion. The two *ccl* atom predicates we have seen are *be a good team* and *be numerous*. Other *ccl* atom predicates are *form a pyramid*, *elect the representative* and *constitute a majority.* This is shown by the similar status of the sentences in the following *a/b* pairs.

(35) a. *All the/no/etc. students formed a pyramid/elected the representative/constituted a majority.

     b. *Every/no/etc. student formed a pyramid/elected the representative/constituted a majority.

Atom predicates also include all distributive predicates like *smile* or *sleep*, as the equivalences below show.

(36) Every/no/etc. student smiled/slept

     ⇔ All the/no/etc. students smiled/slept

A further interesting fact that was pointed out by Dowty (attributing it to Bill Ladusaw) concerns the sentences in (37) below.

(37) a. The students voted to accept the proposal.

     b. Every student voted to accept the proposal.

     c. All the students voted to accept the proposal.

The predicate *vote* leads to a collectivity effect with plural definite subjects as in sentence (37a), where the reported vote need not be unanimous. That is, sentence (37a) is not equivalent to (37b). This non-equivalence, plus the acceptability of sentences like *Mary voted to accept the proposal*, classifies *vote* as a mixed predicate on its subject argument. On the other hand, Dowty and Ladusaw observe that sentence (37c), with an *all* nominal, *is* equivalent to (37b). This clearly characterizes *vote* as an atom predicate. It seems that a similar effect appears also in (38) below with the verb *weigh*.

(38) a. The potatoes in this basket weigh 1 kg.

     b. Every potato in this basket weighs 1 kg.

     c. All the potatoes in this basket weigh 1 kg.

This shows that not only completely collective predicates (e.g. *be a good team*) or distributive predicates (e.g. *smile*) can be atom predicates. Some mixed predicates like *vote* or *weigh* (on their subject argument) are atom predicates as well.

Set predicates, in addition to the predicates *meet* and *gather*, also include *ccl* predicates like *disperse* and *be similar*, as well as reciprocated predicates like *admire each other*. This is demonstrated by difference in acceptability between the following pairs.

(39) a. *Every/no/etc. student dispersed/is similar/admired each other.

     b. All the/no/etc. students dispersed/are similar/admired each other.

With many "mixed" predicates like *lift a piano* there is probably some variation among speakers. For instance, Dowty (1987: 104) recognizes a "collective interpretation" of sentence (40a), which means he reads it as non-equivalent to (40b).

(40) a. All the students in my class performed Hamlet.
    b. Every student in my class performed Hamlet.

Thus, in Dowty's dialect the predicate *perform Hamlet*—and presumably also other mixed predicates such as *lift a piano*—is a set predicate. For convenience, I henceforth refer to this (possible) dialect of English as *Dowty's dialect*. Dowty mentions that some people find collective interpretations in (40a) more natural if the word *together* is added. This seems to be correct also for speakers like Dowty who do not take (40a) and (40b) to be equivalent. Other speakers, however, are stricter and consider (40a) and (40b) to be totally equivalent. For these speakers, only when *together* is added can the sentences become non-equivalent. Using the present terminology, in this dialect, unlike in Dowty's dialect, the predicate *perform Hamlet* is an atom predicate and only the word *together* can modify it into a set predicate. A similar point holds for many other "mixed" predicates like *drink a whole glass of beer*, *lift a piano* or *write a book*.

Moving on to the nominal domain, it is important to note that the criterion we use classifies predicates as *atom* or *set* independently of their morphological number. Thus, plural forms of nominals, verbs and adjectives (in languages where these items have number inflection) get the same classification as their singular forms. For instance, both the singular noun *student* and its plural form *students* are classified as atom predicates due to the equivalence in (41) below. Relational nouns like *colleagues*, *sisters*, *friends* and so on qualify as set predicates according to non-equivalences as in (42a). Another way to obtain a (complex) set nominal is to modify an atom nominal by a set predicate as illustrated in (42b–c).

(41) Every woman is a student
    ⇔ All the women are students

(42) a. ?Every woman is a colleague/sister/friend
       ⇎ All the women are colleagues/sisters/friends
    b. ?Every woman is a similar student
       ⇎ All the women are similar students
    a. *Every woman is a student who met yesterday at school
       ⇎ All the women are students who met yesterday at school

To end the discussion of nominals, consider "group denoting" nouns like *team*, as in the predicate nominal in the following equivalence.

(43) Every group of tall people is a good basketball team
    ⇔ All the groups of tall people are good basketball teams.

This kind of equivalence shows again that predicates like *be a good basketball team* or *be a big group* should belong to the class of atom predicates like *be a good law student* or *sleep*, despite the (arguably misleading) impression that nouns like *team* and *group* semantically differ in their "semantic number" from nouns like *student*.[10]

The following list gives a summary of atom predicates and set predicates according to the criterion we defined above.

(44) Atom predicates:
   a. sleep, smile, get up
   b. be a good team, be numerous, form a pyramid, elect Clinton, constitute a majority, outnumber (both arguments), be alone
   c. vote to accept the proposal, weigh 1 kg.
   d. (in some dialects) perform Hamlet, lift a piano, write a book
   e. student(s), child(ren), shop(s), team(s), committee(s)

(45) Set predicates:
   a. meet, gather, disperse
   b. be similar, be alike, be together
   c. like each other, look at one another
   d. perform Hamlet *together*, lift a piano *together*, write a book *together*
   e. (in Dowty's dialect) perform Hamlet, lift a piano, write a book
   f. colleague(s), brother(s), friend(s), similar student(s), student(s) who met

Note the differences and the similarities between the atom/set distinction and the traditional distributive/collective typology. An atom predicate can be one that is traditionally classified as distributive (e.g. *sleep*), completely collective (e.g. *be a good team*) or mixed (e.g. *vote*). All set predicates in Dowty's dialect are collective (mixed or completely collective). In other dialects all set predicates are completely collective. Logically, in both kinds of dialects all distributive predicates are atom predicates. This situation is graphically illustrated in figure 5.1.

What in my view is attractive in the new atom/set typology is its robustness. The test used to distinguish atom predicates from set predicates is stated in terms of entailments between natural language sentences. These entailments are argued to hold independently of context or lexical choice of other elements in the sentence besides the relevant predicate.[11] If this claim is correct, then the atom/set typology, and not the traditional distributive/collective classification, is a natural criterion for making a "rigid" model-theoretic distinction between denotations of predicates according to their semantic number. This distinction is proposed as a general principle of the lexical semantics of predicates.

(46) **The atom/set principle**
   Denotations of lexical atom predicates range over *atoms*. Denotations of lexical set predicates range over *sets of atoms*.[12]

The atom/set principle can have different implementations within different ontologies of plurals. In the present Bennett typing, it implies that lexical atom predicates denote *et* objects (sets of *e* type elements) whereas lexical set predicates denote *ett* objects (sets of *et* type elements).

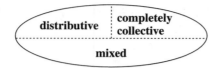

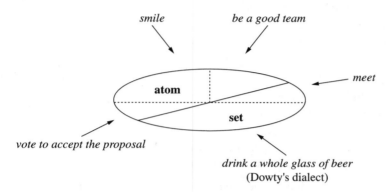

Figure 5.1
Typologies of predicates

The terms "atom predicates" and "set predicates," which classify the linguistic behavior of predicates pre-theoretically only, were of course chosen with this theoretical atom/set principle in mind. Intuitively, it is quite clear that this model-theoretic distinction between atom predicates and set predicates can be used to explain their different behavior. Set predicates lead to collectivity with plural nominals like *all the students* or *no students* because the denotations of these plural nominals range over sets, as will be proposed below. With singular nominals like *every student* or *no student*, whose denotations are assumed to range over atoms, no collectivity effect can appear. Atom predicates, by contrast, do not show collectivity even with the mentioned plural nominals. This is simply explained because the denotation of atom predicates does not encode any information about sets. The following section completes some missing details in the account just sketched.

5.4   The Characterization of Semantic Number

The atom/set distinction between predicates is not the only factor that determines whether a sentence has a collective reading or not. We have already seen that singular sentences clearly fail to exhibit collective interpretations, even when the predicate is a set predicate. Further, plural sentences including flexible nominals like *the students* or *Mary and John* can have a collective interpretation not only with set predicates but also with atom predicates. This section addresses the semantic effects of morphological number and nominal interpretation that, together with the atom/set distinction between predicates, determine whether a sentence has a collective interpretation or not. The emerging general theory of *semantic number* is informally outlined.

5.4.1   Singular predicates versus plural predicates

The effects of morphological number marking on the availability of collective interpretations can be illustrated using the contrasts between the sentences in (47) below and the respective sentences in (48), which are reproduced from the above examples.

(47) $\left\{ \begin{array}{l} \text{All the} \\ \text{No} \\ \text{At least two} \\ \text{Many} \end{array} \right\}$ students met.

(48) $\left\{ \begin{array}{l} *\text{Every} \\ *\text{No} \\ *\text{More than one} \\ *\text{Many a} \end{array} \right\}$ student met.

In standard generalized quantifier theory, pairs of determiners like *every* and *all*, singular *no* and plural *no*, or *more than one* and *at least two* are treated as synonyms. However, contrasts like the ones between (47) and (48) show that something more has to be said about the reasons why collective quantification in English and many other languages is possible with count nominals in the plural but not with count nominals in the singular.[13] As mentioned above, Scha (1981) and Van der Does (1992, 1993) assume that plural determiners can range over sets, while singular determiners cannot. However, this assumption comes only by means of lexical or syntactic stipulations on particular lexical items.

The present proposal differs from both Scha's and Van der Does' systems in taking the *noun* to be the center of the atom/set distinction within the noun phrase. I propose that singular nouns unambiguously range over atoms. The same holds for all other singular intransitive predicates (i.e. verbs and adjectives in the singular). Plural nouns, and all other plural one-place predicates, range over sets of atoms. The set denotation of plural predicates is claimed to be the main source of collectivity effects with plurals. On the other hand, the basic denotation of natural language *determiners* is insensitive to their singular/plural number feature and they all invariably range over atoms as in standard generalized quantifier theory.[14]

The immediate question that arises is of course how the denotation of a plural determiner, ranging over atoms, can combine with the denotation of a plural noun ranging over sets. My answer is based on the type fitting strategy of Partee and Rooth (1983). I propose that a type shifting operator *à la* Scha and Van der Does changes the denotation of the determiner to range over sets, not as a general lifting strategy, but only when the semantic composition with the noun denotation fails. Once its type has changed, the determiner's denotation can compose with the plural noun's denotation so that the whole nominal denotes a quantifier over sets. This quantifier can successfully compose with the main set predicate in the sentence. This is how sentences as in (47) (e.g. *All the students met*) finally get their collective interpretation. Note however that according to Partee and Rooth, type shifting applies *only* when type mismatch occurs. When the noun is in the singular as in (48) (e.g. **Every student met*), it unambiguously ranges over atoms and hence does not trigger any change in the type of the determiner. Consequently, quantification with singular nominals remains unambiguously "distributive."

Let us informally summarize this proposal above as follows.

(49) **The morpho-semantics of number**
   a. Denotations of singular predicates range only over atoms; denotations of plural predicates range over sets of atoms as well.
   b. Type mismatches between denotations ranging over atoms and denotations ranging over sets are resolved using type fitting principles.

How do principles (46) and (49) interact? That is, how do the atom/set classification of the predicate and its singular/plural morphological number together determine its denotation? The key to answering this question is our assumption in principle (46) that the descriptive atom/set classification affects only the *lexical* denotation of the predicate. However, what determines the denotation of the *number inflected* predicate is also its number morphology (singular or plural) as stated in principle (49). What this principle actually makes sure is that the singular and plural number features have meanings that can override the lexical consequences of the atom/set classification of predicates: the singular number feature coerces the denotation of a predicate to range over atoms, even if it is a set predicate. Likewise, the plural number feature allows the denotation of a predicate to range over sets, even if it is an atom predicate.

Formally, principle (49) is implemented using the denotations given to the values of the (possibly covert) number feature. Let us denote these values by +SG and +PL for singular/plural respectively. The denotation of the +SG value is assumed to be the operator mapping any set of sets to the union of its singletons. This singularity operator, referred to as *sg*, is formally defined as follows.

$$\llbracket +\text{SG} \rrbracket = sg_{(ett)(et)} \stackrel{\text{def}}{=} \lambda \mathcal{P}_{ett}.\lambda x_e.\mathcal{P}(\{x\})$$

The +PL value of the number feature is assumed to be interpreted as the *identity map* on predicates.[15]

$$\llbracket +\text{PL} \rrbracket = id_{(\tau t)(\tau t)} \stackrel{\text{def}}{=} \lambda X_{\tau t}.X \quad \text{where } \tau = e \text{ or } \tau = et$$

For sake of presentation let us ignore for a while the $(et)(et)$ type of +PL and use only its $(ett)(ett)$ type.

The result of these assumptions about the denotations of +SG and +PL is that the lexical *ett* denotation of set predicates can always compose directly with the denotation of the number feature. However, with number inflected *atom* predicates the *et* type of the lexical predicate and the type of the number feature (either +SG or +PL) do not match. To resolve these type mismatch situations we use the commonly assumed *predicate distributivity* (*pdist*) operator as a type fitting operator that changes the type of the predicate from *et* to *ett*. This operator standardly maps a predicate P to the powerset of this predicate minus the empty set. Formally:

$$pdist_{(et)(ett)} \stackrel{\mathrm{def}}{=} \lambda A.\lambda B.\emptyset \neq B \subseteq A$$

In a more complete framework, such operators as *sg*, *id* and *pdist* on one-place predicates should be extended to arbitrary arguments of *n*-place predicates of arbitrary arity. For the sake of clarity I do not take here this technically simple but cumbersome step.

The following examples illustrate the use of the number feature denotations and the *pdist* type fitting operator. Let us first consider the singular and plural forms of the nominal atom predicate *student(s)*.

(50) a. $\llbracket \text{student} \rrbracket = \llbracket \text{student+SG} \rrbracket = \textbf{student}'_{et}\ sg_{(ett)(et)}$ (mismatch)
          $sg(pdist(\textbf{student}')) = \textbf{student}'$ (resolution)
   b. $\llbracket \text{students} \rrbracket = \llbracket \text{student+PL} \rrbracket = \textbf{student}'_{et}\ id_{(ett)(ett)}$ (mismatch)
          $id(pdist(\textbf{student}')) = \lambda A_{et}.\emptyset \neq A \subseteq \textbf{student}'$ (resolution)

In (50a), the lexical *et* type of the noun does not match the *sg* denotation of the singular value of the number feature. Consequently, the *pdist* operator is allowed to apply, and it lifts its type to *ett*. The result of composing *sg* and *pdist* leads us back to where we started: to the lexical denotation of the noun. In (50b) there is also a type mismatch, this time with the plural value +PL of the number feature. The *pdist* operator is allowed to apply, and since the number feature value +PL denotes the identity map, the result is the *ett* predicate *pdist*(**student**′): the set of all non-empty sets of students.

The following analyses illustrate the derivation of meaning for the singular and plural forms of the nominal set predicate *friend(s)*.

(51) a. $\llbracket \text{friend} \rrbracket = \llbracket \text{friend+SG} \rrbracket = sg_{(ett)(et)}(\textbf{friends}'_{ett}) = \lambda x_e.\textbf{friends}'(\{x\})$
   b. $\llbracket \text{friends} \rrbracket = \llbracket \text{friend+PL} \rrbracket = id_{(ett)(ett)}(\textbf{friends}'_{ett}) = \textbf{friends}'$

In these cases type fitting is unnecessary, because the lexical type *ett* of set predicates matches the type of both number values. In (51a), this leads to the predicate holding of the singular elements in the lexical denotation, that is to the entities x s.t. x is a friend (whatever this may mean in the context of utterance). In (51b), the identity map leaves us with the lexical denotation of the predicate: the set of sets of friends (including all possible singletons). I henceforth use the notation **students**′ for plural atomic nominals like *students* as an abbreviation for their derived *ett* meaning *pdist*(**student**′). Likewise, **friend**′ is a convenient notation for the derived *et* denotation *sg*(**friends**′) of the singular set predicate *friend*.

Verbal atom and set predicates are similarly analyzed:

(52) a. $[\![\text{sleeps}]\!] = [\![\text{sleep+SG}]\!] = sg(pdist(\textbf{sleep}'_{et})) = \textbf{sleep}'$
     b. $[\![\text{sleep}]\!] = [\![\text{sleep+PL}]\!] = id(pdist(\textbf{sleep}'_{et})) = pdist(\textbf{sleep}')$

(53) a. $[\![\text{meets}]\!] = [\![\text{meet+SG}]\!] = sg(\textbf{meet}'_{ett})$
     b. $[\![\text{meet}]\!] = [\![\text{meet+PL}]\!] = id(\textbf{meet}'_{ett}) = \textbf{meet}'$

Of course, these analyses assume that the forms *sleep* and *meet* in (52b) and (53b) have the third person feature. Otherwise these forms should be analyzed like the singular forms in (52a) and (53a).

With respect to the analysis of atom predicates in the singular (e.g. *student* or *sleeps*), it was noted that the composition of the singularity feature denotation *sg* with the *pdist* operator always gives the identity function on the *et* domain. This is stated in general below.

Fact 7 For every P_{et}: $sg(pdist(P)) = P$.

This means that in the proposed mechanism singular morphology has no semantic effect on the lexical denotation of atom predicates, just like plural morphology (whose meaning is *id*) does not trigger any change in the denotation of set predicates.

Unlike predicates, all lexical *determiners* are assumed to range over atoms: their type is uniformly the standard $(et)(ett)$. In singular sentences like (54) we get the standard analysis in (55).

(54) No student slept.

(55) $\textbf{no}'_{(et)(ett)}(\textbf{student}'_{et})(\textbf{sleep}'_{et})$
     $\Leftrightarrow \textbf{student}' \cap \textbf{sleep}' = \emptyset$

In singular sentences like (56) below, the denotation of the singular set predicate *meets*, derived using the *sg* operator, leads to the plausible interpretation in (57).

(56) No committee met.

(57) $\textbf{no}'_{(et)(ett)}(\textbf{committee}'_{et})(sg(\textbf{meet}'_{ett}))$
     $\Leftrightarrow \textbf{committee}' \cap \{x_e : \textbf{meet}'(\{x\})\} = \emptyset$

In plural sentences like the following, there is a type mismatch between the $(et)(ett)$ determiner and the *ett* denotation of the plural noun.

(58) No students slept.

(59) No committees met.

This type mismatch is resolved by applying a type fitting operator to the standard denotation of the determiner. This operator, referred to as *determiner fitting* (*dfit*), turns an $(et)(ett)$ determiner over atoms to an $(ett)(ettt)$ determiner over sets. After the application of this operator, the analysis of sentences (58) and (59) is as follows.

(60) $((\textit{dfit}(\mathbf{no}'))(\textit{pdist}(\mathbf{student}')))(\textit{pdist}(\mathbf{sleep}'))$

(61) $((\textit{dfit}(\mathbf{no}'))(\textit{pdist}(\mathbf{committee}')))(\mathbf{meet}')$

The definition of the *dfit* operator is the subject of section 5.5. Meanwhile, it suffices to note that the analysis generated in (60) for (58) (= *no students slept*) correctly turns out to be equivalent to the standard reading of (54) (= *no student slept*) in (55). By contrast, when the set predicate *meet* is involved as in (59) (= *no committees met*), the application of *dfit* in (61) generates a plausible collective analysis, paraphrased roughly by "no two (or more) committees met each other." This reading is of course different than the distributive reading of (56) (= *no committee met*) in (57). In a similar way, the *dfit* operator derives for the plural sentence (63) below a reading that is equivalent to the statement in (63a). By contrast, the singular sentence (62) is modeled by the statement in (62a), which is tautological because of the selectional properties of the predicate *meet*.

(62) *No student met.
    a. $\neg\exists x[\mathbf{student}'(x) \wedge \mathbf{meet}'(\{x\})]$

(63) No students met.
    a. No student participated in a student meeting.

As was remarked above in relation to example (34), plural sentences like (59) do have a "distributive" reading equivalent to their singular correlate. This is the reason for our assumption above that the denotation of the plural morphology feature +PL is ambiguous between the identity map on the *et* domain and the identity map on the *ett* domain. The second reading generates the "collective" analysis of (59) in (61) while the first $(et)(et)$ reading of +PL is responsible for the reading equivalent to (56), whose derivation below is almost identical to (57).[16]

(64) $\mathbf{no}'_{(et)(ett)}(\textit{id}(\mathbf{committee}'_{et}))(\textit{sg}(\mathbf{meet}'_{ett}))$
    $\Leftrightarrow \mathbf{committee}' \cap \{x_e : \mathbf{meet}'(\{x\})\} = \emptyset$

This concludes the exposition of the proposed treatment of the relationships between morphological number and semantic number. The discussion would not be complete, however, without making some empirical remarks about these complex relations. First, principle (49) is intended to deal only with count nouns and not with mass terms, which are the typical singular nominals that do show collectivity effects. For instance, while the count nominal *piece of sugar* in sentence (65a) below distinctly differs from its plural counterpart in (65b), the mass noun *sugar* does show collectivity in (66).

(65) a. All the pieces of sugar are concentrated in this container.
    b. ?Every piece of sugar is concentrated in this container.

(66) All the sugar is concentrated in this container.

Second, it should be noted that non-collectivity with singular count nominals is not a universal phenomenon despite its robustness in English and many other languages. Agnes Bende-Farkas and Anna Szabolcsi (p.c.) point out that Hungarian allows collectivity with some singular count nominals. For instance:

(67) Minden / az összes / a legtöbb / sok   diák   össze-gyűlt
      Every   / the all   / the most / many student together-gathered
      "All the/all the/most of the/many students gathered"

The study of such phenomena is left for further research. I believe however that the insightful cross-linguistic analysis of mass terms in Chierchia (1998b) can be combined with the present proposal to account for such puzzles.

One further remark has to do with the inclusion of singular elements (i.e. singletons) in the *ett* denotation of plural nouns. As mentioned in subsection 4.2.4, it is sometimes very clear that morphological plurality forces an interpretation that involves more than one element. For instance, sentence (68) clearly implies (69).

(68) The students in this room are happy.

(69) There are at least two students in this room.

The present analysis does not capture such effects. One reason is that the set of sets generated by the *pdist* operator as the denotation of plural nouns like *students* includes singletons.[17] Thus, in a situation where there is only one student in the room sentence (68) is counter-intuitively expected to be true if this student happens to be happy. Sentence (69) is of course false in this situation.

Are we to conclude from this problem that plural nouns should not include singularities in their extension? Like many other works on plurality I believe the answer is negative.[18] Consider for instance the following example, due to Krifka (1989).

(70) Do you have children?
      Yes, I have one child. / #No, I have (only) one child.

If the denotation of *children* excludes singularities then it is hard to see how the question in (70) is interpreted the way it is. Or consider a similar example without an interrogative:

(71) Every parent who cares about his children thinks that we should hire John as a teacher.

Suppose that Bill only has one child and he cares about him. Sentence (71) entails that Bill thinks that we should hire John as a teacher. This is unexpected if the noun *children* excludes singularities. The reason is that in this case the value of the nominal *his children* would become empty or undefined for Bill. Consequently, Bill would be excluded from the set of parents quantified over in (71), this fact is not captured.

Another example for the absence of "semantic plurality" with plurals is the following sentence.

(72) Either John or [Mary and Sue] are the thieves who stole Bill's car.

Suppose it turns out that John is the thief who stole Bill's car. Sentence (72) is of course true. However, if the noun phrase *the thieves who stole Bill's car* excludes singularities from its denotation this cannot happen.

   Thus, we are facing some conflicting evidence, which may point to the conclusion that the "more than one" implication of plural nouns is not simply denotational. In the lack of a theory that accounts for the factors that govern such effects I think that a reasonable motivation to prefer the present choice is the following theoretical consideration of Landman (1989). The inclusion of singletons in the denotations of plural nouns allows us to use the *pdist* operator in their definition. As we will see in chapter 6, this operator is independently motivated in the analysis of plurals. Thus, since any theory has to assume some mapping from the denotation of singular nouns to the denotation of plural nouns, a mapping that allows singletons is theoretically more economical than the alternative possibility of excluding them. As will become evident below, this inclusion of singletons is crucial for the present account of plural quantification.

5.4.2 Quantificational nominals versus non-quantificational nominals

So far, we have concentrated on collectivity effects of various predicates with nominals like *all the students* and *no students*. We saw that set predicates show collectivity effects with such nominals, whereas atom predicates do not. This is exemplified below once more using our two prototypical examples for atom predicates and set predicates, but this time with a larger class of nominals.[19]

(73) $\left\{\begin{array}{l}\text{All the}\\\text{Exactly four}\\\text{Between four and ten}\\\text{More/Less than eleven}\\\text{At least/most twelve}\\\text{Few/Many}\\\text{no}\\\text{Most of the/?Most}\end{array}\right\}$ students $\left\{\begin{array}{l}\text{met}\\\ast\text{are a good team}\end{array}\right\}$

However, with many other nominals the contrast between atom predicates and set predicates vanishes. Consider for instance the following sentences.

(74) $\left\{\begin{array}{l}\text{The students}\\\text{Some students I know}\\\text{Five students I know}\\\text{Mary and John}\\\text{A/Some student and a/some teacher I know}\\\text{The student(s) and the teacher(s)}\end{array}\right\}$ $\left\{\begin{array}{l}\text{met}\\\text{are a good team}\end{array}\right\}$

Such collectivity effects with atom predicates like *be a good team* are not explained by the two principles (46) and (49) above. To complete our classification of "collectivity triggers" we should therefore account for these effects and for the origins of the contrast they show between the nominals in (74) and the nominals in (73).

In chapter 4, the distinction between the nominals in (73) and those in (74) was claimed to be a manifestation of the more general distinction made between *rigid nominals* (DPs) and *flexible nominals* (NPs and D's). The subjects of (73) are rigid, hence their only reading is the *quantificational* reading obtained by composing the denotation of an overt SPEC position (a semantic determiner) with the denotation of the noun. By contrast, the flexible nominals in (74) also have a *predicative* reading. I propose that the origin for the contrast between (73) and (74) is that this predicative reading of the nominals in (74) allows the application of a mapping from sets of atoms to atoms. This *impure atom* strategy is due to Link (1984) and Landman (1989, 1996), who allow a plural noun phrase like *the students* or *the committee members* to have an interpretation similar to singular noun phrases like *the group of students* or *the committee*. In a sentence like *the students are a good team*, the set of students is mapped to the atomic element representing the relevant group of students. This *e* type group, and not simply the *et* set of students, is claimed to be a good team. Such a mapping from sets to so-called "impure" atoms captures the collective effect with atom predicates. With rigid nominals as in (73), we assumes that this mapping is not available.

The assumed "impure atom" strategy is modeled as a mapping from predicates of type *ett* (predicates over sets) to predicates of type *et* (predicates over atoms). I use the notation $\downarrow$ to refer to this $(et)(ett)$ operator. Without trying to say more right now about the nature of this mapping, the following analyses use it for exemplifying the compositional meaning derivation for two sentences from (74) above. For relevant notation in these analyses consult chapter 4.

(75) The students are a good team.

   a. $\exists f_{(et)e}[\text{CH}(f) \wedge \langle f \rangle (\downarrow (\textbf{the}^{\text{pl}}_{(ett)(ett)}(\textbf{students}'_{ett})))(\textbf{good\_team}'_{et})]$
   $\textbf{student}'_{et} \neq \emptyset \wedge \exists x \in (\downarrow \{\textbf{student}'\})[\textbf{good\_team}'(x)]$

(76) Five students I know are a good team.

   a. $\exists f[\text{CH}(f) \wedge \langle f \rangle (\downarrow (\textbf{five}'(\textbf{students}')))(\textbf{good\_team}')]$
   $\exists x \in (\downarrow \{A \subseteq \textbf{student}' : |A| = 5\})[\textbf{good\_team}'(x)]$

(77) Mary and John are a good team.

   a. $\exists f[\text{CH}(f) \wedge \langle f \rangle (\downarrow (\text{min}(M \sqcap J)))(\textbf{good\_team}')]$
   $\exists x \in (\downarrow \{\{\textbf{m}', \textbf{j}'\}\})[\textbf{good\_team}'(x)]$

The empirical distinction between rigid nominals and flexible nominals also holds with other atom predicates besides *be a good team*. For instance, we have reviewed above the

Dowty/Ladusaw observation that sentence (37c) (reproduced below as (78a)), with the rigid quantificational nominal *all*, must be interpreted distributively, as equivalent to (78b). Sentence (79), by contrast, allows a collective interpretation, as it is clearly equivalent to neither (78a) nor (78b).

(78) a. All the students voted to accept the proposal.
     b. Every student voted to accept the proposal.

(79) The students voted to accept the proposal.

In a similar way, sentence (80) below states that the total number of *individual* students who voted to accept the proposal is ten. The sentence does not leave open the possibility that the number of students who made an individual affirmative vote was more than ten or less than ten. In other words, quantifiers like *exactly ten students* fully distribute to atoms when they combine with atom predicates. By contrast, sentence (81) contains the set predicate *meet*. This sentence can of course be true in case no single student is in the extension of the predicate.[20]

(80) Exactly ten students voted to accept the proposal.

(81) Exactly ten students met.

As in sentence (78a), with *all*, the rigid nominal *exactly ten students* in (80) differs from a flexible nominal like *the ten students*, which does show collectivity with the atom predicate *vote* in sentence (82) below: this sentence is not equivalent to (83).

(82) The ten students voted to accept the proposal.

(83) Each of the ten students voted to accept the proposal.

The subject of sentence (82) is treated as flexible, hence the analysis above using a mapping from sets to atoms is applicable to derive its collective readings.

5.4.3 Summary of collectivity triggers
Three binary distinctions were argued to trigger collectivity effects in natural language sentences:

1. The *lexical semantic* distinction between predicates that range over atoms and predicates that range over sets.
2. The *morpho-syntactic* distinction between singular number inflected predicates, which range over atoms, and plural predicates, which ambiguously range over either atoms or sets.
3. The *syntactic/semantic* difference between quantificational nominals and non-quantificational nominals (or rigid nominals versus flexible nominals). Non-quantificational nominals ranging over sets can be mapped to denotations ranging over "impure" atoms. Quantificational nominals cannot undergo this process.

To summarize the effects of these three principles, consider what happens in the four cases where an atom/set predicate meets a quantificational/non-quantificational nominal.

1. When a set predicate like *gather* meets a rigid nominal like *every student* or *all the students*, the situation depends on the morphological number of the noun. Singular nouns, like all singular one place predicates in natural language, denote predicates over atoms. Plural nouns, by contrast, can denote predicates over sets of atomic entities. Determiners standardly range over atoms. Consequently, sentences in the singular like *every student gathers* get only the unacceptable interpretation, claiming that the set of students is a subset of the set of atomic entities that gather. Sentences like *every committee gathers* obtain their acceptable interpretation in the same way. With plurals, however, as in *all the students gather*, the noun can denote a predicate over sets, which does not match the atomic denotation of the determiner. This mismatch drives a type fitting operator that changes the denotation of the determiner to range over sets. Consequently, the denotation of nominals like *all the students* can range over sets and thus can combine with denotations of set predicates like *gather* to give meaningful interpretations. Sentences like *all the committees gather* are ambiguous due to the atom/set ambiguity of the plural noun and verb.

2. When an atom predicate like *be a good team* encounters a non-quantificational nominal like *the students*, whose denotation ranges over sets, we get a collectivity effect. This is due to a mapping of the set of students to an impure atom. This process is a *general* one: it can occur with all non-quantificational nominals and all atom predicates. Thus, a non-distributivity effect like the one Dowty observes in the sentence *the children are getting up to watch cartoons* also stems from this "impure atom" strategy.

The two other possibilities are less dramatic:

3. When an atom predicate like *smile* or *be a good team* meets a quantificational nominal like *all the students/committees* or *every student/committee*, the derived interpretation is the standard analysis of generalized quantifier theory. Determiners like *every* and *all* are synonyms. Due to the atomic denotations of nouns such as *student(s)* and *committee(s)*, determiners like *every* and *all* lead to equivalent truth conditions, even when the plural determiner is *dfit* ted into a determiner over sets.

4. When a set predicate like *meet* combines with a non-quantificational nominal like *the students*, we have two possibilities, as in many theories of plurals. One possibility is to let the quantificational denotation of the nominal, which ranges over sets, to combine directly with the set predicate. A more complicated possibility is let the impure atom strategy map the *set* denotation of the NP to an impure atom, as in case 1 above. This also leads to a collective interpretation, this time using the *atom* denotation of *meet*.

Table 5.1 indicates the cases where collectivity is possible and the interpretative strategies that derive it.

Table 5.1
Cases of collectivity

VP	Nominal		
	Singular	Plural	
		Non-quantificational	Quantificational
atom	no	yes (*i.a.*)	no
set	no	yes (*i.a.*/directly)	yes (*dfit*)

Notes: *i.a.* = impure atoms, *dfit* = determiner fitting

5.5 Quantification over Sets

This section studies the interpretation of plural quantificational nominals. As was proposed in the previous section, the plural number of the noun in such nominals triggers the application of a *determiner fitting operator* responsible for the collective interpretation of the sentence. The precise nature of this reading, and the proper way to define the *dfit* operator that derive it are the subject of this section.

Subsection 5.5.1 introduces the type fitting operator that is responsible for collective readings with plural determiners. Subsection 5.5.2 argues for the empirical adequacy of this process in many aspects, but proposes to refine it using an additional quantificational strategy over *witness sets*, which is needed in order to capture some further puzzles of quantification with plurals. Subsection 5.5.3 summarizes the general type fitting strategy that emerges, and motivates a simple principle of *quantifier fitting*, in parallel to the determiner fitting and predicate fitting (distributivity) mechanisms. Subsection 5.5.4 remarks on the central issue of monotonicity with plural determiners and subsection 5.5.5 briefly discusses some remaining hard problems with multiple occurrences of plural quantificational nominals in coordinations and transitive constructions.

5.5.1 Fitting determiners to quantification over sets

The previous sections have specified the factors that govern collective interpretations by concentrating on the type of singular predicates and plural predicates. We may turn now to another central question of this chapter: what is the collective interpretation of sentences where a quantificational nominal combines with a set predicate and how is it derived? Consider for example sentence (84) below.

(84) Exactly five students met.

Both the plural noun *students* and the verb *meet* have a reading where they denote *ett* predicates. Under this interpretation, the plural noun denotes the set of sets *pdist*(**student**$'$), which is abbreviated as **students**$'$; and the plural form of the verb *meet* denotes the *ett* predicate **meet′**. The determiner *exactly five* standardly denotes the relation **exactly_5′** that holds between *et* predicates whose intersection is of cardinality five. The resolution of the type mismatch between the determiner and the noun is the point where quantification over sets comes into play. Unlike the Scha/Van der Does ambiguity approaches, I would like to propose that there is a *uniform* process that adjusts the (*et*)(*ett*) determiner to its *ett* arguments. Conceptually, the result of this process is that both arguments are lowered to *et* predicates so ordinary quantification can apply. This is obtained in two steps, which are illustrated below for sentence (84).

Step 1 (intersection)   The verb denotation **meet′** is modified by intersecting it with the noun denotation **students′**. We get the set **meet′** ∩ **students′**, the set of all non-empty sets of students that met. As will be explained below, this operation is motivated by the *conservativity* property of quantification in natural language.

Step 2 (union)   The two sets of sets that serve as arguments of the determiner are both unioned. Thus, the set of sets **students′** is lowered to the set ∪ **students′**, which is just the singular noun denotation **student′**. Analogously, the intersection set of sets **meet′** ∩ **students′** is lowered to ∪(**meet′** ∩ **students′**), which is the set of students who participated in a set of students that met. This notion of *participation* is taken to be central to the semantics of plurals.

The resulting reading is calculated in (85) and paraphrased in (86).

(85) **exactly_5′**(∪**students′**)(∪(**meet′** ∩ **students′**))
    ⇔ **exactly_5′**(**student′**)(∪{$A \subseteq$ **student′** : $A \neq \emptyset \wedge$ **meet′**(A)})
    ⇔ **exactly_5′**(**student′**)({$x_e : \exists A \subseteq$ **student′**$[x \in A \wedge$ **meet′**$(A)]$})
    ⇔ $|\{x \in$ **student′** $: \exists A \subseteq$ **student′**$[x \in A \wedge$ **meet′**$(A)]\}| = 5$

(86) The number of students who participated in a student meeting is five.

The determiner fitting operator *dfit* implements the two step strategy in (85) by lifting the standard (*et*)(*ett*) determiner to a determiner over sets of type (*ett*)(*ettt*). The formal definition of the *dfit* operator is the following.

(87) **Determiner fitting**
    $dfit \stackrel{\text{def}}{=} \lambda D_{(et)(ett)}.\lambda \mathcal{A}_{ett}.\lambda \mathcal{B}_{ett}.D(\cup\mathcal{A})(\cup(\mathcal{A} \cap \mathcal{B}))$

The type lifting format is technically convenient. Moreover, subsection 5.5.5 shows an advantage of the lifting strategy for the analysis of nominal coordination.

    The reading derived in (85) is of course the result of applying the *dfit* operator to the determiner as follows:

(88) *dfit*(**exactly_5′**)(**students**)(**meet′**)

This is the same reading that is derived by the **N** lifting operator of Scha and Van der Does when the **N**-lifted determiner applies to the *et* set **student′** and the *ett* predicate **meet′**. Formally:

(89) $\mathbf{N}(D)(A_{et})(\mathcal{B}_{ett}) \Leftrightarrow dfit(D)(pdist(A))(\mathcal{B})$

Note however three differences between the Scha and Van der Does lifting strategy and the present proposal:

1. The *dfit* operator derives a determiner that is of a "symmetric" type, where both the nominal phrase (e.g. *students*) and the verb phrase (e.g. *meet*) are of type *ett*. S&D allow only the verb phrase to range over sets, but not the nominal. The advantage of the present approach is obvious when we consider plurals like *all the friends* and *no students who met*, where the nominal is analyzed as being of type *ett*.
2. The *dfit* operator applies according to Partee and Rooth's type-fitting strategy and therefore it is not obligatory like S&D's lifting operators.
3. In the proposed system, the *dfit* operator is the only mechanism responsible for collective readings of quantificational plurals. By contrast, as mentioned above, S&D use a variety of lifting operators.

The implications of these points will be clarified as we go along. Before moving on to empirical matters, it is important to clarify the intuitive background behind the definition of the *dfit* strategy and its relations with generalized quantifier theory.

Conservativity as intersection   Step 1 of the *dfit* process, where the verb denotation is intersected with the noun denotation, is closely related to the *conservativity* property of determiners in generalized quantifier theory. There are various ways to conceive of this familiar notion. A linguistically attractive one is to view it as an *empirical generalization* on quantification in natural language. Consider a sentence of the form Det-N-VP. Conservativity in its simplest formulation claims that any sentence of this form is semantically equivalent to a sentence of the same form where the verb phrase is replaced by an expression that has the effect of intersecting the original verb phrase denotation with the noun denotation. One option to get such an effect is conjunction, as the equivalence in (90) below illustrates. Another option is relative clause formation, as exemplified by the equivalence in (91). Yet another intersective strategy is using "intersective" adjectives like the adjective *pregnant* in (92). It is commonly agreed that equivalence patterns similar to (90) to (92) apply with *all syntactic determiners* in natural language.

(90) Every student is a woman $\Leftrightarrow$ Every student is a student and a woman

(91) Every student arrived $\Leftrightarrow$ Every student is a student who arrived

(92) Every student is pregnant $\Leftrightarrow$ Every student is a pregnant student

The exact statement of conservativity as a generalization on equivalences in natural language is a dull syntactic task. The semantic insight behind it, however, is clear and highly surprising: there is no a priori reason why we should expect conservativity equivalences to be as prevalent as they are in natural languages.[21]

The common way to account for conservativity equivalences is by appealing to an *internal* property of natural language determiners. This is the model-theoretic definition used so far in this book, repeated below.

(93) A determiner denotation D_E is conservative iff for every $A, B \subseteq E$:
$$D_E(A)(B) \Leftrightarrow D_E(A)(A \cap B).$$

Under this perspective, conservativity appears in natural language because, so it happens, the denotations of all natural language determiners are conservative functions. As far as I know there is no theory that clearly accounts for *why* this happens to be the case.[22]

Although I will not offer here an account of the conservativity of determiners either, I would like to point out an alternative, less standard way to approach to this notion, as being *external* to the meaning of natural language determiners.[23] Suppose that by some means of syntax or by way of semantic composition the second argument of a determiner is always intersected with the first argument before application occurs. Thus when the denotations of the determiner, the noun and the verb phrase are D, A and B, respectively, the meaning of the sentence is not $D(A)(B)$ as usual, but rather $D(A)(A \cap B)$. This accounts for conservativity equivalences as well. Crucially, however, this is so even if the denotation of the determiner D is *not* a conservative function as defined in (93). For instance, the classical denotation of the determiner *every* is the subset relation as defined in (94a). Suppose, for sake of the mental exercise, that the denotation of *every* is the *identity* relation as defined in (94b) below.

(94) a. $subset(A)(B) = 1 \Leftrightarrow A \subseteq B$
  b. $id(A)(B) = 1 \Leftrightarrow A = B$

(95) a. $[\![every]\!] = subset$:
  $[\![every\ student\ arrived]\!] = 1$
  $\Leftrightarrow subset(\mathbf{student'})(\mathbf{student'} \cap \mathbf{arrive'}) = 1$
  $\Leftrightarrow \mathbf{student'} \subseteq \mathbf{student'} \cap \mathbf{arrive'}$
  $\Leftrightarrow \mathbf{student'} \subseteq \mathbf{arrive'}$
  b. $[\![every]\!] = id$:
  $[\![every\ student\ arrived]\!] = 1$
  $\Leftrightarrow id(\mathbf{student'})(\mathbf{student'} \cap \mathbf{arrive'}) = 1$
  $\Leftrightarrow \mathbf{student'} = \mathbf{student'} \cap \mathbf{arrive'}$
  $\Leftrightarrow \mathbf{student'} \subseteq \mathbf{arrive'}$

Given an intersective procedure as described above, both possibilities lead to the correct analysis of a sentence like *every student arrived* as expressing a subset relation between the two relevant sets. This is shown in (95a–b) using the corresponding definition of *every* in (94a–b). The identity relation, however, is not a conservative determiner denotation, as can be easily verified.

Getting back to plurals, the present *dfit* operation is based on the latter view of conservativity. More formally, when both the noun and the verb phrase predicates are *pdist*ributed *et* predicates, what we get is a classical conservativity equivalence that does not hinge on a conservative denotation of the determiner. This is formally stated below.

Proposition 8 For any determiner D, for all $A, B \subseteq E$: $dfit(D)(pdist(A))(pdist(B)) \Leftrightarrow D(A)(A \cap B)$.

Of course, since we assume that all predicates, singular and plural, can denote *et* predicates without being lifted by the *pdist* operator, we still have to assume the standard conservative denotations for determiners in the non-lifted case. However, if the "intersective" view on conservativity as external to the determiner denotation is correct, it may turn out that the intersection step within *dfit* is a manifestation of a more general process in natural language. I will not try to get into this point any deeper here.

Empirically interesting questions about conservativity with plurals emerge when we consider cases where one of the arguments of the determiner is a set predicate. Intuitively, the following pairs of sentences are equivalent.

(96) a. All the lines are parallel.
  b. All the lines are parallel lines.

(97) a. All the students who met yesterday at the nightclub are rich.
  b. All the students who met yesterday at the nightclub are rich students who met yesterday at the nightclub.

(98) a. All the students who met yesterday at the nightclub are similar.
  b. All the students who met yesterday at the nightclub are similar students who met yesterday at the nightclub.

The intersective process within the *dfit* strategy accounts for such equivalences, which are not even expressible using the standard conservativity restriction in (93) on *(et)(ett)* determiner denotations. Below we will see more motivation for assuming that conservativity equivalences standardly hold also with plural quantification.

Participation as union The intersective strategy in step 1 of the *dfit* operation still does not resolve the type mismatch between the determiner and its *ett* arguments, although as we will see below it is a prerequisite for a semantically sound resolution of the mismatch. To do that we appeal to the notion of *participation* as in Link (1983: 310), which is also the intuitive background for Dowty's subentailment idea. Link and Dowty, however, introduce participation operators as new semantic primitives. Instead, I propose to use the simple *union* operation on *ett* predicates. Thus, a singularity x participates in a meeting if and only if it belongs to a set A in the extension of *meet*. Put differently: $x \in \cup\mathbf{meet}'$. However, it would be a mistake to use *only* a union strategy in order to resolve the type mismatch between the determiner and its arguments. For instance, the meaning of sentence (99) cannot be modeled as in (100), paraphrased in (101).

(99) All politicians are similar.

(100) **all$'$**($\cup$**politicians$'$**)($\cup$**similar$'$**)

(101) Every politician belongs to a set of similar things.

To see the problem, suppose that every politician is similar to his mother, but no politician is similar to any other politician. Sentence (99) is clearly false, but (101) is true. The predictions we get once we use the intersective strategy before unioning the *ett* predicates are more adequate. For instance, in the situation just described the formula (102) and its paraphrase in (103) are both false.

(102) **all$'$**($\cup$**politicians$'$**)($\cup$(**politicians$'$** $\cap$ **similar$'$**))

(103) Every politician belongs to a set of one or more similar *politicians*.

This is certainly an improvement. However, is the *dfit* strategy an empirically sound procedure *in general*? The next subsection answers this question affirmatively, after some elaborations and refinements.

5.5.2 The empirical adequacy of determiner fitting

In this subsection I examine more closely the implications of the *dfit* strategy. Some potential problems are addressed and it is argued that the mechanism above handles them in a satisfactory way. However, an additional problem motivates a modification of the quantificational strategy by adding a (conditioned) existential quantifier over witness sets.

Collectivity and counting considerations   Before moving on to problems for the *dfit* strategy, let us first address one challenge to the above classification of collectivity triggers that it explains. As summarized in table 5.1, the proposed theory predicts that plurality of a quantificational nominal is a sufficient condition for it to exhibit collectivity effects with set predicates. A case where this condition holds but the sentence does not seem to get a collective interpretation is following.

(104) ?Less than two students have gathered in the hall.

Although the verb is a set predicate, and although both the noun and the verb are plural, hence can be assigned the *ett* type, the sentence does not seem to have any acceptable interpretation. The reason for this becomes obvious once we consider the reading that the *dfit* operator generates:

(105) *dfit*(**less_than_two$'$**)(**students$'$**)(**gather$'$**)

$\Leftrightarrow$ **less_than_two$'$**($\cup$**students$'$**)($\cup$(**students$'$** $\cap$ **gather$'$**))

$\Leftrightarrow$ $|\{x_e : \exists A \subseteq$ **student$'$**$[x \in A \wedge$ **gather$'$**$(A)]\}| < 2$

In words: the number of students who participated in a student gathering (in the hall) is less than two.

Taking into account also the lexical selection properties of the verb *gather*, the possibility that only one student participated in a student gathering is of course ruled out—this could have only happened if one student "gathered alone," which the predicate *gather* disallows. Thus, statement (105) can only be used as equivalent to the statement in the following (acceptable) sentence, which the *dfit* strategy correctly models.

(106) No students gathered in the hall.

I believe that upon some reflection, most speakers would accept the equivalence between (105) and (106) as a valid prediction. Reasonably, sentence (105) seems unacceptable at first only because it is a very cumbersome way to convey the statement in (106).

Vague monotonicity of set predicates and conservativity   Consider the following sentence, which simplifies an example from Van der Does (1992: 34).

(107) Exactly one hundred children met near Amsterdam.

Suppose that only one meeting took place near Amsterdam and that it consisted of exactly one hundred children as well as some adults. Van der Does takes this description to entail (107), which is quite likely. Assume that the denotation of the verb phrase in this situation is **meet'** $= \{A\}$, where A the set of people who participated in the meeting. Under this assumption the *dfit* operator makes (107) false. The reason is that the intersective strategy within *dfit* takes into account only the sets in the denotation of the verb phrase that consist exclusively of children. The set $\{A\} \cap$ **children'** is empty since A includes also non-children. Thus, under the assumption we have made about the denotation of the predicate, sentence (107) is modeled as false in the situation described. Does this show that the intersective strategy in the *dfit* operator or in Scha's **N** operator is problematic? Like Van der Does (1993: 537–538) and unlike Van der Does (1992), I think there are reasons to doubt it.[24]

The tentative assumption we made about the denotation of the predicate *meet near Amsterdam* in the given situation is based on mere intuition. Crucially, this intuition is not a fact about entailment. It is highly questionable if as language speakers we may have such fine-grained intuitions about (model) theoretical constructs like denotations of set predicates. I would say that sentence (107) is indeed false in case we are willing to accept that the set A met but its subset of one hundred children did not meet. However, this is quite unlikely given lexical (world) knowledge about the verb *meet*. When a set of people meets it is hard to imagine how relatively big subsets of this set could possibly not have met. For instance, consider the strange effect in the following sentence.

(108) #Mary, Sue, John and Bill met yesterday at school but Mary, Sue and John didn't meet yesterday at school.

For similar reasons, in the situation described above it is implausible that the denotation of the predicate in (107) was actually $\{A\}$ as tentatively assumed. It is likely that the subset of one hundred children in A is also in the denotation of the predicate **meet'**. In this case, the intersection **meet'** $\cap$ **children'** is not empty after all. After unioning it we get a set of one hundred children and consequently (107) is treated as *true* by the *dfit* strategy.

Thus, the predicate *meet* is not a very good candidate for checking the predictions of the *dfit* operator. As an extreme example that further clarifies the point consider the predicate *be similar*. This predicate reasonably shows complete downward monotonicity up to the level of doubletons: a speaker being told that a set A is in the extension of *similar* is likely to infer that any subset of A with at least two members is also in this extension. Suppose now we want to check the adequacy of our treatment of sentence (109) below using a situation S in which there is only one set of similar things.

(109) Exactly three girls in this room are similar.

Assume this unique set of similar things includes exactly three girls and one boy. The problem is obvious: given the monotonicity of the predicate *similar*, such a situation is highly unlikely to exist—sets including any two or more of the four children are also in the extension of *similar*. More accurately, in order to construct an entailment with an antecedent that describes situations like S we would have to use a conjunction of natural language sentences that includes sentences like the following.

(110) a. Mary, Sue, Ruth and John are similar.
         b. Mary, Sue, and Ruth are *not* similar.

However, sentences (110a) and (110b) contradict each other due to the monotonicity of the predicate *similar*, hence "naive" judgments about entailment become practically impossible.

As we see, there is little hope to check fine-grained predictions of the *dfit* process using predicates like *meet*, *be similar* or *gather*. We may refer to these predicates as *(vaguely) n-bounded downward monotone*. For instance, the predicate *be similar* shows 2-bounded downward monotonicity, which can be described using the following meaning postulate.

(111) $\forall A, B[[\textbf{similar'}(A) \wedge B \subseteq A \wedge |B| \geq 2] \rightarrow \textbf{similar'}(B)]$

Fortunately, however, not all set predicates have such confounding monotonicity properties. For instance, the predicate *drink together a whole glass of beer* is clearly non-monotone, as the contingency of (112) shows.

(112) Mary, Sue, John and Bill drank together a whole glass of beer. Mary, Sue and John did not.

In a situation where Bill participated actively in the joint effort of drinking the beer, (112) is perfectly acceptable. We can now test the adequacy of the *dfit* strategy using the following sentence.

(113) Exactly five girls drank together a whole glass of beer.

Suppose that there was only one set, A, whose members drank beer together and that A consists of some five girls *and a boy*. In such a situation sentence (113) is clearly false. To check the predictions of the *dfit* strategy it becomes now reasonable to assume that the denotation of the predicate in (113) is simply $\{A\}$. No other denotation is likely in this situation, as the consistency of the sentences in (112) shows. Thus, the *dfit* strategy correctly expects (113) to be false, since $\{A\} \cap \mathbf{girls'} = \emptyset$.

These considerations mean that for the truth of (113) we are interested only in sets of *girls* that drank beer together and not in any "mixed" set of girls together with other things. This supports the intersective strategy within *dfit*, as well as the above claim that conservativity equivalences standardly hold also with set predicates. Thus, we may now safely conclude that sentences (114) and (113) are correctly predicted to be equivalent.

(114) Exactly five girls are girls who drank together a whole glass of beer.

The clearly non-monotone behavior of the predicate *drink together a whole glass of beer* helps to test many other intricate properties of quantification over sets. I will use such predicates occasionally for this purpose.

Concluding, I should emphasize that the monotonicity of predicates, although important for the general interpretation procedure, is not a *formal* semantic matter. Hence, it is irrelevant for the formulation of the *dfit* operator. For instance, from sentence (110a) and the assumption that every girl except Mary, Sue and Ruth is not similar to any other girl, sentence (109) still does not formally follow in the system. This is as it should be, since this type of entailment is not general with set predicates, as exemplified above using the predicate *drink together a whole glass of beer*. With a meaning postulate like (111), the entailments with the predicate *similar* are treated correctly.

Nothing was said above about the *reasons* for the lexical semantic monotonicity differences between set predicates. An hypothesis put forth by Tanya Reinhart (p.c.) is that this kind of monotonicity is related to the aspectual class of the predicate: all *stative* predicates like *be similar* or *meet* are (vaguely) monotone. Eventive predicates like *drink a whole glass of beer* can be non-monotone.[25] This hypothesis may be true as far as I know, and if so, it might help to explain the monotonicity behavior of set predicates. Serious investigation of these questions must wait however for another occasion.

Quantification over atoms   As mentioned above, both Scha and Van der Does assume that standard "distributive" quantification is needed for all determiners. In Van der Does' proposal this is implemented using the **D** lifting operator that adjusts a determiner to quantification over singletons. This is absolutely necessary in the S&D systems for singular determiners like *every*. However, as we have already seen (cf. (34a)), the distributive analysis is useful for plural determiners as well. To mention another motivation for this analysis,

Figure 5.2
Sets of students drinking beer

consider the following sentence, which is similar to (113) but does not include the *together* adverbial.

(115) Exactly five students drank a whole glass of beer.

Truth of this sentence may obtain independently of the joint actions of students by taking into account only students who drank a whole glass of beer by themselves. Consider for instance a situation where there was a set of five students such that each of them drank a whole glass of beer. In addition, there were also three students who drank *together* a whole glass of beer. This situation is graphically illustrated in figure 5.2, where a circle stands for a beer-drinking set. Intuitively, sentence (115) is true under this situation. In the "Dowty dialect" (see the discussion following example (40) above, page 204) the predicate *drink a whole glass of beer* is a set predicate. Thus, the *dfit* strategy, like Scha's **N** reading, expects the sentence to be false, because the total number of students who participated in sets of students that drank beer was eight, not five. Thus, we also need a strategy that does not take into account "collective actions." In the present proposal this is captured by the *et* denotations of the plural noun *students* and the main predicate. With these readings, no lifting operation applies, and sentence (115) is analyzed as in (116) below.[26]

(116) **exactly_5′(student′)**$(sg(\textbf{drink\_gl\_beer}'))$
  $\Leftrightarrow$ $|\textbf{student}' \cap sg(\textbf{drink\_gl\_beer}')| = 5$
  $\Leftrightarrow$ $|x \in \textbf{student}' : \textbf{drink\_gl\_beer}'(\{x\})| = 5$

Is there a modificational strategy?   A perennial issue in the literature on plurality concerns the existence of a modificational reading for numerals and other determiners. In the Scha and Van der Does frameworks this is the interpretation obtained using the $\mathbf{C}_a$ lift on standard determiners. This lift interprets sentences (117) and (118) as in (117a) and (118a) respectively.

(117) Five students met.
    a. There is a set of five students and this set met.

(118) Exactly five students met.
    a. There is a set of exactly five students and this set met.

Should the system generate these existential-modificational readings? The present analysis answers positively for (117) but negatively for (118). *Bare* numerals like *five* denote predicate modifiers. Noun phrase like *five students* are interpreted as quantifiers using the existential choice function mechanism as explained in chapters 3 and 4. By contrast, *complex* numerals like *exactly five*, as well as the other determiners in (73), denote standard determiners of generalized quantifier theory. Thus, in cases like (118) only the *dfit* strategy can lead to a collective reading. This process, like the **N** lift of Scha and Van der Does, does not generate any modificational reading like (118a). Rather, we get only the interpretation in (85)/(86) above, which requires that the *total* number of students who participated in student meetings is exactly five. Is this distinction between bare numerals and complex numerals well-motivated? Is there indeed motivation for a modificational strategy also with "real determiners"? For the following reasons I propose an affirmative answer to the first question and a negative answer to the second question.

Simple monotonicity tests   The modificational strategy gives an upward monotone analysis of all quantifiers. For instance, both (117a) and (118a) are true in a situation where there were many sets of students that met, independently of their number and their size, as long as one of them contained exactly five students. This is OK for (117) but problematic for (118). To see this, it is easier to use a "specificity creating" context as in the following examples. We observe that while (119a) is a felicitous continuation of (119), a similar continuation of (119) as in (120a) is impossible, as the two sentences contradict each other.

(119) Five students I know and respect met at school yesterday.
     a. Also some other students I know and respect met at school yesterday.

(120) *Exactly* five students I know and respect met at school yesterday.
     a. #Also some other students I know and respect met at school yesterday.

Existential scope   In subsection 3.3.5 it was argued that although bare numerals easily show existential wide scope beyond syntactic islands, complex numerals do not. If a modificational interpretation were adopted also for the latter, it would have been natural to expect the choice function mechanism to apply to them, generating a non-existing wide scope effect.

The determiner "no"   While it is easy to devise a modificational interpretation for most determiners, it is quite clear that this is not the general strategy for plural quantification. Reconsider the following sentence.

(121) No/exactly zero teachers are similar.

A modificational attempt to paraphrase this sentence as in (122) is of course absurd.

(122) There is an empty subset of the set of teachers and this (the) empty set is in the extension of *similar*.

Collective atom predicates   As shown above by the sentences in (73) vis-à-vis the sentences in (74), complex numerals do not allow a collective reading with atom predicates while bare numerals do. This is illustrated again by the contrast below.

(123) Eleven students I know are the football team that won the cup.

(124) *Exactly eleven students I know are the football team that won the cup.

This contrast is accounted for in section 5.6 below using the predicative reading of the indefinite subject in (123). If the same reading for the subject existed also in (124), using a modificational reading of *exactly eleven*, it would become harder to draw such a distinction and to account for the contrast.

Distributive atom predicates   This is the Van Benthem problem mentioned above, which is the strongest motivation I know to avoid modificational readings. When the set predicates of sentences like (118) or (121) are replaced by a distributive atom predicate like *sleep*, any modificational analysis known to me that is not equipped with some ad hoc stipulations has disastrous consequences for the clear monotonicity properties of the sentence. For instance, in any simple modificational strategy a sentence like *exactly five students slept* is not predicted to contradict the sentence *exactly fifty students slept*.

The witness condition   There is one point where the modificational strategy does have an advantage over the *dfit* strategy. Consider the following sentence.

(125) All the rocks are similar.

The *dfit* strategy only requires that in (125) every rock is similar to *some* other rock. This is shown by the derivation in (126).

(126) $dfit(\mathbf{all'})(\mathbf{rocks'})(\mathbf{similar'})$
$\quad \Leftrightarrow \mathbf{all'}(\cup\mathbf{rocks'})(\cup(\mathbf{rocks'} \cap \mathbf{similar'}))$
$\quad \Leftrightarrow \mathbf{all'}(\mathbf{rock'})(\{x : \exists A \subseteq \mathbf{rock'}[x \in A \land \mathbf{similar'}(A)]\})$
$\quad \Leftrightarrow \forall x[\mathbf{rock'}(x) \rightarrow \exists A \subseteq \mathbf{rock'}[x \in A \land \mathbf{similar'}(A)]]$

However, as Scha's and Dowty's analyses predict, sentence (125) entails sentence (127).

(127) The rocks are similar.

The relevant interpretation we get for (127) claims that the set of rocks $\mathbf{rock'}$ is in the extension of the set predicate $\mathbf{similar'}$.[27] The proposition in (126) does not guarantee that. Hence, the entailment (125) $\Rightarrow$ (127) is not accounted for. Intuitively, the *dfit* strategy does not expect (125) to make any claim about the entire set of rocks. Only subsets of this set are required to contain similar members.[28]

Another aspect of the problem can be observed using a more complex example like the following.

(128) Exactly five students drank together a whole glass of beer.

This sentence requires that some group of *five* students drank a whole glass of beer. To see this, consider a situation where John and Bill drank together one glass of beer and Mary, Sue and Ruth drank together another one. Assume no other glasses of beer were drunk. Sentence (128) is false (or highly marked) in such a situation. The *dfit* strategy does not respect this judgment: in the described situation we have **drink_gl_beer**$'$ = {{**j**$'$, **b**$'$}, {**m**$'$, **s**$'$, **r**$'$}}. Thus ∪(**drink_gl_beer**$'$ ∩ **students**$'$) is just the set {**j**$'$, **b**$'$, **m**$'$, **s**$'$, **r**$'$} and (128) is incorrectly modeled as *true*. In the modificational strategy, by contrast, we require in (128) that there is a set of five students that drank a whole glass of beer together, hence (128) is correctly treated as *false* in the situation just described.

My conclusion from these facts is that something is missing from the definition of the *dfit* operator, although no independent modificational strategy is required. In a quantificational structure like *D students met*, the *dfit* strategy considers correctly all the sets of meeting students. However, it only counts the number of elements in these sets and does not put any additional condition on their size. The modificational strategy does that, but does not take into account all the sets of meeting students, which leads to the problems summarized above. The ambiguity lines of Scha and Van der Does enjoy the merits of both strategies, but of course they must also inherit their demerits. There is however a way to combine the two strategies into one lifting operator that does not suffer from these problems.

The notion that will be useful for defining the combined strategy is the *witness set* definition of Barwise and Cooper (1981).

Definition 18 (witness set)   Let $D \in \wp(\wp(E) \times \wp(E))$ be a determiner over E and let A and W be subsets of E. We say that W is a *witness set* of D and A and denote $wit(D)(A)(W)$ iff $W \subseteq A$ and $D(A)(W)$ holds.

For example, the only witness set of the determiner **every**$'$ and the set **man**$'$ is the set **man**$'$ itself. A witness of **some**$'$ and **man**$'$ is any non-empty subset of **man**$'$. We sometimes sloppily refer to a set W as a witness set of the *quantifier $D(A)$*.[29]

Let us now add to the *dfit* strategy a condition that is henceforth referred to as the *witness condition*.

(129) **The witness condition**

In a quantificational structure D, A, B where D is an $(et)(ett)$ determiner and A and B are ett predicates, if the intersection set $A \cap B$ is not empty then it contains a witness set of D and ∪A.

In formula, we define the relation *witc* between D, A and B as follows.

(130) $witc \stackrel{\text{def}}{=} \lambda D.\lambda A.\lambda B.[A \cap B \neq \emptyset \rightarrow \exists W \in A \cap B[D(\cup A)(W)]]$

Read: the witness condition holds between D, A and B.

In type lifting format, we use the *dfit* lift conjoined with the witness condition as defined below. The resulting operator is referred to as $dfit_w$.[30]

(131) $dfit_w \stackrel{\text{def}}{=} \lambda D.\lambda A.\lambda B.dfit(D)(A)(B) \wedge witc(D)(A)(B)$

Let us turn now to the consequences of the witness condition. Sentence (125) is now analyzed as equivalent to the conjunction of (132a) and (132b) below.

(132) a. Every rock participates in a set of similar rocks.

b. If there is any set of similar rocks then there is a set W of similar rocks such that every rock is in W.

Sentence (132a) paraphrases the *dfit* condition, equivalent to Scha's neutral reading. Sentence (132b) paraphrases the additional witness condition. Together they simply claim that whenever the set of rocks is not empty it is in the extension of *similar*. Formally:

(133) $dfit_w(\mathbf{all'})(\mathbf{rocks'})(\mathbf{similar'})$

$\Leftrightarrow \mathbf{all'}(\cup\mathbf{rocks'})(\cup(\mathbf{rocks'} \cap \mathbf{similar'}))$

$\wedge\, [\mathbf{rocks'} \cap \mathbf{similar'} \neq \emptyset \to \exists W \in \mathbf{rocks'} \cap \mathbf{similar'}[\mathbf{all'}(\cup\mathbf{rocks'})(W)]]$

$\Leftrightarrow \forall x[\mathbf{rock'}(x) \to \exists A \subseteq \mathbf{rock'}[x \in A \wedge \mathbf{similar'}(A)]]$

$\wedge\, [\exists B \neq \emptyset[B \subseteq \mathbf{rock'} \wedge \mathbf{similar'}(B)]$

$\to \exists W \neq \emptyset[W \subseteq \mathbf{rock'} \wedge \mathbf{similar'}(W) \wedge \mathbf{rock'} \subseteq W]]$

$\Leftrightarrow [\mathbf{rock'} \neq \emptyset \to \mathbf{similar'}(\mathbf{rock'})]$

Ignoring as usual the case where there are no rocks, these are the same truth conditions sentence (127) gets in the present approach to plural definites.[31]

In sentence (128) the analysis using $dfit_w$ is as follows.

(134) $dfit_w(\mathbf{exactly\_5'})(\mathbf{students'})(\mathbf{drink\_gl\_beer'})$

$\Leftrightarrow \mathbf{exactly\_5'}(\cup\mathbf{students'})(\cup(\mathbf{students'} \cap \mathbf{drink\_gl\_beer'}))$

$\wedge\, [\mathbf{students'} \cap \mathbf{drink\_gl\_beer'} \neq \emptyset$

$\to \exists W \in \mathbf{students'} \cap \mathbf{drink\_gl\_beer'}[\mathbf{exactly\_5'}(\cup\mathbf{students'})(W)]]$

$\Leftrightarrow |\{x \in A : A \subseteq \mathbf{student'} \wedge \mathbf{drink\_gl\_beer'}(A)\}| = 5$

$\wedge\, \exists W \subseteq \mathbf{student'}[\mathbf{drink\_gl\_beer'}(W) \wedge |W| = 5]$

The first conjunct in the simplified formula is achieved by the *dfit* operation and guarantees that *exactly* five students participated in sets of students drinking beer. The second conjunct is a result of the witness condition and it verifies that there exists at least one such set constituted by exactly five students.

The non-emptiness requirement in the antecedent of witness condition(al) guarantees that it becomes vacuously true in cases of downward monotone quantifiers. Linguistically, this makes sure that in cases like (135) we do not make any undesired statement like (135a). Instead, only requirement (135b) is added to the *dfit* analysis of the sentence, which is trivially satisfied when *dfit* applies.

(135) No students are similar.

a. Incorrect addition to the *dfit* strategy: there is a set of zero similar students.

b. Vacuously true addition, provided the *dfit* strategy: *if* there is any non-empty set of similar students then there is a set of zero similar students.

In general, the witness condition is trivially satisfied with any determiner that is downward monotone on its second argument. Formally:

Proposition 9   If a determiner D is downward monotone on its second argument then $dfit_w(D) = dfit(D)$.

Proof $dfit_w(D) \subseteq dfit(D)$ by definition for any determiner D.
Assume now that $dfit(D)(\mathcal{A})(\mathcal{B})$ holds.
Thus, $D(\cup\mathcal{A})(\cup(\mathcal{A} \cap \mathcal{B}))$. (i)
Assume $\mathcal{A} \cap \mathcal{B} = \emptyset$. Then $dfit_w(D)(\mathcal{A})(\mathcal{B})$ trivially holds.
Otherwise, pick any $W \in \mathcal{A} \cap \mathcal{B}$. Hence we have $W \subseteq \cup(\mathcal{A} \cap \mathcal{B})$.
By (i) and downward monotonicity of D we have $D(\cup\mathcal{A})(W)$.
Thus $dfit_w(D)(\mathcal{A})(\mathcal{B})$ holds.

The witness condition totally avoids the Van Benthem problem. For instance, in (136) there is no problematic additional requirement like (136a). The only possible addition is (136b), which is harmless due to the definition of the *dfit* strategy.

(136) No students are happy.
      a. Incorrect addition to *dfit*: there is a set of zero happy students.
      b. Vacuously true addition to *dfit*: *if* there is any set of happy students then there is
         a set of zero happy students.

In general, when $\mathcal{A}$ and $\mathcal{B}$ are distributed *et* predicates then $dfit_w$, like the original *dfit* operator (cf. proposition 8), generates the standard truth conditions. Formally:

Proposition 10   For any determiner D, for all $A, B \subseteq E$:
$dfit_w(D)(pdist(A))(pdist(B)) \Leftrightarrow D(A)(A \cap B)$.

Proof $dfit_w(D)(pdist(A))(pdist(B))$
$\Leftrightarrow D(\cup pdist(A))(\cup(pdist(A) \cap pdist(B)))$
      $\wedge [pdist(A) \cap pdist(B) \neq \emptyset \quad \rightarrow \exists W \in pdist(A) \cap pdist(B)[D(\cup pdist(A))(W)]]$
$\Leftrightarrow D(A)(A \cap B) \wedge [A \cap B \neq \emptyset \rightarrow \exists W \subseteq A \cap B[D(A)(W)]]$.
But given $D(A)(A \cap B)$, the additional condition is met for $W = A \cap B$. Hence:
$\Leftrightarrow D(A)(A \cap B)$.

To summarize, the witness condition starts to do semantic work only in cases where the determiner is not downward monotone on its second argument and one of its arguments is a set predicate. This is necessary in view of the "existence" requirement in cases like (125) and (128). Some more cases like this are given below.

(137) More than six/between four and six/most of the students drank together a whole
      glass of beer.

(138) More than six/between four and six/most of the students who drank together a whole
      glass of beer got drunk.

A note on witness sets, discourse anaphora and maximality   As shown above, the witness condition improves the empirical adequacy of the *dfit* strategy in some problematic cases of collectivity without bringing the well-known ills of unrestricted existential techniques. Conceptually, however, the situation is far from satisfactory: while the *dfit* strategy itself is well-motivated by considerations of conservativity in generalized quantifier theory, the additional witness condition is a stipulation in need for independent motivation. Such a motivation comes from work by Szabolcsi (1997), who concentrates on some problems of nominal interpretation in Hungarian.

Szabolcsi distinguishes between different syntactic positions for nominals in Hungarian, which affect their interpretation. For instance, according to Szabolcsi the nominal in (139a), translated roughly as *more than six boys*, can appear in two different pre-verbal positions that are referred to as *DistP* and *PredOp*. By contrast, the nominal in (139b), which in English gets the same translation, can appear only in the PredOp position in Hungarian.

(139) a. több, mint hat fiú
       b. hatnál több fiú

Szabolcsi proposes that all nominals in a DistP position are interpreted using an existential quantifier over witness sets (without a conditional as in the witness strategy above). This mechanism is used to account for the possibility of cross-sentential anaphora as in (140), which in Szabolcsi's treatment gets the interpretation in (141).

(140) More than six students passed the exam. They prepared well.

(141) $\exists W \in wit(\textbf{more\_than\_6}')(\textbf{student}')[pdist(\textbf{pass}')(W) \wedge pdist(\textbf{prepare}')(W)]$

The existential quantifier is introduced using a DRT style treatment of the witness set variable W.

There are two important properties of this analysis:

1. Szabolcsi claims that all nominals that can appear in a DistP position in Hungarian are upward monotone. Thus, existential quantification over witnesses cannot generate the Van Benthem problem, which almost does not arise in these cases.[32]
2. The anaphora in cases of nominals in a DistP position is analyzed as *non-maximal*. For instance, in (140) the pronoun does not necessarily refer to *all* the students who passed the exam. Rather, when its antecedent is in a DistP position it corresponds to a witness set, which can be *any* set of more than six students who passed.

While these factual claims may be correct, Szabolcsi's account of the above nominals is distinguished from the treatment of nominals that are not in a DistP position, including all the non-upward-monotone nominals. For instance, consider the cross-sentential anaphora in (142). In these cases anaphora is "maximal," that is, *they* refers to *all* the students who passed the exam.

(142) Less than six/between six and ten/exactly six students passed the exam. They were the only ones who prepared well.

For the treatment of such cases, Szabolcsi (correctly) refrains from using her witness mechanism and appeals to the DRT framework of Kamp and Reyle (1993).

The present approach, unlike Szabolcsi's, does not take bare numerals like *three* to denote determiners. Bare numeral indefinites basically denote predicates and the mechanism interpreting them is the choice function category shift of chapter 4, rather than the witness strategy, which is designated for purely quantificational nominals. Unlike Szabolcsi, I thus suggest that it is the latter case that motivates a (maximal) witness set analysis, rather than the first one. The main motivation for this revision is the intricate relations that exist between the problem of maximal anaphora and the interpretation of collective quantifiers. Consider for example the following sentence.

(143) Between ten and thirty students drank together a whole glass of beer.

Consider now two situations. In situation S_1 there were two different sets of twelve students each, and each set drank a whole glass of beer. Situation S_2 minimally differs from S_1 in that each set consists of *twenty* students. Intuitively, sentence (143) is equally odd in both situations. However, the $dfit_w$ strategy expects the sentence to be true in S_1 but false in S_2. This is because of the total numbers of relevant students: twenty four in S_1 and forty in S_2. Note that the witness condition is satisfied in both situations, as in both of them there is *some* set of between ten and thirty students that drank together a whole glass of beer.

I would like to suggest that the unacceptability of sentence (143) in the given situations is of the same sort of the unacceptability of definites when their uniqueness requirement is not met (see subsection 4.2.4). There may be a maximality requirement related to the witness strategy, which also accounts for the maximal anaphora in (142). Concentrating on sentence (143), in both situations S_1 and S_2 there is more than one maximal witness relevant for the interpretation of the sentence, which I suggest is the reason for the oddity/falsity of the sentence in these situations. To rule out such situations, we may add to the witness condition a *unique maximum* requirement of the same sort that applies to plural definites. A revised version of the witness condition using such a requirement is formalized below as a *maximal witness condition (mwitc)*.

(144) $mwitc \overset{\text{def}}{=} \lambda D \lambda \mathcal{A} \lambda \mathcal{B}. \mathcal{A} \cap \mathcal{B} \neq \emptyset \rightarrow \exists W \in \mathcal{A} \cap \mathcal{B}[\max(wit(D)(\cup\mathcal{A}) \cap \mathcal{B}) = \{W\}]$

For instance, in sentence (143) we get the following condition.

(145) $\textbf{students}' \cap \textbf{drink}' \neq \emptyset \rightarrow \exists W \in \textbf{students}' \cap \textbf{drink}'$
$[\max(wit(\textbf{between\_10\_and\_30}')(\cup\textbf{students}') \cap \textbf{drink}') = \{W\}]$

In words: if there is any set of students that drank together a whole glass of beer then there is such a (unique) set of between 10 and 30 students that contains any other set of between 10 and 30 students that drank together a whole glass of beer. This requirement makes sentence

(143) *false* in situations S_1 and S_2 as both situations include two maximal sets. This is a "Russellian" implementation of the uniqueness condition.

An alternative technique that I will not develop here is to impose the "unique maximum" requirement as a Strawsonian presupposition and consider sentences like (143) as semantically undefined in situations that do not satisfy this requirement. This suggests that the sort of unacceptability observed in (143) with situations S_1 and S_2 is closely related to the puzzling status of sentence (146) in these situations.

(146) The students who drank together a whole glass of beer became drunk.

It is very hard to make sense of (146) in such situations for there is no unique maximal set of students that drank together a whole glass of beer. This follows from the Sharvy/Link maximality-based treatment of definites. Thus, maximality and uniqueness are common requirements for definite descriptions, collective quantification and anaphora. As in subsection 4.2.4, I must defer a more thorough investigation of these factors to another occasion and refer the reader to Rullmann (1995) for a study of maximality in other linguistic domains.

5.5.3   The general type fitting perspective

The present proposal makes a type-theoretical difference between denotations ranging over atoms and denotations ranging over sets. Accordingly, it is proposed that type mismatches between the two kinds of denotations are resolved by Partee and Rooth's *type fitting* strategy. There are three important differences between this strategy and the *category shifting* principles proposed in chapter 4:

1. Type fitting changes the *type* of an expression. Category shifts change its semantic category in the sentence.
2. Type fitting *lifts* the type of a denotation. Category shifts may leave the type unchanged. In principle they may even lower it.
3. Type fitting is subject to the coercion principle of Partee and Rooth: it is *type driven*. Category shifts are *syntax driven* in the subclass of flexible predicative nominals, but not with rigid nominals.

In principle, each semantic category (determiner, predicate, quantifier etc.) should have a (unique) type fitting operator responsible for resolving atom-set mismatches.

The type fitting approach helps to account for a phenomenon that remained unexplained by the mechanism of chapter 4. Consider the following sentence.

(147) All these children as well as every other child lifted a piano.

This sentence may be interpreted collectively for the first conjunct, but it must be interpreted distributively for the second conjunct. That is, the sentence does not entail (148a) but it does entail (148b).

(148) a. Each of these children lifted a piano.
　　 b. Every other child lifted a piano.

The general point that sentence (147) comes to exemplify is that two nominal conjuncts do not necessarily get the same distributive/collective interpretation.[33] This is problematic for the analysis we have assumed so far, where the only collective interpretation of nominals like *all these children* is of type *ett* while the only distributive interpretation of *every other child* is of type *ett*. A natural way to solve this problem arises once we fill in a gap in the proposed type fitting paradigm and add a type fitting principle for quantifiers, in addition to the *dfit* and *pdist* operators that deal with determiners and predicates respectively. The following lifting operator from *ett* quantifiers to *ettt* quantifiers completes the picture.

(149) **Quantifier fitting**
$$qfit \stackrel{\text{def}}{=} \lambda Q_{ett}.\lambda \mathcal{A}_{ett}.Q(\{x : \{x\} \in \mathcal{A}\})$$

This operator has a similar effect to the Scha/Van der Does **D** operator on determiners: both operators care only of singletons in the extension of the predicate. Using the *qfit* operator we can analyze sentence (147) as follows.

$$(dfit_w(\mathbf{all'})(\mathbf{children'}) \sqcap qfit(\mathbf{every'}(\mathbf{o\_child'})))(\mathbf{lift\_piano'})$$

$$\Leftrightarrow \mathbf{child'} \neq \emptyset \land \mathbf{lift\_piano'}(\mathbf{child'}) \land \forall x \in \mathbf{o\_child'}[\mathbf{lift\_piano'}(\{x\})]$$

Note that the application of *qfit* is motivated here by the type mismatch between the conjuncts. Note further that *qfit* is semantically sterile when the *ett* predicate to which the lifted quantifier applies is a *pdist*ributed *et* predicate. Alternatively, when this predicate is a non-*pdist*ributed *ett* predicate (hence the denotation of a set predicate), the *qfit* operator leads the same reading generated without *qfit*, using the *sg*-lowered *et* denotation of the predicate. Formally:

(150) a. $qfit(Q_{ett})(pdist(A_{et})) \Leftrightarrow Q(A)$
　　 b. $qfit(Q_{ett})(\mathcal{A}) \Leftrightarrow Q(sg(\mathcal{A}))$

　　The three type fitting strategies are summarized in table 5.2. Each of the operators applies to a different semantic category and adjusts its type for ranging over plural individuals.

Table 5.2
Type fitting strategies

	Singular		Plural
Determiner	$(et)(ett)$	$\stackrel{dfit_w}{\Longrightarrow}$	$(ett)(ettt)$
Predicate	et	$\stackrel{pdist}{\Longrightarrow}$	ett
Quantifier	ett	$\stackrel{qfit}{\Longrightarrow}$	$ettt$

5.5.4   A note on the monotonicity of plural determiners

A traditional domain of inquiry that was not extensively studied here is the issue of *monotonicity*. This domain is especially interesting because collective quantification in certain cases does not obey classical inference patterns with quantifiers. For instance, sentence (151a) does not entail (151b): it is possible that there is a whole glass of beer drunk by the set of all students while there is no such glass that the set of *rich* students drank. This is in contrast to the classical downward monotone behavior of *all* on its first argument, demonstrated by the entailment in (152).

(151) a. All the students drank together a whole glass of beer
       b. $\not\Rightarrow$ All the rich students drank together a whole glass of beer.

(152) a. All the students arrived
       b. $\Rightarrow$ All the rich students arrived.

This lack of monotonicity with *all* when it combines with collective predicates is accounted for by both the *dfit* and the *dfit$_w$* operators. For a systematic characterization of monotonicity with collective quantifiers, see Ben-Avi and Winter (2001).

5.5.5   Coordination, scoping and cumulative strategies with plural quantification

Sentences that involve multiple plural quantifiers are highly puzzling. Consider for instance the following sentence.

(153) Exactly four boys and exactly five girls drank together a whole glass of beer.

There are many effects involved in the interpretation of such sentences. Let us try to tease them apart. Consider first the sentences in (154), whose meanings are easier to paraphrase: they are both equivalent to sentence (155).

(154) a. Exactly four boys as well as exactly five girls drank together a whole glass of beer.
       b. Both exactly four boys and exactly five girls drank together a whole glass of beer.

(155) Exactly four boys drank together a whole glass of beer and exactly five girls drank together a whole glass of beer.

This equivalence is accounted for by application of *dfit$_w$* operators to both determiners and a simple boolean coordination of *ettt* quantifiers. Also in sentence (153) such an analysis is highly plausible, which is verified by the fact that each of the sentences in (154) and (155) entails (153). Incidentally, these are illustrations for the advantages of starting quantification over sets at the determiner level: in this way we get two collective quantifiers that can easily be coordinated in the boolean way.

Consider now sentence (156), which illustrates a more complicated aspect relevant for the interpretation of (153).[34]

(156) Every boy and every girl drank together a whole glass of beer.

I propose that the interpretation of such sentences is obtained by application of the standard scope mechanism to each of the conjuncts.[35] The two variables that remain as "traces" for the two nominals are treated as Montagovian individuals. Application of the **C** operator (= a choice function plus minimum) to the boolean coordination of such principal filters generates a desired collective reading, as illustrated below.

(157) every boy (λx.every girl ($\lambda y.x$ and y drank beer))
$\quad$ **every$'$(boy$'$)(λx.every$'$(girl$'$)(λy.C($\lambda A.A(x) \sqcap \lambda B.B(y)$)(drink_gl_beer$'$)))**
$\quad \Leftrightarrow$ **every$'$(boy$'$)(λx.every$'$(girl$'$)(λy.drink_gl_beer$'$($\{x, y\}$)))**
$\quad \Leftrightarrow$ $\forall x \in$ **boy$'$** $\forall y \in$ **girl$'$[drink_gl_beer$'$($\{x, y\}$)]**

The scoping operation gives here the two quantifiers scope over their conjunction, which may seem to violate the coordinate structure constraint. However, in Winter (1996a) it is argued that this is not quite correct, for reasons that I do not repeat here. Moreover, a similar device is needed for the interpretation of the anaphora in (158) (see also Roberts (1987: 166)) and for obtaining the wide scope reading of the second conjunct in (159) over the first conjunct, as paraphrased in (159a).

(158) Every professor and every student of his drank a whole glass of beer together.

(159) A student and every professor drank together a whole glass of beer.
$\quad$ a. Every professor drank a whole glass of beer together with a (potentially different) student.

Further, in standard Arabic sentences like (156) can be translated as in (160) below using the suffix *ya* on the verb. This is a special suffix indicating "couple" agreement with the subject. With this *ya* suffix, my Arabic informants report that the meaning of the sentence clearly involves every possible couple consisting of a boy and a girl. This meaning is correctly analyzed in (157) above. For unknown reasons, ordinary plural agreement as English (as well as the Arabic plural suffix *u*) makes the sentence a bit vaguer than what expected by this analysis.

(160) kul$\quad$walad w$\quad$kul$\quad$bint iltaqa-*ya*
$\quad\quad$every boy$\quad$and every girl met-PAIR

$\quad\quad$"Every couple that consists of a boy and a girl had a meeting"

$\quad$ Applying in sentence (161) below a similar scoping device to the one assumed for (156) gives the two interpretations paraphrased in (161a–b), depending on the relative scope of the quantifiers.

(161) Exactly one boy and exactly one girl met.
$\quad$ a. The number of boys who met exactly one girl is exactly one.
$\quad$ b. The number of girls who met exactly one boy is exactly one.

The interpretation like (161a) is hard to get and the interpretation in (161b) is virtually impossible. The same effect is observed in transitive constructions like (162).

(162) Exactly one boy met exactly one girl.

While an object narrow scope reading is possible in (162), a wide scope reading is not. A relevant factor is that independently of these judgments, a prominent reading in such cases is the familiar *cumulative* reading paraphrased following Scha (1981) in (163).

(163) Exactly one boy met a girl and exactly one girl met a boy.

While I do not have any explanation to offer for the cumulative effect,[36] I think it is clear that any account of the scopal relations between quantifiers that generates this effect would have to do it also for cases like (161) under the scoping assumption. Thus, when the two nominals *exactly one boy* and *exactly one girl* are scoped out of the conjunction, they may cumulate using the same mechanism that applies in (162). This mechanism should generate a reading for (161), derived roughly as follows.

(164) [exactly one boy]$_1$ [exactly one girl]$_2$ [x_1 and x_2 met]

The cumulation mechanism should generate from the two nominals *exactly one boy* and *exactly one girl* a cumulative reading using the same method that is adopted for sentences like (162). A similar cumulative analysis should apply to sentence (153) as well.

Note that a cumulative reading is unlikely in (156) for the same (unknown) reason it does not occur in a transitive construction like (165), which does not read as equivalent to (166).

(165) Every boy met every girl.

(166) Every boy met a girl and every girl was met by a boy.

Getting back to sentence (153), this sentence may exhibit yet another puzzling effect: it may have a reading asserting that a group of nine children drank together a whole glass of beer, with a requirement that no other children participated in sets of children drinking beer. I assume that this option, if it exists, reflects cumulation of two *collective* quantifiers of type *ettt* that are obtained by application of the *dfit*$_w$ strategy. In order to determine the motivation for such an analysis we should consider simple transitive constructions and see if they show such a complicated cumulative effect. Thus, we should find transitive predicates that function as set predicates for *both* arguments. I do not know any clear example for such a predicate. Van der Does (1993: 538) considers cases like *exactly four men lifted exactly two tables*.[37] However, the verb *lift* is probably an atom predicate in its object position as witnessed by the possible equivalence in (167). Moreover, even in the "Dowty dialect" this predicate may become an atom predicate also in its *subject* position when its object is a numeral, as the possible equivalence in (168) may show.

(167) John lifted all the tables $\overset{?}{\Leftrightarrow}$ John lifted every table

(168) All the students lifted exactly two tables
    $\overset{?}{\Leftrightarrow}$ Every student lifted exactly two tables

The latter effect raises also the question of the correct way to model processes that map set predicates to atom predicates and vice versa. In the example above we see that the numeral objects turns the predicate *lift*, which can treat its subject like a set predicate (cf. *lift a piano*), into a possible atom predicate *lift exactly two tables*. In other cases we see that a *together* adverbial can map an atom predicate like *be happy* to a set predicate like *be happy together*. The principles that underly these processes are left for further research. I speculate that the question may be related to the problem of aspectual composition.

5.5.6 Conclusion: collectivity in generalized quantifier theory

The question of how precisely to treat plural quantificational nominals when they appear combined with set predicates is empirically and theoretically challenging. In this section I followed two principles in the analysis of this problem:

1. There is no revision in the basic assumption of GQ theory that determiners denote relations between sets of atomic individuals. Collectivity with plural determiners is a by-product of type fitting processes that resolve mismatches created by morphological plurality.
2. Conservativity is more than an accidental property of natural language determiners. It is (at least partly) a realization of an intersective compositional process that is especially operative in cases of collective quantification.

Thus, both collectivity and conservativity are treated as *external* to the denotation of determiners. In this way, we not only prevent the need to modify fundamental principles in the theory of quantification, we also capture the strong relations between collectivity and morphological plurality.

5.6 On Bunch-Denoting Nouns and Atom Constitution

As shown above, the proposal to let atom predicates in natural language denote predicates over *e* type individuals enables us to make a simple distinction between them and set predicates. The distinction accounts for the different semantic behavior of the two classes of predicates when combined with a purely quantificational nominal like *all the students*. In such cases atom predicates show a well-behaved distributive behavior according to classical generalized quantifier theory. However, with non-quantificational nominals (i.e. the flexible nominals of chapter 4), we have seen that atom predicates do show a collective behavior. This is illustrated again in the following sentences.

(169) Mary and John are a nice couple.

(170) The students are a good team.

(171) Eleven students I know are the team that won the cup.

(172) The problems are numerous.

(173) The children are getting up to watch cartoons.

(174) The students voted to accept the proposal.

For the interpretation of such sentences I assumed that a set can be mapped to an "impure" atom it constitutes. For instance, in sentence (170) the set of students that corresponds to the subject is mapped to an atom in the extension of the noun *team*. The need for such a procedure is not very controversial in contemporary semantic literature that deals with sentences like (169) to (171), which involve nouns like *couple* or *team*. With Link (1984), Landman (1989, 1996), and Verkuyl (1994), however, I assume that collectivity in (172), and moreover in (173) and (174), is a result of a process where a set of atoms is treated as a new atom that can have new properties of its own. Thus, I assume that the mapping to "impure" atoms is a *general* one and not restricted to sentences with "collective nouns" like *couple* or *team*. Following Landman's works, I locate the mapping operation within the noun phrase. Unlike Landman and Link, and more like Barker (1992) and Schwarzschild (1996), I do not take this mapping as having any significant implications for the structure of models of plurality.

These assumptions on "impure atoms" are necessary for the present account of atom predicates. The last "minimal ontology" point, following Barker and Schwarzschild, is a matter of personal choice. I will not be able to develop here a complete account of the problems involved in this hard domain. Instead I will express some general ideas and outline a partial account that suits well the analysis in previous sections. I will briefly compare this line to the suggestive ideas in Schwarzschild (1996: ch. 9). For more discussion of this issue, the reader is referred to Barker (1992), Landman (1989, 1996), Link (1984), and Moltmann (1997: ch. 3).

The main problem under debate is the semantic status of singular nouns like *team*, *committee* and *couple*, and their relations with the semantics of plural noun phrases like *the students*. Following Schwarzschild, let us neutrally refer to the entities in the extension of the firstly mentioned singular nouns as *bunches*, instead of the loaded term "impure atoms."[38] A central piece of evidence for the study of bunches concerns the semantic relations between sentences like (175a) and (175b).

(175) a. The committee voted to accept the proposal.

       b. The members of the committee voted to accept the proposal.

What are these relations? In this particular example there is little doubt about the entailment from (175a) to (175b): it is quite impossible to imagine a situation where a committee votes to accept a proposal but its members do not. Of course, it is possible that (175a) is true while some committee member or other did not vote to accept the proposal, but so is the case also in (175b). Note however that the other direction of the entailment, from (175b) to (175a), does not hold. For instance, even if all the members of the committee voted to accept the proposal it might still have been a personal vote that had nothing to do with the official role of the committee. In such a situation (175b) is true whereas (175a) is false.

So far matters seem clear, but this is no longer the situation when we consider the following example, after Schwarzschild (1996: 173).

(176) a.   The committee is composed of two judges and a fireman.
       b.   #The members of the committee are composed of two judges and a fireman.

If in (176), as in (175), the (a) sentence entails the (b) sentence then it is unclear why (176a) is perfectly fine while (176b) is unacceptable. Note that also opposite cases exist where the plural nominal gives rise to an acceptable sentence whereas the bunch denoting nominal does not. This is shown in (177), after Schwarzschild (1996: 174).

(177) a.   #The committee has foreign sounding last names.
       b.   The members of the committee have foreign sounding last names.

Barker and Schwarzschild conclude from such facts that there should be *no extensional relation* between the denotation of a singular noun phrase like *the committee* and the denotation of a plural like *the committee members*. Thus, for Barker and Schwarzschild the first nominal simply denotes an *e* type entity like any other simple singular definite. The plural definite standardly denotes an *et* set of entities.[39] Furthermore, there is no formal semantic relation between the singular individual and the plural individual. This proposal expects cases like (176) and (177) but does not account for the entailment observed in (175). Schwarzschild (1996: 187–192) discusses two options to evaluate this result. One option is to consider semantic relations as in (175) as irrelevant for formal semantic purposes. Under this approach such relations are similar to the one that may exist between Schwarzschild's examples in (178), a relation that most semanticists would reasonably consider to be irrelevant for linguistic theory.

(178) a. Bill is in Texas.
       b. Bill's brain is in Texas.

A second option that Schwarzschild considers is to follow Landman (1989), who argues that relations as in (175) should be accounted for using a general intensional theory of descriptions.

I consider the Barker/Schwarzschild basic approach of "no extensional relation" between bunches and sets to be semantically appealing. Unfortunately, I do not think it can be maintained. One reason is that this basic approach is not preserved in the actual analyses that Barker and Schwarzschild propose. For instance, in view of cases like (169) to (171), Schwarzschild concludes that there *is* in fact a formal semantic relation between bunches and sets.[40] Consider for instance sentence (170), repeated below.

(179) The students are a (good) team.

Assume, with Schwarzschild, that the noun *team* denotes an *et* predicate over *e*-type entities (atoms) and that the subject *the students* denotes a plurality, say an *et* set consisting of *e*-type atoms. These two objects are not the same semantic entity, but some semantic relation between them is clearly required if we want to analyze the compositional semantics of sentences like (179). This is the point where Schwarzschild has to withdraw the "no relation" thesis. Schwarzschild (1996: 179) tentatively proposes to account for cases like (179) using the following analysis.[41]

(180) $\exists x_e \in \textbf{team}'_{et} \forall y_e [y \in \textbf{the\_students}'_{et} \leftrightarrow \text{part-of}(x)(y)]$

The semantic nature of the part-of relation between singularities introduced in (180) is not clarified. Schwarzschild assumes that it is contributed by the copula in (179), or, more generally, by the predicative nominal construction (cf. Schwarzschild (1996:181)). In more accurate compositional terms, we may describe Schwarzschild's proposal as using an operator from *et* predicates, (e.g. the denotation of the noun *team*) to *ett* predicates over sets (e.g. the denotation of the construction *be a team*). This operator, which I denote ↑, maps a predicate A_{et} to a set that consists of all the *et* sets whose members are precisely the ones that stand in the part-of relation to a member of *A*. This ↑ operator is defined below, together with Schwarzschild's stipulation about its circumstances of activation.

(181) $\uparrow_{(et)(ett)} \overset{\text{def}}{=} \lambda A_{et}.\lambda B_{et}.\exists x \in A[B = \text{part-of}(x)]$

(182)   The ↑ operator is applicable to any NP in a predicative position.

Unlike the Barker/Schwarzschild general approach, this move is not very appealing. As soon as we realize that the radical version of the "no relation" thesis has to be renounced in this way, the system becomes quite ad hoc. For instance, Schwarzschild does not explain why the postulated part-of relation applies only with predicative nominals and not with other predicates or with other nominals. Moreover, I think that despite Schwarzschild's skeptical analogy with the sentences in (178), where no entailment exists,[42] there are some interesting truth-conditional regularities with bunch denoting nominals. These point to the conclusion that the relation between bunches and sets should be more operative in natural language than what Schwarzschild's stipulation in (182) takes it to be. Consider for instance the following example, which is based on the discussion in Schwarzschild (1996: 174).

(183) a. The Math department has a car.
       b. The members of the Math department have a car.

Schwarzschild points out that sentence (183b) does not entail (183a) and concludes that this is a case where a bunch and the corresponding set "do not share the predicate." What this terminology obscures, however, is that an entailment in the opposite direction, from (183a) to (183b), does hold: there is a clear sense in which the members of the department have a car in case the department has one (even if this is an "institutional car"). Schwarzschild's part-of strategy does not apply in such cases and hence the entailment is not accounted for.

In general, most examples known to me show this kind of entailment.[43] I therefore propose the following conjecture.

(184) **The bunch-set conjecture**

Let $S_1 = \mathrm{NP}_1$ VP be a sentence with a bunch denoting NP_1 (e.g. *the committee*). Let $S_2 = \mathrm{NP}_2$ VP be a minimally different sentence with a corresponding plural NP_2 (e.g. *the committee members*). Then S_1 entails S_2.

Crucially, this hypothesis seems to be refuted by cases like (176). Let me speculate that also in such cases, where one of the sentences is unacceptable, the conjecture semantically holds. I assume that sentence (176a) *does* entail (176b) and that the unacceptability of examples like (176b) should follow from pragmatic considerations. For instance, since sentence (176b) has a distributive reading (which in this case is incoherent), it is not only more wordy than (176a), but also more ambiguous.

Independently of the (open) status of the conjecture above, we have seen that a shift between bunches and sets is needed. For this purpose I propose a modification of Schwarzschild's part-of strategy. The modification involves two aspects. First, instead of the primitive part-of$_{e(et)}$ relation between bunches and their constituting atoms let us use a primitive relation constitute$_{e((et)t)}$ between bunches and sets that constitute them. The relation constitute$(x)(B)$ between a bunch x and a set B intuitively means that x "consists of" the elements in B. A bunch now is an atom that may be related in this way to more than one set of other atoms. Second, instead of a lifting operator from *et* to *ett*, I propose an opposite strategy, from *ett* to *et*, using the constitute relation. This operation can apply to any NP with a predicative denotation, and not only to nominals in predicative positions as in Schwarzschild's proposal. Thus, instead of Schwarzschild's assumptions as paraphrased in (181) and (182), we adopt the following assumptions.

(185) The relation constitute$_{e((et)t)}$ is a given relation between e type atoms and et type sets. Read constitute$(x)(B)$ as "B constitutes x."

(186) $\downarrow_{(ett)(et)} \stackrel{\text{def}}{=} \lambda \mathcal{A}_{ett}.\lambda x_e.\exists B \in \mathcal{A}[\text{constitute}(x)(B)]$

(187) The $\downarrow$ operator is applicable for any predicative nominal denotation.

Under these assumptions sentence (179) is analyzed as in (188) below. Crucially, the $\downarrow$ operator applies now to the predicative denotation $\mathbf{the^{pl}}(\mathbf{students'})$ of the definite *subject*, whose semantics was analyzed in subsection 4.2.4.

(188) $\exists f_{(et)e}[\text{CH}(f) \wedge \langle f \rangle(\downarrow (\mathbf{the^{pl}}(\mathbf{students'_{ett}})))(\mathbf{team}_{et})]$

$\Leftrightarrow \exists x \in (\downarrow (\mathbf{the^{pl}}(\mathbf{students'})))[\mathbf{team'}(x)]$

$\Leftrightarrow \exists x \in (\downarrow (\lambda A.\max(\mathbf{students'})(A) \wedge |\max(\mathbf{students'})| = 1))[\mathbf{team'}(x)]$

$\Leftrightarrow \exists x \exists B[\max(\mathbf{students'})(B) \wedge |\max(\mathbf{students'})| = 1$
$\qquad \wedge \text{constitute}(x)(B) \wedge \mathbf{team'}(x)]$

$\Leftrightarrow \mathbf{student'} \neq \emptyset \wedge \exists x[\text{constitute}(x)(\mathbf{student'}) \wedge \mathbf{team'}(x)]$

A similar analysis is available in other cases of flexible nominals. For instance, sentence (171), with a bare numeral indefinite, is analyzed as follows.

(189) $\exists f[\text{CH}(f) \wedge \langle f \rangle (\downarrow \textbf{eleven}'(\textbf{students}'))(\textbf{team}')]$
$\Leftrightarrow \exists x \exists B[B \subseteq \textbf{student}' \wedge |B| = 11 \wedge \text{constitute}(x)(B) \wedge \textbf{team}'(x)]$

The obvious semantic question is how to define the constitute relation. I would like to propose a radical answer: to leave it undefined. This relation may be treated as a *non-logical* constant.[44] Thus, a statement like constitute$(x)(B)$ has no ontological implications as for the relations between the entity x and the set B. The constitute relation is similar to denotations of natural language predicates like *run* or *kill*. The only difference is that constitute in the above use is not an expression of English, but it is covertly introduced by the compositional mechanism via the $\downarrow$ operator. As usual with non-logical constants, constitute may have intricate *logical* relations with other non-logical constants. For instance, the denotations of the verbs *run* and *move*, like those of the verbs *kill* and *die* are logically related by the following rules, which are often modeled as lexical semantic assumptions (meaning postulates).

(190) $\textbf{run}'_{et} \subseteq \textbf{move}'_{et}$ (everything that runs moves)

(191) $\forall x[\exists y[\textbf{kill}'(x)(y)] \rightarrow \textbf{die}'(x)]$ (everything that is killed dies)

In a similar way, the artificial relation constitute may be logically related to the denotation of various English expressions. One possible connection that comes to mind is with the denotation of the English verbs *constitute* and *consist of*. A more interesting relation for our purposes is the one between (the artificial relation) constitute and the denotation of the English expression *(to be a) member of*. We refer to the $e(et)$ denotation of this expression using the relation $\textbf{member\_of}'$. Let us stipulate that for every model, for every x_e, if the set of entities $\textbf{member\_of}'(x)$ is non-empty then it constitutes x. In formula, we adopt the following meaning postulate.

(192) $\forall x_e[\textbf{member\_of}'(x) \neq \emptyset \rightarrow \text{constitute}(x)(\textbf{member\_of}'(x))]$
(everything that has members is constituted by its members)

Using this meaning postulate we can account for entailments like the ones observed in (175) and (183). For instance, the sentences in (175) get the following analyses. For the simplicity of notation assume that exactly one committee exists and that the denotation of the noun phrase *the committee* is therefore $\textbf{c}'_e$. Sentence (175a) then simply denotes the proposition in (193a). Sentence (175b) is analyzed as in (193b).

(193) a. $\textbf{vote}'(\textbf{c}')$
       b. $\exists f_{(et)e}[\text{CH}(f) \wedge \langle f \rangle (\downarrow (\textbf{the}^{\text{pl}}(pdist(\textbf{member\_of}'(\textbf{c}'))))) (\textbf{vote}')]$
           $\Leftrightarrow \textbf{member\_of}'(\textbf{c}') \neq \emptyset \wedge \exists x_e[\text{constitute}(x)(\textbf{member\_of}'(\textbf{c}')) \wedge \textbf{vote}'(x)]$

Using the (reasonable) lexical semantic assumption that any committee in the denotation of an extensional verb like *vote* must have at least one member (at the time of voting), proposition (193b) logically follows from (193a) and the meaning postulate in (192). Alternatively, if the requirement **member_of'(c')** $\neq \emptyset$ in (193b) is analyzed not as part of the assertion of the utterance in (175b) but as a presupposition, then the remainder of the proposition in (193b) follows directly without the stipulation mentioned above.

Crucially, the constitute relation allows one atom to be constituted by more than one set. This provides us with an analysis of another example by Schwarzschild.

(194) The guests this evening will be couples from Hungary.

Schwarzschild (1996: 180) argues that such examples show that the location of the shift between bunches and sets must be the predicate. Using the constitute shift this is no longer the case. This is because we allow an atom constituted by the set denotation of *the guests* to be constituted also by a set of atoms in the denotation of *couples*. (The latter atoms may of course consist of doubletons of other atoms). Formally, we can apply the $\downarrow$ operator to both the subject and the predicate in (194). This is illustrated below.

(195) $\exists f[CH(f) \wedge \langle f \rangle(\downarrow (\textbf{the}^{\text{pl}}(\textbf{guests}')))(\downarrow \textbf{couples}'))]$
$\quad \Leftrightarrow \textbf{guest}' \neq \emptyset \wedge \exists x \exists B \neq \emptyset$
$\quad [\text{constitute}(x)(\textbf{guest}') \wedge B \subseteq \textbf{couple}' \wedge \text{constitute}(x)(B)]$

A similar analysis (cf. (197)) holds also for the "opposite" case of sentence (196), which as far as I can tell is problematic for Schwarzschild's approach.

(196) The couples in the room are guests of the institute.

(197) $\exists f[CH(f) \wedge \langle f \rangle(\downarrow (\textbf{the}^{\text{pl}}(\textbf{couples}')))(\downarrow \textbf{guests}')]$
$\quad \Leftrightarrow \textbf{couple}' \neq \emptyset \wedge \exists x \exists B \neq \emptyset$
$\quad [\text{constitute}(x)(\textbf{couple}') \wedge B \subseteq \textbf{guest}' \wedge \text{constitute}(x)(B)]$

Note that there is no a priori reason why a single bunch should not be constituted by two different sets. For instance, both sentences (198a) and (198b) can be true when the people referred to in the first sentence are just the couples referred to in the latter.[45]

(198) a. These people are the organizing committee.
$\quad$ b. These couples are the organizing committee.

A part-of relation like Schwarzschild's, which induces for every bunch at most one constituting set, is not capable of capturing such effects.

The main reason for Schwarzschild to avoid general application of a mapping between sets and bunches is his "union theory" of *and*. Subsection 2.2.3 reviewed the debate between the "union theorists" (e.g. Schwarzschild (1996)) and the "group theorists" (e.g. Landman (1989)) concerning sentences as in (199) and (200).

(199) The cards below ten and the cards from ten up are separated.

(200) The cows and the pigs were separated.

If, as proposed above, any predicative nominal can be mapped to a bunch, then nothing blocks an analysis of such sentences where each plural conjunct is mapped to a separate bunch. Consequently, these sentences get a "set of bunches" analysis. This might seem to lead us back to Landman's position that Schwarzschild challenges. There are however two important differences between the situation we are facing now and Landman's 1989 proposal. The first point has to do with the ontological status of bunches. If my proposal that the constitute relation is a non-logical constant is tenable, then there is no "set of sets" structure in the *e* domain. A bunch corresponding to a noun phrase like *the students* is not connected in any logical way to individual students. The connection depends on the interpretation of the non-logical relation constitute. In other words, a sentence like *These students are the organizing committee* is not more ontologically revealing about the denotation of *the organizing committee* than what the sentence *These students surrounded the building* reveals about the denotation of *the building*. What both sentences specify is a class of models according to the interpretation of three non-logical expressions: a plural nominal, a singular nominal and a two-place predicate: constitute or *surround* respectively. The difference is that the first predicate is not morphologically realized.

The second point concerns the *motivation* for a "structure" over the *e* domain as induced by the constitute relation. Such a motivation does not come from cases like (199) or (200), as Schwarzschild convincingly argues. However, these sentences also do not argue *against* a "bunch of bunches" analysis: Schwarzschild's argument is only that a "nested" ontology of plurals is not necessary to deal with these sentences. Like Landman (2000), I believe that the motivation for a set-to-atom mapping may come from other kinds of evidence. In our case, the "non-logical structure" on the *e* domain is motivated by examples like (179), as Schwarzschild himself observes. As we have seen, the necessity to invoke such a mechanism in the present system also comes from the collective interpretation of sentences with other atom predicates and other flexible nominals.

5.7   A Case Study: *Every*, *All*, *The* and *Member of*

The differences between singular universal nominals like *every student* or *each student*, plural universal nominals like *all the students* and plural definites like *the students* have puzzled linguists and philosophers for a long time (see Vendler (1967: 72) among others). Within a general framework of plural quantification and a new typology of predicates, this chapter has proposed a solution to this puzzle. While *all* and *every* are taken to be synonyms, which in some languages are even expressed by the same morpheme, semantic differences between them appear due to the difference in their morphological number. Plural definites sometimes seem close in their meaning to nominals with *all*, but atom predicates reveal a significant difference between the two cases: while a plural definite can be mapped to a

Table 5.3
Entailments with atom predicates and set predicates

(i)	a	b	c	d	(ii)	a	b	c	d
a		⇍	⇍	⇍	a		⇍	⇍	⇍
b	⇐		⇐	⇐	b	⇐		⇐	⇐
c	⇍	⇍		⇐	c	⇍	⇍		⇐
d	⇍	⇍	⇐		d	⇍	⇍	⇍	

bunch, an *all* nominal can not. A semantic relation is maintained in this way between bunch denoting nominals like *the committee* and set denoting nominals like *the members of the committee*.

By way of recapitulation, let us summarize the general entailment patterns that appear with these four kinds of nominals and two kinds of predicates. When the predicate is an atom predicate as in (201) the pattern is as summarized in table 5.3(i). For instance, the entailment (201d) $\Rightarrow$ (201b) is described by the "$\Leftarrow$" symbol in column *d* and row *b* of the table. With a set predicate as in (202) the entailments are summarized in table 5.3(ii).[46] The tables differ only with respect to the validity of the entailment from (c) to (d).

(201) a. The committee walked.
    b. The members of the committee walked.
    c. All the members of the committee walked.
    d. Every member of the committee walked.

(202) a.   The committee met.
    b.   The members of the committee met.
    c.   All the members of the committee met.
    d.   #Every member of the committee met.

This entailment pattern is accounted for using the following analysis. In both (201) and (202) the sentences in the singular under (a) and (d) are unambiguous, as given in the corresponding analyses in (203) and (204) below.

(203) a. $\mathbf{walk'(c')}$
    b. i. $\exists f[\mathrm{CH}(f) \wedge \langle f\rangle^d(\mathbf{the^{pl}}(pdist(\mathbf{member\_of'(c')})))(\mathbf{walk'})]$
      ii. $\exists f[\mathrm{CH}(f) \wedge \langle f\rangle(\mathbf{the^{pl}}(pdist(\mathbf{member\_of'(c')})))(pdist(\mathbf{walk'}))]$
      iii. $\exists f[\mathrm{CH}(f) \wedge \langle f\rangle(\downarrow \mathbf{the^{pl}}(pdist(\mathbf{member\_of'(c')})))(\mathbf{walk'})]$
    c. i. $\mathbf{all'(member\_of'(c'))(walk')}$
      ii. $dfit_w(\mathbf{all'})(pdist(\mathbf{member\_of'(c')}))(pdist(\mathbf{walk'}))$
    d. $\mathbf{every'(member\_of'(c'))(walk')}$

(204) a. $(sg(\mathbf{meet'}))(\mathbf{c'})$

    b. i. $\exists f[\mathrm{CH}(f) \wedge \langle f \rangle^d (\mathbf{the}^{\mathrm{pl}}(pdist(\mathbf{member\_of'}(\mathbf{c'}))))(sg(\mathbf{meet'}))]$

      ii. $\exists f[\mathrm{CH}(f) \wedge \langle f \rangle (\mathbf{the}^{\mathrm{pl}}(pdist(\mathbf{member\_of'}(\mathbf{c'}))))(\mathbf{meet'})]$

      iii. $\exists f[\mathrm{CH}(f) \wedge \langle f \rangle (\downarrow \mathbf{the}^{\mathrm{pl}}(pdist(\mathbf{member\_of'}(\mathbf{c'}))))(sg(\mathbf{meet'}))]$

    c. i. $\mathbf{all'}(\mathbf{member\_of'}(\mathbf{c'}))(sg(\mathbf{meet'}))$

      ii. $dfit_w(\mathbf{all'})(pdist(\mathbf{member\_of'}(\mathbf{c'})))(\mathbf{meet'})$

    d. $\mathbf{every'}(\mathbf{member\_of'}(\mathbf{c'}))(sg(\mathbf{meet'}))$

The sentences under (b) are three-way ambiguous. One reading, in the corresponding (b)(i)'s, is obtained by distributing the subject nominal using the $\langle \ \rangle^d$ category shift of chapter 4. Another reading, under (b)(ii), is obtained by direct application of the subject denotation to an *ett* predicate denotation, which in (201b) is derived by *pdist*ribution of the atom predicate *walk*. This makes (203b)(i) and (203b)(ii) equivalent, but not (204b)(i) and (204b)(ii). A third reading for these sentences is obtained by mapping the set corresponding to the subject to a bunch as in the (b)(iii) propositions. When it comes to the *all* nominals in (201c) and (202c), both sentences are modeled as two-way ambiguous. One reading is obtained by picking up the *et* denotation of the nominal and the verb. These (c)(i) readings are equivalent to the corresponding (d)'s. A second reading is obtained by taking the *ett* denotation of the nominal and the verb and *dfit*ting the determiner. In (203c)(ii) this leads to an equivalent reading to (203c)(i) because the atom predicate *walk* must be *pdist*ributed to achieve this. By contrast, in (204c)(ii) the interpretation is not equivalent to (204c)(i) because the set predicate *meet* is originally of type *ett*. There are some other readings additional to the ones given above, which are obtained using the *qfit* operator. These readings do not generate, however, any new propositions. The ways these analyses account for the entailments summarized in table 5.3 should now be clear from the discussion throughout this chapter.

5.8   Summary of Chapter 5

This chapter studied the implications of the basic distinction between atoms and sets of atoms for the typology of predicates and the semantic interpretation of morphological number and quantified nominals. A distinction was drawn between predicates that show collectivity with plural quantifiers and predicates that do not. Predicates of the first kind are called *set predicates* while predicates of the second kind are called *atom predicates*. It was shown that this distinction is independent of the traditional classification of predicates as distributive or collective. It was proposed that the lexical semantic distinction between the two classes directly corresponds to the chosen terminology: atom predicates lexically range over atoms whereas set predicates range over sets of atoms. Morphological number further affects the realization of the predicate's denotation in the sentence: the actual denotation of both atom predicates and set predicates in the *singular* ranges unambiguously over atoms.

Plural predicates, by contrast, are ambiguous and range either over atoms or over sets. The connection between the lexical denotation of predicates, which is insensitive to number marking, and the denotation of the number inflected predicate in the sentence, is maintained by the denotations of the number features +SG and +PL and the *pdist* type-fitting operator. Quantification over sets of atoms is obtained in this system by means of a uniform type fitting operator called *dfit*, which applies to standard determiners. This operator, which maps standard atom-based determiners into set-based determiners, is triggered by the *ett* type of plural nouns. It is proposed that once a *witness condition* is appropriately added to the system, the *dfit* operator correctly captures collectivity effects with quantificational nominals. However, with non-quantificational nominals, an additional strategy mapping sets to "impure atoms" is needed in order to explain the collective interpretation of such nominals when combined with atom predicates. This strategy, based on the constitute relation between sets and atoms, is proposed as a non-logical process that does not affect the logically "flat" structure of the *e* domain.

Chapter 6
On Distributivity

The aim of this chapter is to summarize the general approach to distributivity phenomena that emerges from the proposals in the previous chapters. Against common assumptions, section 6.1 argues that the phenomenon of distributivity that needs a compositional explanation does not simply consist of the implications that a predicate carries for sub-parts of its plural arguments. Rather, it is claimed that only cases where a plural nominal takes scope over another element in the sentence constitute relevant evidence about the formal semantic nature of distribution. This more restricted notion of distributivity is referred to as *quantificational distributivity*. Following previous works, it is proposed that in certain cases this phenomenon must be derived by the application of covert operators of the sort introduced in chapters 4 and 5. Two central questions about the nature of these operators are addressed in sections 6.2 and 6.3. Section 6.2 addresses the debate between *atomic* approaches to distributivity and *non-atomic* approaches and argues for the first kind of analysis. It is claimed that quantificational distributivity shows only atomic behavior and that for this reason atomic distributivity operators are advantageous. Section 6.3 addresses the location of distributivity operators in the compositional analysis of the sentence. Using some new data, it is proposed that such operators should be located both on the nominal and on the predicate. Section 6.4 summarizes the different origins of quantificational distributivity in the system developed in the previous chapters, which conforms to the proposed view on distributivity.

6.1   The Motivation for Distributive Readings

Reconsider the sentences below.

(1) a. The girls met.
     b. The girls are a good team.

(2) The girls slept.

Sentences as in (1) are analyzed by assuming a plural individual denotation for the definite *the girls*. The predicate applies to this plural individual or to a bunch it constitutes (see section 5.6). Scha (1981) argues that a similar analysis is useful also for sentences like (2) with "distributive" predicates. The reason is that sentence *the girls slept* in (2) is not precisely equivalent to the sentence *every girl slept* in (3) below.

(3) Every girl slept.

As Dowty (1987) also argues (cf. subsection 5.2.1 above), sentences with plural definites are in general rather vague with respect to their implications for singularities that support the definite. Intuitively, however, there is still a potential semantic difference between the sentences in (1) and sentence (2). Although, as Scha and Dowty point out, there is no entailment from (2) to (3), an entailment in the opposite direction does hold (assuming as usual there are at least two girls). However, also in this respect it is hard to know if (2) contrasts with (1): the universal statements made by the sentences in (4) below are unacceptable for reasons that were argued to be pragmatic (cf. subsection 2.3.6). Thus, any study of their entailment relations is practically problematic.

(4) a. *Every girl met.
    b. *Every girl is a good team.

However significant the semantic difference between the sentences in (1) and sentence (2) may be (which I doubt), it does not need to be regarded as a truth conditional fact about plurals. Many similar semantic contrasts appear with singular nominals as well. For instance, consider the following sentences.

(5) My car is slow.

(6) My car is wet.

Sentence (6) is entailed by the sentence *every part of my car is wet*. By contrast, the sentence *every part of my car is slow* is rather incoherent and does not seem to entail (5). Such phenomena are likely to stem from what is often called the *lexical semantics* of the adjectives *slow* and *wet*—the plausible denotations of such predicates in everyday situations. While the adjective *slow* is inappropriate for describing many parts of a car, we can easily imagine situations where any relevant car part is wet. Thus, the difference between (5) and (6) is unlikely to indicate any logical distinction between the kind of propositions that these sentences convey.

Getting back to (1) and (2), the situation is quite similar: predicates like *meet* or *be a good team* are unlikely to hold of individual girls, by contrast to the predicate *sleep*. Moreover, predicates like *sleep* (or *be wet*) may have a "cumulative" property that guarantees that whenever all the parts of an object are asleep (wet), so is the object itself. This lexical semantic assumption may be the source of semantic relations like the one between (3) and (2).

Such considerations, which I think are completely sound, underly Scha's approach to distributivity with plural definites. I refer to this line as the *vagueness approach* to distributivity.

(7) **The vagueness approach**
    Sentences with plural definites *uniformly* involve predication over plural individuals
    and any "distribution subentailment" they may show is vague and appears due to lexical
    properties of the predicate.

Note that this simple idea involves two independent claims. The claim that all natural
language predicates can in principle take plural individuals directly or indirectly (via
bunches) was accepted and supported in chapter 5. The vagueness approach in (7) is more
radical than that and furthermore contends that predication over pluralities is all we need
to account for the truth-conditional semantics of plural definites (and other plurals). This
second assumption is unfortunately problematic as mentioned already in chapter 3. Let us
dwell a bit more on the reasons that led to its rejection.

Consider again the following sentence.

(8) The girls are wearing a dress.

According to the vagueness approach this sentence is unambiguously interpreted as in (9)
below. The predicate denoted by the verb phrase *wear a dress* takes as an argument the set
G, the plural individual denoted by the subject *the girls*. Alternatively, we may assume that
the set G is mapped to a bunch, which is however irrelevant for our purposes here.

(9) $[\![$are wearing a dress$]\!]$
    $= \lambda x.\exists y \in \mathbf{dress'}[\mathbf{wear'}(y)(x)]$ $[\![$the girls are wearing a dress$]\!]$
    $= [\![$are wearing a dress$]\!](G)$
    $\Leftrightarrow \exists y \in \mathbf{dress'}[\mathbf{wear'}(y)(G)]$

Given this analysis there is no lexical assumption on the denotation of the verb *wear* that can
guarantee that (8) is true when every girl is wearing a *different* dress, as intuitively required.
The reason for that, in accurate terms of entailment, is that the proposition derived in (9)
is also the meaning assigned to the following (incoherent) sentence under our tentative
analysis.

(10) #There is a dress that the girls are wearing.

Since the proposition that the vagueness approach assigns to (10) is the same proposition
it also assigns to (8) in (9), this analysis fails to account for the obvious non-equivalence
between (8) and (10). Intuitively, in (8) the subject takes *quantificational* scope over the
indefinite object, which allows every girl to wear a different dress. In (10) such a reading is
impossible, reasonably due to the position of the plural within a Complex NP island that is
c-commanded by the indefinite.

Phenomena such as in (8), which are referred to as *Q-distributivity*, have occasionally
been pointed out in the literature on plurals.[1] The popular example in (11) concisely
illustrates the puzzle. While sentence (11) is entailed by both (11a) and (11b), it entails
neither of these sentences.

(11) The girls lifted a piano.
     a. Every girl lifted a (potentially different) piano.
     b. There is a piano that the girls lifted.

The problem is how to let (11) be true in situations where *only one* of the sentences in (11a) and (11b) is true. Similar problems appear with other simple transitive constructions containing various types of object nominals.

(12) The TAs were paid exactly $7000 last year. (Lasersohn (1989))

(13) The men ate most of the courses.

(14) The dogs chased fewer than ten cats.

The common solution is to assume, contra Scha's vagueness approach, that plural definites can optionally contribute a quantifier over singularities or other subparts of the plural individual they denote. One popular assumption is that a sentence like (11) should be modeled as *ambiguous* between (11a) and (11b), which accounts for the entailment pattern.

    Another example for Q-distributivity is the way plural definites behave when "binding" plural pronouns.[2] Consider for instance the following sentence.

(15) The leaders think they are smart.

Sentence (15) can be true in cases where the leaders in question do not even know each other. In fact, (15) is entailed by the following sentence, under the relevant anaphora resolution.

(16) Every leader thinks he is smart.

If the subject of (15) denotes a plural individual then the only natural way to analyze the plural pronoun is as coreferential to this group. Assume, for instance, that the leaders under discussion are Bush and Clinton. Sentence (16) is likely to be true, and so is (15) under the relevant interpretation. However, with anaphora resolution using "group coreference," (15) is analyzed as equivalent to (17), which is not so likely to be true.

(17) Bush and Clinton think that Bush and Clinton are smart.

A better analysis of (15) can be obtained if the sentence is assumed to have a reading equivalent to (16), where the subject contributes a universal quantifier that "binds" the pronoun.

    Yet another test for Q-distributivity is the behavior of plural nominals with predicate disjunction. Consider for instance the following example.

(18) The children in group *A* are only singing. But the children in group *B* are dancing or singing.

Under Scha's vagueness approach the second sentence in (18) is analyzed as in (19), where C_B is the set of children in group *B*. This is the same analysis as of the sentential disjunction in (20).

(19) $(\mathbf{dance}' \sqcup \mathbf{sing}')(C_B)$
      $\Leftrightarrow \mathbf{dance}'(C_B) \vee \mathbf{sing}'(C_B)$

(20) The children in group B are dancing or the children in group B are singing.

Thus, the vagueness approach predicts that (20) conveys the same proposition as the second sentence in (18). This is of course problematic: in a situation where half the children in group B are dancing and the other half are singing, sentence (18) may be true, but (20) is false or highly strange. This fact is another indication that a plural definite like *the children* can be interpreted as a quantifier taking scope over other elements in the sentence, this time a disjunctive VP: the meaning difference between (18) and (20) is similar to the difference between the following pair of sentences.

(21) a. Every child is dancing or singing.
      b. Every child is dancing or every child is singing.

To conclude, the motivation for an optional analysis of plural definites using quantification over singularities does not come from simple sentences like *the girls slept*, where Scha's vagueness approach may be sufficient. Quantification over singularities (or any other subparts of plural individuals) is motivated by Q-distributivity phenomena. This is officially stated below.

(22) **Distributivity methodology**
      Quantification over subparts of a plural individual is easier to attest when the plural NP in question is semantically interpreted as a quantifier taking scope over another element in the sentence (an indefinite, a pronoun, a disjunction etc.).

This principle has been followed in previous chapters at points where critical questions about distributivity were raised. It is useful to keep it in mind as we move to even more intricate problems involving this elusive notion.

6.2 Atomic Distributivity versus Non-atomic Distributivity

Modeling Q-distributivity requires quantification over subparts of a plural individual. One of the main debates in the plurality literature concerns the proper definition of these parts. Two possibilities were explored:

1. Q-distributivity involves universal quantification over *atomic* parts of the plural individual. In this approach a distributive interpretation of a plural definite like *the girls* has similar semantic effects to nominals like *each of the girls* or *every girl*. In set-theoretical treatments of plural individuals this simply means that Q-distributivity should be modeled using a universal quantifier over the elements of a set. Atomic distributivity is adopted in Bennett (1974), Link (1983), and Roberts (1987), among many others, and explicitly argued for against non-atomic views in Lasersohn (1989, 1995) and Lønning (1991).

Figure 6.1
Boys and wheels

2. Q-distributivity involves universal quantification over arbitrary parts of the plural individual, including *non-atomic* parts. This line adopts a more general distributivity operator
that allows different modes of quantification. Each mode specifies a certain partition (or
"cover") of the plural individual into atomic or non-atomic subparts. This mode determines
the entities over which the universal quantifier ranges. Works that defend and implement
this idea include Gillon (1987, 1990), Van der Does and Verkuyl (1995), Verkuyl and Van
der Does (1996) and Schwarzschild (1996: ch. 5) among others.

The empirical debate between the two approaches concentrates on sentences as in (23) (after
Gillon). Similar examples are given in (24).

(23) a. The composers wrote musicals.
      b. Rodgers, Hammerstein and Hart wrote musicals.

(24) a. The boys are holding wheels.
      b. John, Bill and George are holding wheels.

Consider for instance the situation depicted in figure 6.1 and assume that the boys in the
picture are John, Bill and George. The sentences in (24) are both true in this situation.
This points out that the sentences in (24) are both entailed by the following sentence.

(25) John and Bill are holding a wheel (together) and Bill and George are holding a wheel
      (together).

Can we on the basis of such examples reach a decision with respect to the atomic/ non-atomic
nature of distributivity? Proponents of the non-atomic line argue that this is the case and
that the non-atomic view proves preferable. The reasoning that underlies this conclusion is
basically the following. Under the atomic analysis of distributivity the sentences in (24) are
analyzed as two-way ambiguous between the propositions in (26). Proponents of the non-
atomic view hold that such propositions are insufficient for describing the truth-conditions
of the sentences in (24).

(26) a. **hold_wheels′**$(\{\mathbf{j'}, \mathbf{b'}, \mathbf{g'}\})$
      b. $\forall x \in \{\mathbf{j'}, \mathbf{b'}, \mathbf{g'}\}[\mathbf{hold\_wheels'}(x)]$

According to non-atomic analyses, the sentences in (24) should involve quantification over subparts of the plural individual denoted by the plural subject. Ignoring subtle differences between various versions of this approach, this "partitioning" of the plural individual can be achieved using *covers* of a set as defined below.[3]

Definition 19 (cover)   Let A be a set. We say that a set $\mathcal{C} \subseteq \wp^+(A)$ is a *cover* of A iff $\cup\mathcal{C} = A$. This relation is denoted by $COV(A)(\mathcal{C})$.

Using this definition, the sentences in (24) are analyzed as follows.[4]

(27) $\exists \mathcal{C} \in COV(\{\mathbf{j}', \mathbf{b}', \mathbf{g}'\}) \forall X \in \mathcal{C}[\mathbf{hold\_wheels}'(X)]$

This proposition is argued to describe better the truth-conditions of the sentences than the C/D ambiguity in (26): using the cover $\{\{\mathbf{j}', \mathbf{b}'\}, \{\mathbf{b}', \mathbf{g}'\}\}$ of the set of boys, proposition (27) gives a more fine-grained "semantic description" of the situation in figure 6.1. Hence, this analysis is argued to be preferable for capturing the meaning of sentences as in (24) (or (23)).

Like Lasersohn and Lønning, I see no justification for this conclusion. One flaw in this claim, as Lønning points out, is that the argument is not based on entailment judgments. The C reading as roughly given in (26a) is vague with respect to *how* the boys are holding the wheels. Given more accurately, the statement this reading makes is (28) below.[5] This is the same analysis of sentence (29), which intuitively is just as good as sentence (24a) for describing figure 6.1.

(28) $\exists A \subseteq \mathbf{wheel}'[A \neq \emptyset \wedge \mathbf{hold}'(A)(\{\mathbf{j}', \mathbf{b}', \mathbf{g}'\})]$

(29) There are wheels that the boys are holding.

In Scha's vagueness approach, a statement like $\mathbf{hold}'(A)(B)$ does not necessarily say anything about how the elements of B hold the elements of A. Entailments like (25) $\Rightarrow$ (24a/b) can be viewed as similar to entailments like (3) $\Rightarrow$ (2), as indicating only lexical properties of the predicates *hold* or *sleep*. Thus, such entailments are not very telling as for the formal nature of Q-distributivity.

However, we should not give up too easily the attempt to decide on the atomicity question. In view of the methodological principle in (22), consider the following examples.[6]

(30) a. The boys are holding a wheel.
      b. John, Bill and George are holding a wheel.

The sentences in (30) are distinctly worse than the sentences in (24) in the situation of figure 6.1 and they are not entailed by sentence (25). This is expected by the atomic treatment of distributivity but not by the non-atomic approach. According to the atomic line sentence (30a), for instance, is two-way ambiguous between the readings that are assigned to the following sentences.

(31) Every boy is holding a wheel.

(32) There is a wheel that the boys are holding.

Both sentences are quite as bad as (30a) for describing the situation in figure 6.1. This shows that it is reasonable to suppose, as in the above view, that sentences (31) and (32) paraphrase two different readings of sentence (30a). By contrast, according to the non-atomic view sentence (30a) should have been much better in this situation than both (31) and (32). This is because the same cover that is relevant for the interpretation of (24a) in the analysis (27), is relevant for the analysis of (30a) as well. This prediction of the non-atomic analysis is not borne out.

Another way to look at the problem is using the familiar notion of *cumulative reference*, which is a name sometimes used for entailments as in (33).

(33) a. Boy 1 is holding a wheel; boy 2 is holding a wheel; boy 3 is holding a wheel.
    b. $\Rightarrow$ Boys 1, 2 and 3 are holding a wheel.

This entailment is accounted for by the atomic Q-distributive reading of the conclusion in (33b). The non-atomic view expects a more general entailment pattern. For instance, the sentences in (34a) are expected to entail sentence (34b) (= (33b)).

(34) a. Boys 1 and 2 are holding a wheel; boys 2 and 3 are holding a wheel.
    b. Boys 1, 2 and 3 are holding a wheel.

However, as the situation in figure 6.1 shows, such a more general entailment pattern is not attested. Hence, there is no motivation for a non-atomic Q-distributive reading of sentence (34b).

Similar weaknesses appear for all other examples I am aware of that were used to argue for non-atomic Q-distributivity. A possible exception is the following example from Schwarzschild (1996: 65).

(35) The men wrote musicals. They were paid exactly $2000 per musical.

Suppose that the men referred to are Rodgers, Hammerstein and Hart. Rodgers and Hammerstein wrote some musicals and for each musical they were paid $2000 as a collective payment for their joint effort. The same holds for Hammerstein and Hart. Schwarzschild points out, contra Lasersohn (1989), that the sentences in (35) are both true in this situation. This may be correct, but I think the effect is similar to what happens in the following sentence, which I do not see how to model using the cover analysis.

(36) The composers were paid exactly $2000 for each musical.

Here, when the nominal *each musical* takes wide scope over the definite *the composers*, this definite can be interpreted as "dependent," meaning roughly *the composers who wrote the musical*. This is a well-known property of the semantics of definites (see Partee (1989)), and it therefore is an alternative possible origin for the reading that Schwarzschild points out in (35).

Schwarzschild (1996: 107) brings another interesting example as a supporting piece of evidence for non-atomic distributivity:

(37) The prisoners on the two sides of the room could see each other.

Schwarzschild points out that sentence (37) can be false in case there are prisoners on both sides of the room and there is an opaque barrier between the two groups of prisoners. This is argued to be a case where quantification over groups of prisoners is required and not over individual prisoners. To convince ourselves that this conclusion is warranted, let us follow principle (22) and consider the following variation.

(38) The prisoners are hitting each other with a stick.

Suppose again that we have two groups of prisoners, who are this time engaged in a violent dispute. Each group of prisoners is using a large stick in order to hit the members of the other group. Interestingly, by contrast to the cases we mentioned above, now it seems possible that each group is using a different stick. Thus, Schwarzschild's claim on non-atomic distributivity in (37) is supported. Still, I doubt that this fact on the interpretation of reciprocals has any clear implication for the formulation of *covert* distributivity operators: it is possible that the semantics of the reciprocal itself is the one responsible for non-atomic distributivity in (38). The behavior of reciprocals in Hebrew supports this hypothesis. Hebrew has (at least) three types of reciprocal expressions, exemplified by the sentences in (39). These three sentences are candidates for the translation of (38).

(39) a. ha-asirim   makim exad et   ha-šeni   be-makel
        the-prisoners hit   one ACC the-second in-stick

   b. ha-asirim   makim ze et   ze be-makel
      the-prisoners hit   this ACC this in-stick

   c. ha-asirim   makim ele et   ele be-makel
      the-prisoners hit   these ACC these in-stick

The reciprocals *exad et ha-šeni* and *ze et ze* in sentences (39a-b) are composed of morphemes in the singular. In (39c), the reciprocal *ele et ele* ("these ACC these") is the plural form of the reciprocal *ze et ze* ("this ACC this") in (39b). Importantly, among the sentences in (39) only (39c) can be interpreted as true in the situation described above, involving quantification over plural subsets of the set of prisoners. By contrast, the sentences in (39a-b) imply that individual prisoners were using different sticks to hit each other and are consequently odd in the relevant situation. This shows that in Hebrew the possibility to get distribution to sub-parts of a plurality with reciprocals depends on the choice of the overt reciprocal expression. Hence, this sort of evidence, although relevant for the semantics of reciprocals, is unlikely to be an indication for the atomic/non-atomic formulation of a covert distributivity operator.

   The remainder of the debate between the atomic approach and the non-atomic view is conceptual. In Verkuyl and Van der Does' joint works the motivation is to eliminate the ambiguity that the atomic view assumes. For Schwarzschild, the atomic approach is not pragmatically sensitive enough. Without trying to get into lengthy methodological discussions, I think it is fair to say that in these respects non-atomic views do not improve the situation too much. The analysis of Verkuyl and Van der Does involves complicated quantificational techniques. Schwarzschild's analysis appeals to pragmatic factors that determine the relevant cover, but these factors are not accounted for. The atomic analysis, by contrast, is simple and easily falsifiable. The ambiguity it generates, although not too appealing, is combinatorically manageable. As far as I can see, no data that have been shown in the literature so far justify the introduction of further complications on top of such an atomic mechanism. For more problems concerning the (possibly *polyadic*) nature of distributivity operations, see Winter (2000a).

6.3   The Compositional Sources of Q-Distributivity

There are various techniques to introduce distributivity operators into the compositional interpretation process. The most relevant nominals for testing quantificational distributivity are the flexible nominals of chapter 4, including plural definites like *the boys* and simple conjunctive nominals like *John and Bill*.[7] Interesting empirical differences appear between the following general approaches to these nominals.

1. Such nominals are ambiguous between plural individuals (a collective reading) and universal quantifiers over singularities (a distributive reading).
2. Such nominals unambiguously denote plural individuals. Q-distributivity may come from the application of a distributivity operator (atomic or non-atomic) to the predicate in the sentence.

For an extensive survey of the literature on this topic see Lasersohn (1995: ch. 7). A central point made in chapter 3 above is that if the nominal ambiguity assumption is adopted it cannot come only from lexical ambiguity, at least as far as simple numeral indefinites like *three boys* are concerned. The ambiguity is better captured by an additional covert operator. The reason is the double scope observation of subsection 3.3.2. Thus, the main decision concerns the location of a *distributivity operator*.[8]

Most recent works on plurality choose to locate a distributivity operator on the predicate. The main motivation for this decision comes from examples like the following.[9]

(40) The girls met in the bar and smoked a cigarette.

In intuitive terms, sentence (40) shows collectivity with the first VP conjunct but Q-distributivity with the second conjunct. To establish this claim, suppose that the only source of Q-distributivity in (40) may come from ambiguity of the plural subject *the girls*. Under the plural individual reading sentence (40) would be analyzed as equivalent to (41a). The universal quantifier reading would allow to paraphrase sentence (40) by the incoherent sentence in (41b).

(41) a.   The girls met in the bar and there is a cigarette that they smoked.
       b.   *Every girl met and every girl smoked a cigarette.

However, neither of these sentences is entailed by (42) below, which does however entail (40).

(42) The girls met in the bar and every girl smoked a cigarette.

The conclusion is that in a compositional framework Q-distributivity in (40) must come from the second conjunct and not from the subject as tentatively assumed above. This general argument for Q-distributivity at the predicate level seems pretty solid, although examples like (40) are practically quite hard to construct.

Interestingly, as far as I know the extensive discussion of this topic in the literature has ignored the opposite question: can we make a case for a distributivity operator on nominals using symmetric examples of nominal coordination? The answer is positive. Consider the following context. You and I own an institute that prepares pregnant women to the birth of their child. Also the women's spouses are invited to participate in the course. Now, suppose that I mention some women who followed such a course. Suppose further that Mary and John are a couple that participated in the same class. Consider now the following sentence.

(43) The women I mentioned and [Mary and John] had a baby last week.

The only coherent reading of this sentence is Q-distributively for the first nominal conjunct and collectively for the second conjunct. However, atomic distributivity at the predicate level expects only two readings of sentence (43): a C reading as paraphrased in (44) below and a D reading as in (45). Neither of these sentences captures the "mixed" effect in (43): unlike (43) they are both reasonably incoherent.

(44) #There is a baby that the women had and there is a baby that Mary and John had.

(45) #Every woman had a baby, Mary had a baby and John had a baby.

This is an argument in favor of the location of a distributivity operator within the nominal. How decisive is this argument? The answer depends on the solution to the atomic/non-atomic puzzle. If, as argued above, one should adopt the atomic view on distributivity, then nominal distributivity seems necessary to account for sentences like (43).[10] However, this conclusion does not necessarily follow if we are willing to adopt a non-atomic approach to distributivity located on the predicate as proposed by Schwarzschild (1996: ch. 5). Intuitively, with such a formulation of distributivity we could pick a cover of the set $\textbf{woman}' \cup \{\textbf{m}', \textbf{j}'\}$ that distributes to individual women but leaves the doubleton $\{\textbf{m}', \textbf{j}'\}$ intact. Such a cover is what we need in (43) and there is no technical reason why not to introduce it at the predicate level as Schwarzschild proposes. However, we have seen in subsection 6.2 some reasons not to adopt non-atomic distributivity: if non-atomic distributivity is used in (43) it is not clear how to block it in (30), where it was shown to overgenerate. Moreover, it is possible that non-atomic operators generate other distributivity effects that are not observed in natural language. Consider the following sentence in a similar context to example (43).

(46)   ?The women I mentioned and [Mary and John] were the best class we had this year and had a baby last week.

The speakers I consulted consider this sentence quite incoherent. However, a technique that allows predicate distribution using covers might allow the first VP conjunct in (46) to be interpreted using the "one cell" cover {**woman**$'$ ∪ {**m**$'$, **j**$'$}}, while the second VP conjunct could be interpreted using the same cover tentatively used above for sentence (43). Thus, the sentence is expected to be coherent. This cannot happen in the atomic view on distributivity: whatever element we choose to distribute in sentence (46) using an atomic distributor we get a pragmatically incoherent statement. For instance, consider what happens when we want to generate from (46) a coherent Q-distributive assertion that every woman had a (different) baby. If we distribute the nominal conjunct *the women* we get incoherent distribution with the VP conjunct *were the best class*. Alternatively, if we try to distribute the predicate *had a baby*, we get incoherent distribution for the nominal conjunct *Mary and John*.

Thus, sentences of the type given in (46) could in principle show a kind of "super-distributivity" that cannot be captured by atomic distributivity, neither on the nominal nor on the predicate. Non-atomic distribution of predicates allows such effects. However, this reading does not seem to appear in (46) and I do not know any other examples that show such effects. Concluding, I think that the considerations above show that Q-distributivity data alone favor atomic distributors located both within the nominal and within the predicate over a non-atomic distributor located only on the predicate. The next subsection summarizes the treatment of Q-distributivity in the present system, which has independent motivation for such a configuration.

6.4   Distributivity in the Present Analysis: Recapitulation

The system developed in chapters 2 to 5 contains the following assumptions on distributivity.

1. All predicates can in principle take plural individuals as arguments indirectly (using the "impure atom" strategy) or directly (in the case of set predicates).
2. Q-distributivity is atomic and appears both within the nominal and within the predicate.

The motivation for these assumptions did not directly come from Q-distributivity phenomena, but from more general considerations in the proposed system. That all predicates can take plural individual arguments was motivated in chapter 5 by the collectivity effects that appear with many non-collective predicates. Atomic Q-distributivity within the nominal was motivated in chapter 4 as a means to derive collective interpretations of plural nominal coordinations. At the predicate level, atomic Q-distributivity was justified in chapter 5 as a general type fitting mechanism connected to morphological plurality of natural language predicates (nouns, verbs and adjectives). The discussion above shows that these assumptions are motivated also by (Q-)distributivity facts. This subsection reviews the way distributivity principles are motivated and implemented in the proposed system and brings some more data relevant to this proposal.

6.4.1   Predication over plural individuals

The assumption that all predicates can take plural individuals as arguments is motivated by the fact that most predicates, "distributive" and "collective" alike, fail to show distributivity equivalences with plural definites. This is the essence of Dowty's argument quoted under (27) in chapter 5 (page 200). Dowty's remark makes it plain that it would be a mistake to assume the following sentences are equivalent.

(47) The children are sleeping.

(48) Every child is sleeping.

This lack of equivalence is accounted for in the system proposed above. This is because there are two different ways in the proposed system for predicates to take plural individual arguments. Obviously, *set* predicates like *meet* can take plural individuals (sets) directly. However, also *atom* predicates like *sleep* or *be a good team* may show collectivity effects with predicative nominals when the denotations of such nominals are mapped to denotations that range over bunches. The first process is well-motivated for all set predicates and all plural nominals. The second process was motivated for some atom predicates and some flexible nominals. What is its general status? In other words: can all atom predicates and all flexible nominals show collective behavior in this way? As shown by the examples in (74) from chapter 5 (page 213), all flexible nominals show a collective behavior with atom predicates like *be a good team*. What about other atom predicates? An especially interesting case, because of its seemingly extreme distributive nature, is the case of atom predicates like *sleep* and conjunctive nominals like *Mary and Sue*. The assumption that sentences like (49) below have a collective reading contradicts the (a priori reasonable) empirical claim in chapter 2 that this sentence shows a "distributivity equivalence" with sentence (50).

(49) Mary and Sue are sleeping.

(50) Mary is sleeping and Sue is sleeping.

No theory known to me accounts both for the lack of equivalence between (47) and (48) while respecting the (apparent) equivalence between (49) and (50). In fact, however, the assumption about the equivalence between (49) and (50) may be too simplistic, like the parallel assumption on the "universal quantifier" behavior of plural definites with distributive predicates. I believe Dowty's aforementioned remark on plural definites holds for all flexible nominals, including conjunctive nominals like *Mary and Sue*. The more we are likely to conceive of such nominals as bunch denoting, the less likely the equivalence becomes. Consider for instance the following context.[11] Assume that you have two children, Mary and Sue. One evening, when a guest comes by to your place you say to him: "We have to be quiet tonight: Mary and Sue are sleeping." Your assertion (= (49)) does not entail sentence (50). It may happen that one of the girls happens to be awake and you vaguely refer to the "collection" of your daughters. This is of course impossible in sentence (50). I take it that the strong equivalence impression between (49) and (50) may come from pragmatic reasons: in most circumstances the explicit mention of the singularities in (49) would make it quite misleading to assert the sentence when one of the two girls is not sleeping in fact.

Consider similar cases, after an example by Fred Landman (p.c.).

(51) Groenendijk and Stokhof are talking (at the conference).

(52) Simon and Garfunkel are singing (in the Central Park).

These sentences demonstrate again the "Kolkhoz collectivity" effect discussed by Verkuyl (1994). Sentence (51) does not necessarily mean that both well-known semanticists are talking. Maybe only one of them is doing the talk and the other handles the overhead projector. Similarly, in (52), only Garfunkel may be singing while Simon is playing the guitar. Of course, once we use arbitrary names like *Mary and Sue*, the collectivity effect vanishes when the sentence is uttered "out of the blue." This is plausibly because there is no salient bunch these names refer to that is as famous as the G&S couple or the S&G couple.

There is however a class of atom predicates where distributivity equivalences are much more robust. This is the class of predicate nominals. For instance, it is very hard to imagine a context where sentence (53a), with the predicate nominal *singers*, does not have the same truth value as (53b).

(53) a. Simon and Garfunkel are singers.
      b. Simon is a singer and Garfunkel is a singer.

A highly relevant fact is that while verbs and adjectives often accept bunch denoting nominals as their argument, animate nouns like *singer* never do. Consider for instance the contrast in (54) below.

(54) a. The couple is sleeping/talking/singing/hungry/happy.
      b. *The couple is a singer/a girl/a teacher.

Thus, given the proposal of section 5.6 it is hardly surprising that the equivalence in (53) is so robust: since the singular common noun *singer* does not take bunches in its extension (witness (54b)), sentence (53a) cannot get any collective reading due to bunch constitution. The sentence may of course still become true by virtue of direct application of the *ett* predicate denoting the noun *singers* to the set $\{s', g'\}$. However, by definition of this plural noun denotation (cf. section 5.4.1), this correctly entails that Simon is a singer and Garfunkel is a singer. Why should animate nouns like *singer* contrast with verbs and refuse to take bunches in their extension is of course an intriguing (but separate) question, which I leave for further research.

6.4.2   Quantificational distributivity

There are three possible origins of Q-distributivity in the system of chapters 2 to 5:

1. The boolean interpretation of *and* conjunctions within the nominal.
2. Also within the nominal, a distributive determiner:
   a. With flexible nominals, this is the $\langle f \rangle^d$ distributed choice function category shift of chapter 4.
   b. With rigid nominals, this is the standard denotation of determiners like *every*, *all* or *exactly five* in generalized quantifier theory, retained in subsection 5.5.2.
3. The *pdist* type fitting operator on predicates.

The first way to derive Q-distributivity does not need any argumentation in a boolean framework: it follows from the cross-categorial semantics of *and*. This kind of Q-distributivity is trivially reflected in the syntax of coordination. In many senses it is similar to the "distributivity" of nominals like *every woman* or *each man*, which is completely unsurprising with the standard denotation of the determiner.

The second origin for Q-distributivity within the nominal, using the distributed CF operator, allows the denotation of flexible nominals to range over singularities. This was motivated in chapter 4 by the need to *collectivize* such nominals in boolean *and* coordinations (see sections 4.2.3 and 4.2.5). As we have seen above, atomic accounts of Q-distributivity independently have to adopt such an operator within the nominal for cases like (43).

The *pdist* type fitting operator is one of the building blocks of the plural quantification system in chapter 5. It allows atom predicates to be lifted so that they range over sets. This is needed for deriving the denotation of plural nouns (e.g. *women*) from the denotation of the corresponding singular noun (e.g. *woman*). In Bennett's typing, this distributivity lift is also required for coordinations of simple atom predicates and set predicates like *smile and disperse*, *sleep or meet*, *neither sing nor gather*, etc. Moreover, recall the familiar observation that this is needed, independently of Bennett's typing, for sentences like (40) above.

These three strategies for deriving Q-distributivity should in principle be distinguishable. We have seen ways to tell nominal distributivity from predicate distributivity. Let us mention some ways to distinguish between the two sources of nominal distributivity. One of the main differences between these options was observed in subsection 2.3.7 (page 62): NP conjunctions like *Mary and Sue and John* allow "non-atomic" distributive readings according to the parsing of the conjunction. This interpretation is easily obtained by the boolean analysis of *and*. A similar kind of "non-atomic" distributivity appears with the conjunctive nominal *the authors and the athletes* in Schwarzschild's example (40a) in chapter 2 (page 41). By contrast, it was argued in subsections 2.3.7 and 6.2 that "flat" conjunctions like *Mary, Sue and John* or simple denotations like *the women* can show only *atomic* distributivity. This contrast is accounted for by the simple structural considerations of subsection 2.3.7 in chapter 2 and the atomicity of the distributivity operations adopted in subsequent chapters.

There is another potential difference between the two strategies of nominal distribution. In Dalrymple, Hayrapetian, and King (1998) it is claimed that the Russian sentence (55) below, with a conjunctive subject, has both a collective reading as in (55a) and a (less prominent) distributive reading as in (55b). By contrast, sentence (56), where the subject is a simple plural, allows only a collective reading as in (56a).

(55) Petja   i   Vasja   vyigrali $100.
     Petja-NOM   and Vasja-NOM   won $100
     a. "$100 total was won."
     b. "$200 total was won."

(56) Mal'čiki   vyigrali $100.
     boys-NOM   won $100
     a. "$100 total was won." (Only reading)

According to the present proposal, this contrast may show a difference between the availability of distributivity operations, which are the only way to derive distributivity in (56), and boolean conjunction, which is simply the meaning of the Russian coordinator *i*. Dalrymple et al.'s point may show that in Russian only the latter strategy of generating distributivity is available.

6.5 Summary of Chapter 6

This chapter summarized the motivations and the details of the treatment of distributivity in previous chapters. It was first argued that not any distributivity phenomenon with plurals is relevant for truth-conditional semantics, but only cases of *quantificational* (Q) distributivity, where a plural takes scope over another element in the sentence. Once this criterion is employed, it is proposed that an *atomic* formulation of distributivity operators is empirically sufficient. It was shown that such operations are needed within both the predicate level and the nominal. The elements that introduce them in the proposed analysis are boolean conjunction, distributive determiners and choice functions and the distributivity operator on predicates.

Chapter 7
Conclusions

The starting point of the investigations in this book was the boolean approach to natural language semantics that evolved from Montague's work. In this framework syntactic structures are directly interpreted in the model using a compositional procedure that involves no intermediate level of logical representation. In boolean semantics, all noun phrases denote generalized quantifiers, and coordination and negation are uniformly treated using the cross-categorial operators of boolean algebras. The main objective of this book was to examine how suitable these assumptions are for the linguistic theory of coordination, plurality and scope. It was argued that the boolean framework is appropriate for a comprehensive semantic analysis of these phenomena, provided that it is augmented by *flexibility principles*—semantic operations that have no phonological realization.

We have identified three kinds of flexibility principles that are needed for the analysis of coordination, plurality and scope in boolean semantics:

1. *Logical principles* These are principles such as Function Application that constitute the "Logical Base" of meaning composition. These principles are free to apply in any syntactic environment and they are not governed by economy considerations.

2. *Type fitting principles* These principles apply as a "last resort" when the principles in the logical base fail, a situation referred to as "type mismatch." Such operations lift the type of an expression but do not affect its *semantic category* (e.g. quantifier, predicate or determiner).

3. *Category shifting principles* These principles may derive quantifiers from predicates and vice versa, although they do not necessarily change the type of the denotation they apply to. Their application is not triggered by type mismatch but by syntactic factors.

The logical base of meaning composition was not the main focus of this book, though it was recognized that some extensions to the simple Ajdukiewicz Calculus are certainly required. Category shifting principles were extensively studied in chapters 2, 3 and 4. It was proposed that the flexibility of some nominals is derived using two category shifting principles: the *minimum* operator of chapter 2 maps quantifiers to predicates; the *choice function* mechanism of chapter 3 maps predicates to quantifiers. The combination of these two principles explains three seemingly independent phenomena: the apparent "non-boolean" interpretation of *and*, the exceptionally wide scope of indefinite and disjunctive nominals and the interpretation of nominals in predicative positions. The restrictions on these category shifting principles were argued to follow from the DP structure of nominals. It was argued that only nominals that can be analyzed as D's or NPs allow the application of category shifting operators. This class of expressions was referred to as *flexible* nominals.

Type-fitting principles were used as the basic tool for lifting denotations that range over atoms—*e*-type based predicates, quantifiers and determiners—to corresponding denotations that range over sets. This was especially useful in capturing puzzling semantic effects with *rigid* plural nominals—nominals that are unambiguously analyzed as DPs, and which have only a quantificational interpretation. The model-theoretic distinction between atoms and sets was also shown to be relevant for the typology of natural language predicates. A novel truth-conditional criterion was developed in order to distinguish between atom predicates and set predicates, and it was shown that it is substantially different and more robust than the traditional distributive/collective typology. The relations between morphological number and semantic number were captured using different meanings to the singular/plural value of the number feature. Under the type-fitting paradigm, these make sure that singular predicates range over atoms whereas plural predicates (also) range over sets.

Of course, the proposed theory has its limitations, and many important problems have not been successfully treated or have been altogether left for further research. Below I list some of the remaining problems that seem especially important.

• The exact way to treat wide scope disjunction was not fully clarified. The proposed treatment using choice functions applies to disjunctions of nominals, but not to disjunctions of other categories (e.g. adjectives or verbs) that show wide scope behavior as well. The restrictions on the application of category shifting may also lead to problems in the generality of the choice function treatment of disjunctions: *either . . . or* disjunctions may possibly disallow category shifting just like *both . . . and* conjunctions, but they surely do show wide scope effects.

• The precise relationships between DP structure and restrictions on category shifting has not been sufficiently studied. The proposed classification of flexible nominals and rigid nominals should be syntactically substantiated.

• The interaction between multiple quantifiers and plurality should be further studied. This includes the familiar puzzles of cumulative quantification (e.g. *three people won thirteen medals*), as well as the collective interpretation of conjunctions of rigid nominals (e.g. *every man and every woman met*).

• Further attention should be given to the maximal witness condition of plural quantification. It seems evident that this effect is related to well-known problems of maximal reference with anaphora, and it is not simply part of the type-fitting paradigm. However, the precise definition and linguistic status of this condition have not been studied here.

- The similarity between the atom/set distinction in the plurality system and the event/state distinction in the aspectuality system seems evident, but the nature of these possible relations should be examined in detail.

At a more general level, there are further questions concerning compositionality and flexibility that are raised by the proposals in this book. First, the problem of dealing with variables in a compositional way, which is currently studied in categorial frameworks, has important ramifications for the possibility to implement choice functions within a strictly compositional system. The proposal in the appendix of chapter 3 is certainly not satisfactory as a general solution to this problem. The status of flexibility principles within a compositional framework also deserves more attention. While logical flexibility principles and type-fitting principles can simply be conceived of as parts of the meaning composition module—a necessary part of any compositional system, the status of category-shifting principles is less clear. One possibility, which was assumed in the illustrative toy grammar presented in chapter 4, is that category-shifting principles are simply the denotations of phonologically null positions within the DP. This assumption should be supported by linguistic motivation for the postulated empty positions. Another alternative is to look for broader motivations for the triggering of category shifting principles, without appeal to empty categories. In order to explore this alternative, a possibly useful perspective is the following. In a non-flexible compositional framework, semantic types are often merely an easy tool for classifying denotations, but they are not strictly needed in the system. However, in the proposed flexible theory, types are needed in order to block undesired interpretations, and hence they are not redundant. Is there a way to formulate a type system where only necessary typing is preserved and where category shifting principles are altogether eliminated, and formulated as type-fitting principles?

All these problems surely require much more research by both linguists and logicians. The closer relationships between the two disciplines that have been established in recent years make it likely that such efforts would lead to fruitful results. In this book I tried to show that Boolean Semantics, which is one of the prominent logical approaches to natural language semantics, is more than an elegant mathematical theory inspired by natural language. Its linguistic motivations and its unrivaled simplicity are a good starting point for any descriptively adequate linguistic theory of meaning. Flexible semantic interpretation is a strategy that aims to extend boolean semantics into such a theory. The status of flexibility principles in boolean semantics is not yet fully understood, but I believe that by establishing their usefulness, this book has opened some new directions for future research of this question.

Notes

Chapter 2

1. The pre-theoretic notion of "distributive predication" is intuitively related to, but not to be confused with, the formal distributive laws of boolean algebras.

2. To avoid confusion at later stages it should be mentioned that in the revised boolean theory that emerges from subsequent chapters, as in other theories of plurals, equivalences as in (1) will have a substantially different status than the equivalences in (2) and (3). To obtain the first equivalence the following chapters will have to appeal (at least partly) to pragmatic factors, as will be clarified in chapter 6. For the sake of this chapter, however, this theoretical subtlety is irrelevant.

3. Yet another challenge for boolean semantics that Krifka mentions is Link's example *John and Mary are husband and wife*. In this case also the semantics of relational nouns should be taken into account and not only the meaning of *and*. For instance, one should like to know why the sentence *John and Mary are husband and sister* is ruled out.

4. The problem is pointed out by Lasersohn (1995: 282–283).

5. Krifka's proposal is technically criticized in Winter (1998), where it is shown that the analyses in Krifka (1990: 174–175) and Section 6 do not follow from the definitions.

6. This is not a completely accurate restatement of Landman's actual proposal. See below.

7. In section 5.6 we will find reason to readopt some (significantly changed) version of Landman's approach, on other grounds than sentences like (36) or (37).

8. "The air will be hot and humid in $\{e, e'\}$ if $[\![\text{hot and humid}]\!](\{e, e'\}) = 1$, $\Theta_{\text{hot, subj}}(e)(\text{a})$ and $\Theta_{\text{humid, subj}}(e')(\text{a})$."

9. See also Winter (1995) for an account of such effects.

10. Lasersohn (1995: 46–47) mentions a modification by Schein (p.c.) which, with considerable complications, may avoid this problem.

11. Later in this book, in chapter 5, such nominals will be less ambiguously referred to as "bunch denoting."

12. In the sequel such simple facts are stated without proof.

13. A filter $F \subseteq A$ is an *ultrafilter* iff for every $x \in A$: $x \in F$ or $\overline{x} \in F$ but not both. Of course, "a principal ultrafilter" means "a principal filter that is also an ultrafilter."

14. Later in the book, in chapter 5, we will refer to this resolution of type mismatch using type shifting operators as *type fitting*.

15. Montague Raising is an instance of a general *type-lifting* operation, which is derivable by the Lambek Calculus. See Van Benthem (1991).

16. For other expressions, however, P&R do give empirical motivation for their non-uniform typing strategy. They argue that sentences like *John caught and ate a fish* motivate only a $e(et)$ typing of the extensional transitive predicates, although such predicates require type lifting when they are conjoined with intensional predicates.

17. This is reminiscent of the definition of non-boolean conjunction in Hoeksema (1983), but there are some major differences. See subsection 2.3.8.

18. However, perhaps this strategy is still needed also in the present account, in order to deal with examples like Hoeksema's (22) (page 35). See the speculative discussion in subsection 5.5.5.

19. The sentence probably does have a *reading* that has this entailment, but this is irrelevant as the sentence *per se* does not entail that.

20. Note that we do not take "group-denoting" singular NPs like *the crowd* into account. The semantics of these NPs is the major problem in defining the class of *ccl* predicates.

21. I am grateful to Danny Fox and an anonymous reviewer for suggesting this to me. See Gazdar (1979: 60) for one of the many explorations of the Gricean perspective on disjunction.

22. As mentioned in subsection 2.3.1, this aspect of the system will be modified in chapter 5, where also distributive predicates will get the $(et)t$ type. The same holds for the type considerations with collective predicates below.

23. Two important problems concern the exact position of the coordinator and the possibility of representing these coordinations using structurally equivalent trees with only binary branching nodes.

24. Sentence (107a) does not require the man John met to be different than John himself, as intuitively required. This is however a general effect with indefinites, which normally refer to novel discorse entities. Here this effect is strengthened by the selectional restrictions of the predicate *meet*, which does not allow a "singular" argument like *John*.

Chapter 3

1. Note that the derivation of the VP meaning involves more than the function application of the Ajdukiewicz calculus. This will be accounted for by the saturation mode of composition in section 3.7.

2. See Kempson and Cormack (1981) and Ruys (1992: 6–16), among others, for attempts to determine whether there is any pre-theoretical reason to assume that sentences like (1) have more than one reading.

3. *Meta-level* because we don't want the disjunction between different readings of an ambiguous sentence to become its only reading. For instance, if a sentence S_1 is the negative counterpart of a sentence S_2 this does not imply that S_1 reads unambiguously as the formal negation of the disjunction of S_2's readings. In fact, given the scope of natural negation, S_1 will often be assumed to have more readings than S_2. *Disjunction* because in the propositional boolean algebra **2** it holds that if $S_1 = x_1 \vee \cdots \vee x_n$ and $S = y_1 \vee \cdots \vee y_m$, then $S_1 \leq S$ iff [if $x_i = 1$ for some i, $1 \leq i \leq n$, then $y_j = 1$ for some j, $1 \leq j \leq m$].

4. See e.g. Veltman (1985) or von Fintel (1996), and the references therein.

5. One way to follow principle 1 is to replace *every woman* in (25a) by *exactly one woman*. Then the WS reading with material implication does not entail the NS reading, even when one ignores marginal situations of vacuous satisfaction.

6. See remarks on some proposals in section 3.3.3 below.

7. But see Hendriks (1993: 95–108) for an interesting hypothesis.

8. I am using "representationalist" here in the sense proposed in section 1.2, as the general idea that syntactic operations should be postulated for representing semantic facts (not necessarily at a semantic level of representation).

9. See Ruys (1992: 102–103) for a concise description of more facts.

10. For more general doubts about the notion of specificity see Higginbotham (1987: 64–66), Ludlow and Neale (1991), Ruys (1992: 96–100).

11. As mentioned above, Ruys's proposal is exceptional in that he does not consider his illustrative representational mechanism to be a semantic theory.

12. Hilbert's program influenced instantial logics and logics of arbitrary objects. See Meyer-Viol (1995) and Fine (1985) for extensive developments of these two perspectives. In linguistics the epsilon tradition has been persistently followed in works of the "Konstanz School" on anaphora and (in)definites (see e.g. Egli and Von Heusinger (1995) and the references therein).

13. For the time being, marginal situations where there are less than two girls are ignored.

14. See subsection 3.3.5 and chapter 5 for more on complex numerals.

15. Curiously, Scha (1981) also assumes a similar ambiguity of numeral indefinites although, as mentioned above, unlike Bennett he takes definites to be unambiguously collective.

16. Note that the *at least* interpretation is assumed only for NPs in *argument* positions. Bare numerals in *predicate* positions do entail exactness as shown and accounted for in subsection 4.3.5. Further, note that the *at least* interpretation does not appear with the numeral *zero*, probably because *at least zero* is tautological.

17. This particular example is from Ruys (2000). Ruys (1992) contains many other examples in support of what I henceforth call the *Ruys observation*.

18. This example still does not follow the methodological principle 1 in (15), because the existential WS distributive analysis in (54c) may entail reading (54b) under some analyses. However, this point is unlikely to matter for the experiment, as mentioned below, because sentence (53) is unacceptable, contrary to what would be expected if the analysis in (54c) was available. Moreover, example (60) below is a case where the WS-distributive analysis does not entail the WS-collective reading and still this analysis is shown to be ill-motivated.

19. The facts discovered by Ruys were not originally described in these terms. However, Ruys's work is the source of this generalization. The remarks in Schein (1993: 205–206 and fn. 35) seem to suggest a similar generalization.

20. We assume that there are also other, lower candidate positions for the existential closure of the CF g variable. However, for the WS reading of the plural only (61) is relevant.

21. This is the original proposal in the prepublished version of Reinhart (1997). Because of the problems pointed out below, in the final version of her article Reinhart is less confident about the possibility of eliminating operational distributivity.

22. Thanks to Eddy Ruys for a discussion that led to the discovery of the effect exemplified here.

23. In subsection 3.3.3 it will be claimed that indefinites should get standard restricted scope, like other NPs. In section 3.4 the individual yielded by the CF will be wrapped up in a generalized quantifier, which is another motivation for this assumption.

24. Kamp and Reyle (1993: 348) stipulate that distribution is part of the process of *syntactic* predication. Consequently, it does not escape adjunct islands to take scope over conditionals, for example.

25. See also Fox (1995) for an insightful analysis of relevant scope problems in the context of VP ellipsis.

26. Note that not only plurals, also singular NPs headed by *exactly one* are reluctant wide-scope-takers in comparison to *each* and *every*.

27. This interpretation may be achieved by Montague raising (see page 52) the f (**man$'$**) entity into a quantifier. However, for other reasons the next section proposes that choice functions should generate such quantifiers directly, so the Montague raising operator is dispensable.

28. I do not have clear intuitions about what happens when the article *some* in (104a) is replaced by the numeral *one*. Perhaps *one* is more similar in its (limited) scope potential to *exactly one*, as Kratzer (1998) remarks.

29. Below we will see that the decision does not become easier once this factor is eliminated.

30. This is because in an empty universe, statement (129a), with a widest scope existential closure of the CF variable, is false, whereas (128b) is standardly treated as true.

31. A similar observation was made by Reinhart (1992) for functional questions (see below) with *wh* in situ. Reinhart's example is (i)—a complex variation on an example by Engdahl (1986).

(i) Who remembers which lady will be offended if we invite which of her philosophical rivals?
    Answer: I remember which lady will be offended if we invite her Deconstructionist rival.

Reinhart did not notice that the relevant reading in this example is not generated by her choice function analysis. This happens for reasons similar to the ones that make (139) unsuitable for (136).

32. The similarity between wide scope indefinites and functional readings is anticipated by Groenendijk and Stokhof (1984: 196–201), who discuss examples like: *Every man loves a woman. It's his mother.*

33. I am using here a modeltheoretic version of the general definition in Meyer-Viol (1995: 21). However, Groenendijk and Stokhof, among others, use the term *Skolem functions* for *ee* functions. This is only a terminological difference, since the *ee* functions referred to are the result of applying a Skolem function of arity 1 (of type $(e(et))(ee)$) to a restriction predicate with one free variable (of type $e(et)$).

34. This is the view of the variable-free approach to anaphora. See section 3.7.

35. See Dowty et al. (1981: ch. 6) and Gamut (1991b) for an introduction into the treatment of intensionality in Montague Grammar, which is essential background for the discussion in this subsection.

36. The formula in (154) describes the determiner obtained by composition of existential closure with the meaning of the indefinite article in the variable free implementation developed in section 3.7 below.

37. This proof was greatly simplified thanks to a proposal by an anonymous reviewer.

38. See Reichenbach (1947: 266–274), Davidson (1967), Kamp and Reyle (1993: 73) and Partee (1987), among others.

39. A similar problem in the analysis of temporal preposition was dealt with in Pratt and Francez (2001) using a rule of "pseudo-application" generalizing standard function application.

40. In this case, the COND rule is useful for basically the same purpose as the "Geach rule" (Van Benthem (1991: 36)), which is used by Jacobson (1999) for similar "percolation" effects.

41. The format of the application rule that is given here requires an addition of a *Cut* rule to the system (see e.g. Van Benthem (1991)).

Chapter 4

1. As in previous chapters, I use for the time being the conventional term "NP" when informally referring to nominal syntactic units. In section 4.3 this term will used only in a narrower technical sense for referring to a special level within the DP analysis of nominals.

2. In figure 4.1, I omit the intensional operators *pred* and *nom* in Partee's original diagram. I also ignore the operator THE, which corresponds to the Russellian determiner denotation of the definite article. For convenience, I also employ shorter names for Partee's operators.

3. See Quine (1960: 97, 114–115), Higginbotham (1987: 49) and Zaring (1996), as well as the references therein.

4. This is the *identity function* on predicates, and should not be confused with *be of identity*.

5. Kamp, however, does not dismiss the possibility that the denotation of an *et* adjective may change from one sentence to the other due to contextual factors. This analysis may also be responsible for the failure of the entailment, but without lifting the type of the adjective.

6. Keenan and Faltz' analysis differs from Montague's proposal in EFL, which in extensional terms amounts to the assignment of $\lambda M_{(et)(et)}.\lambda x.(M(\lambda y.\top))(x)$ as the meaning of the copula. Thus, Jumbo is taken to be small iff Jumbo is a small entity. Some differences between the predictions of Montague's definition and K&F's definition can be gleaned from Montague (1970: 211–213) and Keenan and Faltz (1985: 140).

7. Partee does not discuss the problems that motivated the modificational type for these categories and does therefore not decide whether other types besides *et* are needed.

8. The same holds for (15a) and (20), but then relative to the Montague/Keenan and Faltz treatment of adjectives, which will not be discussed here.

9. Strictly speaking, this is not true for the Hebrew indefinite in (21), which lacks an article and hence need not be interpreted as a quantifier to begin with. However, the absence of the article also in *argument* positions (cf. (3)) is still problematic for Montague's treatment.

10. See Keenan and Stavi (1986) for the basic denotation of these constructions. Extensive discussions of the derivation of this semantics can be found in Hoeksema (1996), Lappin (1996) and Moltmann (1995).

11. Partee mentions the sentence *this house has been every color*, given by Williams (1983) as an example for his claim that the (un)grammaticality of nominals in predicative positions is not determined by the determiner alone. However, for reasons that I will not repeat here, Partee argues that such examples are irrelevant for the evaluation of her approach. The same holds for the present proposal.

12. Eddy Ruys mentions a potential problem for this speculation: in the example *this man is none other than John* negation is less likely to be analyzed at the predicate or sentence level.

13. The result in page 132 shows when the Existential Choice Closure (ECC) operator saturates a lifted choice function $\langle f \rangle$, what we get is the standard existential determiner. Thus, the free introduction of $\langle f \rangle$ and ECC leads to the existential raising operator **E** of the Partee triangle.

14. Roger Schwarzschild (p.c.) points out the impossibility of plural NP *disjunction* in predicative positions as in the following examples.

(i) *These (two) women/Mary and Sue are an author *or* a teacher.

If this sentence is analyzed as grammatically well-formed, we expect a coherent reading due to the distributive reading of the subject. However, I speculate that the unacceptability of such sentences is purely a matter of number agreement between the subject and the predicate *be an author or a teacher*, which must be singular. This speculation is supported when the subject of (i) is replaced by other plural NPs like *no women*, *all the women* or *less than two women*, which does not ameliorate the sentence. However, singular NPs like *every woman* or *each of these two women* lead to acceptable sentences.

15. This so-far possible derivation will be formally ruled out in section 4.4.

16. An analysis like (40a) is useful for deriving the "two groups" reading of sentences like *the women and the men earned $5000*. Analyses similar to (40b) will be used for treating "appositional" conjunctions in section 4.3.

17. In chapter 6 it will be argued that also the more commonly assumed distributive analysis of plural *predicates* is justified.

18. See Gamut (1991a: 158–164) for a brief historical survey of the Russell/Strawson debate.

19. Link's exposition of his * operator suggests that he takes this denotation of plural nouns to be semantically prominent. However, Link also uses a "proper" denotation of plural nouns that excludes singleton sets. For more on plural nouns see section 5.4.1.

20. Contrary to what might be suspected, the use of choice functions does not create scope ambiguities with definites. In the case of definites, CFs apply only to the empty set or to a singleton set. There is therefore only one quantifier to which a CF can map the restriction set: the empty quantifier or the principal filter generated by the singleton set, respectively. Thus the scope of the existential closure operator that applies to the CF does not matter (unless in the linguistically irrelevant case where the universe is empty.) I do not give here the proof of this fact.

21. The problem goes in fact deeper than mere type mismatch: also a "distributed" version of E of type $(ett)(ett)$ would not work, since it would still give the disjunction scope that is narrower than the collectivizing min operator.

22. Some of these examples were pointed out earlier in this book.

23. See Jackendoff (1977) for an early discussion of problems in this domain.

24. In subsequent chapters, which do not concern the syntax of nominals, I will return to the traditional "NP" terminology.

25. For a somewhat different proposal about the relations between the semantics of DPs and their internal structure see Zamparelli (1996) as well as the references therein.

26. This classification is not completely adequate. As we shall see in section 4.5, some rigid nominals can also be analyzed using a predicative category PRED. However, when they are analyzed as DPs, these rigid nominals, unlike flexible nominals, always have a quantificational reading.

27. Eddy Ruys points out that in order to obtain this prediction we do not have to assume full categorial identity in coordinations, but only *X-bar level* identity. This more permissive assumption may be needed to account for coordinations of "unlike" categories as in Sag et al. (1985) (see page 142).

28. This is a variation of a proposal by Danon (1996), who suggests that simple numerals are basically nouns. See also Reinhart (1997) for relevant discussion. Eddy Ruys mentions constructions like *the*

fewer than three girls and *John and Mary's between ten and thirty grandchildren*, which may challenge this syntactic distinction between complex and simple numerals.

29. Eddy Ruys and Craig Thiersch point out that in possessives like *my father's friend* the "determiner" position is complex although the nominal should be classified as flexible. I do not address here the analysis of such constructions in the present proposal. Note however, that possessives like *every student's friend* are rigid, so it must be the *possessor* that determines the classification of the nominal and not simply the possessive construction.

30. Neijt's stronger hypothesis is that *both . . . and*, *either . . . or* and *neither . . . nor* coordinate only "major phrases." Thus, she excludes also lexical categories from being conjoined in complex coordinations. Neijt recognizes some counter-examples to this claim, like *either in or on the chest*.

31. Because the accusative marker does not appear before *Sara*, this sentence has a grammatical, but irrelevant, "ellipsis" reading: *Dan knows Rina and Sara as well knows Rina*.

32. Thanks to Tanya Reinhart for discussion.

33. Sentence (119a) can mean that I found John *for* my strongest supporter, which is irrelevant for our purposes. Even more irrelevant is an "appositional" reading the sentence has: "I found my strongest supporter, who is John."

34. Without the contrastive context (*not you*) sentence (122) becomes slightly marked when the copula is omitted. Rapoport (1987: 116) claims that such cases are completely ungrammatical. This disagrees with Doron, as well as with my own judgment and the reactions of other Hebrew speakers I consulted.

35. This is similar to a proposal in Barwise and Cooper (1981).

36. I thank Edit Doron for her help in formulating these tests.

37. Whether this "non-coreference" is an *entailment* of (139) or just a pragmatic implicature is not really crucial for us. Throughout this book I assume that plural number only implies semantic plurality, but does not entail it. For some remarks on this issue see section 5.4.1.

38. What the above examples do not show is that also *a*/bare indefinites that are interpreted wide scope resist appositional conjunction. I do not know a simple test that would decisively support or refute this assumption.

39. A similar prediction would have been derived if we allowed the predicate nominal *no teacher* to scope over the subject. I cannot address here the principles that should prevent this interpretation.

Chapter 5

1. Like Dowty, I ignore throughout this chapter the subtle differences between nominals such as *all the girls*, nominals such as *all girls* and cases of floating *all*, as in *the girls all arrived*.

2. The reason for the replacement of the individual-level predicate *be a good team* by a similar stage-level predicate is explained in note 19 below.

3. Similar weaknesses exist also in the attempts of Taub (1989) and Brisson (1997) to deal with Dowty's data using the notions of aktionsarten (Taub) and pragmatic weakening (Brisson). Like Dowty and Link, also these works concentrate on *all* and neglect other plural determiners that behave the same with respect to the distinction under discussion between predicates.

4. Van der Does (1992) considers a third collective analysis but (inconclusively) dismisses it in his 1993 paper. See in subsection 5.5.2 the discussion following sentence (107).

5. The *a* originally stands for *adjectival*, which I use here to distinguish C_a from the C operator of chapter 2.

6. Van der Does (1992: ch. 4) tries to avoid the problem by ruling out the C_a reading with distributive predicates using a syntactic mechanism. This may be a correct description of the problem, but it is hardly a solution.

7. Furthermore, it may also become clear why all *ccl* predicates have to be collective. Suppose that some predicate *blik* were *ccl* and distributive. By definition of *ccl* predicates, sentences like *Mary/John blik* would have been unacceptable, hence so would also (reasonably) be the conjunction *Mary blik and John blik*. By distributivity of *blik*, also the sentence *Mary and John blik* would have had to be unacceptable. Such a predicate like *blik* that is unacceptable with both singular nominals and plural nominals would not be very useful in natural language.

8. As explained above, this is what Dowty's analysis of subentailments implicitly assumes. A similar assumption is also implicit in the works of Taub (1989) and Brisson (1997).

9. When nouns or adjectives are substituted for PRED, we may need (in some languages, like English) to add a *be* verb in front of the predicate in (33), and in case it is a singular noun, also an indefinite article.

10. The assumption concerning the "atomic" status of nouns like *team* or *group*, following the works of Barker (1992) and Schwarzschild (1996), is crucial for the proposal in section 5.6.

11. There is a problem for this claim. Gilad Ben-Avi (p.c.) points out that the atom/set criterion as stated above implicitly assumes that the noun within the nominal argument (e.g. *student(s)* in (33)) is itself an atom predicate. When this is not the case (e.g. when we substitute *similar cat(s)* for *student(s)*), as in the following examples, even a predicate like *be asleep* can counter-intuitively be classified as a set predicate, due to the non-equivalence between (i) and (ii).

(i) All the similar cats are asleep.

(ii) Every similar cat is asleep.

This typological problem can be overcome (without circularity) using a more sophisticated statement of the atom/set criterion. However, this would be unnecessary for the present purposes.

12. The reason for the focus on *lexical* atom and set predicates will become clear in the next subsection. In cases of predicates with more than one argument, principle (46) relates to each argument separately, though formal details are obviously missing. For instance, we have seen above that the transitive predicate *elect* is atomic on its subject argument, hence this argument is assumed to be an element of E. Whether a predicate is an atom predicate or a set predicate on its *object* argument should be tested independently. For instance, the predicate *see* should be classified as atomic on its object argument due to equivalences as between the sentences *John saw every student* and *John saw all the students*. However, further discussion of this point must be deferred to another occasion.

13. About mass terms and the cross-linguistic status of this generalization see some remarks below.

14. Cross-linguistically, this uniformity is not less plausible than the alternative idea of distinguishing between meanings of plural determiners and singular determiners. Many languages use the same morphology for singular determiners and their plural correlates. Consider for instance the singular/plural English determiner *no* (as in *no student/s*), or the singular/plural Hebrew determiner *kol* ("each"/"all"). In such cases it is natural to assume that both items are just one and the same morpheme, unspecified for the number feature, in a similar way to words like the English nouns *fish* and *sheep*.

15. Incidentally, this is just the denotation assumed in section 4.4 for the copula *be*.

16. When the nominal in such plural sentences as (59) is a set predicate, a "distributive" reading is *not* derived by the present system. For instance, the sentence *No friends slept* does not get an analysis equivalent to *No friend slept*. This is because no principle fits the lexical denotation **friends$'_{ett}$** to the $(et)(et)$ identity meaning of the plurality morpheme. This property of the system may turn out to be problematic. If it is, the problem can be solved either by stipulating that *sg* is a covert type fitting principle or by letting all lexical predicates be ambiguous between *et* and *ett*. Both assumptions are inelegant, and at present I don't see enough justification for adopting any of them.

17. Another reason might have been the *et* denotation of a plural noun like *students*, equivalent to its singular form *student*. Thus, a noun phrase like *the students* might have perhaps ended up meaning *the student*. However, in chapter 4 I assume that plural definite articles have only the $(ett)(ett)$ type definition given on page 154, so the *et* meaning of the noun *students* cannot generate the problematic effect because it must be lifted first to combine with the article.

18. In this I follow Schwarzschild (1996: 5, fn. 1), Sternefeld (1997: 308) and Krifka (1989: 85), among others, and disagree with Verkuyl (1981, 1993) and Chierchia (1998b), where singularities are excluded from the denotations of common nouns. While the system is compatible with Verkuyl's motivations, it remains to be seen if Chierchia's suggestive analysis of mass terms can be re-implemented without his "no singularities" assumption on the denotation of plural nouns.

19. With the indefinite subjects in (73) and the "individual level" predicate *be a good team*, some speakers get acceptable generic readings. For instance, the sentence *exactly four students are a good team* may be read as *to be exactly four students is to be a good team*. However, any coherent reading besides this generic reading is strictly impossible. To support this claim, replace the predicate by a "stage level" predicate like *are the team that won the cup yesterday*, which does not give rise to generic readings. This makes the sentence completely uninterpretable.

20. In terms of entailment, while (80) is equivalent to (i) below, (81) is clearly not equivalent to (ii).

(i) There are ten students such that each of them voted to accept the proposal and no other student voted to accept the proposal.

(ii) *There are ten students such that each of them met and no other student met.

21. As an example for the logically contingent status of conservativity, the case of *only* as in *only students arrived* is a well-known potential counter-example for this property. It is commonly agreed, however, that *only* should not qualify as a syntactic determiner.

22. The proposal that seems to me closest to explaining the conservativity of determiners is the observation by Keenan and Stavi (1986) that the set of conservative determiners over a given domain is a closure of a small set of "basic" determiners under the boolean operators of *meet*, *join* and *complement*. However, Keenan and Stavi do not explain the arguments for choosing their class of "basic" determiners.

23. Gennaro Chierchia argued for a similar idea in a course given at Utrecht University in winter 1996, relating it to the "copy theory of traces."

24. In his 1992 dissertation, Van der Does follows the preliminary remark in Van Benthem (1991: 68), where a Scha-like **N** operator as well as a "non-intersective" collectivizer are proposed.

25. For the state/event distinction see Dowty (1979), Hinrichs (1986) and Verkuyl (1993), among others. Pauline Jacobson (p.c.) informs me that a similar connection between collectivity and aspectuality was observed in an unpublished joint work by her and Sam Bayer. Also Taub's (1989) work, mentioned above, stresses this connection, which still need to be studied further.

26. For simplicity of notation, I use here *sg* as an operator on a complex predicate. However, recall the remark on page 209 that such a derivation may be obtained by a generalized definition of *sg* to *n*-ary predicates, which is independently needed.

27. Sentence (127) also gets pragmatically unacceptable readings using the distributivity operator *pdist* applied to $sg(\textbf{similar}')$ or the $\langle f \rangle^d$ category shift applied to the NP. Further, in (127) we may also have the "impure atom" reading around (see section 5.6). These readings are irrelevant however for capturing the entailment. Refer to section 5.7 for a case study that summarizes the available readings for definites in the system.

28. Some analyses of plural definites, notably Schwarzschild (1996), would not take this to be a problem, as they contend that also (127) does not make any claim on the entire set of rocks but only on subsets that *cover* it. However, in chapter 6 I will argue that the "cover" analysis of plural definites is under-motivated.

29. Barwise and Cooper define witness sets on quantifiers explicitly, but they reach the argument *A* indirectly by defining what they call a *live on set* of the quantifier. This complication is unnecessary for our purposes.

30. As will be proposed below, the witness condition be given a linguistic status that is different than the status of the *dfit* as a type-fitting operator, though the present implementation using the combined $dfit_w(D)$ operator may mask this claim.

31. When there are no rocks (125) gets in (133) a *true* value. This might be overridden by the presence of the definite article in the subject *all* THE *rocks*.

32. "Almost," because if we use Szabolcsi's unconditioned existential strategy then in a situation where no student arrived a tautological sentence like *at least zero students arrived* is analyzed as false (or perhaps undefined), under the standard assumption that an empty set cannot be in the extension of predicates like *arrive*.

33. This is reasonably true in general, not only for the complex coordination in (147). However, when *as well as* is replaced by a simple *and* we may get collectivity *in between* the conjuncts, as discussed in subsection 5.5.5, which complicates the semantics considerably (with *or*, entailment relations do not allow to show the point to begin with). See also subsection 6.3 for a similar motivation for nominal distributivity with definites.

34. This is the same effect that was exemplified by Hoeksema (1988) and reproduced in example (22) of chapter 2.

35. This scoping intuition appears already in Hoeksema's (1988) analysis of such sentences, using the LP calculus. See subsection 2.2.2.

36. See Landman (2000) for a recent proposal.

37. See also Van der Does and Verkuyl (1995: 49).

38. I consider this term infelicitous. In the proposal below there is no sense in which the atom corresponding to a nominal like *this team* is more "impure" than an atom corresponding to a nominal like *this student*.

39. In fact, Barker and Schwarzschild do not assume a type distinction between singulars and plurals. This is irrelevant for our purposes here, however.

40. Barker has different motivations for establishing such a relation: constructions like *a committee of women* and the possibility in some English dialects to get plural agreement with bunch denoting nominals (e.g. *The committee are old*). I do not address these interesting problems here.

41. I simplify a bit Schwarzschild's actual proposal for the sake of exposition.

42. Imagine for instance that Bill is an intelligent alien who reached Texas, while his behavior is controlled from distance by a brain held in a small capsule on Mars.

43. Barker attributes a similar observation to Landman (1989), but only for a restricted set of predicates.

44. For an extensive recent study of the distinction between logical and non-logical objects see Keenan (1996a).

45. Fred Landman (p.c.) points out that this is a *necessary* condition for (198a) and (198b) to be consistent. For instance, if one of the people referred to in (198a) is not in any of the couples referred to in (198b), it is impossible for both sentences to be true. This evidently shows that there is more to be said on the constitute relation than I am able to do here.

46. The entailment relations with (202d) are obscured here by obvious factors. Things become very clear however with set predicates (in the "Dowty dialect") like *lift a piano* or nominals like *every committee/all the committees*.

Chapter 6

1. See Dowty (1987: fn. 1) (referring to Peter Lasersohn, p.c.), Kamp and Reyle (1993: 322), Lasersohn (1995: 76, 131) and Lønning (1987: 226), among others.

2. See Heim et al. (1991) and Kamp and Reyle (1993: ch. 4) for more on this issue.

3. Recall for this definition that $\wp^+(A) = \wp(A) \setminus \{\emptyset\}$, the set of all non-empty subsets of A.

4. Schwarzschild (1996) does not use existential quantification over covers as in (27) but assumes that the relevant cover is pragmatically determined. This point is irrelevant for our present purposes.

5. If semantic plurality is encoded in the denotation of plural nouns like *wheels* then the statement in (28) should include the requirement $|A| \geq 2$ (see section 5.4.1). This is irrelevant for our discussion, however.

6. A similar point is made by Lønning (1991).

7. Other purely quantificational nominals involve distribution effects that were accounted for in chapter 5.

8. There is a possible alternative of imposing a collectivity operator. I do not know any advantage of this possibility.

9. The general point is due to Dowty (1987) and/or Roberts (1987). See Lasersohn (1995: ch. 7, fn. 7) for the complex chronology of these examples.

10. When proofreading this book I realized that this argument is in fact incorrect. Under the assumptions of chapter 5, the conjunct *Mary and John* in (43) can be mapped to a bunch, and then distribution at the predicate level may lead to the desired interpretation, without having to separately distribute the conjunct *the women I mentioned* within the subject NP.

11. Thanks to Tanya Reinhart.

References

Abney, S. P. (1987). *The English Noun Phrase in its Sentential Aspect*. Ph.D. thesis, Massachusetts Institute of Technology.

Abusch, D. (1994). The scope of indefinites. *Natural Language Semantics*, 3:88–135.

Ajdukiewicz, K. (1935). Die syntaktische konnexität. *Studia Philosophia*, 1:1–27.

Barker, C. (1992). Group terms in English: representing groups as atoms. *Journal of Semantics*, 9:69–93.

Bartsch, R. (1973). The semantics and syntax of number and numbers. In J. P. Kimball, editor, *Syntax and Semantics*, volume 2. Seminar Press, New York, London.

Barwise, J., and Cooper, R. (1981). Generalized quantifiers and natural language. *Linguistics and Philosophy*, 4:159–219.

Beghelli, F. (1993). A minimalist approach to quantifier scope. In *Proceedings of the 23th conference of the Northeast Linguistic Society*.

Beghelli, F. (1995). *The Phrase Structure of Quantifier Scope*. Ph.D. thesis, University of California Los Angeles.

Ben-Avi, G., and Winter, Y. (2001). A characterization of monotonicity with collective quantifiers. To appear in *Proceedings of Formal Grammar and Mathematics of Language 7*, FGMOL.

Ben-Shalom, D. (1993). Object wide scope and semantic trees. In *Proceedings of Semantics and Linguistic Theory, SALT3*.

Bennett, M. (1974). *Some Extensions of a Montague Fragment of English*. Ph.D. thesis, University of California Los Angeles.

Brisson, C. (1997). On definite plural NPs and the meaning of *all*. In *Proceedings of Semantics and Linguistic Theory, SALT7*.

Carlson, G. N. (1977). *Reference to Kinds in English*. Ph.D. thesis, University of Massachusetts at Amherst.

Carlson, G. N., and Pelletier, F. J. (1995). *The Generic Book*. University of Chicago Press, Chicago.

Carpenter, B. (1997). *Type-Logical Semantics*. MIT Press, Cambridge, Massachusetts.

Chierchia, G. (1993). Questions with quantifiers. *Natural Language Semantics*, 1:181–234.

Chierchia, G. (1998a). Reference to kinds across languages. *Natural Language Semantics,* 6:339–405.

Chierchia, G. (1998b). Plurality of mass nouns and the notion of 'semantic parameter'. In S. Rothstein, editor, *Events and Grammar*. Kluwer, Dordrecht.

Chierchia, G., and McConnel-Ginet, S. (1990). *Meaning and Grammar: An Introduction to Semantics*. MIT Press, Cambridge, Massachusetts.

Cleese, J., and Booth, C. (1989). *The Complete Fawlty Towers*. Pantheon Books.

Cooper, R. (1975). *Montague's Semantic Theory and Transformational Syntax*. Ph.D. thesis, University of Massachusetts at Amherst.

Corblin, F. (1997). Les indéfinis: variables et quantificateurs. *Langue Française*, 116:8–32.

Dalrymple, M., Hayrapetian, I., and King, T. H. (1998). The semantics of the Russian comitative construction. *Natural Language and Linguistic Theory*, 3:597–631.

Dalrymple, M., Kanazawa, M., Kim, Y., Mchombo, S., and Peters, S. (1998). Reciprocal expressions and the concept of reciprocity. *Linguistics and Philosophy*, 21:159–210.

Dalrymple, M., Kanazawa, M., Mchombo, S., and Peters, S. (1994). What do reciprocals mean? In *Proceedings of Semantics and Linguistic Theory, SALT4*.

Danon, G. (1996). The syntax of determiners in Hebrew. Unpublished master thesis, Tel-Aviv University. Available at http://www.tau.ac.il/~danon/thesis.html.

Davidson, D. (1967). The logical form of action sentences. In Rescher, N., editor, *The Logic of Decision and Action*. University of Pittsburgh Press, Pittsburgh. Reprinted in D. Davidson, *Essays on Actions and Events*. Clarendon Press, London, 1980.

Dik, S. C. (1968). *Coordination: Its Implication for the Theory of General Linguistics*. North-Holland, Amsterdam.

Doron, E. (1983). *Verbless Predicates in Hebrew*. Ph.D. thesis, The University of Texas at Austin.

Dowty, D. (1979). *Word Meaning and Montague Grammar: The Semantics of Verbs and Times in Generative Semantics and in Montague's PTQ*. D. Reidel, Dordrecht.

Dowty, D. (1987). Collective predicates, distributive predicates and *all*. In *Proceedings of the Eastern States Conference on Linguistics, ESCOL3*.

Dowty, D., Wall, R., and Peters, S. (1981). *Introduction to Montague Semantics*. D. Reidel, Dordrecht.

Egli, U., and von Heusinger, K. (1995). The epsilon operator and e-type pronouns. In U. Egli, P. E. Pause, C. Schwarze, A. von Stechow, and G. Wienold, editors, *Lexical Knowledge in the Organization of Language*. John Benjamins, Amsterdam-Philadelphia.

Engdahl, E. (1980). *The Syntax and Semantics of Questions in Swedish*. Ph.D. thesis, University of Massachusetts at Amherst.

Engdahl, E. (1986). *Constituent Questions: The Syntax and Semantics of Questions with Special Reference to Swedish*. D. Reidel, Dordrecht.

Farkas, D. (1981). Quantifier scope and syntactic islands. In *Papers from the 17th regional meeting of the Chicago Linguistic Society, CLS17*.

Farkas, D. (1997). Evaluation indices and scope. In A. Szabolcsi, editor, *Ways of Scope Taking*. Kluwer, Dordrecht.

Fine, K. (1985). *Reasoning with Arbitrary Objects*. Blackwell, Oxford.

Fodor, J. D., and Sag, I. (1982). Referential and quantificational indefinites. *Linguistics and Philosophy*, 5:355–398.

Fox, D. (1995). Economy and scope. *Natural Language Semantics*, 3:283–341.

Gamut, L. T. F. (1991a). *Logic, Language and Meaning*. Volume 1. University of Chicago Press, Chicago.

Gamut, L. T. F. (1991b). *Logic, Language and Meaning*. Volume 2. University of Chicago Press, Chicago.

Gazdar, G. (1979). *Pragmatics: Implicature, Presupposition, and Logical Form*. Academic Press, New York.

Gazdar, G. (1981). Unbounded dependencies and coordinate structure. *Linguistic Inquiry*, 12:155–184.

Gillon, B. (1987). The readings of plural noun phrases in English. *Linguistics and Philosophy*, 10:199–219.

Gillon, B. (1990). Plural noun phrases and their readings: a reply to Lasersohn. *Linguistics and Philosophy*, 13:477–485.

Groenendijk, J., and Stokhof, M. (1984). *Studies on the Semantics of Questions and the Pragmatics of Answers*. Ph.D. thesis, University of Amsterdam.

Groenendijk, J., and Stokhof, M. (1989). Type shifting rules and the semantics of interrogatives. In G. Chierchia, B. Partee, and R. Turner, editors, *Properties, Types and Meanings*, volume 2. Kluwer, Dordrecht.

Halmos, P. R. (1963). *Lectures on Boolean Algebras*. Van Nostrand, Princeton, New Jersey.

Heim, I., and Kratzer, A. (1997). *Semantics in Generative Grammar*. Blackwell.

Heim, I., Lasnik, H., and May, R. (1991). Reciprocity and plurality. *Linguistic Inquiry*, 22:63–101.

Hendriks, H. (1993). *Studied Flexibility: Categories and Types in Syntax and Semantics*. Ph.D. thesis, University of Amsterdam.

Hepple, M. (1991). *The Grammar and Processing of Order and Dependency: A Categorial Approach*. Ph.D. thesis, University of Edinburgh.

Higginbotham, J. (1987). Indefiniteness and predication. In E. J. Reuland and A. G. B. ter Meulen, editors, *The Representation of (In)definiteness*. MIT Press, Cambridge, Massachusetts.

Hilbert, D., and Bernays, P. (1939). *Die Grundlagen der Mathematik II*. Springer, Berlin. Second edition, reprint, 1970.

Hinrichs, E. (1986). *A Compositional Semantics for Aktionsarten and NP Reference in English*. Ph.D. thesis, Ohio State University.

Hintikka, J. (1986). The semantics of *a certain*. *Linguistic Inquiry*, 17:331–336.

Hoeksema, J. (1983). Plurality and conjunction. In A. ter Meulen, editor, *Studies in Modeltheoretic Semantics*. Foris, Dordrecht.

Hoeksema, J. (1988). The semantics of non-boolean *and*. *Journal of Semantics*, 6:19–40.

Hoeksema, J. (1996). The semantics of exception phrases. In J. van der Does and J. van Eijck, editors, *Quantifiers: Logic and Language*. CSLI Publications, Stanford.

Horn, L. R. (1972). *On the Semantic Properties of Logical Operators in English*. Ph.D. thesis, University of California Los Angeles.

Jackendoff, R. (1977). *X̂-Syntax: A Study of Phrase Structure*. MIT Press, Cambridge, Massachusetts.

Jacobson, P. (1999). Towards a variable-free semantics. *Linguistics and Philosophy*, 22:117–185.

Janssen, T. M. V. (1983). *Foundations and Applications of Montague Grammar*. Ph.D. thesis, Mathematisch Centrum, Amsterdam.

Kamp, H. (1975). Two theories about adjectives. In E. Keenan, editor, *Formal Semantics of Natural Language*. Cambridge University Press, Cambridge.

Kamp, H., and Reyle, U. (1993). *From Discourse to Logic: Introduction to Modeltheoretic Semantics of Natural Language, Formal Logic and Discourse Representation Theory*. Kluwer, Dordrecht.

Keenan, E. (1996a). Logical objects. Unpublished ms., University of California Los Angeles. To appear in C. A. Anderson and M. Zeleny, editors, *Logic, Language and Computation: Essays in Honor of Alonzo Church*. Kluwer.

Keenan, E. (1996b). The semantics of determiners. In S. Lappin, editor, *The Handbook of Contemporary Semantic Theory*. Blackwell.

Keenan, E., and Faltz, L. (1978). *Logical Types for Natural Language*. UCLA Occasional Papers in Linguistics 3, Department of Linguistics, UCLA.

Keenan, E., and Faltz, L. (1985). *Boolean Semantics for Natural Language*. D. Reidel, Dordrecht.

Keenan, E., and Stavi, J. (1986). A semantic characterization of natural language determiners. *Linguistics and Philosophy*, 9:253–326.

Keenan, E., and Westerståhl, D. (1996). Generalized quantifiers in linguistics and logic. In J. van Benthem and A. ter Meulen, editors, *Handbook of Logic and Language*. Elsevier, Amsterdam.

Kempson, R. M., and Cormack, A. (1981). Ambiguity and quantification. *Linguistics and Philosophy*, 4:259–309.

Koppelberg, S. (1989). General theory of boolean algebras. In J. D. Monk and R. Bonnet, editors, *Handbook of Boolean Algebras*, volume 1. Elsevier, Amsterdam.

Kratzer, A. (1998). Scope or pseudoscope? Are there wide scope indefinites? In S. Rothstein, editor, *Events and Grammar*. Kluwer, Dordrecht.

Krifka, M. (1989). Nominal reference, temporal constitution and quantification in event semantics. In R. Bartsch, J. van Benthem, and P. van Emde Boas, editors, *Semantics and Contextual Expression*. Foris, Dordrecht.

Krifka, M. (1990). Boolean and non-boolean 'and'. In L. Kálmán and L. Pólos, editors, *Papers from the Second Symposium of Logic and Language*. Akaemiai Kiado, Budapest.

Lakoff, G. (1970). Repartee. *Foundations of Language*, 6:389–422.

Lakoff, G., and Peters, S. (1969). Phrasal conjunction and symmetric predicates. In D. A. Reibel and S. E. Schane, editors, *Modern Studies in English*. Prentice-Hall, Englewood Cliffs, N.J.

Lambek, J. (1958). The mathematics of sentence structure. *American Mathematical Monthly*, 65:154–169.

Landman, F. (1989). Groups I & II. *Linguistics and Philosophy*, 12:559–605, 723–744.

Landman, F. (1996). Plurality. In S. Lappin, editor, *The Handbook of Contemporary Semantic Theory*. Blackwell.

Landman, F. (2000). *Events and Plurality: The Jerusalem Lectures*. Kluwer, Dordrecht.

Lappin, S. (1996). Generalized quantifiers, exception phrases and logicality. *Journal of Semantics*, 13:197–220.

Larson, R. K. (1985). On the syntax of disjunction scope. *Natural Language and Linguistic Theory*, 3:217–265.

Lasersohn, P. (1989). On the readings of plural noun phrases. *Linguistic Inquiry*, 20:130–134.

Lasersohn, P. (1995). *Plurality, Conjunction and Events*. Kluwer, Dordrecht.

Link, G. (1983). The logical analysis of plurals and mass terms: a lattice theoretical approach. In R. Bauerle, C. Schwarze, A. and von Stechow, editors, *Meaning, Use and Interpretation of Language*. De Gruyter, Berlin.

Link, G. (1984). Hydras: on the logic of relative constructions with multiple heads. In F. Landman and F. Veltman, editors, *Varaities of Formal Semantics*. Foris, Dordrecht.

Link, G. (1987). Generalized quantifiers and plurals. In P. Gärdenfors, editor, *Generalized Quantifiers*. D. Reidel, Dordrecht.

Liu, F. (1990). *Scope Dependency in English and Chinese*. Ph.D. thesis, University of California, Los Angeles.

Lønning, J. T. (1987). Collective readings of definite and indefinites noun phrases. In P. Gärdenfors, editor, *Generalized Quantifiers*. D. Reidel, Dordrecht.

Lønning, J. T. (1991). Among readings: some remarks on 'among collections'. In van der Does, J., editor, *Quantification and Anaphora II*. DYANA deliverable 2.2.b, Edinburgh.

Ludlow, P., and Neale, S. (1991). Indefinite descriptions: in defense of Russell. *Linguistics and Philosophy*, 14:171–202.

May, R. (1977). *The Grammar of Quantification*. Ph.D. thesis, Massachusetts Institute of Technology.

Meyer-Viol, W. P. M. (1995). *Instantial Logic*. Ph.D. thesis, Utrecht University. ILLC dissertation series, Amsterdam.

Moltmann, F. (1995). Exception sentences and polyadic quantification. *Linguistics and Philosophy*, 18:223–280.

Moltmann, F. (1997). *Parts and Wholes in Semantics*. Oxford University Press, New York.

Montague, R. (1970). English as a formal language. In B. Visentini et al., editors, *Linguaggi nella Società e nella Technica*. Edizioni di Communità, Milan. Reprinted in R. Thomason, editor (1974), *Formal Philosophy: selected papers of Richard Montague*. Yale, New Haven.

Montague, R. (1973). The proper treatment of quantification in ordinary English. In J. Hintikka, J. Moravcsik, and P. Suppes, editors, *Approaches to Natural Languages: Proceedings of the 1970 Stanford Workshop on Grammar and Semantics*. D. Reidel, Dordrecht. Reprinted in R. Thomason, editor (1974), *Formal Philosophy: Selected Papers of Richard Montague*. Yale, New Haven.

Nam, S. (1991). *N*-ary quantifiers and the expressive power of NP compositions. In J. van der Does and J. van Eijck, editors, *Generalized Quantifiers: Theory and Application*. Dutch network for language, logic and information, Amsterdam.

Neijt, A. H. (1979). *Gapping: A Contribution to Sentence Grammar*. Ph.D. thesis, Utrecht University.

Partee, B. (1987). Noun phrase interpretation and type shifting principles. In J. Groenendijk, D. de Jong, M. and Stokhof, editors, *Studies in Discourse Representation Theories and the Theory of Generalized Quantifiers*. Foris, Dordrecht.

Partee, B. (1989). Binding implicit variables in quantified contexts. In *Papers from the 25th regional meeting of the Chicago Linguistic Society, CLS25.*

Partee, B. and Rooth, M. (1983). Generalized conjunction and type ambiguity. In R. Bauerle, C. Schwarze, and A. von Stechow, editors, *Meaning, Use and Interpretation of Language.* De Gruyter, Berlin.

Payne, J. (1985). Complex phrases and complex sentences. In T. Shopen, editor, *Language Typology and Syntactic Description: Complex Constructions*, volume 2. Cambridge University Press, Cambridge.

Pratt, I., and Francez, N. (2001). Temporal prepositions and temporal generalized quantifiers. *Linguistics and Philosophy,* 24:187–222.

Quine, W. V. O. (1960). *Word and Object.* John Wiley & Sons, New York.

Quine, W. V. O. (1966). Variables explained away. In his *Selected Logic Papers.* Random House, New York.

Rapoport, T. R. (1987). *Copular, Nominal and Small Clauses: A Study of Israeli Hebrew.* Ph.D. thesis, Massachusetts Institute of Technology.

Reichenbach, H. (1947). *Elements of Symbolic Logic.* Macmilan Company, New York. Reprint 1956.

Reinhart, T. (1983). *Anaphora and Semantic Interpretation.* Croom Helm, London, Sydney. Second edition, reprint, 1987.

Reinhart, T. (1992). Wh-in-situ: an apparent paradox. In *Proceedings of the eighth Amsterdam Colloquium.*

Reinhart, T. (1997). Quantifier scope: how labor is divided between QR and choice functions. *Linguistics and Philosophy*, 20:335–397.

Roberts, C. (1987). *Modal Subordination, Anaphora, and Distributivity.* Ph.D. thesis, University of Massachusetts at Amherst.

Rodman, R. (1976). Scope phenomena, 'movement transformations' and relative clauses. In B. H. Partee, editor, *Montague Grammar.* Academic Press, New York.

Rooth, M., and Partee, B. (1982). Conjunction, type ambiguity and wide scope *or.* In *Proceedings of the first West Coast Conference on Formal Linguistics, WCCFL1.*

Ross, J. R. (1967). *Constraints on Variables in Syntax.* Ph.D. thesis, Massachusetts Institute of Technology.

Rullmann, H. (1995). *Maximality in the Semantics of WH-Constructions.* Ph.D. thesis, University of Massachusetts at Amherst.

Russell, B. (1919). *Introduction to Mathematical Philosophy.* George Allen and Unwin, London. Reprint, 1953.

Ruys, E. G. (1992). *The Scope of Indefinites.* Ph.D. thesis, Utrecht University.

Ruys, E. G. (2000). Weak crossover as a scope phenomenon. *Linguistic Inquiry,* 30:587–620.

Sag, I., Gazdar, G., Wasow, T., and Weisler, S. (1985). Coordination and how to distinguish categories. *Natural Language and Linguistic Theory*, 3:117–171.

Scha, R. (1981). Distributive, collective and cumulative quantification. In J. Groenendijk, M. Stokhof, T. M. V. and Janssen, editors, *Formal Methods in the Study of Language.* Mathematisch Centrum, Amsterdam.

Schein, B. (1992). Conjunction reduction redux. Unpublished ms., University of Southern California.

Schein, B. (1993). *Plurals and Events*. MIT Press, Cambridge, Massachusetts.

Schwarzschild, R. (1992). Types of plural individuals. *Linguistics and Philosophy*, 15:641–675.

Schwarzschild, R. (1996). *Pluralities*. Kluwer, Dordrecht.

Sharvit, Y. (1997). *The Syntax and Semantics of Functional Relative Clauses*. Ph.D. thesis, Rutgers University.

Sharvy, R. (1980). A more general theory of definite descriptions. *Philosophical Review*, 89:607–624.

Sikorski, R. (1964). *Boolean Algebras*. Springer-Verlag, Berlin. Second edition.

Sternefeld, W. (1997). Reciprocity and cumulative predication. In F. Hamm E. and Hinrichs, editors, *Plurality and Quantification*. Kluwer, Dordrecht.

Szabolcsi, A. (1987). Bound variables in syntax: are there any? In *Proceedings of the Sixth Amsterdam Colloquium*.

Szabolcsi, A. (1997). Strategies for scope taking. In A. Szabolcsi, editor, *Ways of Scope Taking*. Kluwer, Dordrecht.

Taub, A. (1989). Collective predicates, aktionsarten and *all*. In E. Bach, A. Kratzer, and B. Partee, editors, *Papers on Quantification*. University of Massachusetts at Amherst.

Thijsse, E. (1983). On some proposed universals of natural language. In A. ter Meulen, editor, *Studies in Modeltheoretic Semantics*. Foris, Dordrecht.

Van Benthem, J. (1986). *Essays in Logical Semantics*. D. Reidel, Dordrecht.

Van Benthem, J. (1991). *Language in Action: Categories, Lambdas and Dynamic Logic*. North-Holland, Amsterdam.

Van der Does, J. (1992). *Applied Quantifier Logics: Collectives, Naked Infinitives*. Ph.D. thesis, University of Amsterdam.

Van der Does, J. (1993). Sums and quantifiers. *Linguistics and Philosophy*, 16:509–550.

Van der Does, J., and van Eijck, J. (1996). Basic quantifier theory. In J. van der Does and J. van Eijck, editors, *Quantifiers: Logic and Language*. CSLI Publications, Stanford.

Van der Does, J., and Verkuyl, H. (1995). Quantification and predication. In K. van Deemter and S. Peters, editors, *Semantic Ambiguity and Underspecification*. CSLI Publications, Stanford.

Veltman, F. (1985). *Logics for Conditionals*. Ph.D. thesis, University of Amsterdam.

Vendler, Z. (1967). *Linguistics in Philosophy*. Cornell University Press, Ithaca, New York. Reprint, 1968.

Verkuyl, H. (1981). Numerals and quantifiers in X-bar syntax and their semantic interpretation. In J. Groenendijk, M. Stokhof, and T. M. V. Janssen, editors, *Formal Methods in the Study of Language*. Mathematisch Centrum, Amsterdam.

Verkuyl, H. (1993). *A Theory of Aspectuality*. Cambridge University Press, Cambridge.

Verkuyl, H. (1994). Distributivity and collectivity: a couple at odds. In M. Kanazawa and C. J. Piñón, editors, *Dynamics, Polarity and Quantification*. CSLI Publications, Stanford.

Verkuyl, H., and van der Does, J. (1996). The semantics of plural noun phrases. In J. van der Does and J. van Eijck, editors, *Quantifiers: Logic and Language*. CSLI Publications, Stanford.

Von Fintel, K. (1996). Conditionals in dynamic context. Unpublished ms., Massachusetts Institute of Technology.

Williams, E. (1983). Semantic vs. syntactic categories. *Linguistics and Philosophy*, 6:423–446.

Winter, Y. (1995). Syncategorematic conjunction and structured meanings. In *Proceedings of Semantics and Linguistic Theory, SALT5*.

Winter, Y. (1996a). A unified semantic treatment of singular NP coordination. *Linguistics and Philosophy*, 19:337–391.

Winter, Y. (1996b). What does the strongest meaning hypothesis mean? In *Proceedings of Semantics and Linguistic Theory, SALT6*.

Winter, Y. (1997). Choice functions and the scopal semantics of indefinites. *Linguistics and Philosophy*, 20:399–467.

Winter, Y. (1998). *Flexible Boolean Semantics: Coordination, Plurality and Scope in Natural Language*. Ph.D. thesis, Utrecht University.

Winter, Y. (2000a). Distributivity and dependency. *Natural Language Semantics*, 8:27–69.

Winter, Y. (2000b). What makes choice natural? In U. Egli and K. von Heusinger, editors, *Reference and Anaphoric Relations*. Kluwer, Dordrecht.

Zamparelli, R. (1996). *Layers in the Determiner Phrase*. Ph.D. thesis, University of Rochester.

Zaring, L. (1996). "Two *be* or not two *be*": identity, predication and the Welsh copula. *Linguistics and Philosophy*, 19:103–142.

Zimmermann, T. E. (1986). Transparent adverbs and scopeless quantifiers. In J. Groenendijk, D. de Jongh, and M. Stokhof, editors, *Foundations of Pragmatics and Lexical Semantics*. Foris, Dordrecht.

Zimmermann, T. E. (1991). Scopeless quantifiers and operators. In J. van der Does J. and van Eijck, editors, *Generalized Quantifiers Theory and Application*. Dutch network for language, logic and information, Amsterdam.

Zwarts, J. (1992). *X′-Syntax–X′-Semantics: On the Interpretation of Functional and Lexical Heads*. Ph.D. thesis, Utrecht University.

Index

Current Studies in Linguistics

Samuel Jay Keyser, general editor